'The reader
must understand'

'The reader must understand'

Eschatology in Bible and theology

Edited by K. E. Brower and M. W. Elliott

APOLLOS (an imprint of Inter-Varsity Press),
38 De Montfort Street, Leicester LE1 7GP, England

First published 1997

British Library Cataloguing in Publication Data
A catalogue record for this book is available from the British
Library.

ISBN 0-85111-460-1

Typeset in Great Britain by Tyndale House, Cambridge

Printed in Great Britain by Creative Print and Design Group

Contents

Preface

'A loss of nerve in the face of extremists.'
'The disappearance of the topic from the academy.'

Could these be the reasons that preaching on what might be called eschatological matters has largely disappeared from pulpits of 'respectable' churches? Or is it because scholars have produced such a plethora of definitions that 'eschatology' has become an 'Alice in Wonderland' kind of word?

Whatever the case, the church is impoverished if, because of difficulties in definition, it abandons the field to eccentrics and cranks, or, worse, simply ignores this part of biblical teaching and Christian theology. Without balanced preaching and clear teaching on the purposes of God centred in Christ as they move towards His goal for all things, the church finds itself proclaiming a gospel which is entirely time-bound within the present. It promises more than God delivers now, thereby alternately raising and dashing the hopes of broken and needy people. Equally damaging is the other extreme: the proclamation of a gospel which offers only 'pie in the sky by-and-by'. In this version, the world loved by God, and for which Christ died, is simply abandoned as the elect sit back and wait for the return of Christ.

Both these versions of the gospel are deficient. Without the firm hope for the future, symbolized by and inaugurated in the resurrection of Christ, the church's message proves to be fraudulent. And without the reality of God's action in Christ and its impact on this present age, the church seems to be a complete irrelevancy, only interested in conversation with itself. Its message to the world is drowned in the despair of human existence without God.

The members of the Tyndale Fellowship have set their faces firmly against this abandonment of eschatology, believing that a fresh examination of aspects of this theme is particularly timely. This book includes many of the papers devoted to the theme of eschatology which were read at the third Triennial Plenary Conference of the Tyndale Fellowship at Swanwick, Derbyshire, in July 1997. They address the topic from the broad categories of Bible and theology.

The book begins with an introductory essay which gives a broad perspective on the theme, followed by two essays in biblical theology. The first takes a comprehensive look at the overarching theme of 'new creation' while the second develops the eschatological significance of God's call of a people to be a kingdom of priests and a holy nation. Essays on the presence of a personal hope in Israelite faith and the notoriously difficult Gog and Magog passages in Ezekiel follow. New Testament papers include two which look at eschatology in the Gospel of Mark with particular attention to Jesus and the temple. The conference included lively interaction on the vexed problem of the fate of the lost; three papers in the book reflect this debate. Essays looking at Pauline eschatology and the Apocalypse round out the New Testament discussion.

The final chapters address the topic from a theological perspective. One looks at the theme of hope in the past thirty years. Not least amongst theologians of hope has been Jürgen Moltmann; a critique of his most recent work, *The Coming of God*, is offered. An integrative examination of science and the eschatological hope is followed by two essays which point to the significance of eschatology for Christian mission and ethics.

The unifying and underlying belief in these essays is the confidence that God's good purposes will come to fruition in His time and His way. Our conviction is that the reader must understand this message if the proclamation of the gospel is to be biblically based and powerful in our world today.

The book would not have appeared without the tireless work of the staff at Tyndale House, Cambridge. Their expertise in producing camera ready copy for the publishers was invaluable. Heartfelt gratitude is also given to Dr Bruce Winter and Denise Jillions for their ready advice and encouragement to the editors.

November 1997   Dr Kent E. Brower
                                                 Dr Mark W. Elliott
                                                 (Editors)

Introduction

UNDERSTANDING THE TIMES

Mark W. Elliott

'The Reader Must Understand'; to translate this way gives more force
to the imperative in Mark 13:14 than does the 'normal' translation:
'*Let* the reader understand'.[1] Pharisees and Sadducees were criticized
for not reading the signs of the times (Mt. 16:3). For the Christian
today, with Paul we 'see in a mirror, darkly'; but Paul's emphasis
was as much on 'see' as on 'darkly' (1 Cor. 13:12). Eschatology gives
us something to be understood. Too often in recent times Christians
have neglected eschatology, whether in sermons or as a section in a
Dogmatics. The church seems preoccupied with the urgent matters of
the here and now, and is in danger of losing sight of where it is,
ultimately, going. As Ben Witherington reminds us (chap. 7), the
emphasis in Paul is on the Lord Jesus who has been and is revealed
to us (if obscurely at points), not on a dark and fearful future.
Christians are called to give a reason for their hope, and that means
understanding something about how what God has done ties up
with what will happen to the world and to them.

    As Ernest Lucas notes with reference to the work of H.
Bertens (see chap. 14), practitioners in the humanities who opine that
there can be no precise or absolute truth in any science (while
asserting this claim with perfect confidence) stray embarrassingly far
outside their jurisdiction. However, despite these qualifiers, there is
some truth in the 'postmodern' diagnosis: information overload and
the lack of connection between fields of knowledge, the feeling that
feeling has to triumph over reason, the sense of having to surf the

---

[1] ὁ ἀναγινώσκων νοείτω.

pacy flow of life in order to avoid drowning – all leading to a
syndrome of anxiety often immune to scientific analysis.[2] By way of
compensation, a sort of secular-spiritual eschatology encourages us
that the tension of living humanely while under the material
pressures of competition and stress is making us somehow more
'spiritual' people. Here is a new, strange kind of postmillennialism
for the year 2000 and beyond.[3]

Continuity and Discontinuity

According to the apostolic presentation, the old world is passing
away and a new one coming. God has always been in the renewing
business, ever since the early days of creation. With the New
Testament this now has cosmic, earth-shattering implications – but
the shattering is done in order to set things right.[4] As Stephen
Williams has said elsewhere[5] in response to Oliver O'Donovan's
emphasis on the continuity between this creation and the new
creation, it becomes very difficult to tell (with any great amount of
meaningfulness) just how the world to come – and the humans
within it – will be different and how they will be the same as before.[6]
O'Donovan's thesis is made partly as a response to the world-
denying tendencies within traditional evangelicalism (and thus he
emphasizes sin as existing not so much in that which is, as in our *view*

---

[2]Already in the 1960s, *e.g.* in N. Cohn's book, *The Pursuit of the Millennium*
(London: Pimlico, 1970).

[3]I sense something of this in Pannenberg's tracing of a development of the
human spirit through the ages; early modernity's (or was it the Reformation's?)
breaking of the hierarchy of orders of being made a sense of immediate relating
to 'the divine' possible; late modernity has seen an 'ethicization' of society – and
what we have to look forward to is an increasingly rarefied and self-conscious
existence. See his *Metaphysics and the Idea of God* (Edinburgh: T. & T. Clark, 1990).

[4]See the essays of Greg Beale (chap. 1) and Bruce Winter (chap. 16) in this
volume.

[5]S. Williams, 'Evangelicals and Eschatology: A Contentious Case', in A. N. S.
Lane (ed.), *Interpreting the Bible: Essays in honour of David F. Wright* (Leicester:
Apollos, 1997), 291-308. The theme of 'love' rather than 'victory for continuity' is
perhaps to be our watchword: see Williams, below (chap. 12).

[6]In this volume, Richard Bauckham (chap. 13) concurs with Jürgen Moltmann's
plea for remembering the goodness of ('earthy' or 'physical') creation which
traditional dogma has overlooked. But he raises the point that the millenarian
tradition seems to abandon this in preference for a step up into a final heavenly
'new creation', as if the millennial kingdom on earth were a stepping stone, a
buffer state, a chrysalis before the final butterfly.

and use of that which is). However, it also operates out of a ('later Barthian')[7] concern that the resurrection of the humanity of Christ be understood to have changed reality for everyone. This is an understanding of resurrection as being out of death and which starts in the hearts of believers – to be fulfilled in the spiritual body of which Paul speaks in 1 Corinthians 15:35ff. Until the eschaton, there is not an automatic process at work; rather, the good news is that there is a power of possibility for change which goes deep, issuing in action which embodies the Lord's teaching (see Gordon Thomas, chap. 2). What is of value will be preserved. God can be trusted to be the judge of what is valuable.

Recently, N. T. Wright has attempted to show that many New Testament prophecies from the mouth of Jesus concerning the end-times refer particularly to the events of AD 70.[8] The New Testament seems to say slightly less than it used to about the final days of the world as a whole. There has been a similar trend in Old Testament studies over the last decade, with once apparently eschatological texts shown to be using cosmic imagery in a metaphorical way in order to say something more dramatically but also more truthfully about the restoration of ancient Israel in a foreseeable future.[9] Daniel Block (chap. 4) argues that Ezekiel 38–39 is not about the end of everything, but is about a provisional end. It is a summit which is not the top; not a 'false' summit, but one from which we can see what or where the top is, even if it appears a little obscured by the cloud. Eschatological passages in the Old Testament give its readers a chance to take eschatological bearings, and set a pattern for understanding what that end will be like.

Irenaeus had a place for the millennium in his scheme of showing the Lordship of God over His creation – that, in a sense, the millennium on earth would be not so much an 'interim' order to get God and people used to each other, as the proof that God is at home in what He has made.[10] What biblical eschatology distributes across

---

[7]See O. O'Donovan, *Resurrection and Moral Order: An Outline for Evangelical Ethics* (Leicester: Apollos, 2nd edn., 1994). *Cf.* Karl Barth, *Christ and Adam: Man and humanity in Romans 5* (Edinburgh: Oliver & Boyd, 1956). Of course it might be described as 'Athanasian', and is strongly present in Orthodox soteriology.

[8]N.T. Wright, *Jesus and the Victory of God* (London: SPCK, 1996). For dialogue with his position, see the essays of K. E. Brower (chap. 5) and C. Fletcher-Louis (chap. 6) in this volume.

[9]See M. A. Sweeney, *Isaiah 1-39 with an introduction to prophetic literature* (FOTL; Grand Rapids: Eerdmans, 1996), 314.

[10]Irenaeus, in A. Rousseau *et al.*, *Irénée de Lyon. Contre les hérésies, Livre V*, Sources Chrétiennes 152-153 (Paris: Cerf, 1969).

all its forms is a state of mind that longs for God's intervention, that God's will would be done on earth, here and now before the end itself comes. This is a belief in a kind of backward causation in which the Holy Spirit comes from the end of time to draw things to a conclusion and a change, all the time inviting humans to take part by ethical response, which is one of watching in the light of the judgment. The judgment we do not know; but we know the Judge and so we aim to keep in His ways. When He comes, will He find faith on the earth? The lamentable state of western Christianity is perhaps thrown into relief by the fate of the Christian faith in the original 'Bible lands'. Western Christians have largely abandoned any political messianism since it tends to encourage ideas of crusading and of some *Tausendjahres Reich*.[11] In its place is the United Nations' ideal of human rights and justice for all; one does not have to be a cynic to hold that this is often upheld only when the economic interests of the capitalist world are at stake.[12]

Spirituality: AD 1000 and AD 2000

The Catholic teaching on eschatology was sober,[13] even before it (in the person of Aquinas) had to encounter the theories of Joachim of Fiore. What seems sure is that the church said more about what *not* to believe than what was to be expected. Popular piety feared the end and military rulers used the drama of the end-times to build up their reputation; but commentaries on the Apocalypse or 2 Thessalonians tended to avoid the issue by dwelling at a level of abstraction. They remained stoutly in the tradition of Augustinian refusal (aided by Jerome) to get excited about the idea of a millennium, at least an imminent one. Eschatology in any vibrant form (*i.e.* that suggested the end-times were at hand) came to be regarded as a subset of heresiology, or was obviously the weapon of the rulers who were trying to assert themselves over other rulers home and abroad. (For

---

[11]An over-close identification of the work of God and humans was particularly a problem for Eastern European mystical theology (*e.g.*, that of Angelus Silesius). Ernst Benz argued that this 'bad' theology prepared the way for this century's totalitarianism (*Endzeiterwartung zwischen Ost und West: Studien zur Christlichen Eschatologie* [Freiburg: Rombach, 1973], 249f.).

[12]Of course, this might be seen as 'a good thing'. *Cf.* Francis Fukuyama, *The End of History and the Last Man* (London: Hamish Hamilton, 1992).

[13]To judge from the *Handbuch der Dogmengeschichte* volume by Ludwig Ott, *Eschatologie in der Scholastik* (Freiburg: Herder, 1990). It is also instructive that Aquinas's *Summa Theologiae* has no part devoted to 'the last things'.

example, the Franks and their successors in the West appear to have borrowed the interpretation of 'the restraining one' [2 Thes. 2:6] from Byzantium.) Thus it was neither a commentary nor a treatise but a letter to an ambitious queen asking for an explanation of the end-times which was perhaps the most striking text of an eschatological nature in the latter days of the first millennium.[14] A search for a *theological* encounter with the issues around the end of the first millennium is not encouraging.[15] Eschatology had more to do with spirituality, how to cope with fear, presumption, or indifference that the idea of 'the last times' produced.

Today, the figure of the Antichrist is no longer present in western churches, either because we have become desensitized to evil (so, Bernard McGinn) or perhaps simply because the church has cried 'wolf in sheep's clothing!' once too often.[16] There is a hesitancy to trace God's hand in history for fear of too easily identifying Him with a nation, a party, a way of life, even a religion. The spirit which inspired Troeltsch has come of age. Perhaps it is inevitable that there should be a retreat to personal religion – but even there the signs of God's advent are not always easy to see. Concerns are less cosmic and outward-looking, often manifested in a tendency for defensive-ness and the need to save what we have. Out of this the God of hope calls us to generosity.

One of the key questions concerning the millennium is: should it make us either (1) optimists, believing either (a) that we can inaugurate the millennium and so hasten Christ's postmillennial return or (b) that we hasten His premillennial return by preaching His imminent coming, or (2) pessimists, retreating to our wisdom, our attempts to find meaning, hoping to be as a community a light on the hill, as individuals salt in the earth – until He comes? Perhaps both attitudes are to be taught, producing expectancy of a sober sort; certainly one which believes this world is the one worthy (in God's eyes) to be transformed. What seems clear (although not beyond threat of contradiction) is that how one views the future makes a

---

[14]See B. McGinn, 'Adso of Montier-en-Der: Letter on the Origin and Time of the Antichrist', in *idem*, *Apocalyptic Spirituality* (London: SPCK, 1980), 89-96, esp. 93.

[15]For eastern Christian views, see Cyril Mango, *Byzantium* (London: Weidenfeld & Nicolson, 1980), chap. 11 ('The future of mankind'). For the West, see (*e.g.*) Johannes Fried, 'L'attesa della fine dei tempi alla svolta del millenio', in Ovidio Capitani and Jürgen Miethke (eds.), *L'attesa della fine dei tempi nel Medioevo* (Bologna: il Mulino, 1990), 37-86.

[16]Candidates have included Justinian, Mohammed, the Pope.

difference as to how one lives now.[17] But the gospel includes a requirement that what life after death will be and will not be like is explained.

Ultimate Doctrine

But when it comes to what the church should teach, to *dogma* as distinct from spirituality, it is perhaps with the doctrine of hell and eternal judgment, one half of the truly *last* things that we ought to be concerned. Evangelicals are known, notorious perhaps, for a refusal not to take this question seriously, to see it as a mountain to be climbed, or at least gazed at, because it is there. Of course, the goodness and generosity of the God of Jesus Christ is to be defended against attacks. Yet God's grace is not bound: He has mercy on whom He wills (Rom. 9). Tony Gray and Peter Head present differing responses to the paper of Earle Ellis (chaps. 9-11). What is the second *death*, if not a termination of existence? Why should souls last for ever? Is even their maker not allowed to 'end' them if He has made them? It is perhaps not right to rely over much on intertestamental literature as background for our New Testament interpretation (after all, many of these books are apocryphal, not even deuterocanonical, precisely *because* of the 'fanciful' nature of their content).[18] Yet, *per contra*, is the Old Testament any more admissible – especially when the interpretation of relevant texts concerning the afterlife is disputed;[19] or are the writings of Ignatius, Irenaeus, Athanasius *et al.* really such important witnesses, even if they are Christian? Augustine's (hardly platonizing) point was that it is the duration of resurrection *bodies* not souls which enables suffering to be eternal.[20] (Moreover, the notion of disembodied souls

---

[17]*Cf.* Mark Noll, *A History of Christianity in the United States and Canada* (Grand Rapids: Eerdmans, 1992), 376ff. *Cf.* also Howard Peskett, chap. 15 in this volume, on the relationship (could it be dialectical?) between 'pre-millennial urgency' and 'post-millennial optimism'.

[18]See B. M. Metzger, *An Introduction to the Apocrypha* (New York: OUP, 1957); R. T. Beckwith, *The Old Testament Canon of the New Testament Church* (Reading: SPCK, 1985).

[19]As early as Origen's interpretation of *The Witch of Endor*; challenged by Eustathius (see E. Klostermann, *Origenes, Eustathius von Antiochien und Gregor von Nyssa über die Hexe von Endor* [Bonn-Berlin, 1912], 16-62). In 1 Sa. 28 did Saul only think he saw the shade of Samuel? On the OT 'personal eschatology', see Philip Johnston in this volume.

[20]*De civitate Dei* 21:3: 'mirabile est enim, dolere in ignibus, et tamen vivere...sed sempiterna mors erit, quando nec vivere anima poterit Deum non habendo, nec

awaiting the resurrection is not such a medieval 'platonizing' development, but arose from a need to explain what happened to the early Christian martyrs.) Are statements such as that in Revelation 14:9-11 ('And the smoke of their torment will go up for eternity') not clear enough?[21] *Which bits* of the language of such a 'hard text' are metaphorical anyway? The 'smoke going up'? 'For eternity'? The torment? Evangelicals can be glad that in wrestling with, or disagreeing over the meaning of, these texts they take them seriously and thus believe that whatever it is, there is such a thing as divine judgment.

This book seeks to help readers bring their own ideas of the eschaton into congruence with the apostolic witness in such a way that their re-shaped ideas help make this life itself more meaningful. Knowledge of the shortness of time and the judgment of a good God *can* make people appreciate this life more; believing there is a heaven can encourage us to radical action or to quiet trust, as appropriate. Faith is not certainty, but it is accompanied by a certain surety of sense. On that faith, informed by the knowledge of ultimate things, He will build His church.

---

doloribus corporis carere moriendo. Prima mors animam nolentem e corpore, secundo mors animam nolentem tenet in corpore.'

[21] ὁ καπνὸς τοῦ βασανισμοῦ αὐτῶν εἰς αἰῶνας αἰώνων ἀναβαίνει. (For a preliminary attempt to make sense of the Apocalypse, see A. Garrow in this volume, chap. 8.)

Section A

BIBLICAL THEOLOGY

Chapter 1

THE ESCHATOLOGICAL CONCEPTION OF NEW TESTAMENT THEOLOGY[1]

Greg K. Beale

There have been many New Testament theologies written in the twentieth century. Some theologies have emphasized a general redemptive-historical or 'already and not yet' eschatological paradigm. It is upon the basis of such a theological focus that the proposal of this article begins. Though these eschatological approaches have seen 'new creation' as a facet of eschatology, none have attempted to understand eschatology exhaustively as 'new creation'. The present thesis proposes to do just this, and to contend that the perspective of the 'already and not yet', latter-day new creation is the heuristic lens for understanding all of the major doctrines of the New Testament. Such a thesis sheds new light on the theology of the New Testament.

Is the quest for a centre for a comprehensive biblical theology so fraught with difficulties that it ought to be abandoned in favour of a multiperspectival approach? Or is the quest still open to a fresh search which builds on previous attempts, avoiding some of the pitfalls into which they fell?

This essay sets out the view that *new creation* is a plausible and defensible centre for New Testament theology, and that it is a needed refinement of the 'inaugurated eschatology' centre previously proposed by others. The challenges facing a single theme approach should not be underestimated. If a single theme approach

---

[1]The essay originated in my inaugural address on the occasion of being installed as Professor of New Testament at Gordon-Conwell Theological Seminary (19 March, 1993). I am thankful to my colleagues at Gordon-Conwell Theological Seminary and the Tyndale Fellowship for their helpful evaluative comments on this paper especially to Moisés Silva, Scott Hafemann and Phil Towner.

is to succeed, it will have to show how the single theme can be related to (1) the various major theological ideas of the New Testament and (2) the various New Testament books themselves. The paper will set out a response to the first challenge, but the limits of this study do not allow for much of a response to the second. An appendix entitled 'Methodological issues for a single-centre biblical theology'(pp. 45-52) will respond more fully to the challenges. I hope that those who disagree with my proposed centre will see it, at least, as a helpful paradigm which sheds new light on the New Testament.

'Already and Not Yet': Eschatology as the Starting-Point for the New Proposal

I am developing an approach to New Testament theology which builds partly on those scholars who have established that an 'already and not yet' eschatological scheme is crucial to understanding the New Testament. My thesis goes beyond this perspective by attempting to define the general notion of eschatology specifically as new creation. My presupposition is that the entire canon is the proper, inspired database for doing biblical theology, though this essay focuses on the New Testament.

The starting-point of my approach, in agreement with others before me, is that to understand the New Testament in its full richness we must have a keen acquaintance with how the biblical authors viewed the 'end-times'. This may sound like an extreme proposition. After all, can we not have an excellent understanding of the New Testament without knowing about exactly how the world is going to end? Are not questions about the time of the rapture, tribulation and millennium secondary to the salvation which Christ accomplished at the cross? We would answer these questions with a 'yes' *if* the end-times *were* a period coming only at the final phase of history. Indeed, many Christians assume that the end-times pertain only to the future end of history, so that Christ's death and resurrection are events which happened at His first coming and are not closely connected with those events leading up to His second coming.

Such a popular understanding that the latter-days refers only to the yet future end of the world needs radical adjustment. New Testament scholarship over the past few decades has made great strides in increasing our understanding that the beginning of Christian history was perceived by the first Christians as the beginning of the end-times. There is, however, still much to be done in synthesizing this work, developing a New Testament theology in the light of such work, and refining the focus of eschatology in its relation to New Testament theology.[2] New Testament scholarship has still been atomistic enough to prevent serious broad theological reflection on the entire New Testament corpus (though there are some significant exceptions, such as N. T. Wright's work). Along these lines, as late as the mid-1980s, D. C. Allison could complain that the history of New Testament theology was responsible for influencing scholars to focus specifically on the atoning nature of Christ's death and not pay sufficient attention to its eschatological ramifications. He continued,

> Christian theology has rarely grappled seriously with the eschatological presuppositions that permeate the New Testament, and although the twentieth century is the century of Albert Schweitzer, contemporary students of the New Testament have yet to explore *fully* the importance of eschatological language for the early followers of Jesus.[3]

A good place to begin is with a brief survey of explicit eschatological language in the New Testament. The phrase 'latter days' and its synonyms occur approximately twenty-seven times in the New Testament, and only sometimes refer exclusively to the very end of history as we typically think of it. These phrases, however, are also used often to describe the end-times as beginning *already* in the first century. A survey of these phrases will lay the foundation for the idea that all doctrine in the New Testament is essentially eschatological in nature, so that even the general scholarly perspective of the eschatological 'already and not yet' will be seen to need significant refinement. It will also require the church to reassess the popular view of eschatology as dealing only with the future.

---

[2]For recent articles (and relevant bibliography) summarizing the eschatology of the Gospels, Paul and the rest of the New Testament, see D. C. Allison, 'Eschatology', in J. B. Green, S. McKnight and I. H. Marshall (eds.), *Dictionary of Jesus and the Gospels* (Downers Grove and Leicester: IVP, 1992), 206-209; L. J. Kreitzer, 'Eschatology', in G. F. Hawthorne, R. P. Martin and D. G. Reid (eds.), *Dictionary of Paul and his Letters* (Downers Grove and Leicester: IVP, 1993), 253-269; G. K. Beale, 'Eschatology', in P. H. Davids and R. P. Martin (eds.), *Dictionary of the later New Testament and its Developments* (Downers Grove and Leicester: IVP, 1997). See also D. E. Aune, 'Early Christian Eschatology', in D. N. Freedman (ed.), *The Anchor Bible Dictionary* (New York: Doubleday, 2nd edn. 1992), 594-609.
[3]Allison, *The End of the Ages Has Come* (Philadelphia: Fortress, 1985), 169 (italics added).

The first observation about these more technical end-time phrases is that they are alluding to identical phrases in the Old Testament. Therefore, the meaning of the Old Testament expression 'latter days' must be understood before the New Testament use can be explained fully. In the Old Testament this wording is prophetic and refers to a future time when: (1) there will be a tribulation for Israel consisting of oppression (Ezk. 38:14-17ff.), persecution (Dn. 10:14ff.; 11:27–12:10), false teaching, deception and apostasy (Dn. 10:14ff.; 11:27-35); (2) after the tribulation Israel will seek the Lord (Ho. 3:4-5), they will be delivered (Ezk. 38:14-16ff.; Dn. 10:14ff.; 12:1-13) and their enemies will be judged (Ezk. 38:14-16ff.; Dn. 10:14ff.; 11:40-45; 12:2); (3) this deliverance and judgment will occur because a leader (Messiah) from Israel will finally conquer all of its Gentile enemies (Gn. 49:1,8-12; Nu. 24:14-19; Is. 2:2-4; Mi. 4:1-3; Dn. 2:28-45; 10:14-12:10); (4) God will establish a kingdom on the earth and rule over it (Is. 2:2-4; Mi. 4:1-3; Dn. 2:28-45) together with a Davidic king (Ho. 3:4-5); (5) after the time of tribulation and persecution, Daniel 11–12 says there will be a resurrection of the righteous and unrighteous (so Dn. 11:30-12:3ff.).[4]

The Old Testament also expresses eschatological hopes without using the technical vocabulary of 'latter days', 'end-times', and so on. For example, Joel 2:28ff. refers to the 'pouring out of God's Spirit' in the coming period of restoration, and this hope can be found elsewhere in the Old Testament as well.[5] Likewise, Isaiah 65:17-18 and 66:22 refer to the coming new creation of the cosmos without utilizing formal eschatological terminology.

The New Testament repeatedly uses precisely the same phrase 'latter days' as found in the Old Testament prophecies. And the meaning of the phrase is identical, except for one difference: in the New Testament the end-days predicted by the Old Testament are seen as beginning their fulfilment with Christ's first coming. All that the Old Testament foresaw would occur in the end-times has begun already in the first century and continues on into our present day. This means that the Old Testament prophecies of the great tribulation, God's deliverance of Israel from oppressors, God's rule over the Gentiles and the establishment of His kingdom have been set in motion by Christ's life, death, resurrection and formation of the Christian church. The resurrection marked the beginning of Jesus'

---

[4]In addition to Dn. 10:14, *cf.* also eschatological terms such as 'time of the end' in Dn. 8:19; 11:40.
[5]The Joel 2 prophecy is introduced by the phrase 'after this' which is eschatologically charged, as evident from Acts 2:17 rendering Joel's phrase by 'in the last days'.

messianic reign, and the Spirit at Pentecost signalled the inauguration of His rule through the church (see Acts 1:6-8; 2:1-43). On the other hand, persecution of Jesus and the church indicated the beginning of the final tribulation. What the Old Testament did not foresee so clearly was the ironic reality that the kingdom *and* the tribulation could co-exist at the same time: for example, John says in Revelation 1:9, 'I, John, your brother and fellow-partaker in the tribulation and kingdom and perseverance which are in Jesus.' Therefore, the latter days do not take place only at some point in the future but occur throughout the whole church age, which means we in the twentieth century are still experiencing the latter days, as strange as that may sound to some people.

The first time the wording 'last days' appears in the New Testament is Acts 2:17. Here, Peter understands that the tongues being spoken at Pentecost are a beginning fulfilment of Joel's end-time prophecy that a day would come when God's Spirit would gift not merely prophets, priests and kings, but all of God's people. Peter says,

> For these men are not drunk as you suppose, for it is only the third hour of the day; but this is what was spoken of through the prophet Joel: 'And it shall be *in the last days*, God says, that I will pour forth of My Spirit upon all mankind . . .' (Acts 2:15-17a; *cf.* Joel 2:28).

In 1 Corinthians 10:11, Paul says that the Old Testament was written to instruct the Corinthian Christians about how to live in the end-times, since upon them 'the ends of the ages have come'. And in Galatians 4:4 he refers to Jesus' birth as occurring 'when the fullness of the time came' in fulfilment of the messianic prophecies. Likewise, in Ephesians 1:7-10 and 1:20-23 'the fullness of the times' alludes to when believers were redeemed and Christ began to rule over the earth as a result of His resurrection. The expressions 'the last times' and 'end days' in 1 Timothy 4:1ff. and 2 Timothy 3:1ff. refer to the presence of tribulation in the form of false, deceptive teaching. That the latter days in 1 and 2 Timothy is not a reference only to a distant, future time is evident from recognizing that the Ephesian church is already experiencing this latter-day tribulation of deceptive teaching and apostasy (see 1 Tim. 1:3-4, 6, 7, 19-20; 4:7; 5:13-15; 6:20-21; 2 Tim. 1:15; 2:16-19; 2:25-26; 3:2-9).

The author of Hebrews proclaims in his opening two verses that in his own day, 'in these last days', Jesus had begun to fulfil the Psalm 2 prophecy that God's Son would judge the evil kingdoms and receive the earth as an inheritance from His Father (*cf.* Ps. 2:1-12 with Heb. 1:2-5). In like manner, in Hebrews 9:26 he says 'at the consummation of the ages He (Christ) has been manifested to put away sin by the sacrifice of Himself'. And James 5:1-9 warns his readers not to trust in riches, because the 'last days' have come. He attempts to motivate his audience to trust in Christ and not worldly possessions by imparting to them a comprehension of what God has accomplished through Christ in these 'last days'.

In identical fashion, 1 Peter 1:19-21 says that Christ has died as a sacrificial lamb and been resurrected 'in these last times'. 2 Peter 3:3 also reflects the same outlook as Paul's on the end days when it is pronounced that 'in the last days mockers will come with their mocking' (see 1 Tim. 4:1; 2 Tim. 3:1). That this is not mere prophecy of the future but description of the present is clear from noticing that Peter recognizes that the mockers are presently spreading false teaching in the church which he is addressing (2 Pet. 3:16-17; note the imminent threat of false teachers in 2:1-22). Jude 18 has exactly the same idea (cf. Jude 4, 8, 10-13). In a similar context of false teaching, 1 John 2:18 says, 'Children, it is the last hour; and just as you heard that antichrist is coming, even now many antichrists have arisen; from this we know that it is the last hour.' These 'antichrists' were manifesting themselves by attempting to deceive others through erroneous teaching (see 1 Jn. 2:21-23, 26; 4:1-5). Indeed, one of the indications that the latter-day tribulation is continuing during the present inter-advent period is the pervasive presence of false teaching within the purported covenant community.

This brief survey demonstrates that the last days predicted by the Old Testament began with Christ's first coming, although there is other terminology besides 'latter days' in many other passages which could also be adduced as further evidence (e.g., see Paul's use of 'now' in 2 Cor. 6:2; Eph. 3:5, 10). There are also many passages conveying eschatological concepts but which do not use technical eschatological expressions. Christ's life, death, resurrection and establishment of the church community have ushered in the fulfilment of the Old Testament prophecies of the tribulation, the Messiah's conquering of Gentile enemies, Israel's deliverance and the long-expected kingdom. In this initial phase of the end-times, Christ and the church begin to fulfil the prophecies concerning Israel's tribulation and end-time kingdom because Christ and the church are seen by the New Testament as *the true Israel* (see Rom. 2:25-29; 9:6, 24-26; Gal. 3:29; 6:15-16; Eph. 2:16-18; 3:6; 1 Pet. 2:9; Rev. 1:6; 3:9; 5:9-10).[6] This notion of radical inaugurated fulfilment is best expressed by 2

---

[6]See further H. K. LaRondelle, *The Israel of God in Prophecy* (Berrien Springs: Andrews University Press, 1983).

Corinthians 1:20: 'For as many as may be the promises of God [in the Old Testament], in Him [Christ] they are yes.'

Of course, there are passages in the New Testament which speak of the future consummation of the present latter-day period: for example, the bodily resurrection of all people, the destruction of the present cosmos, the creation of a completely new heavens and earth, the final judgment, the eternal Sabbath, and so on. The New Testament writers assert that Christians experience only a part of what will be completely experienced in the final form of the new heavens and earth. There is what some call an 'already-and-not-yet' dimension of the end-times. In this respect Oscar Cullmann has metaphorically described Jesus' first coming as 'D-day', since this is when Satan was decisively defeated. 'V-day' is the second coming, when Jesus' enemies will totally surrender and bow down to Him. Cullmann put it this way: 'The hope of the final victory is so much more vivid because of the unshakeably firm conviction that the battle that decides the victory has already taken place.'[7]

But the point of the present discussion is that the great end-time predictions have already begun the process of fulfilment. William Manson has well said,

> When we turn to the New Testament, we pass from the climate of prediction to that of fulfilment. The things which God had foreshadowed by the lips of His holy prophets He has now, in part at least, brought to accomplishment . . . The supreme sign of the Eschaton is the Resurrection of Jesus and the descent of the Holy Spirit on the Church. The Resurrection of Jesus is not simply a sign which God has granted in favour of His son, but is the inauguration, the entrance into history, *of the times of the End*.

> Christians, therefore, have entered through the Christ into the new age . . . What had been predicted in Holy Scripture as to happen to Israel or to man in the *Eschaton* has happened to and in Jesus. *The foundation-stone of the New Creation has come into position*.[8]

Therefore, the apostles understood eschatology not merely as futurology but as a mindset for understanding the present within the

---

[7]Cullmann, *Christ and Time* (Philadelphia: Westminster, 1964), 87.
[8]Manson, 'Eschatology in the New Testament', in *Eschatology* (Four Papers Read to *The Society for the Study of Theology*), Scottish Journal of Theology Occasional Papers No. 2 (Edinburgh: Oliver and Boyd, 1953), 6 (my italics in the last sentence). Though this sounds like 'over-realized eschatology', Manson qualifies it by saying, 'The End has come! The end has not come!' (*ibid.*, 7).

climaxing context of redemptive history. That is, the apostles understood that they were already living in the end-times and that they were to understand their present salvation in Christ to be already an end-time reality. *Every aspect of their salvation was to be conceived of as eschatological in nature.* To put this another way, every major doctrine of the Christian faith has an end-time tint. This means that the doctrine of eschatology in New Testament theology textbooks should not merely be one among many doctrines. Furthermore, eschatology should not be placed at the end of New Testament theology textbooks or at the end of chapters dealing with the different New Testament corpuses because it purportedly describes only the very end of the world as we know it. Rather, the doctrine of eschatology should be part of the title of such a textbook, since every major theological concept breathes the air of a latter-day atmosphere. Perhaps, the title of a biblical theology of the New Testament could read 'New Testament Theology as Eschatology.' For the same reason systematic theology textbooks should not place eschatology as the last chapter, but should integrate it into discussion of other New Testament doctrines.

New Creation as the Refinement of the 'Already and Not Yet' Eschatological Centre

When viewed through end-time spectacles, our understanding of most of the traditional doctrines is not so much changed as radically enriched. But how are some of the crucial doctrines of our faith so enriched when seen as eschatological doctrines? The concluding part of W. Manson's above quotation is a good place to start answering this question. He said the *resurrected* Christ as 'the foundation-stone of the New Creation has come into position'.

We should think of Christ's life, and especially his death and resurrection as the central events which launched the latter days. These pivotal events of Christ's life, death and resurrection are eschatological because they launched the beginning of the new creation. The end-time new creation has not been recognized sufficiently heretofore as the basis of a biblical theology of the New Testament, and it is this concept which has the potential to refine significantly the general scholarly view of the eschatological 'already and not yet'.

Of course, the Old Testament prophesied that the destruction of the first creation and the re-creation of a new heavens and earth were to happen at the very end of time. Christ's work reveals that the end of the world and the coming new creation have begun in his death and resurrection: 2 Corinthians 5:15 and 17 says Christ 'died and rose again . . . so that if any are in Christ, they are a new creation, the old things have passed away; behold, new things have come'. Revelation 1:5 refers to Christ as 'the first-born from the dead' and then Revelation 3:14 defines 'first-born' as 'the beginning of the [new] creation of God'.[9] Likewise, Colossians 1:18 says that Christ is 'the first-born from the dead' and 'the beginning' so that 'he himself might come to have first place in everything'. In Galatians 6:14-15, Paul says that his identification with Christ's death means that he is a 'new creation'.

Indeed, the resurrection was predicted by the Old Testament to occur at the end of the world as part of the new creation. God would make redeemed humanity a part of the new creation by recreating their bodies through resurrection (cf. Dn. 12:1-2). Of course, we still look forward to the time when our bodies will be raised at Christ's final parousia, and we will become part of the consummated new creation. Christ's resurrection, however, placed Him into the beginning of the new creation. The resurrected Christ is not merely spiritually the inauguration of the new cosmos, but He is literally its beginning, since He was resurrected with a physically resurrected, newly created body. When Matthew 27:50 narrates Jesus' death, Matthew immediately adds in verses 51-53, 'the earth shook; and the rocks split, and the tombs were opened; and many bodies of the saints who had fallen asleep were raised; and coming out of the tombs after His resurrection they entered the holy city and appeared to many'. These strange phenomena are recorded by Matthew to signal to his readers that Christ's death was the beginning of the end of the old creation and the inauguration of a new creation. Likewise, 1 John 2:17-18 can say 'the world is passing away . . . it is the last hour'. Christ's death is not just any death, but it is the beginning of the destruction of the entire world, which will not be consummated until the very end. Likewise, 1 Corinthians 15:22-24 says the resurrection launched in Christ will be consummated when He returns.

New creation is in mind wherever the concept of resurrection occurs, since it is essentially the new creation of humanity. The equivalence of resurrection with new creation is apparent also from

---

[9]For the notion of new creation in the 2 Cor. 5 and Rev. 3 texts, see G. K. Beale, 'The Old Testament Background of Reconciliation in 2 Corinthians 5-7 and Its Bearing on the Literary Problem of 2 Cor. 6:14-7:1', *New Testament Studies* 35 (1989), 550-581, and *idem*, 'The Old Testament Background of Rev 3.14', *New Testament Studies* 42 (1996), 133-152.

noticing that three of the four most explicit new creation texts in the
New Testament refer to Christ's resurrection (2 Cor. 5:14-17; Col.
1:15-18; Rev. 1:5 and 3:14), while the fourth refers to His death (Gal.
6:14-15; 2 Cor. 5:14-17 likely also includes both the death and
resurrection as a part of the new creation). These are significant
observations, since the idea of resurrection occurs so much
throughout the New Testament; likewise Christ's death can be seen
as part of the process of new creation, as hinted at just above in the
Matthew 27 discussion, and as will be explained further below.
Likewise, mention of Christ's death throughout the New Testament
probably carries connotations of the beginning destruction of the old
world which paves the way for the new. In the light of these
observations, new creation also can be seen as a more dominant
notion than one might at first think.

In the light of what we have said so far, we can state the
overriding idea of New Testament theology, especially in Paul and
Revelation, but also in the Gospels and the rest of the New
Testament. The idea is this: *Christ's life, and especially death and
resurrection through the Spirit, launched the glorious end-time new creation
of God*.

It is at this precise point that I hope to build on the
foundational work of such theologians as Geerhardus Vos,[10] Oscar
Cullmann,[11] Herman Ridderbos,[12] and George Eldon Ladd.[13] They
also recognized that Christ's redemptive work inaugurated the latter
days and that the eschatological period would be consummated at
some point in the future.[14] These scholars understood that

---

[10]*The Pauline Eschatology* (Grand Rapids: Baker, 1979); see also *Redemptive History
and Biblical Interpretation. The Shorter Writings of Geerhardus Vos*, ed. R. B. Gaffin
(Phillipsburg, NJ: Presbyterian and Reformed, 1980), *passim*.
[11]Cullmann, *Christ and Time*.
[12]*The Coming of the Kingdom* (Philadelphia, PA: Presbyterian and Reformed
Publishers, 1962); *Paul: an outline of his theology* (Grand Rapids: Eerdmans, 1975).
[13]*Presence of the Future* (Grand Rapids: Eerdmans, 1974).
[14]Though there were a few others who held this view. These scholars brought
together the polar positions of A. Schweitzer and C. H. Dodd, who believed
respectively that the end-times were imminent but not yet fulfilled, and, on the
other hand, that the latter-days had fully arrived in the coming of Jesus (for a
brief overview of the two positions, see Aune, 'Eschatology', 599-600, who also
cites J. Jeremias and W. G. Kümmel as holding a synthesis of the two
perspectives). Interestingly, Vos appears to be the first European or American
scholar to espouse an 'already and not yet eschatology' as a major theological
approach to Paul! Recently, C. M. Pate has developed Vos's view of eschatology
as the framework within which to understand Pauline theology in a more

eschatology was a crucial influence upon the thinking of the New Testament writers. More specifically, Richard Gaffin in his book *The Centrality of the Resurrection*[15] affirms that the resurrection as an end-time event is the all-encompassing thought in Paul. Seyoon Kim in his *The Origin of Paul's Gospel*[16] explains why the resurrection dominated Paul's thinking: it was because of the lasting impact of the risen Christ's confrontation with Paul on the Damascus Road.

But these scholars did not attempt to explain in programmatic fashion how inaugurated eschatology relates to and sheds light on the major theological doctrines of the New Testament.[17] *Nor did they see that the controlling conception of eschatology was new creation.* William Dumbrell is the only consistent exception to this, since he sees creation as the central theme of both Old and New Testaments: all of the Old Testament works toward the goal of new creation, and the New Testament begins to fulfil that primary goal.[18]

Dumbrell identifies five related themes, which are 'interrelated through their common relation to the Bible's wider concept of government and the Kingdom of God'.[19] He traces five major themes throughout both testaments: (1) new creation, (2) new covenant, (3) new temple, (4) new Israel and (5) new Jerusalem.[20]

---

thoroughgoing manner than before, though he does not interact with Vos (*The End of the Ages Has Come. The Theology of Paul* [Grand Rapids: Zondervan, 1995]).
[15](Grand Rapids: Baker, 1978).
[16](Grand Rapids: Eerdmans, 1982).
[17]Though Ridderbos (*Paul*) and Pate (*End of the Ages Has Come*) have made a good attempt at this in Paul.
[18]See his *The Search for Order* (Grand Rapids: Baker, 1994); *The End of the Beginning* (Homebush West NSW, Australia: Lancer, 1985); *cf.* his Old Testament theology, *Covenant and Creation* (Nashville: Thomas Nelson, 1984).
[19]*The End of the Beginning*, 'Introduction'. Interestingly, in his recent article on biblical theology, Scobie surveys past proposals of 'centres' for Old Testament, New Testament and the entire canon, and he criticizes them all, except for Dumbrell's, though he does say that Dumbrell's is 'not a full-fledged Biblical Theology'(180). Scobie surveys such significant centres for a canonical biblical theology as 'covenant', 'kingdom' and 'life', and for the New Testament he discusses such centres as 'the Christ event', 'christology', 'justification' and 'reconciliation.' Scobie himself offers a biblical-theological scheme of the entire canon not too different from Dumbrell's. In fact, what he does is to combine the numerous suggestions for a 'single centre' and organizes them broadly into four groups, which become the basis for his multi-thematic approach: (1) God's creative order; (2) God's servant (Christ); (3) God's people; (4) God's way (ethics). Scobie is apparently attracted to Dumbrell's view because it seems also to be multi- perspectival.
[20]For an expansion of the following summary of Dumbrell, see my review of his *The End of the Beginning* in *Themelios* 15 (1990), 69-70.

Each theme is not to be viewed as of equal importance, but they are the most important ones in the Bible for him. The new Jerusalem is the symbol of government and those governed; the new temple is the seat of government; the new covenant is the instrument of government; the new Israel reveals those governed and their role; and the new creation is a final comprehensive presentation of both the governed and the Governor.

Dumbrell rightly opts for new creation as the most comprehensive idea and the summary of the other four. The entire scheme of the Bible is structured around the movement 'from creation to new creation by means of divine redemptive interventions', climaxing in Christ's death, resurrection and second coming which concludes all things.[21] Dumbrell asserts that redemption is always subordinate to creation in that it is the means of reintroducing the conditions of the new creation.[22] All events since the fall are to be seen as a process leading to the reintroduction of the original creation. Dumbrell is correct in understanding new creation as the dominating notion of biblical theology because new creation is the goal or purpose of God's redemptive-historical plan; new creation is the logical main point of Scripture, which points further to new creation as the main lens of a canonical biblical theology.

There are, nevertheless, weaknesses in Dumbrell's approach. His work is too much of a sweeping brush-stroke which surveys broad themes (with brief summaries of important passages), does not work trenchantly at the exegetical level (though it was not intended to be such a work),[23] does not try organically to relate the major New Testament doctrines specifically to Christ's life, death and resurrection, nor does it attempt to explain specifically how the notion of new creation relates organically to the major New Testament ideas and doctrines. Nowhere is there a sufficiently precise explanation of how Christ's life, death and resurrection relate to or inaugurate the new creation.

Despite these weaknesses, Dumbrell's is the best canonical biblical theology which I have read. Although Dumbrell does not provide a specific answer, his thesis demands that the question concerning how Christ's death and resurrection relate to new creation be answered in a clear and thorough manner, thus

---

[21]*End of the Beginning*, 166, 196.

[22]*Ibid.*, 84-185, 191, 194.

[23]*E.g.*, there needed to be serious discussion of texts in the New Testament which actually associate Christ with the language of new creation (especially Gal. 6:14-18; 2 Cor. 5:14-17; Eph. 2:13-25 [*cf.* 1:20-23 and 2:10]; Col. 1:15-18; Rev. 3:14 [*cf.* with 1:5]).

supporting the view that the movement toward new creation is the centre of the New Testament.

My own view is broadly similar to Dumbrell's, but I am trying to establish the centrality of new creation in a much more exegetical and theologically trenchant manner. My thesis is that the major theological ideas of the New Testament flow out of the concept that *Christ's life, and especially death and resurrection through the Spirit, launched the end-time new creation for God's glory*. Each significant theological idea in the New Testament gains its fullest meaning within the framework of this overriding idea and is but a facet of it. We can think of Christ's life, and particularly death and resurrection, as a diamond which represents the new creation. The various theological ideas are the facets of the diamond, which are inseparable from the diamond itself. Some examples follow of how this is so, and how the eschatological enhancement of the various doctrines also gives insight into the practical application of these doctrines to our lives.

This idea of new creation is clearest in Paul and the Apocalypse, but is also apparent, I believe, elsewhere in the New Testament. It must also be acknowledged that the actual terminology 'new creation' does not occur much even in Paul, but, as noted above, the notion of resurrection is central in Paul, it is the climactic goal of the four Gospels, and resurrection is essentially a part of new creation; indeed, resurrection *is* the new creation of humanity.

Although the phrase 'new creation' does not appear often,[24] we should beware of assuming that for an idea to be prevalent the technical term usually associated with the idea must be used often. E. P. Sanders has cautioned in this regard:

---

[24]In fact, the actual phrase καινὴ κτίσις occurs only twice (2 Cor. 5:17 and Gal. 6:15), though paraphrastic variants of the phrase occur six times ('creation itself will be set free' in Rom. 8:20, 'new heavens and a new earth' in 2 Pet. 3:13, 'beginning of the creation of God' in Rev. 3:14, 'a new heaven and a new earth' in Rev. 21:1, and 'I am making all things new' in Rev. 21:5), and the theme occurs explicitly (along with the word 'create' and synonyms) in several other passages: Eph. 2:10-17; Col. 1:15-20; 3:10-11; Mt. 19:28 has παλιγγενεσία ('regeneration, rebirth') which likely refers to the creation of a new cosmos (so D. C. Sim, *Apocalyptic Eschatology in the Gospel of Matthew* [SNTS Monographs 88; Cambridge: Cambridge University Press, 1996], 111-114), and Tit. 3:5 employs the same word to refer to the believers' part in the regenerated cosmos, which is emphasized by the directly following phrase in 3:5, '*renewing* by the Holy Spirit', a likely reference to the Spirit's creation of people by giving them new life (which is made explicit in the 'eternal life' of 3:7); *cf.* also Ja. 1:18: 'He brought us forth by the exercise of His will through the word of truth in order that we should be a certain first fruit among His creatures.'

> It has frequently been urged as evidence against the primacy of the covenantal conception in 'late Judaism' that the word 'covenant' does not often appear . . . Word studies are not always deceptive, but they can be, and this one is . . . I would venture to say that it is the *fundamental nature of the covenant conception which largely accounts for the relative scarcity of appearances of the term 'covenant' in Rabbinic literature.*[25]

N. T. Wright, in his now well-known recent work, *The New Testament and the People of God*, appeals to Sanders at this point to argue for the pervasive presence of the 'covenant' concept in the Old Testament, even though the word also does not occur there in massive numbers.[26] Likewise, the infrequent use of the word 'creation' in the Old Testament and the rare use of the phrase 'new creation' in the New Testament does not mean that the idea is rare.

Some will conclude that to reduce the centre of the New Testament down to new creation is to add yet another reductionistic New Testament theology to those previously proposed, and that we must be content with a multi-perspectival approach.[27] I think, however, that the 'centre' I am proposing is supported by the broad sweep of canonical thought, wherein the Bible begins with original creation which is corrupted, and the rest of the Old Testament is a redemptive-historical process working toward a restoration of fallen creation. This approach is partially validated by the simplicity of its narrative story-line.

One could question the present thesis by asking how the central idea of new creation relates to the Gospels. In addition to earlier comments in this paper, it should be pointed out that the penultimate and ultimate climaxes of all the Gospels respectively are Jesus' death and resurrection, which, taken together, clearly relate to the notion of new creation. Therefore, all of the prior material in the Gospels is selected in one way or another to work toward their penultimate and ultimate goals. In this light, it may also not be coincidental that Βίβλος γένεσις ('The book of the genealogy') at the very beginning of Matthew (1:1) may do double duty to introduce

---

[25]*Paul and Palestinian Judaism* (London: SCM, 1977), 420ff.
[26](London: SPCK, 1992), 260.
[27]Of course, though I have mentioned some other New Testament theological approaches, the limits of the present study prohibit a serious attempt to survey and evaluate these and additional approaches, but it is a worthy task, and some have done it (*e.g.*, G. Hasel, *New Theology: Basic Issues in the Current Debate* [Grand Rapids: Eerdmans, 1978], and Scobie more recently, but not as thoroughly).

both the directly following genealogy of Jesus *and* the entire book, with the sense of the 'Book of the New Genesis by Jesus Christ.'[28]

How does the idea of 'kingdom' in the Gospels relate to new creation? The two could be different images and connote different ideas. Both, however, are two sides of one coin. Kingship was to be a role of Adam in the original creation, and this is to be a feature of the consummated new creation according to Revelation 11:15 and 22:5. In the original creation of Genesis 1–2 Adam was to be God's vicegerent, representing Him on earth. Recall that images of kings in the Ancient Near East represented the authority of kings themselves, and so it was with Adam. The *doctrines of Christ as the Last Adam, and the image of God and God's son and Messiah* are to be understood as references to Christ re-establishing a new creation as God's new, reigning vicegerent, since the first creation was commenced with a human also called Adam, who was in the image of God and called God's son.[29] As such, Christ is the Son of Adam, or 'the Son of Man', who has begun to do what the first Adam should have done and to inherit what the first Adam should have, including the glory reflected in God's image. And, of course, Daniel 7, where 'Son of Man' is prominent, makes allusions both to Genesis 1–2 and to Psalm 8. Paul can say that Christ's followers also reflect the renewed divine image and glory, as well as possessing sonship, because Christ has regained these things Himself (Rom. 8:18-23, 29-30; Eph. 4:25; Col. 3:10).

The first Adam should have obeyed and subdued the entire earth, but he did not. After the flood, Noah was commissioned to subdue the earth, but he had his own 'fall' in a garden-like

---

[28]W. D. Davies and D. C. Allison, *The Gospel According to Saint Matthew*, I (ICC; Edinburgh: T. & T. Clark, 1988), 149-155, who suggest that early Jewish readers would have been reminded of the beginning of the Old Testament Book of Genesis and of the beginning of the first creation narrative (*cf.* Gen. 5:1; 2:4). There is little doubt that the phrase 'In the beginning' at the introduction of John alludes, at least in part, to Yahweh's creative word in Genesis 1, especially because of the following imagery of 'the light shining in the darkness'. Perhaps Mk. 1:1 echoes the same background with his use of Ἀρχή.

[29]See D. J. McCartney, '*Ecce Homo*: The Coming of the Kingdom as the Restoration of Human Vicegerency', *Westminster Theological Journal* 56 (1994), 1-21, who contends that Jesus' beginning establishment of the kingdom in the Gospels and the remainder of the New Testament is to be primarily understood as 'the *reinstatement of the originally intended divine order for earth, with man properly situated as God's vicegerent*' (p. 2); in this connection he discusses Jesus as 'son of Man', 'son of God' and last Adam.

environment, also in connection with the image of nakedness.[30]
Subsequently, God created a corporate Adam, Israel, who was to be
obedient to God in the promised land, which the Old Testament
refers to repeatedly as 'like the garden of Eden'. They were to go out
from the promised land and subdue the rest of the earth. Appropriately, Israel was called by Adamic names, like 'Son of Adam (Man)'
and 'Son of God'. Israel had her 'fall' at the golden calf episode, the
effects of which were devastating for the nation's destiny. Instead of
subduing the earth, she was subdued by it. Lastly, God raises up
another individual Adamic figure, Jesus Christ, who finally does
what Adam should have done, and so He inaugurates a new creation
which will not be corrupted but find its culmination in a new
heavens and earth. And His titles of 'Son of God' and 'Son of Man'
also allude to Him, not only as the Last Adam, *but also as true Israel*.

In this connection, Wright provides some corroborating
evidence. He says,

> (1) At the large-scale level, Jewish covenant theology claims that the
> creator has not been thwarted irrevocably by the rebellion of his
> creation, but has called into being a people through whom he will
> work to restore his creation . . .

> (2) At a smaller-scale level, Israel's own sufferings, which create
> problems within covenant theology itself ('If our god is sovereign,
> why are we suffering?'), are answered from within the same
> covenantal doctrine: we are suffering because of our infidelity to the
> covenant, but our god will remain faithful and will restore us.

> (3) At the individual level . . . the sufferings and sins of individual
> Jews may be seen in the light of the continual provision of
> forgiveness and restoration, as a kind of oft-repeated small-scale
> version of the great restoration which was expected. Here the
> sacrificial system gains its full significance.[31]

According to Wright, the complex of covenantal ideas (of
monotheism, election and eschatology) 'gave Israel a particular
understanding of who precisely she was as a people within the

---

[30]For various aspects of the Noah narrative as recapitulations of the Adam
narrative, see W. A. Gage, *The Gospel of Genesis. Studies in Protology and
Eschatology* (Winona Lake, Indiana: Carpenter Books, 1984), 8-16.
[31]*The New Testament and the People of God*, 260.

purposes of the creator God'.[32] Israel's covenantal call made her understand herself as the true humanity of the Creator. If Abraham and his descendants are viewed as the means by which the Creator deals with the sin of Adam, and consequently with evil in the cosmos, 'Israel herself becomes the true Adamic humanity'.[33] Wright then shows how Abraham, Isaac, Jacob and Israel have applied to them Adam's commission in Genesis 1:28 (*e.g.*, Gn. 12:2ff.; 17:2, 6, 8; 22:16ff.), though the original command to 'be fruitful' becomes a promise and Adam's dominion over nature becomes Israel's possession of Canaan and supremacy over enemies. Wright says Exodus 19:6 affirms that Israel was to be a people having a corporate priestly function through which the creation would be blessed by the Creator.[34] He adds that the theme of Israel as an Adamic figure intended to bless the world occurs also in the prophets[35] and in Wisdom literature (in obtaining 'wisdom' Israel would become the true humanity which God had originally intended to come about).[36]

For Wright, the belief in resurrection in the first century AD also suggests that Israel believed she would be raised to be true humanity.[37] In this respect, the covenantal purpose of Israel has as its basic goal the deliverance and restoration of the whole created order. To miss this observation is to misunderstand the significance of Israel's fundamental beliefs of monotheism and election. The second level of God's covenantal purpose is his intention to recreate and reconcile Israel herself.[38] The Jews' hope for a resurrection was, in reality, a part of a broader hope in the renewal of the entire creation. The last resurrection would be at the same time the reconfirmation of the covenant and of the creation. Israel's restoration would take place within a restored created order.[39]

Therefore, Wright's recent focus is more on the penultimate role of Israel's restoration from their captivity than on the restoration of the cosmos; though he states that Israel's restoration is to lead to the restoration of the cosmos, he is not clear that the final goal is a fully renovated new heavens and earth (he says the New Testament

---

[32]*Ibid.*, 262.

[33]*Ibid.*, 262, and *cf.* 263.

[34]*Ibid.*, 263.

[35]*Ibid.*, 264.

[36]*Ibid.*, 265; he observes that the same is true in the book of Daniel and in Qumran (*ibid.*, 265-266).

[37]*Ibid.*, 266.

[38]*Ibid.*, 268.

[39]*Ibid.*, 332.

merely 'hints' at this final goal).[40] My purpose is to see New Testament theology more within the framework of the restoration of the creation, but Wright's recent work provides a good penultimate support for this focus.

The theological point of new creation is to underscore that God's glorious presence will be with his people in a way as never before, when their sin formerly prohibited experience of that presence. The inaugurated new creation in Christ allowed them to begin to experience the intimate presence of God, but only in the consummated new creation will that presence be fully experienced: 'behold, the tabernacle of God is with men, and he will tabernacle with them' (Rev. 21:3), and 'they will see his face, and his name will be on their forehead' (Rev. 22:4).

How Does the Centre of New Creation Illuminate Various Major Doctrines of the New Testament?

A brief survey of some major theological ideas and doctrines shows how they can be related organically to this proposed theological 'centre' of *Christ's life, and especially his death and resurrection through the Spirit, as the beginning of the glorious latter-day new creation of God.*

First, *missiology.* Recall the commission of Adam, Noah and Israel. They were all to obey God and go to the ends of the earth and subdue it. Of course, after Adam's 'fall', Israel's commission to subdue the earth includes shining their light in the world's spiritual darkness and judging nations who refuse to accept their light. Adam,

---

[40]*Ibid.*, 141-142. Among the 'hints' he mentions are Rom. 8; 1 Cor. 15, and parts of Revelation. 2 Pet. 3 should certainly be added to the list. Several Old Testament texts, and many New Testament passages, speak explicitly of the future physical resurrection of the saints, which is certainly a partial reference to a future, consummated new creation, since physically resurrected bodies are newly created bodies, and the way saints will inhabit a broader new creation is through resurrection. I believe this is more than a 'hint' of a consummated physical, new creation. It is true that the New Testament does not often refer to the broader new creation within which resurrected saints will live, but the notion is explicit when it is discussed (see the above-mentioned texts). Though Wright's work is immensely illuminating, it seems that he has de-emphasized the final goal of the 'story-line' and virtually collapsed it all into Christ's death and resurrection. Even G. B. Caird, Wright's mentor, who has a similar emphasis at this point as Wright, nevertheless acknowledges that the metaphorical use of end-of-the-world dissolution imagery in application to judgment of sinful nations within space-time history reflects the biblical authors' presupposition that the creation had a literal beginning and would have a literal ending (*e.g.*, see Caird, *The Language and Imagery of the Bible* [Philadelphia: Westminster, 1980], 244, 256-260).

Noah and Israel all failed to subdue, but Christ, the Last Adam and true Israel perfectly obeys, dies, rises, not only as new Israel (the focus of Wright), but also as a new creation, and the church, as His risen body, carries on the commission of the true Adam and Israel to subdue the earth for God as His vicegerent. Consequently, 'mission' or going to the ends of the earth is to be an intrinsic mark of the true church. This is why the church receives the 'Great Commission' in Matthew 28:19-20 from Christ, who bases it on His own authority given to Him as *Son of Man* (*i.e.*, 'Adam') by God (so Mt. 28:18 in allusion to Dn. 7:14).

Second, *christology*. This is seen especially in the nature of Christ's ministry of miracles as a facet of the new creation. Christ's miracles of healing not only inaugurated the end-time kingdom, but signalled the beginning of the new creation, since the healings were a beginning reversal of the curse of the old fallen world. The miracles were a sign of the inbreaking new creation where people would be consummately healed. Those He healed, and especially raised from the dead, foreshadowed His own resurrection. Christ's resurrection was the first-fruits of all believers. They, like Him, would be raised with perfected, restored bodies at the very end of the age, when the new world would be ushered in. The repeated and dominating notion of the kingdom in the Gospels is one of the main ways by which the Evangelists express ideas about the new creation.[41]

In addition, Christ's ministry of casting out demons was an expression of His beginning, though decisive, defeat of Satan, who had brought creation into captivity through his deception of Adam and Eve. This is the significance of the parable of the binding of the strong man (Mt. 12:29). Of course, His victory over Satan's temptations in the wilderness was the basis for His subsequent victories over the demons. It is certainly not coincidental that in resisting the Devil in the wilderness He is depicted by the Gospel writers as doing what Israel should have done in their wilderness wanderings,[42] and even what Adam should have done in the Garden of Eden.[43]

---

[41]I will have to defend this more below, but fuller defence must await future publication where the scope allows elaboration.

[42]Jesus responds to each of the three temptations by quoting a passage from Deuteronomy, which refers to what Israel should have done in the wilderness, but did not do.

[43]Jesus' three responses also allude to the temptation of Eve in Eden, which may be apparent from considering their themes (the fruit of the tree seemed good for food = the bread temptation; the tree was 'a delight to the eyes' = temptation to jump off the pinnacle of the temple and be delivered by angels before Jerusalem's onlookers; 'the tree was desirable to make wise' = the temptation to

Therefore, when Jesus exorcised demons, 'he was doing what Adam should have done'[44] in Eden by casting out the Devil and his forces.

Also, with respect to christology, the notions of Christ as Son of Man, Son of God and Messiah are crucial in understanding Jesus' role as the reinstater of God's vicegerency originally designed for Adam, but this has already been commented on above.

Third, *pneumatology*. The doctrine of the Holy Spirit is a full-blown new creation notion: the Old Testament prophesied that the Holy Spirit would be given as a gift at the end of the world and its first benefit would be to raise the saints from the dead. The Spirit set Christ apart at the beginning of His ministry, raised Him physically from the dead (Rom. 1:4), and raises people spiritually now (Rom. 8:6, 10-16; *cf.* 6:4-5), and will do so bodily at the second coming (Rom. 8:11). Indeed, the Holy Spirit is what causes Christians to be existentially linked with the new world to come. Christians partake of the blessings of the future new world through the Holy Spirit.

How did such an apparently esoteric eschatological idea affect the earliest Christians? One of the gifts which the Old Testament promised that the Holy Spirit would give to the saints in the new creation was perfect righteousness. The Spirit was to set them apart from the old, sinful world and would make them perfect in righteousness. Paul especially affirms that Christians have received the Spirit and His various gifts, but they will not receive the gift of personal, sinless perfection until Christ returns. Nevertheless, the Holy Spirit has come into our hearts to begin to work end-time

---

rule over the earth) (see. S. C. Glickman, *Knowing Christ* [Chicago: Moody Press, 1980], 56-58). Luke's ending of his genealogy with Jesus being related to 'the son of Adam, the son of God', directly preceding the temptation narrative, points further to Jesus as an Adamic figure in the temptation, as does Mark's apparently off-hand comment that immediately after the temptation, Jesus 'was with the wild beasts', apparently residing in peace with them (Mk. 1:13).

[44]McCartney, '*Ecce Homo*', 10. McCartney also mentions that Jesus' proclamations of the kingdom are expressions that the vicegerency lost with the first Adam was now being announced, and His power over nature was another example of exercising dominion over the earth as God's vicegerent, which the first Adam should have exercised (*ibid.*, 10). *Cf.* also M. G. Kline, *Kingdom Prologue* (South Hamilton, MA: Gordon-Conwell Seminary, 1989), 65-67, who makes the suggestive observation that 'the tree of the discernment of good and evil' in Genesis 2 refers to Adam's duty to discern between good and evil, so that when the Serpent entered the Garden, he was to judge the Serpent as an evildoer. Kline supports this partly by adducing other texts which refer to a discerning between 'good and evil' as the exercise of 'a legal-judicial kind of discrimination' (Is. 5:20, 23; Mal. 2:17), such as 'a king engaged in rendering judicial decisions' (2 Sa. 14:17; 1 Ki. 3:9, 28).

righteousness in us. Until the Spirit perfects us at the end of time, we should be very uncomfortable when we sin. The Spirit of righteousness in us cannot abide in harmony with indwelling sin. Paul tells the Ephesians that if they sin, they 'will grieve the Holy Spirit of God'. And if the Spirit is in us, then we should grieve along with Him when we sin. If we are really Christians, then the Spirit should convict us of our sin. If saints are not *characteristically* grieved by and convicted about sin, can we be confident that the eschatological Spirit is really in us?

Another eschatological feature of the Spirit is Paul's reference to 'the fruits of the Spirit' in Galatians 5. This phrase is best seen against the background of Isaiah's repeated prophecies that in the new creation there would be abundant fruitfulness. Isaiah often interprets this fruitfulness to be godly attributes, such as righteousness and holiness and trust in the Lord, and joy and peace.[45]

Fourth, *regeneration*. This doctrine is usually understood to mean being born again through faith and being given a new nature. When regeneration is seen through the lens of new creation, it is none other than being transformed into a new latter-day creation: again, 2 Corinthians 5:17 says, 'If any are in Christ, they are a new creation; the old things have passed away; behold, new things have come.' That text is a direct allusion to Isaiah 65:17, which is one of the most well-known prophecies of new creation in all of the Old Testament. Just as God sovereignly and irresistibly brought the first creation into being, so He brings irresistibly the new creation into being. The first Adam was not pleading with God to be created. Rather, God brought him into being and Adam reacted by worshipping. So the creation of a new humanity in the second creation also occurs by God's will and not autonomous human effort. This is one reason Paul says in 2 Corinthians 4:6, 'God, who said, "Light shall shine out of darkness," is the One who has shone in our hearts to give the light of the knowledge of the glory of God in the face of Christ.' This is none other than God imparting resurrection life to His people.

Fifth, *sanctification*. This is usually understood as the process of a Christian growing in righteousness, being set apart from sin and set apart to holiness. The Greek word ἁγιάζω can mean 'set apart'. But with the 'glasses' of eschatology we can see that sanctification involves being set apart from the 'old world' characterized by sin and set apart to the new creation.[46]

---

[45]*Cf.* Is. 11:1-5; 32:13-18; 44:2-4; 61:3, 11; 65:8, 17-22 with Gal. 5:22-25, and 6:14-16.
[46]I do not intend to imply here that ἁγιάζω always or even often has the technical meaning 'set apart'.

This means that if Christians have been truly regenerated, they have become new creatures and have been transferred spiritually into the new creation. Accordingly, Ephesians 2:10 says, 'We are His creation, created in Christ Jesus for good works which God prepared beforehand that we should walk in them.' This demands the practical conclusion that genuine Christians will surely, though perhaps slowly, bear fruits of righteousness.[47]

All true believers are part of the new creation.[48] This means that the struggle within the believer is not a conflict between the 'old man' and the 'new man', in which the 'old man' may win out most of one's Christian life. Instead, 2 Corinthians 5:17 says, 'If any are in Christ, they are a new creation, the old things have passed away; behold, new things have come.' True Christians are new creatures who struggle, not with an 'old man' or unbelieving self, but who struggle with indwelling sin and sinful habit patterns of their old way of life, a struggle in which they will surely, though perhaps slowly, win. The presence of such sin within will not ultimately prevail over the ability of our regenerate nature to produce the fruit of righteousness. People who profess faith but never bear fruit should have no assurance that they are genuine Christians or inhabitants of the new creation. The regenerate life of a Christian must eventually shine through.

Sixth, *justification*. This is a doctrine which pertains to the last judgment concomitant with the destruction of the cosmos. This doctrine can be viewed in purely legal terms whereby Christ bore the eternal wrath of God as our penal substitute so that we could be

---

[47]Cf. Ja. 1:18, which refers to Christians as having been created as a 'first fruit' among God's creation, with 3:13-18, which says that 'the fruit of righteousness is sown in peace in those doing peace', so that those who are part of God's new creation are expected to bear fruits. Also in 3:13-18, and elsewhere in James, is the idea that believers are to be characterized by 'wisdom,' which is plausibly best understood in the light of those in the new creation walking wisely according to the original wisdom which Adam and Israel (so Proverbs) should have possessed. (Cf. T. C. Penner, *The Epistle of James and Eschatology* [JSNTSupp. 121; Sheffield: Sheffield Academic Press, 1996], who does not focusing on new creation, argues that the eschatological dimensions of the opening and closing sections of the epistle define and shape the middle segment, so that 'James should be understood as eschatological community instruction' [*ibid.*, 258].)

[48]This conclusion bears upon the present 'Lordship-salvation' debate in North America: some argue that the New Testament affirms there are two kinds of Christians: radically 'unspiritual Christians' and 'spiritual Christians'. They go on to say that genuine Christians may remain characteristically unrighteous their whole life. According to this view, Christians can gain assurance of salvation without ever bearing any fruit of righteousness.

declared righteous. When we see justification in the light of inaugurated eschatology, we see that the final judgment which unbelievers will face in the future has been pushed back for believers to the cross in the first century. Believers have already passed through the last judgment when Christ suffered eternal hell for them on the cross.

When Matthew 27:50 narrates Jesus' death, Matthew immediately adds in verses 51-53, 'the earth shook; and the rocks split, and the tombs were opened; and many bodies of the saints who had fallen asleep were raised; and coming out of the tombs after His resurrection they entered the holy city and appeared to many'. These strange phenomena signal to Matthew's readers that Christ's death was the beginning of the end of the old creation and the inauguration of a new creation. Is it accidental that Matthew 27:51, describing the tearing in two of the veil of the temple, directly precedes the language of cosmic dissolution and resurrection in verses 51b-53? Josephus says that on the outer veil of the temple was needlework portraying the starry heavens (*Wars* 5.5.4; *Ant.* 3.6.4; 3.7.7). Therefore, the tearing of the veil may be suggestive of the beginning destruction of the old cosmos. This is consistent with the following ideas: (1) the Old Testament notion that the temple was a microcosmic model of the true divine macrocosmic temple in heaven; (2) Jesus' statements in John 2 that, after the destruction of the Herodian temple, his own resurrection body was the beginning rebuilding of the new temple promised to be rebuilt at the time of the new creation in Ezekiel; (3) the Old Testament represents the sky as a curtain or tent (Ps. 104:2; Is. 40:22; *cf. b. B. Mes. 59a*) and other Old Testament and New Testament texts speak of the 'rending' of the heavens on 'the Day of the Lord'.[49] In the light of this Matthean imagery, it is consistent that right on the heels of 1 John 2:2 concerning Christ being a propitiation for sins, 1 John 2:17-18 can say 'the world is passing away . . . it is the last hour'.

Therefore, justification is related to new creation in that the last judgment paves the way for new creation; the last judgment is not merely the punishment of the wicked, but it is also inextricably linked to God's judgment of the old cosmos by which he destroys the sin-tainted and corrupted world. Therefore, in that the last judgment

---

[49]Jb. 14:12 [LXX]; Ps. 102:26; Is. 34:4; 63:19 (64:1); Hg. 2:6; *Sib. Or.* 3:82; 8:233, 413; Mt. 24:29 par.; Lk. 21:25; 2 Pet. 3:10; Rev. 6:14; so D. C. Allison, *End of the Ages Has Come,* 32-33, who suggests that, against the background of the preceding references just cited and in the light of Josephus' information about the veil, that rending of the curtain in Mark 15:38 indicates cosmic dissolution imagery, though R. H. Gundry, *Mark* (Grand Rapids: Eerdmans, 1993), 971-972, demurs. The Mt. 27 context makes this suggestion even more attractive.

has been pushed back to the cross and has begun there, so also the destruction of the cosmos has begun there (so Gal. 6:14-15).

Justification, however, does not refer only to a declaration of not guilty because Christ has taken one's final judgment upon Himself. The Old Testament and Judaism expected God to bring about a perfect righteousness among His people in the eschaton. In justification, Christ does not merely suffer the punishment of sinners, but He provides a perfect righteousness for them; His righteousness is transferred to them. Romans 5:12ff. and 2 Corinthians 5:21 likely include reference to a positive covenantal righteousness which is bestowed on God's people. It is not by chance that both of these contexts contain overt resurrection and new creation language: respectively, Jesus as the Last Adam in Romans 5 and 'new creation' in 2 Corinthians 5:17.[50]

Seventh, *reconciliation*. This is almost synonymous with new creation, but ultimately must be seen as a subcategory of it. The traditional formulation of this doctrine has revolved around the notion of God's hostile wrath having been diverted from us to Christ, so that we are *reconciled* to God and are able to come into a peaceful relationship with Him. The end-time colour of this doctrine is highlighted by recalling the Old Testament prophecies of the new creation. Isaiah 11:6-12 and 65:17, 25 predict that when the new creation comes there will be peace, not only between God and humanity but between hostile humans themselves. The fruit of reconciliation with God is reconciliation among people: according to Isaiah 11 and 65 hostile animals will dwell in harmony, such as the wolf and the lamb, the lion and the ox. The predicted harmony of the animals in both Isaiah texts serves merely to point to the peace among traditionally hostile people groups, like Jew and Gentile.

Reconciliation could be understood as a result of new creation, and hence a goal of God's new order, and, therefore, more all-encompassing; however, since, according to the biblical view, new creation continues eternally, it is part and parcel with reconciliation and the two co-exist together for ever. Indeed, reconciliation is only one facet of the new creation, since other distinct realities apart from reconciliation are part of the new creation (*e.g*, the reign of the saints is part of the new order, but it is not to be confused with reconciliation; the two are different).

---

[50]*Cf*. also Rom. 4:25, which affirms that Christ 'was raised with a view toward our justification', which may have in mind the declaration of righteousness that consists in the resurrection life of the new creation.

The rallying cry of the New Testament is 'There is no distinction between Jew and Greek' (Acts 15:9; Rom. 10:12; Eph. 2:16-19). The reason instructions are directed to husbands and wives, parents and children, and slaves and masters in Ephesians 5 and Colossians 3 is because these were three typical human relationships which had become fragmented due to the fall; and it is no coincidence that Ephesians (ch. 2) and Colossians (ch. 1) refer explicitly to the reconciliation of people to God and to one another, employing restoration notions from Israel's restoration promises, and new creation imagery. These same relationships, however, experience peace again for all those in Christ, the beginning of the new creation. The pillars of alienated relationships holding up the old fallen world were knocked down by Christ, and Christ established a new world which has only one pillar and that pillar is Christ Jesus Himself.

The mark of genuine faith among those in the new spiritual creation is that of unity because they are part *of the one Christ*: Ephesians 2:15-16 asserts that Christ made 'the two into *one* new man, thus establishing peace' and reconciled Gentile and Jew 'in *one* body to God through the cross'. Alienation and division are no longer the rule in the new order in fulfilment of the Isaianic new creation prophecies.

There are to be no nationalistic distinctions any more in Christ, like Jew or Gentile, African or American, Asian or European. In the new creation the 'old things', like old ethnic and nationalistic identifications, 'have passed away; behold, new things have come' in Christ, the beginning of the new creation. Therefore, in the new cosmos of Christ's church the emphasis is *theological* unity in Christ and not ethnic diversity. The goal of the church is not primarily to identify *within herself* many ethnic diversities. That would be to return to the old, sinful world's way of recognizing things. Rather, the true church seeks to evangelize many ethnic diversities outside of itself, so that they all may identify with the one Christ and find the peace of the new creation in theological unity. Revelation 5:9 says of Christ, 'for you were slain, and did purchase for God with Thy blood *some from every tribe and tongue and people and nation.*'

The New Testament doctrine of 'affirmative action' is to affirm all the diversity of redeemed humanity as one in Christ. As 1 Corinthians 12:13 says, 'For by one Spirit we were all baptised into one body, whether Jews or Greeks, whether slaves or free,' and Galatians 3:27-28 says likewise, 'for all of you have clothed yourselves with [the one] Christ. There is neither Jew nor Greek, there is neither slave nor free, there is neither male nor female; for you are all one in Christ Jesus.' Our common bond is the unified

interpretative lens on christology, Scripture (its authority), and the
world (its need of reconciliation) which the Spirit of Christ has
imparted to us. *To emphasize in the church ethnic diversity or to
emphasize theologies which depend on unique aspects of ethnic diversity
more than emphasizing theological unity in Christ is to resist the forward
moving redemptive-historical direction toward reconciliation and unity in
the new creation.* And what is this theological unity to be underscored
at all costs? Romans 10:8-13 summarizes it:

> The word of faith which we are preaching [is] that if you confess
> with your mouth Jesus as Lord, and believe in your heart that God
> raised him from the dead, you shall be saved; for with the heart man
> believes resulting in righteousness, and with the mouth he
> confesses, resulting in salvation. For the Scripture says, 'Whoever
> believes in him will not be disappointed.' For there is no distinction
> between Jew and Greek; for the same Lord is Lord of all, abounding
> in riches for all who call upon him; for 'Whoever will call upon the
> name of the Lord will be saved.'

Consequently, reconciliation is not some abstract theological
concept, but has far-reaching practical implications for the way
people-groups relate within the church of Jesus Christ.

Eighth, the *Law*. Especially in Paul, the Law not only relates
to the new age, but can best be understood in the light of the
beginning destruction of the old creation and the emergence of the
renovated creation. In this respect, the notion of the Law is bound up
with the idea of reconciliation discussed in the preceding section. The
most obvious place where this can be seen is in Ephesians 2:13-18.
Verses 14-15 are the crucial verses, where it says that Christ made
Jew and Gentile one 'by having loosed the dividing wall of the
barrier' and 'by having nullified in his flesh the Law of commandments in decrees'. This likely refers not to Christ's nullification of the
whole Law, but only part of the Law, as I believe the remainder of
Ephesians bears out, since Paul repeatedly quotes and alludes to Old
Testament moral Law. Christ has abolished that part of the Law
which divided Jew from Gentile, so that they could become one.
Gentiles no longer need to adapt the signs and customs of national
Israel to become true Israelites: they do not need to move to
geographical Israel to become Israelites, but they need only move to
Jesus, the true Israel; they do not need to be circumcised in flesh, but
in the heart by Christ's death, which is their true circumcision, since
it cuts them off from the old world and sets them apart to the new (*cf.*
Col. 2:10-14; Gal. 6:14-15); Gentiles do not need to make pilgrimage to
Israel's temple to get near to God, but they merely need to make

pilgrimage to Jesus, the true temple, of which the Ephesian Christians were a part (see Eph. 2:20-22). This is the significance of defining the 'mystery' in Ephesians 3:6 as Gentiles being 'fellow-heirs and fellow members of the body and fellow-partakers of the promise'.

The parallel passage to Ephesians 2:13-18 in Colossians 2 defines the 'decrees' (δόγμα) of Ephesians 2:15 which Christ abolished as the external nationalistic expressions of the Law: food, drink festivals, new moons, or Sabbaths (see Col. 2:15-17, 20-21). Colossians 2:20-21 even refers to these 'decrees' with the verbal form of δόγμα: '[why] do *you submit yourself to decrees* [δογματίζω] – do not handle, do not taste, do not touch, which things are all destined for perishing with the consuming, according to the commandments and doctrines of men.' Note what Colossians says they died to: ἀπὸ τῶν στοιχείων τοῦ κόσμου ('from the elements of this world'). There is much debate about the meaning of στοιχεῖα in Paul (plural of στοιχεῖον, occurring in Paul only in Gal. 4:3, 9 and Col. 2:8, 20). Many see it referring to demonic powers, and this is possible. The most usual meaning of στοιχεῖα in the Greek world, however, is the four basic elements of the cosmos: air, fire, water and earth.[51] How could this basic meaning have relevance for Colossians 2?[52] The old fallen order was based on cosmic 'elements'. These 'elements' were 'elements of division', ultimately held in place by the Devil and his evil forces.

Now that Christ has come, however, and has launched a new cosmos, the old cosmos has begun to be destroyed and the new is in place. The only element or fundamental building block of the new creation is Christ. And, since there is only one Christ of which the new creation consists and upon which it is built, then there can be only one new created people subsisting in that renovated creation. The elements of divisiveness which sustained the sinful structure of the old world have been decisively decimated by Christ and He has replaced them by Himself as the only foundational pillar of the new world. This is what Galatians 6:14-16 has in mind: through the cross of Christ

the world has been crucified to me, and I to the world. For neither is circumcision anything or uncircumcision, but a new creation. And

---

[51] As, for example, illustrated in 2 Pet. 3:10, 12, though here the 'elements' of the cosmos are destroyed by means of fire.

[52] For the notion of στοιχεῖα as demonic powers, the four elements of the universe, supernatural powers in some way connected to the four elements, among other possible views, see C. E. Arnold, 'Returning to the Domain of the Powers: *STOICHEIA* as Evil Spirits in Galatians 4:3, 9,' *Novum Testamentum* 38 (1996), 55-76, who cites extensive bibliography.

as many as *walk by the elements* (στοιχήσουσιν) of this rule, peace and mercy be upon them – even upon the Israel of God.

That is, as many as conduct their lives on the foundational element of Christ are partakers of the new creation, and they will experience the peace promised to occur in the forthcoming new heavens and earth.

We could picture Christ as a hermeneutical filter through which the Law must pass in order to get to the new creation. Those parts of the Law which are nationalistic in nature or are overt nationalistic tags distinguishing Israelites ethnically from other people-groups are too large or misshapen to be able to pass through the filter. Those parts of the Law more moral and less ethnic in nature are able to pass through the filter. This appears to be the significance of 1 Corinthians 7:19: 'Circumcision is nothing, and uncircumcision is nothing, but *what matters is* the keeping of the commandments' (so NASB). This is parallel with Galatians 6:15 and 5:6 which both begin with the same negative statement about circumcision, and then respectively add in the contrastive clause 'a new creation' and '[in Christ Jesus] . . . faith working through love'. The 'commandments' to be kept in Christ, in the new creation, are summed up in the statement 'love your neighbour' (*cf.* Gal. 5:6 with 5:14), and are those which are in contrast to what distinguishes people ethnically, which must, therefore, exclude those parts of the Law distinguishing Israelites as a unique racial group.[53]

This renewed order in Galatians 6 and Ephesians 2, as well as Colossians 2, in which Jews and Gentiles become unified and at peace is a reflection of Isaiah 11 and 66, where there also is a prophecy that Jews and Gentiles will be unified and at peace with one another in the coming new cosmos.

Therefore, because of the Old Testament prophecy of new creation which has begun fulfilment in Christ, there can be no longer any nationalistic distinctions; the only distinguishing element is Christ. Those nationalistic distinctions entailed in the Law are no longer valid. This is why Paul quotes only from the moral Law, or when he quotes other facets of the Old Testament Law (such as the civil), he uses it in a typological or non-theocratic manner in employing it within the covenant community of the church (*e.g.*, see his use of Deuteronomy in 1 Cor. 5:13).

Consequently, understanding how Christ has instituted the new creation also gives insight into understanding what parts of the Old Testament Law relate to the new age and what parts do not.

---

[53]The parallelism between 1 Cor. 7:19, Gal. 5:6 and 6:15 has been pointed out by D. P. Fuller, *The Unity of the Bible* (Grand Rapids: Zondervan, 1992), 348-349.

Ninth, *ecclesiology* is affected in a variety of ways. For example, worship on the last day of the week in the Old Testament has now changed to the first day of the week because Christ's resurrection occurred on the first day of the week and His resurrection inaugurated the eternal rest promised in the new creation. The continuation of a Sabbath, a day of 'worshipful rest' on Sunday, is a sign reminding us that the spiritual 'rest' of the new creation has begun in Christ. Sabbath worship on Sunday reminds us to look forward to the time when our eschatological rest will be consummated in the final form of the new creation when Christ returns the final time (this is what Heb. 3–4 looks forward to and the idea of perseverance in that epistle is to be construed primarily within this sabbatarian-creation framework).

Baptism and the *Lord's Supper*, which N. T. Wright would refer to as the 'symbols' associated with the biblical 'story',[54] are also charged with notions of new creation. Baptism connotes the believer's identification with Christ's death and resurrection:[55] the old man (position in Adam) was crucified with Christ and Christians have risen with him in 'newness of life' (*e.g.*, Rom. 6:3-11). In addition, two other significant New Testament discussions of 'baptism' compare it with Noah's salvation through water (1 Pet. 3:20-21) and Israel's exodus through water (1 Cor. 10:1-2), both of which have been discussed above as major parts of the overall story line of 're-creation'.[56] Also important in this regard is the description of salvation in Titus 3:5 through baptismal *and* new creation imagery: 'by the washing of regeneration (παλιγγενεσία) and renewing by the Holy Spirit'.[57]

---

[54]*The New Testament and the People of God*, 447-448.

[55]See O. Cullmann, *Baptism in the New Testament* (Studies in Biblical Theology No. 1; Naperville, Ill.: A. R. Allenson, 1950), 9-22, for the foundation of baptism being in Christ's death and resurrection.

[56]See M. G. Kline, *By Oath Consigned* (Grand Rapids: Eerdmans, 1968), 63-83, for fuller discussion of the relationship of these two Old Testament events as a background through which to understand baptism. Against this Old Testament backdrop, baptism can be seen as 'a sign of the eschatological ordeal' (*ibid.*, 79). Subsequently, in support of Kline, Wright has observed that Exodus typology and Christ's death and resurrection are associated with baptism, and that baptism was 'the mode of entry into the eschatological people . . . *because it* had to do with Jesus, who had himself brought Israel's history to its appointed destiny, and who as Messiah summed up Israel in himself' (*The New Testament and the People of God*, 447).

[57]Not coincidentally, the term παλιγγενεσία refers in Philo to the renewal of the earth after the flood and in Josephus to the return of Israel from captivity (see note 78 below). Likewise, Wisdom 19:6 describes the Exodus event as the time

Likewise, the Eucharist evokes new creation imagery. It was part of the weekly worship service on the first day of the week in which Christians remembered Christ's resurrection on the same first day of the week, which, as we just saw, set in motion the Sabbath rest intended for Adam in the first creation.[58] Christ's Last Supper and the Eucharistic meal of the early church were overtly linked to Israel's Passover and, hence, the Exodus.[59] Perhaps not coincidentally, Jewish tradition associated the Passover with the original creation and the coming future destruction and renovation of the cosmos, when the Messiah would come[60] and God's kingdom

when 'the whole creation was again renewed in its own kind anew' (see further note 83 below).

[58]Justin Martyr (*Dial.* 138) says that the eight people preserved through water in the ark 'were a symbol of the eighth day [Sunday, the first day of the week], wherein Christ appeared when He rose from the dead . . . For Christ, being the first-born of every creature, became chief of another race regenerated by Himself through water and faith'; accordingly, the fathers viewed Sunday as 'the eighth day going beyond the present "week" into the future age', so that it is natural that believers could be understood already tasting 'the life of the new creation in the bread and wine of the eucharist' (G. Wainwright, *Eucharist and Eschatology* [New York: Oxford University Press, 1981], 77, who also observes the Justin reference in this connection). 'The earliest reason given for celebrating Sunday is that it is the day of the resurrection (*Ep. of Barnabas*, 15.9)', and, 'according to Justin (*1 Apol.* 67), Christians also believed they were commemorating both the first creation, which was on the first day of the creation week, and the resurrection of Christ, who rose on the first day of the week' (P. G. Cobb, 'The History of the Christian Year', in C. Jones, G. Wainwright, E. Yarnold and P. Bradshaw [eds.], *The Study* of Liturgy [London: SPCK and New York: Oxford University Press, 1992], 457).

[59]See J. Jeremias, *The Eucharistic Word of Jesus* (New York: C. Scribner's Sons, 1966), 15-88, who sees a Passover background eliciting a context of *Heilsgeschichte* and of 'promise and fulfilment' for Jesus' Last Supper (*cf. ibid.*, 88). 1 Cor. 5:6-8 refers to Christ as the Passover sacrifice, 'celebrating the feast, not with old leaven' but with 'new', which Jeremias believes echoes Jesus' own words at the Supper 'this is my body [which is given for you]' (*cf.* Lk. 22:19) and which he sees as an eschatological interpretation of the loaves used in the Passover (*ibid.*, 59-60); *cf.* G. D. Fee, *The First Epistle to the Corinthians* (NICNT; Grand Rapids: Eerdmans, 1987), 218, who sees a possible allusion to the Lord's Supper in 1 Cor. 5:8, and cites others making this suggestion.

[60]Interestingly, 'the Four Nights' midrashic hymn in various versions of the Targum is inserted into Exodus 12, which gives instructions for the Passover meal; this insertion explains what events have taken place or will occur in the future on the same night in which Passover takes place. These events are none other than the key constituent elements of the biblical-theological story line mentioned above in connection with the work of Wright, in which the major stepping-stones from the beginning of biblical history to the end of history are, according to the Targum: (a) the creation of the world in Genesis 1; (b) God's

would be established.[61] Such an association makes it natural that each of the Synoptic accounts of the Last Supper includes a saying by Jesus with respect to the cup that 'I will not drink of this fruit of the vine from now on until that day when I drink it *new* with you in My Father's kingdom [Luke has 'until the kingdom of God comes]' (Mt. 26:29; likewise Mk. 14:25 and Lk. 22:18). This could be a figurative reference echoing the promised fruitfulness of the coming new creation which would be formally inaugurated by the resurrection.[62] This is further pointed to by the reference that the drinking will take place at the time when 'the kingdom comes', a further instalment of the inaugurated end-time kingdom. This saying of Jesus apparently began to be fulfilled during Jesus' resurrection appearances to His disciples.[63]

On the other hand, 1 Corinthians 11:21-34 affirms that when partaking at the Lord's table saints either must judge themselves in order to partake worthily or they will be judged by God in the present. Whichever is the case, however, true believers receive their judgment *now* at the Supper in order that they 'may not be condemned along with the world' at the last judgment' (1 Cor. 11:32). Hence, the Supper contains in itself a beginning form of the last judgment, which will be consummated at the end of time. Consequently, as G. Wainwright concludes, the Lord's Supper is

---

covenantal dealings with Abraham, which are described figuratively with cosmic conflagration imagery; (c) the Passover; (d) when the earth reaches its appointed time to be dissolved, at which time the Messiah will come to redeem Israel (so Targum Neofiti Exodus 12; likewise Targum Pseudo-Jonathan Exodus 12; *cf.* the various translations in M. McNamara and R. Hayward, *Targum Neofiti 1: Exodus* and M. Maher, *Targum Pseudo-Jonathan: Exodus* [in *The Aramaic Bible* 2; Collegeville, Minn.: Liturgical Press, 1994], J. W. Etheridge, *The Targums of Onkelos and Jonathan Ben Uzziel on the Pentateuch* [New York: KTAV, 1968], 479-481, and M. McNamara, *The New Testament and the Palestinian Targum to the Pentateuch* [Analecta Biblica 27; Rome: Pontifical Biblical Institute, 1966], 210-211). For other eschatological hopes, including new creation, associated with Passover, see Jeremias, *Eucharistic Word of Jesus*, 58-59, 206-207.
[61]See McNamara, *New Testament and Targum*, 210, who discusses ms. Paris 110 of Targum Pseudo-Jonathan, which inserts 'the Four Nights' segment at Ex. 15:18, which says, 'The Lord will reign forever and ever.'
[62]The Old Testament and Judaism expected abundant fruitfulness in the coming creation, including specifically fruitful 'vineyards' producing 'new wine' (*e.g.*, Is. 62:8-9; 65:17-22; Ho. 14:7-8; Zc. 9:17; 10:7).
[63]According to Acts 10:41, the apostles 'ate and drank with Him after He rose from the dead' (so A. J. B. Higgins, *The Lord's Supper in the New Testament* [Studies in Biblical Theology No. 6; Chicago: A. R. Allenson, 1956], 62).

a projection, from the future . . . of the coming of the Lord . . . who comes to judge and recreate . . . it includes a present moment of judgement and renewal which is the projection of the cataclysm[64] that will inaugurate the universal and incontestable reign of God.[65]

Tenth, *the final tribulation.* How does the idea of a *tribulation* which had begun in the early church but was not consummated fit into the scheme proposed in this study? The Old Testament predicted that a final tribulation would precede the dawning of the new cosmos. For example, Daniel 12:1-2ff. prophesies a time of great distress before the climactic resurrection of the righteous and wicked. While Daniel refers to the coming trial as one in which there will be deception within the covenant community and persecution of non-compromisers, other Old Testament and New Testament texts affirm that the final tribulation will be one in which there will be a breakdown of various parts of the natural order of the cosmos, which will be culminated by complete destruction of the heavens and earth.[66] Against this background, one can see how the final tribulation is but an inextricable prelude to the eventual destruction and recreation of the cosmos. Actual phenomena of cosmic dissolution are not the typical characteristic of the inaugurated phase of the tribulation, rather false teaching and deception are among the predominant expressions. Nevertheless, we have seen above that literal physical phenomena of cosmic break-up were expressed at Christ's death: 'darkness fell upon all the land' (Mt. 27:45) and 'the earth shook; and the rocks were split, and the tombs were opened' (Mt. 27:51). Such literal expressions of initial destruction will again occur at the very end of history when the body of Christ, the church throughout the world, will experience climactic, universal persecution like Christ before it (*cf.* Rev. 11:3-13; 20:7-11). The apparent Old Testament perspective was that (1) deception and persecution were seen to occur at the same general period as (2) the

---

[64]In this respect, *Didache* 10:6, part of the conclusion to the instructions on the Eucharist begun at 9:1, says, 'May grace (= Christ) come, and may this world pass away.'

[65]Wainwright, *Eucharist and Eschatology,* 151 (on this judgment theme, see also *ibid.,* 80-83). For more thorough elaboration on the 'already and not yet eschatological and new creation' nature of the Eucharist argued for in this essay, see *idem, Eucharist and Eschatology, passim,* especially, 37-41, 68-70, 77, 80-83, 106, 147-154.

[66]For New Testament examples, *cf.* Mk. 13:8 and Lk. 21:11, 23-26 ('earthquakes' and 'famines,' which are 'the beginning of birth pangs'). For some Old Testament and especially scattered early Jewish texts which depict similar convulsions of nature, *cf.* Allison, *End of the Ages Has Come,* 5-25.

convulsions of nature, but the New Testament understands these to occur in stages in which the first feature predominates throughout the age, but then the two converge at the very end.

Along with false teaching and deception, Christian 'suffering' as a result of 'persecution' is also an essential feature of the inaugurated end-time tribulation, a theme struck throughout the Synoptics, Paul, 1 Peter and Revelation.[67] When saints refuse to compromise with false teaching, they often must face persecution (cf. Dn. 11:30ff.; Rev. 2:8-17). Every manner of suffering is part of the scheme of the overlap of a fallen world which is passing away in the midst of an inaugurated new world.[68]

The origin of ecclesiology, particularly with respect to the hierarchical structure of the church, is best viewed within the context of the latter-day tribulation of false teaching (note the overt references in 1 Tim. 4:1 and 2 Tim. 3:1 to the end-time trial of deception within the church community). 'Elders' or 'bishops' are needed in order to maintain the doctrinal purity of the covenant community which is always threatened from the infiltration of 'fifth columnist movements'. Titus 1:5-16 gives this as the formal reason for the establishment of elders throughout the churches of Crete, and the same rationale is apparent in 1 and 2 Timothy (cf. 1 Tim. 1:3-7, 19-20 and 4:1-7 with 3:1-15, 5:17 and 6:20-21; cf. 2 Tim. 2:14-18, 23-26). On the other hand, such an ecclesiastical authority structure ensured the Christian community that it was continuing in the truth and life of the kingdom, which would enable it to be strong in accomplishing its mission of witness to the world, which is likely as significant a theme in the Pastorals as is the concern about false teaching.[69] This positive element of 'mission' is part of the larger positive role of the church in its responsibility of carrying out the original Adamic commission to

---

[67] Accordingly, in the Synoptics, suffering is related to following the Son of Man, whose own suffering is rooted in the prophecy of Dn. 7, where the Son of Man, representing true Israel, must suffer persecution (e.g., Mt. 8:18-22); Paul also links the church's sufferings as the 'body' of Christ with her identification with 'Christ's afflictions' (Col. 1:24), as does Heb. (cf. 1:2 and 9:26 with 12:1-7), Ja. (cf. 1:2-4 with 5:1-11), 1 Pet. (cf. 1:5-6 and 1:20 with 2:19-23 and 3:14-5:10) and Rev. (e.g., cf. 1:5-6 with 1:9 and 5:6 with 6:9).

[68] Cf. Rom. 8:18-23 with 8:35-39, where, in the former text, suffering of believers, and of all creation, is viewed as a result of being part of a new creation emerging from the old corrupted creation, which is portrayed by the image of suffering birth pangs.

[69] Indeed, recently R. G. Gruenler, 'The Mission-Lifestyle Setting of 1 Timothy 2:8-15', JETS (forthcoming), has plausibly contended that 'mission' is the dominant theme and concern of the Pastorals, especially highlighting the significance of 1 Tim. 1:10-16 and 2:1-4, among other passages.

subdue the ends of the earth and Israel's similar commission to be priests for and a light of witness to the world.[70] Of course, Acts highlights this eschatological light-bearing mission of the new creation more than any other New Testament book[71] (and the mention of deacons in Acts 6 and elders in Acts 20, at least in part, is to indicate their role in speeding on the spread of the kingdom, and in the latter case also to encourage the elders to guard against false teaching).

Conclusion

As I mentioned earlier, it is likely that some will conclude that to reduce the centre of the New Testament down to the notion of new creation is merely to add to the many reductionistic New Testament theologies already proposed, and that we must content ourselves with a multi-thematic approach. It is my argument, however, that this 'centre' is supported by the broad sweep of canonical thought, wherein the Bible begins with original creation which is corrupted, and the rest of the Old Testament is a redemptive-historical process working toward a restoration of the fallen creation in a new creation. The New Testament then sees these hopes beginning fulfilment and prophesies a future time of fulfilment in a consummated new creation, which Revelation 21:1–22:5 portrays.

Other doctrines could be mentioned. It is appropriate to close with the words of Paul's conclusion to his epistle to the Ephesians: in 6:24 he says: 'Grace be with all those who love our Lord Jesus Christ with a love incorruptible.' Paul is saying that if we really have been created as part of the new creation (*cf.* Eph. 2:10), which is incorruptible, then our love for Jesus will be incorruptible and will never end. Nothing on this corruptible earth can thwart the love of incorruptible new creatures who live in the new creation in Christ.

---

[70]See F. Hawkins, 'Orders and Ordination in the New Testament', in *The Study of Liturgy*, 344-345, which has helped crystallize my own thoughts on these negative and positive factors leading to the establishment of church offices in the New Testament.

[71]*E.g.*, Acts 1:6-8 and 2:17–3:26; 13:47; 26:16-18. See G. K. Beale, 'Eschatology', in *Dictionary of the later New Testament and its Developments*, for the relationship of the eschatology of Acts to the notion of resurrection and new creation.

APPENDIX

Methodological issues for a single-centre biblical theology

After surveying various past proposed 'centres' of each Testament, C. H. H. Scobie warns:

> It is difficult to understand the obsession with finding one single theme or 'centre' for Old Testament or New Testament Theology and still less for an entire Biblical Theology. It is widely held today that the quest for a single centre has failed. An approach which recognises several themes would appear to be more productive and this seems to be the trend in a number of more recent Old Testament Theologies including those of J. L. McKenzie, W. Zimmerli, W. A. Dyrness and C. Westermann.[72]

Scobie criticizes such proposed 'centres' (for a biblical theology) as *kingdom, covenant, history of redemption, presence of God* and *life*. Instead, he believes the future of any biblical theology lies with a multi-perspectival approach. Whenever, as in this paper, a particular centre is proposed as the key to biblical theology, the issue of validation arises. When one centre is offered over others, the magnitude of the problem increases. That centre which is most comprehensive is to be judged as the most probable.

Four validation tests can be considered briefly. First, the proposed centre needs to be shown to be more overarching than other centres, with the others logically sub-categories of it; this can be done through analysis of the nature of the centres themselves and of their relationship to one another. Second, the proposed centre needs to be related to the various major themes of the New Testament documents to see if it adequately comprehends the diversity present throughout the New Testament; if there is a blurring of the focus in some books, then this suggests that the lens is not comprehensive enough; if the focus remains sharp and the lens sheds greater light on the books than other lenses, then it validates itself. It will not result in fuzzy thinking nor in a reductionistic atomism in which it fails to explain the interrelatedness and complexity of concepts.[73] Third, any viable centre must be integrally related to major Old Testament themes,[74] be undergirded by a broad story-line which expresses a theological world-view or belief system about God's relationship with humanity,[75] and be anchored in Christ's death and resurrection. Fourth, each competing centre needs to be analysed in turn for its comprehensiveness to see if it might not be

---

[72]'C. H. H. Scobie, 'Structure of Biblical Theology', *Tyndale Bulletin* 42 (1991), 178-179.

[73]I owe this particular formulation to Phil Towner in his oral response to this paper at the Tyndale Fellowship Triennial Conference on Eschatology in Swanwick, Derbyshire, 1997.

[74]This presupposes not only the Jewish roots of early Christianity, but also the necessity of any good New Testament theology being adequately linked to Old Testament theology.

[75]The criterion of 'story' as essential to a biblical theology has been emphasized recently by Wright, *The New Testament and the People of God, e.g.*, 31-80, 121-144, 215-224.

46   THE READER MUST UNDERSTAND

the most overarching. By its very nature, this test cannot be addressed here.[76]
The first, second and third tests may now be addressed, in a skeletal outline.

With respect to the third criterion, this essay has attempted to root
every aspect of New Testament theology in the Old Testament, especially the
notion of new creation as the recapitulation of the original creation, but on a
grander scale. The recapitulating story-line is: (1) chaos of pre-creation state and
creation/commission of Adam, followed by fall; (2) chaos of deluge and re-
creation/commission of Noah, followed by fall (sins of Noah and his sons); (3)
chaos of Egyptian captivity and plagues of de-creation, followed by re-creation
(at Exodus)/commission of Israel (anticipated by commission of Patriarchs)
followed by fall (golden calf); (4) chaos of captivity in Babylon and in Israel's
own land, followed by re-creation/commission of Jesus the True Israel (in His
life, death and resurrection), followed by no fall of Jesus as Last Adam, and
followed by successful consummation of initial re-creation in eternal new
heavens and earth.[77] This story-line[78] expresses a world-view rich in theological
doctrines.[79] The new creation is rooted in Christ's life, death and resurrection.[80]

How does 'new creation' fare when our second criterion is applied?
This essay has related the centre of new creation to the subject matter of all the
major New Testament corpuses and books in broad contours, suggesting how
this question could be answered in more depth. The reader will have to decide
whether this broad outline holds promise for further developing new creation as
the heuristic device for understanding New Testament theology.

More elaboration is needed to respond adequately to the first criterion:
how do some of the other previously proposed 'centres' *logically* compare to the
new creation thesis and *vice versa*? The following 'centres' are the most viable
contenders, some of which were mentioned above: *kingdom, covenant, promise,
salvation, redemption, history of redemption, new Exodus, justification, reconciliation,
people of God, new temple, life, new Jerusalem / Zion, presence of God* and *God's glory.*

The most prominent competitors with 'new creation' are the notion of
the *kingdom* in the Gospels, as well as justification and reconciliation in Paul. The
kingdom is a major facet of new creation, since Jesus was reinstating the

---

[76]One must depend on the work of scholars who have attempted to demonstrate the viability of
some of the competing centres; likewise, works which have surveyed and evaluated some of the
significant centres must also be used. See especially the works of Hasel and Scobie noted above.
[77]The word παλιγγενεσία ('regeneration, rebirth'), which refers in Mt. 19:28 to the new creation
and kingdom which Christ will bring to completion, is used by Philo to refer to the regaining of
life (Philo, *On the Cherubim* 114; *Posterity of Cain* 124) and to the renewal of the earth after the
cataclysmic flood (*Life of Moses* II, 65), and Josephus employs it with reference to the restoration
of Israel after the Babylonian exile (Josephus, *Ant.* 11, 66; so Sim, *Apocalyptic Eschatology in the
Gospel of Matthew*, 112). See also Dumbrell, *Covenant and Creation*, 100-104 for creation themes
interwoven into the narrative of Israel's exodus from Egypt (especially Ex. 15).
[78]For comparison of this to Wright's own analysis, see the above discussion of his three levels of
covenantal purpose; *e.g.*, note 31 above.
[79]See the theological concepts elaborated upon in the main body of the essay, which were viewed
as facets of the new creation, or of the new re-creation story line.
[80]See E. E. Lemcio, 'The Unifying Kerygma of the New Testament', *JSNT* 33 (1988), 3-17, and
idem, 'The Unifying Kerygma of the New Testament (II)', *JSNT* 38 (1990), 3-11, who contends that
'the unifying kerygmatic centre to the diverse witness of the NT' is six fold: (1) God who (2) sent
(according to the Gospels) or raised (according to the rest of the New Testament witness) (3)
Jesus, (4) followed by a response, (5) towards God, (6) brings benefits. It is significant that,
according to this scheme, Jesus' resurrection is the core of the post-Gospel message.

vicegerency which Adam should have successfully carried out in the original creation. This is a facet of new creation, not more comprehensive nor even synonymous with new creation. The image of the new Jerusalem/Zion and of the new temple in both Testaments alludes to the presence of God in the midst of his victorious *reign*.[81] At the core of the kingdom is rule, and there is certainly more to new creation than ruling.

Reconciliation is a serious contender, since it could be seen logically to be the goal of new creation: the purpose of restoring creation is in order that sinful people could also be restored into relationship with their Creator (see the link between new creation and reconciliation in 2 Cor. 5:17-21). However, new creation is the broad reference to the restoration of the fallen cosmos *within which* there is restoration of humanity's vicegerency and there is reconciliation with God and between alienated humans.

The *new Exodus* is a major theme in portions of the New Testament (especially the Gospels, Paul and the Apocalypse), but it is another metaphor for new creation. The plagues on Egypt which begin the process of the Exodus are designed to indicate a de-creation and situation of chaos from which Israel can emerge through the division of water and earth as a new humanity on the other side of the Red Sea.[82] Just as Israel was a corporate Adam, so their inheritance of the promised land was to be what God had promised to Adam if he had obeyed: full possession of the Garden of Eden, and by extension the ends of the earth. This is why the land promised to Israel is also referred to as the Garden of Eden (Is. 51:3; Ezk. 36:35; Joel 2:3; *cf.* Is. 65:21-23 [LXX]). If Israel had obeyed as a corporate Adam, they would have inherited their own paradisal garden, and, ultimately, the whole earth. They disobeyed, and were, like Adam, disinherited. The golden calf episode was the event which recapitulated the fall of Adam.[83]

All of this is recapitulated in the exile, which is compared to a state of creational chaos, and in the promises of their return from exile, which is compared by Isaiah to another Exodus. But significant features of the fulfilment are delayed since: (1) only a remnant returns; (2) the rebuilt temple does not meet the expectations of the one promised in Ezekiel 40–48 (it is smaller and, perhaps, the divine presence is absent); (3) Israel is still under foreign domination; (4) there is no new creation in which the land is renovated, nor is there a renewed Zion into which the redeemed return from among the Gentiles, nor is there peace among Jew and Gentile. The major features of the restoration promises begin fulfilment in Christ's coming; both Jesus and Paul appeal to Old Testament restoration promises beginning fulfilment in their midst. And because the promises of restoration were coined in new Exodus language, Jesus is seen as

---

[81]So Dumbrell, *End of the Beginning*, 1-34.
[82]Wisdom 19:6 portrays the Exodus as a new creation: 'For the whole creation was again *renewed* [διατυπόω = also fashioned, formed, framed] in its own kind anew' (19:18 adds, 'For the elements were changed in themselves . . .'; on the nuances of διατυπόω, see R. M. Davidson, *Typology in Scripture* [Andrews University Seminary Doctoral Dissertation Series 2; Berrien Springs, Mich.: Andrews University, 1981], 132).
[83]For the events of Israel's sin, judgment and restoration in Ex. 32–34 being a recapitulation of Adam's sin, fall and restoration, see S. J. Hafemann, *Paul, Moses, and the History of Israel* (WUNT 81; Tübingen: J. C. B. Mohr [Paul Siebeck], 1995), 227-231, who also shows that this was the view of Judaism to varying degrees.

launching the realization of those prophecies;[84] and because New Exodus is the initial reinstatement of the primal creation, the New Testament can also refer to the fulfilment of the promises of restoration as the fulfilment of new creation.[85]

The proposed centres of *salvation, redemption* and *justification* are too narrow in comparison to new creation. All three are part of the means used to accomplish the goal of new creation: people are 'saved' from their sinful state, so that the wrath of God will not overwhelm them at the final judgment, and they pass through it, so that they can enter the new creation. *Redemption* is a similar metaphor and plays the same instrumental role in relation to new creation, but it has the nuance of being bought out of slavery to sin and to Satan. Likewise, *justification* is one of the means used to work toward the new cosmos, but it has overtones of a legal metaphor.[86] In the case of all three – salvation, redemption and justification – Christ carries out the action on behalf of His sinful people.

The proposal of *history of redemption*, God's salvific dealings with His people throughout the entire history from the fall of Adam until the final consummation of history, also fits into the same penultimate position as the ideas of salvation, redemption and justification, since all of these are solutions to the predicament of sin which prevents new creation from occurring.

Covenant is a penultimate means to accomplishing the new creation, whether one has in mind the purported covenant of creation made with Adam, or the covenants made with Noah, Abraham, Moses, David, and then the new covenant promised in Jeremiah and inaugurated in the New Testament.[87]

The notion of *promise* has the similar intermediate role of covenant in that covenants are formalizations of earlier salvific promises, though covenants are broader, since they include considerations of stipulations and judgment as well. Although both the promise of redemption in Christ and the new covenant are fulfilled in the new heavens and earth, that condition of fulfilment continues eternally. Nevertheless, the condition of the new creation also exists for ever.

The proposal of the *people of God* as the central New Testament concept is too general and too one-sided, since it does not include sufficient focus on God, Christ and the Spirit.

The theme of *life* is best understood as virtually synonymous with the idea of resurrection and regeneration discussed earlier. Alternatively, if one construes life to refer to the manner of life one lives, then this might fit better under the category of *sanctification*. Whichever is the case, it is still a sub-category of new creation, since it cannot comprehend all other facets of new creation.

The notion of *the presence of God* is very close to reconciliation, since people are reconciled to God's presence, which then reconciles them to one another. God's presence, however, is greater than merely a facet of reconciliation.

---

[84]In addition to N. T. Wright, *ibid., cf.* also W. D. Swartley, *Israel's Scripture Traditions and the Synoptic Gospels* (Peabody, MA: Hendrickson, 1994), 44-153, and R. E. Watts, 'The Influence of the Isaianic New Exodus on the Gospel of Mark' (Ph.D. Thesis, University of Cambridge, 1990; forthcoming in the WUNT series [Tübingen: J. C. B. Mohr (Paul Siebeck)]), who analyse the second Exodus patterns in the Synoptics.

[85]On the dual notion of Christ's death and resurrection as fulfilling both the promises of new creation and the prophecies of Israel's restoration, see Beale, 'Old Testament Background of Reconciliation in 2 Corinthians 5-7', and *idem*, 'Old Testament Background of Rev 3.14'.

[86]For elaboration of the notion of justification, see the extended discussion earlier in the essay.

[87]For this role of the covenants in relation to creation, see the three works of W. J. Dumbrell mentioned earlier (especially *Covenant and Creation*).

Indeed, the divine presence is almost synonymous with God's glory, which refers to the essence of His attributes and very being. Yet God's glorious presence is not co-equal with new creation. God, Christ and the Spirit are the sovereign agents in bringing about new creation and they rule in the new creation. Both images of new Jerusalem/Zion and new temple connote the notions of God's presence and active reign.[88]

The consummated new creation is the overarching reality integrating distinct elements. These were part of the first, pre-fall creation, but go beyond the initial creation because now they exist in *escalated* form with respect to their nature or quality.[89] They include: (1) God's presence and glory, (2) perfected human life (involving resurrection life after the fall), (3) peace (involving reconciliation after the fall), (4) restoration of the material cosmos, (5) righteousness, (6) reign and (7) Sabbath rest; (8) the original primordial command to 'be fruitful and multiply'. Genesis 12 ff. transformed this into a promise to multiply Abraham's seed, which finds its fulfilment in Christ and His many sons (Gal. 3:16, 26-29), all of whom will be finally perfected in the new cosmos.

In sum, eschatology is not merely the end of redemptive or cosmic history or the goal of Israel's hopes or the goal of the individual saint's hopes, but an 'already and not yet new creation in Christ', and all other things associated with eschatology are inextricably linked with 'new creation'.[90] The well-known dictum '*Endzeit als Urzeit*'[91] is on the mark, as is the *Epistle of Barnabas* 6:13, 'Behold, I make the last things as the first things'. Eschatology is protology: the goal of all redemptive history is to return to the primal condition of creation from which humankind fell[92] and then go beyond it to a heightened state, which the first creation did not reach.

But how is the phrase *new creation* used? Is it (1) the strict idea of the specific apocalyptic notion of the dissolution and recreation of the entire cosmos, including the resurrection of people? (2) or, a theological construct in which all eschatological hopes are wrapped up in one theological package? (3) or, the general future hope typical of *Israel's* world-view in which the following are included as the objects of that hope: resurrection, renewal of the cosmos, vindication of Israel, return from captivity, salvation of those believing among the nations, punishment of the wicked nations, and, possibly, other theological themes which need to be linked together? All three senses are used here, and, hence, it refers to the entire network of ideas that belong to renewal of the whole world, of Israel, and of the individual.

---

[88]For this dual idea of temple, see Dumbrell, *End of the Beginning*, 35-76.
[89]See G. K. Beale, *The Book of Revelation* (New International Greek Testament commentary series; Grand Rapids: Eerdmans and Carlisle: Paternoster, forthcoming), on Rev. 21:1–22:5, for discussion of the recapitulated and escalated elements of the final form of the new creation.
[90]See I. H. Marshall, 'Slippery Words I. Eschatology', *ExpT*89 (1978), 264-269, who summarizes nine different ways in which the term 'eschatology' has been used; he concludes that the core definition must include the idea of the awareness that God's promises have begun to be fulfilled in the present but they have not been consummately fulfilled, so that there is still a forward looking aspect as well.
[91]As far as I am aware, this idea was first established in scholarship by H. Gunkel, *Schöpfung und Chaos in Urzeit und Endzeit* (Göttingen: Vandenhoeck & Ruprecht, 1895), *e.g.*, 367-370.
[92]So Allison, *End of the Ages Has Come*, 91.

Does the notion of new creation advance our understanding of already and not yet eschatology?[93] Part of the answer lies in Wright's view of the three levels within the covenantal complex of ideas discussed above: (1) cosmic or worldwide level, in which Israel's role was to be an agent in restoring the fallen creation; (2) a national level, in which Israel suffered because of her own sin and needed restoration herself; (3) the individual level, in which an Israelite received forgiveness and restoration symbolically through the sacrificial system, as a small-scale model of the coming restoration of the nation. These three levels are better viewed *within a complex of new creational ideas*, with the notion of covenant playing a subsidiary role within the complex. This is a sharpening of the understanding of eschatological salvation, and it explains more precisely how eschatological ideas are interrelated.

The central element of the inaugurated new creation is Jesus Christ. This is specific yet general along the lines of the biblical concept of 'the one and the many' or of 'corporate representation'.[94] The beginning of new creation is understood as Christ's life, especially His death and resurrection, so that He is a formative microcosmic model which determines the nature and destiny of people, and the rest of creation, on a macrocosmic scale. What happened to Christ in His life, death and resurrection contains patterns of things which, not only recapitulate earlier Old Testament historical patterns, but embody patterns of things which will happen to His people: for example, with respect to His suffering, resurrection as first-fruits, His names of Son of God (Christians are adopted sons) and Son of Man (*i.e.*, Adam; Christians become true humanity in Christ), being a light to the nations, reception of the Holy Spirit, keeping of the Law, restoration to God's presence from death, Christ's vindication becomes the Christian's justification, and so on.[95] New creation is the New Testament's hermeneutical and eschatological centre of gravity.

Of course, new creation is not *the* key to explaining exhaustively why *all* features appear as they do in the New Testament. There are cultural, linguistic, sociological, political and other factors which are reflected in the New Testament and apparently have nothing to do with 'new creation'.[96] A number of background features from which New Testament authors drew or through which they naturally expressed their ideas, whether Jewish or, especially, Greco-Roman are in mind here.[97] But it is possible that certain background ideas were chosen in order to supplement and enrich the theology of a particular writer. For

---

[93]Towner posed this very question of how 'new creation' is a better general centre than the 'already and not yet eschatological salvation' (as proposed by L. D. Hurst and G. B. Caird in *New Testament Theology* [Oxford: Clarendon, 1994]).

[94]For discussion of this concept, see H. W. Robinson, *Corporate Personality in Ancient Israel* (Philadelphia: Fortress, 1980), and the attached bibliography therein, as well as A. R. Johnson, *The One and the Many in the Israelite Conception of God* (Cardiff: University of Wales, 1960), though the view of 'corporate personality' has been qualified by later critics; it is better to speak of corporate solidarity and representation.

[95]See Wright, *ibid.*, 79, 'Paul is telling . . . the whole story of God, Israel and the world as now compressed into the story of Jesus. . . his use of the Old Testament is designed . . . to suggest new ways of reading well-known stories, and to suggest that they find a more natural climax in the Jesus story than elsewhere' (*ibid.*, 79). There is also a forward-looking aspect which I discuss here.

[96]Towner drew attention to sociological lenses in his response noted earlier.

[97]*E.g.*, *cf.* the works of A. J. Malherbe on various Greco-Roman backgrounds, and *cf.* the on-going New Wettstein projects.

instance, the 'book' of Revelation 5:1ff. is depicted partly through allusion to the Old Testament and partly against the Roman background of testaments or wills. The allusion to Ezekiel 2 carries with it notions of judgment, while the reference to the opening of a Roman seven-sealed will conveys the idea that Jesus has gained for His people an earthly inheritance lost by humanity.[98] Revelation elaborates on this inheritance as none other than receiving a place in the new heavens and earth (*cf.* Rev. 21:1-7 ff.). Likewise, the household code in Ephesians is plausibly referred to because of an overriding concern in the letter about the fragmented condition of fallen humanity, which Christ as the Adamic 'household manager' (*cf.* οἰκονομία in Eph. 1:10; 3:9) has begun to put back together, as He has the rest of the creation (*cf.* Eph. 1:10). The fragmentation of Jews and Gentiles has been breached by Christ's death and resurrection (Eph. 2:1–3:7); healing of the different levels of fractured relationships in the family (= the household) has also begun for those in Christ (*cf.* Eph. 5–6; the household code in Col. serves a similar role).

Were the New Testament writers really conscious of having new creation as the centre of their theology? I believe the answer to this question is 'yes', to varying degrees, since they were all immersed in an Old Testament-Jewish thought-world, which had at its inner ideological core the recapitulating story-line of creation. They all understood Jesus to be the key player in the beginning climax of this redemptive-historical story-line, though they drew the connections in different ways and highlighted diverse aspects of it (emphasizing tribulation, or reconciliation, or kingdom, or mission, and so on).

If these writers did have such a centre consciously in mind, why was it not more explicit? As early Jewish-Christian leaders, they would agree about Jesus playing the crucial role in the initial unfolding of the story-line's creational goal, but they would maintain their own distinct expressions and emphases in formulating their particular versions. Once their unique expressions of how Christ and the church relate to the story-line of creation are clearly understood, the centre of new creation can be seen to have been explicit in their minds.

No New Testament authors wrote with the explicit purpose of trying to produce a theological understanding of their faith, but they wrote primarily because of circumstances and problems in the various churches. Their aim was to solve those problems by appealing to the most germane parts of their underlying theology, so that they express only those parts of their larger theology which were most relevant for addressing the particular circumstances of each situation. This means that we must put pieces of their theological puzzle together. There are enough of the pieces to put most of the puzzle together, but gaps remain.

In summary, the core notion of new creation may be conceived of as a doctrinally thematic skeleton giving shape to the outer 'skin', which consists of various other elements not so closely related organically or thematically to the skeletal biblical-theological structure. In the light of this skeleton-skin meta-phor,[99] this essay contends that the most comprehensive centre of New Testament theology is: *Christ's life, and especially his death and resurrection through the Spirit, is the 'already and not yet' end-time new creation for God's glory.* The glory of

---

[98]The 'book' of Revelation 5 carries other connotations; for fuller discussion see Beale, *Book of Revelation, in loc.*
[99]The aptness of this analogy was suggested by Towner in response to my Tyndale Fellowship conference presentation.

God is the primary goal even within this centre, since every aspect of the consummated new creation is designed to display the divine glory completely in
contrast to the partial manifestation of it on earth during pre-consummation
history (see Num. 14:21; Rev. 21:1–22:5; *e.g.*, 21:10-11, 23).[100]

---

[100]God's glory as the zenith point of new creation has already been anticipated by the other
recapitulating quasi-new creation episodes of redemptive history in the Old Testament. God's
glory or great name is viewed as the goal of the following events: Exodus, Israel's wandering in
the wilderness, conquest of Canaan, building of the temple, exile and promised restoration, Jesus'
life and death, *etc.* (so J. Piper, *Desiring God* [Portland, Or.: Multnomah, 1986], 227-238, who
demonstrates this from various biblical texts, and includes other significant Old and New
Testament events [*e.g.*, the Genesis 1 creation account] in his analysis in order to show that their
goal is also the divine glory). This point deserves an entire section of discussion.

Chapter 2

A HOLY GOD AMONG A HOLY PEOPLE IN A HOLY PLACE: THE ENDURING ESCHATOLOGICAL HOPE

Gordon J. Thomas

In this essay a redefinition of eschatology is proposed as the doctrine of 'ultimate things' rather than of 'last things'. Ultimate reality is not just what will transpire at the end of time, but that which God apparently has always sought to make a present reality. This approach is applied to the idea of holiness in an attempt to demonstrate that throughout Scripture a holy God has always indicated His wish to dwell among a holy people in a holy place. The eschatological call is to mirror God in His holiness.

Eschatology Reconsidered

According to G. B. Caird and L. D. Hurst, 'eschatology' is a term introduced into the English language from Germany in about 1845. They begin their discussion of the term by quoting the definition for it given in the *Oxford English Dictionary* (1891, 1933) as 'The department of theological science concerned with the four last things, death, judgment, heaven and hell.'[1] In his *Anchor Bible Dictionary* article on the subject David L. Petersen defines eschatology as follows:

> Derived from the Gk word *eschatos*, meaning 'last' or 'final', eschatology is teaching about 'the last things.' It refers to a time in

---

[1] G. B. Caird & L. D. Hurst, *New Testament Theology* (Oxford: Clarendon Press, 1995), 243.

the future when the course of history will be changed to such an extent that one can speak of an entirely new state of reality.[2]

Back in 1982, Christopher Rowland undertook an exercise in inductive reasoning in order to redefine the term 'apocalyptic' in his book *The Open Heaven*. The first of his seven conclusions was that: 'A definition of apocalyptic should not be too restricted but attempt to do justice to all the various elements in the literature.'[3] Rowland was arguing that justice had not really been done to all the various elements in the literature covered by the label 'apocalyptic', because the concern of many apocalypses with present realities in the heavenlies had been marginalized by an overemphasis on the study of the destruction and replacement of the present order in the eschaton. One might legitimately argue in a similar vein that a definition of 'eschatology' as the study of last things does not do justice to all the various elements in the literature. As Donald Gowan points out in his *Eschatology of the Old Testament*:

> Although the word literally means 'doctrine of the end', the OT does not speak of the end of the world, of time or of history. It promises the end of sin (Je. 33:8), of war (Mi. 4:3), of human infirmity (Is. 35:5-6a), of hunger (Ezk. 36:30), of killing or harming any living thing (Is. 11:9a).

Gowan then sums up all of the above by suggesting that justification for calling the Old Testament hope 'eschatology' is that it is all about 'the end of evil'.[4]

This redefinition of eschatology is quite helpful, because it captures in its net some of the major concerns of the Old Testament which elude the more restricted usual definition. Since the object of the exercise ought to be to find the best possible ways of doing justice to the biblical text, may one suggest another tweak to the definition of eschatology?

Most scholarly discussions of the subject differentiate between two kinds of dualism implicit in eschatology. There is a temporal dualism which contrasts the present evil age with the

---

[2]D. L. Petersen, 'Eschatology (OT)', in *Anchor Bible Dictionary*, *Vol. 2* (New York: Doubleday, 1992), 575. Petersen adds (576) that the term is used with widely differing meanings: in Greek it meant 'farthest extent in space, final element of time, and last piece of money', and was 'most often innately communal and cosmic in its reference'.

[3]C. Rowland, *The Open Heaven* (London: SPCK, 1982), 70.

[4]D. Gowan, *Eschatology in the Old Testament* (Philadelphia: Fortress Press, 1986), 2.

glories of the age to come in a very linear way. Thus in Hebrews the animal sacrifices belong to the former time, whereas the atoning death of Christ belongs to the latter time. There is also what some have called a spatial dualism, which contrasts earthly and heavenly realities, the most obvious example of which must be the way Hebrews compares the real heavenly sanctuary above with the shadow or copy below. Chronological or temporal dualism, then, works on a horizontal axis; cosmological or spatial on a vertical one.

The problem with the standard definition of eschatology as the doctrine of last things is that it is skewed in the direction of temporal dualism and fails to do justice to the other dimension, the spatial or cosmological. As a cipher for the balance desired, the author's choice of vocabulary in John 3 may be commended. In his conversation with Nicodemus, Jesus says that a person must be born *anothen* – a delightfully ambiguous word which covers both eschatological axes. The rendering 'born again' covers the horizontal or temporal aspect; the rendering 'born from above' covers the vertical or spatial.

Biblical scholarship might do better justice to the material in Scripture by defining eschatology as 'the doctrine of ultimate things'. Ultimate reality is not just what will transpire at the end of time, but that which has always existed in the heavenlies and which God apparently has always sought to make a present reality, according to the Law and the Prophets. This chapter is built around an understanding of eschatology as the study of ultimate things, ultimate realities.[5] It will attempt to deal with the hope of the Old Testament, its partial fulfilment in the first coming of Christ and its consummation at the end of all things. And one way, not the only way, of doing this is by following the idea of holiness as a thread throughout both Testaments. The notion under consideration is that of a holy God among a holy people in a holy place as the enduring eschatological hope of the Scriptures.[6]

---

[5]My suggestion is not a million miles away from Samuel Terrien's outlook. He writes: 'Prophets are usually mistaken for predictors. The prophets of Israel unveiled *not the future but the absolute* ' (*The Elusive Presence* [San Francisco: Harper & Row, 1978], 227; my emphasis).

[6]See Caird and Hurst, who point out that, while the OED definition deals with the ultimate destiny of the individual, the word has come to be understood mainly in a historical sense as covering 'the biblical teaching about the destiny of the world and *the working out of God's purposes in and through his holy people* ' (*New Testament Theology*, 243; my emphasis).

A Holy God among a Holy People in a Holy Place: The Old Testament Picture

A fair case can be made for the thesis that eschatology is in good measure, though by no means entirely, a recapitulation of protology, the study of first things. *Paradise Regained* is not just the name of Milton's sequel to *Paradise Lost*; it is a handy way of summarizing how the language and imagery of the final chapters of Revelation clearly owe much to the Eden story in Genesis. The sweep of the biblical narrative begins with God enjoying fellowship with the sinless man He has created in an unsullied environment and ends with the Lord God the Almighty and the Lamb living among a holy people in a holy city, from which everyone unclean is excluded. At many points in between, God intentionally tries to recreate this picture.

The first time in history that God explicitly reveals himself as holy[7] is in a bush near Mount Horeb to a Midianite-Egyptian-Hebrew shepherd named Moses. A few dramatic events later, He reveals His holiness more fully at the same mountain to Moses' people. Before cutting a covenant with them, God intimates that they are to be a kingdom of priests and a holy nation to Him (Ex. 19:6). In ten well-chosen words[8] God gives the adjective 'holy' some moral content, and in the months and years that follow He articulates through a plethora of case-law[9] precisely how He expects His chosen people to live. The great danger is that if a holy God comes to live among an unholy people, His holiness will consume them. The pyrotechnics at

---

[7]Concerning the holiness of God, J. E. Hartley writes, 'Holiness is not one attribute of Yahweh's among others; rather it is the quintessential nature of Yahweh as God' (*Leviticus* [WBC; Dallas: Word Books, 1992], lvii). The older Old Testament theologian Edmund Jacob, in *Old Testament Theology* (London: Hodder & Stoughton, 1958), 86, wrote in similar vein, 'Holiness is not one divine quality among others, even the chiefest, for it expresses what is characteristic of God and corresponds precisely to his deity.'

[8]*I.e.* the Decalogue.

[9]Whether 'case-law' is the most accurate description of the legislation that follows the Decalogue is open to question. I therefore made a conscious decision to refrain from an exegetical paperchase on two grounds. First, my argument remains unaffected by whatever label one puts on the other laws. Second, biblical theology as an academic enterprise will be smothered at birth if every statement made about any one part of the Bible has to be beyond scholarly dispute. In my judgment, biblical theology has to rely most of the time on the building-blocks provided by a fairly well-established exegetical consensus in order to explore the relation of the parts to the whole biblical picture. Otherwise, if unassailable exegetical expertise in every part of the Bible is a prerequisite, few will dare to attempt the task at all.

Sinai, plus sundry miracles and judgments in the desert, leave the Israelites in little doubt about the awesomeness of God's holiness. The ashes of Nadab and Abihu (Lv. 10:1-3),[10] not to mention those of 250 men who offer incense presumptuously (Nu. 16:35), bear silent but eloquent testimony to the fact that a holy God is a consuming fire (Dt. 4:24). It is this very likelihood which motivates God's refusal to accompany the Israelites on their journey from Sinai to Canaan.[11] A three-fold solution is therefore proposed.

First, God says, 'Have them make me a sanctuary, so that I may dwell among them' (Ex. 25:8). Before the construction of the tabernacle, God goes before or behind the Israelites on the march, but when they stop, it would appear from Exodus 33 that God stays at a safe distance. Thus Moses has to get clear away from the camp in order to enjoy his regular conversations with God in the tent of meeting (Ex. 33:7). This does not satisfy God apparently, who wishes to be central in every respect in the lives of His people. He wants to be among them, not on the periphery of their communal life. The construction of a clean and consecrated place right in the middle of the camp is God's solution. The elaborate restrictions on access to the inner and outer sancta and to the surrounding courtyard establish a *cordon sanitaire* between the holy and dangerous God and the people He chooses to dwell among. Exodus 40:34-35 describes the glorious initial consummation of a holy God's desire to dwell among His people:[12]

> Then the cloud covered the tent of meeting, and the glory of the LORD filled the tabernacle. Moses was not able to enter the tent of meeting because the cloud settled upon it, and the glory of the LORD filled the tabernacle.

Secondly, God commands all the people of Israel to be holy, because He Himself is holy (Lv. 11:44-45; 19:1-2). The book of Leviticus elaborates what David Clines has called the theme of the Pentateuch by spelling out in detail the means by which the relationship now established is to be maintained.[13] The people of Israel, who have been constituted holy by virtue of a covenant-

---

[10] Note God's response: 'I will show myself holy among those who are near me.'

[11] Ex. 33:3: 'I will not go up among you, or I would consume you on the way, for you are a stiff-necked people.'

[12] The people do not create a holy place for a holy God to occupy. Rather, as J. G. Gammie says, 'God is the one who sanctifies tent, altar, and priests. Indeed, the former is set apart, made holy not so much by human action but by the presence of the glory of God' (*Holiness in Israel* [Minneapolis: Fortress Press, 1989], 17).

[13] D. J. A. Clines, *The Theme of the Pentateuch* (Sheffield: JSOT Press, 1978), 50.

relationship with a holy God, are now commanded to become like Him.[14] The Holiness Code spells out in detail that this involves a change in spiritual conduct (no compromise with occultic Canaanite religious practices), in sexual conduct (the expression of sexuality is given clear limits) and in social conduct (the way relatives and neighbours are to be treated is itemized and then summarized in Lv. 19:18). The motivation for such a holy lifestyle is not meant to be the accumulation of merit or the attempt to earn salvation. These people are already redeemed. They are already in covenant-relationship with God. As the Shema goes on to make clear, God wants His people to be holy because they love Him with heart, soul and might (Dt. 6:4-5). In all of this literature faithfulness, love, justice, honesty, kindness and purity emerge as aspects of divine holiness that are to be replicated in the people of God. The most widely-touted definition of holiness as separation (separation from the world and separation to God for sacred purposes) is clearly not a sufficiently comprehensive one.[15]

Thus the Torah is extremely clear that a holy God wishes to dwell among a holy people. But, thirdly, He also wants to dwell in a holy place. It is not sufficient for the tabernacle to be holy; the camp too must be holy. All sources of defilement must be removed. Lepers are to be excluded, for example, because 'they must not defile their

---

[14]The biblical command to the people of God to be holy is perhaps too easily ignored or brushed aside by some Christians, and this despite a steady stream of books which have reiterated the charge over many centuries. It is a command from Almighty God, not just some pious wish. In the worldview of the ancient Israelite there was no accepted doctrine of the afterlife, and therefore the only possible fulfilment of this command was in the here and now. As Caird and Hurst point out, '... most of the books of the Old Testament were written at a time when the Hebrew people had no belief in an afterlife for the individual. For them life meant this life ... Their eschatology was concerned with the vindication in history of the truth and justice of God and of His purpose for Israel and the world' (*New Testament Theology*, 268.) With regard to a full biblical theology, this command is not superseded by New Testament revelation but reiterated explicitly by the apostle Peter (1 Pet. 1:14-16). With regard to hermeneutics, when we bring this command to the touchstone of Christ, we hear him saying, 'Be perfect, therefore, as your heavenly Father is perfect' (Mt. 5:48). Whatever else that means, I think I am fairly confident that it does not imply any watering down of the demands that God makes on his people.

[15]Older scholars sought to get to the heart of holiness by attempting to pin down the etymological derivation of the *qds* and *hagios* word-groups. 'More fruitful is a consideration of the term as the focal point of an idea which emerges by reference to its context and the wider semantic field' (Kent Brower, 'Holiness', in D. R. W. Wood [revision ed.], *New Bible Dictionary* [Leicester: IVP, 3rd edn. 1996], 477).

camp, where I dwell among them' (Nu. 5:3). Excretion must take place outside the camp, because, in the words of Deuteronomy 23:12-14, the camp must be holy, so that God might not see anything indecent among them and turn away from them. The camp is to be characterized not only by cleanness but also by order. Every tribe has its appointed place in relation to the tabernacle (Nu. 2). Cleanness and order – two more colours in the spectrum of God's holiness.

What is the rationale behind all this 'fussiness'? Why exactly does a holy God want to dwell among a holy people in a holy place? The answer does not lie on the surface of the biblical text. Perhaps it can be teased out, however, as an implication of certain texts. An explanation might be made in terms of mirroring and of mission.

Judaism is often described as an aniconic religion, a religion devoid of images of its God. The concept of the image of God does occur, however, in the creation narrative, and has generated much discussion of both a scholarly and a scholastic nature as to precisely which human attributes replicate divine ones, whether image and likeness are to be differentiated, and the extent to which the image has been lost or marred as a result of the fall.[16] One perspective on this sees the individual human as being the sole legitimate image of God.[17] The Eastern Orthodox emphasis on the *perichoresis* or mutual indwelling of the Holy Trinity offers a different way of looking at the matter. If God is not a monad but a tri-personal being-in-communion, then what mirrors Him best is (or are) people-in-communion. A line then opens out through Scripture featuring the people of Israel as the corporate image of God in the world, then the person of Jesus as the image of the invisible God and finally the church as the image of God in the world. How was a world estranged from its maker to know what God was like? Simple: by looking at the Israelites,[18] first of all, and subsequently at Christ and at the church.

This mirroring of God, then, is a crucial aspect of the mission of the people of God. If the telling phrase from Exodus about Israel being chosen as a kingdom of priests and a holy nation is

---

[16]Gordon Wenham provides a compact and helpful summary of alternative interpretations in his *Genesis 1-15* (WBC; Waco: Word Books, 1987), 29-31.

[17]C. J. H. Wright, *Living as the People of God* (Leicester: IVP, 1983), 31: ' … the only image that was "allowed" was the one God had designed and created himself – the image of God, man himself.'

[18]On this point I concur with Chris Wright, who writes that in giving laws, 'God's purpose . . . was not just righteous individuals, but a new community who in their social life would embody those qualities of righteousness, peace, justice and love which reflect God's own character and were his original purpose for mankind' (*Living as the People of God*, 35).

reconsidered for a moment, what can be learnt? A priest exercises a mediatorial role between God and the people, so who are a kingdom of priests to mediate between? One another and God? It makes more sense to understand them as being called to mediate between God and the nations,[19] thus fulfilling the promise to Abraham that through his seed all the nations would be blessed.[20] Corporately, collectively, communally, in their shared living, Israel is called to model the life of the Godhead, to live out the love and goodness and justice of God for the nations to see and be drawn to. But they can only be a kingdom of priests in so far as they are also a holy nation.[21] If they are indistinguishable from their neighbours in their spiritual, sexual and social conduct, the mission of God is 'dead in the water'.

Space precludes discussion of how a holy temple in a holy city in a holy land eventually supplants a holy tabernacle in a holy camp, but the theophany at the dedication of Solomon's Temple in 1 Kings 8:10 is a development of the motif established at Sinai. Such landmark events as these dominate the Israelite religious imagination for centuries to come. In later years the imagery used to convey the eschatological hope nearly all looks back to the past. It describes the future like a new Eden (Is. 11:6-8; 51:3; Ezk. 36:35), like a new Exodus (Is. 4:5; 52:11-12) or like a new Davidic monarchy (Is. 9:6-7; 11:1-3; Je. 23:5). In all these pictures God is redeeming his people again, God is restoring order in society, God's law is being assimilated by people who wish to keep it (Je. 31:33).

The repeated ministry of the prophets during the monarchy is to call Israel back to the standards of Torah,[22] back to their true vocation of being a holy nation in a holy place, among whom a holy God lives. Israel's corporate election as a priestly kingdom and holy nation is the main issue. If she falls short of her calling, God's saving purposes for the nations are frustrated. Only by maintaining God's standards in her public life can Israel mediate a true knowledge of YHWH to others. The only way this can happen is by a devout obedience to Torah and a resolute avoidance of being contaminated by pagan religion and pagan moral values. The words and actions of

---

[19]See S. Terrien, *The Elusive Presence*, 125: '... Israel in its entirety becomes "a holy nation", because Israel's vocation is to become the priest of the King of history. Israel, the covenant people, is to mediate the presence of Yahweh to the world.'
[20]An idea whose Old Testament climax is found in Is. 66:18-21.
[21]See Chris Wright, *Living as the People of God*, 43: 'Their very existence and character as a society were to be a witness to God, a model or paradigm of his holiness expressed in the social life of a redeemed community.'
[22]*E.g.* Mal. 4:4: 'Remember the law of my servant Moses, the statutes and ordinances that I commanded him at Horeb for all Israel.'

the prophets are aimed therefore at exposing the various ways in which Israel's holiness has been compromised. These include:

1. Idolatry – which abuses God's sacrificial self-giving love. It breaks the first commandment of the Decalogue (to have no other gods before YHWH). It also breaks the great commandment of the Shema to love God supremely. Since love is the heart of the covenant-relationship, the prophets often portray idolatry as adultery (Ho. 4:12, 9:1; Je. 5:11, 13:27), as infidelity to a marriage which has taken place at Sinai between YHWH and His bride Israel. What is the contradiction here? God is faithful but Israel, who is meant to image Him, is unfaithful.

2. Iniquity – which distorts the moral picture of God's character which Israel is meant to portray (Ho. 4:1-3; Mi. 6:10-12; Je. 9:4-6). The contradiction? God is good but Israel is wicked.

3. Injustice – which perverts the moral order of a society that is meant to demonstrate a restored creation-order in its relationships between people. Injustice prevents any possibility of making wrong things right again (Am. 5:11-12; Mi. 3:1-3; Je. 5:28). Righteousness is a term which describes these right relationships and one which therefore often goes hand in hand with justice (Am. 5:24, Is. 28:17, 48:18, 56:1). The contradiction here? God is just but his representative, Israel, is unjust.

Of all of these, perhaps the chief obstacle to the fulfilment of God's wishes in Israel's history is the continual, corrupting influence of pagan idolatry,[23] rather than any suggestion of hereditary depravity resulting from the fall. Thorough-going exposure of children to the teachings of Torah is the medicine against corruption recommended by both the Torah (Dt. 6:4-9) and the Wisdom-tradition (Ps. 119; Pr. 22:6). Divine discipline is a remedial method used by God to sanctify both individuals (Pr. 3:11-12) and nation (Dt. 8:2-5).

When sound biblical teaching fails, God's righteous judgment, announced so frequently by the prophets, is designed to restore Israel to her former state. An escalating series of sanctions is built into the covenant to achieve the necessary turnaround. If famine, drought, plague and sword fail, the last resort is exile from the land. The very act of expelling the rebellious nation from the land has sanctification as its objective. Exile cleanses the land of that which, and of those who, defile it. Exile purifies a people by leaving a remnant, who will be fit to reoccupy the land.

---

[23]This is the case even in the isolation of the wilderness wanderings. The supreme act of rebellion, the making of the golden calf at Sinai, mimics Egyptian, and prefigures Canaanite, iconography.

Cleansing and restoration are therefore integral to the eschatological hope of the prophets, and they are not for the far-off distant future, but for some time closer at hand. Therefore complicated calculations, which attempt to identify precisely when the prophets predicted that the kingdom of God would come to earth in its fullness are a waste of time. As suggested earlier, eschatology in the Old Testament has more to do with ultimate, than with last, things. The ultimate hope is not linked to any particular time. It is not millennia or even centuries away. More often than not, the prophets refer to 'that day', the ever-recurring day of the LORD, when the suzerain breaks into history to call His wayward vassals to account. God's kingdom is right overhead at all times; God can break into history at any time and re-establish it. The prayer of Isaiah 64:1 is for YHWH to tear open the heavens and come down.

The prerequisite for such a deliverance is often portrayed as one sincere act of turning back to YHWH and a repudiation of oppression and injustice in public life, which seems to be virtually all the prophets think it will take (Am. 5:14-15; Ho. 10:12; Joel 2:12; Zp. 2:1-3; Is. 1:16-20; Je. 3–4 *etc.*). This will bring about the restoration of Israel's fortunes, which has been promised in the covenant (Dt. 30:3) and echoed both by prophets (Am. 9:14; Je. 29:13-14) and by psalmists (Ps. 126).

However, acts of national repentance are few and far between and often very short-lived. After the catastrophic fall of Jerusalem, the exilic prophets find the key to the fulfilment of the eschatological hope to be a new covenant predicted in Jeremiah 31:31-34. When this happens, YHWH will put His law inside people and write it on their hearts. Instead of hating God's commandments as a painful duty, people will want to keep them. The desire to do so will come not from outside but from inside. The same kind of idea is expressed by Ezekiel (36:22-36), who foresees Israel's regathering from among the nations as bringing several spiritual changes in its wake: the cleansing of Israel from all her uncleannesses and from all her idols; the reception by Israel of a new tender heart (of flesh rather than stone); the reception by Israel of God's Spirit within her; righteous living by Israel (God would cause them to walk in His statutes); right relationship with God ('you shall be my people and I will be your God').

It is hard to imagine a more complete description of sanctification, comprised of cleansing, filling and communion. The interesting aspect for our purposes is to note that Ezekiel does not appear to envisage all this in the far-off distant future, but as following Israel's return from exile in Babylon. Jeremiah's words are likewise located in the middle of a section, chapters 30-33, which is often labelled something like 'Jeremiah Foretells Israel's Restoration'. Entire sanctification, the making of a holy people in a holy land fit for a holy God to live among, is portrayed by the prophets as the action of God, if not in the here and now, at least in the near future. Such bright prospects are viewed as imminent because the recent cataclysmic judgement is interpreted as an effective instrument of catharsis, where the nation's defilement is concerned.

The fulfilment of the eschatological hope can be expressed then in precisely this way: it is of a holy God dwelling in the midst of a holy people in a holy land (Joel 2:27, 3:17, Is. 12:6, 60:19-21). A textbook example of this idea is found in Ezk. 37:25-28, which reads:

> They shall live in the land that I gave to my servant Jacob, in which your ancestors lived; they and their children and their children's children shall live there forever; and my servant David shall be their prince forever. I will make a covenant of peace with them; it shall be an everlasting covenant with them; and I will bless them and multiply them, and will set my sanctuary among them forevermore. My dwelling place shall be with them; and I will be their God, and they shall be my people. Then the nations shall know that I the LORD sanctify Israel, when my sanctuary is among them forevermore.

Those who have been regathered from exile, reanimated and sanctified by the breath/Spirit of God, are to be reconstituted as the dwelling-place of a holy God in their own land in order that the nations will get the message about what God is like. The outcome of the sanctification of Israel will be the accomplishment of God's missionary purpose for Israel. God's glory will be revealed throughout the whole world (Is. 11:9, 40:5). All nations will acknowledge His authority, and will participate in the worship of Him (Mi. 4:1-4; Is. 66:18-21). In other words, the corporate sanctification of Israel is expected to lead to the corporate sanctification of the nations, and therefore to a universal state of righteousness, justice and peace. Sadly, Israel fails to live up to her privileges and responsibilities as the servant of YHWH and, as the New Testament reveals, the eschatological hope of holiness comes to depend on Messiah for its fulfilment.

A Holy God among a Holy People in a Holy Place:
The New Testament Picture

The witness of the Gospels to God's yearning for a people who will
live holy lives is reiterated in a variety of ways. In Matthew, Jesus is
able to demand a greater righteousness than that of scribe and
Pharisee (Mt. 5:20) because He has come to fulfil the law and the
prophets (Mt. 5:17). The eschatological hopes of a new heart and new
spirit under a new covenant expressed by Jeremiah and Ezekiel are
fulfilled as Jesus takes the eucharistic cup and announces it as His
blood of the new covenant (Mt. 26:28).[24] Mark depicts the life of the
holy people of God as a gathering about the holy one of God, a
following of Him on His way to the cross, a self-denying, cross-
bearing servant lifestyle demanded right now. In the *Benedictus*, Luke
records Zechariah's prophetic expectation 'that we, being rescued
from the hands of our enemies, might serve him without fear, in
holiness and righteousness before him all our days' (Lk. 1:74-75).

In the Fourth Gospel the dwelling-place of God among His
people is neither tabernacle nor temple but the body of the incarnate
Logos, presented in John 1:14 as the one who tabernacled among
them and displayed God's glory. Then in John 2:19-21 the destroyed
and resurrected body of Jesus is cryptically proffered as the
replacement of Herod's temple, a point reinforced in the conversation
with the woman at the well in chapter 4:23. The woman's attempt to
hide behind an age-old quibble about the correct mountain on which
to worship God is scotched by Jesus' declaration that neither Mount
Gerizim nor the temple mount in Jerusalem is any longer the
divinely-appointed place of worship.

---

[24]Most scholars appear to agree these days that biblical eschatology is best
expressed as the end having broken into the middle of time or of a tension
between the 'already' and the 'not yet'. However, the consensus that the
purposes of God will all ultimately be accomplished is broken by disagreement
between Christian traditions as to what is included in the 'already' and what
remains in the 'not yet' of sanctification. In my opinion, the eschatological
shortcoming of a thoroughgoing Augustinian pessimism regarding the
possibility of God's people living holy lives in the present is that it represents an
under-realized eschatology. It speaks as though Jesus did not inaugurate the new
covenant by his death on the cross. The problem with sinless perfectionism, on
the other hand, is that it conveys an over-realized eschatology. People's
relationship with God may be an experience of the life of the ages here and now,
but we do not yet see all things under Jesus' feet. Rather, as the church has
always affirmed, the battle with the world, the flesh and the devil is ongoing and
unremitting until the parousia, the general resurrection and the great white
throne of judgment.

If Jesus combines in His own person the presence of a holy God and the holy dwelling-place, what of the holy people? The moral and ethical demands are as high as ever in the Fourth Gospel. Those who love Jesus must keep His commandments, and again this is a means of demonstrating love and of remaining in intimate communion with Jesus. The metaphor of branches abiding in a vine (Jn. 15) is then intensified in chapter 17 into a picture of the mutual indwelling of Father, Son and believers. There can be no stronger statement regarding a holy God's desire to live among a holy people than the perichoretic language of Jesus' high priestly prayer (Jn. 17:20-23), amplifying His words in John 14:20: On that day you will know that I am in my Father, and you in me, and I in you.'

Out of people full of selfishness, faithlessness and failure, Jesus welds the new covenant community. In Acts 2, Luke records how this motley crew, together now in one place, experience the eschatological outpouring of the Spirit upon all flesh, as prophesied by Joel. The Paraclete is no longer merely with them; He is in them (thus fulfilling Jesus' words in Jn. 14:17) and He is between them,[25] as the basis of their fellowship with one another. When the holiness that has been given by virtue of the Holy Spirit filling them all and purifying their hearts by faith (Acts 15:9) is threatened by the duplicity of Ananias and Sapphira, the Spirit acts as ruthlessly to stamp out corruption as YHWH himself did in Joshua's day, when the sin of Achan compromised the holiness of the people of God (Jos. 7).

The doctrinal expositions in the Pauline epistles repeatedly extol the full sufficiency of Christ's death and resurrection to deal with sin in all its aspects, by contrast with the impotence of the law. The attendant ethical exhortations stress in a variety of ways that Christians are called to live up to their privileged position as members of the body of Christ, as stones in a holy temple, which is a dwelling place for God (Eph. 2:22). A telling phrase at the beginning and end of Romans sums up the advantage of the gospel of Christ over the Torah. The purpose of the gospel concerning the whole Christ-event as delivered to the apostles is 'to bring about the obedience of faith' (Rom. 1:5; 16:26). That means to bring about faithful obedience to God, to make such a thing a present reality.

Many scholars down through the centuries have interpreted Romans 7:14-25 as Paul's current and normative experience of the struggles and repeated defeats of the Christian life,[26] but there are

---

[25]Cf. Augustine's term *vinculum caritatis*, whereby he portrayed the Holy Spirit as the bond of love between the Father and the Son.

[26]C. E. B. Cranfield, for example, is emphatic that 'it presents the experience of Christians generally, including the very best and most mature' (*Romans*, Vol. 1

several problems with this line of interpretation.[27] The 'obedience of faith' in the Prologue and Epilogue has already been mentioned. To that could be added the total absence of any christological or pneumatological references in these verses. If the normal Christian life is of necessity one of spiritual impotence, frustration and defeat, then one wonders how the new covenant can be one whit better than the old. The Jews knew what God required but could not or would not do it. Are Christians, according to Paul, in exactly the same boat?[28] Jeremiah and Ezekiel were apparently expecting God to write His Torah on people's hearts by His Spirit, thus making obedient and holy living both desirable and possible for the new covenant community.

The writer to the Hebrews has no reservations about the superiority of the new covenant, about the utter sinlessness (Heb. 4:15) of the fully divine (Heb. 1:3) and fully human (Heb. 2:17) son and high priest. None either about the total efficacy of the ultimate and unrepeatable sacrifice for sin (Heb. 9:26a) or about the completeness of the cleansing and sanctifying of believers achieved by that death. Thus Hebrews 10:14 declares that 'by a single offering he has perfected for all time those who are sanctified'. The author calls upon his readers to lay aside sin and follow in Jesus' footsteps (Heb. 12:1-2), to accept God's fatherly discipline (Heb. 12:5-11), to pursue peace with everyone and the holiness without which no-one will see the Lord (Heb. 12:14). What Christ has done for them must be matched by what they allow Him to do in them. There must be a real and not just a relative change.

[ICC; Edinburgh: T. & T. Clark, 1975], 344). More recently, J. I. Packer concurs in *A Passion for Holiness* (Nottingham: Crossway Books, 1992), 150-151. Nevertheless, the Reformed tradition in which both these eminent scholars stand is far from encouraging Christians, in Cranfield's phrase, 'to wallow complacently in our sins' (*Romans*, 1.358). Likewise, the spirit of Packer's book totally justifies its title.

[27]On such a massively-contested interpretative crux, the would-be biblical theologian sometimes seems in a no-win situation. The choice is between completely sidestepping knotty exegetical problems, offering a sketchy comment or two, and being sucked back into the quagmire of biblical studies and aborting the attempt to perceive the 'big picture' of the Bible to which biblical theology aspires. My decision is to touch only lightly on contentious issues, rather than abandon the quest for the overall picture.

[28]See W. G. Kümmel's trenchant question: 'How is it to be explained that our Christianity differs so widely from the Pauline one that we actually recognise ourselves in the picture of the Pauline non-Christian?' cited in J. Lambrecht, *The Wretched 'I' and Its Liberation: Paul in Romans 7 and 8* (Louvain: Peeters Press / Eerdmans, 1992), 88.

It is an interesting challenge to consider on the basis of the evidence of the Johannine literature how much sin the apostle John would have tolerated in the Johannine community. It seems likely from the texts we have that he would have had zero tolerance. Certainly there appears to be no acceptance of anything less than true doctrine and holy living in the letters to the seven churches in Asia. The avowed intention of the first epistle is that the readers may not sin. The battle lines between light and darkness drawn by earlier Jewish apocalyptists are clear.[29] In this last hour (1 Jn. 2:18), marked by antichrists and lawlessness, the devil and his children are on one side; God and His children on the other. Sinning is natural for the former group; it is unnatural for the latter group. God's *sperma*, God's seed, abides in His children. Unlike those exegetes who interpret this as an allusion to God's word or Spirit or an agricultural metaphor,[30] this writer takes this to be a daring sexual metaphor worthy of John Donne.[31] The context is all about children and parenthood. The metaphor, if a sexual one, is consistent with the new birth metaphor in John 3. Its implication is that holy living is not only possible but natural for the child of God, because the child bears what we in this generation might call the father's genetic blueprint.

The Petrine letters also have a great deal to say about the need for the people of God to be holy. In the second epistle there is a striking phrase about escaping from the corruption that is in the world because of passion and becoming partakers of the divine nature (2 Pet. 1:3-4) – a concept not a million miles away from sharing in the *perichoresis* of the Godhead or of being in Christ or of being filled with all the fullness of God or of having God's seed in us. The time frame for this experience is ambiguous in these verses because of the word 'promises', which might be present or future. However, the time frame in chapter 3 verses 11 and 12 is unequivocally present. Having referred to the imminence of the coming day of the Lord, the author writes: 'Since all these things are to be dissolved in this way, what sort of persons ought you to be in leading

[29]'In Jewish apocalyptic expectation the final period would be without sin on the part of those who were close to God' (R. E. Brown, *The Epistles of John* [ABC: New York: Doubleday, 1982], 415).

[30]I. Howard Marshall lists a large number in a footnote below his own statement that 'John is using the metaphor of a seed planted in the ground which produces new life', adding that: 'There is some doubt whether the seed is intended to signify the Holy Spirit (Jn. 3:6, 9) or the Word of God (Lk. 8:11; Jas. 1:18, 23; 1 Pet. 1:23, 25). Probably these two ideas are to be linked together' (*The Epistles of John* [NICNT; Grand Rapids: Eerdmans, 1978], 186).

[31]Such as his invitation to God to ravish him in Holy Sonnet XIV 'Batter my heart, three-person'd God.'

lives of holiness and godliness, waiting for and hastening the coming of the day of God...?'

Conclusion

It is possible to speak about two kinds of human holiness – imputed[32] (*i.e.* credited to our account in heaven) and imparted[33] (*i.e.* given in part to us to enjoy here and now). The problem with this way of thinking is that it lays all the responsibility on God as the giver. He imputes. He imparts. Humans remain passive. It might be more helpful to think of human holiness as relational and required, if these terms reflect the pattern of biblical teaching more fully.

Typical of many scholars, W. T. Purkiser writes, 'God alone is holy in himself. All other holiness is derived from a relationship with Him.'[34] To be successful, any relationship requires whole-hearted commitment on both sides (*e.g.* a marriage). In this case, it requires God to give Himself fully to His people and His people to respond fully to Him. It is hard to see what more God could have given than the Torah, His Son and His Spirit. It is easy on the other hand to see what God has always demanded in return. Jesus' restatement of the greatest commandment cannot be bettered. God has always required wholehearted love of Himself and of our neighbour here and now in this life.

Besides an unclouded relationship with Himself, which is both gift and requirement, God lays other ethical demands on His people. Worship of God requires acceptability to Him – having clean hands and pure hearts. Fellowship with God requires compatibility with Him – being holy as He is holy. Mission for God requires resemblance to Him – representing Him accurately.

---

[32]That is, if righteousness is regarded as a partial synonym of holiness.

[33]Chick Yuill, *We Need Saints: A Fresh Look at Christian Holiness* (London: International Headquarters of the Salvation Army, 1988), 13: 'The holy life is possible, only because God has conferred his own holiness upon us.' See also David Peterson, *Possessed by God: A New Testament Theology of Sanctification and Holiness* (NSBT; Leicester: Apollos, 1995), 23: 'Holiness cannot simply be acquired by human effort. It is a status or condition which God imparts to those whom he chooses to bring into a special relationship with himself through covenant and redemption.'

[34]W. T. Purkiser, *Exploring Christian Holiness*, Vol. 1 (Kansas City: Beacon Hill, 1983), 19. In similar vein, J. E. Hartley writes, 'Because only Yahweh is intrinsically holy, any person or thing is holy only as it stands in relationship to him. Thus there are degrees of holiness depending on the proximity of an item or person to Yahweh' (*Leviticus*, lvii).

This brief survey of a few aspects of the Bible's teaching on holiness has attempted to make the case that what God has always wanted has been to be a holy God dwelling among a holy people in a holy place. The journey through Scripture has moved from the Garden of Eden to the tabernacle at Sinai and cast a fleeting glance at the temple in Jerusalem. With the incarnation, the person of the holy God and the holy place where He chooses to live among His people have been conflated. In the post-Pentecost era the holy people and holy place have been conflated. But the story of God ends in the book of Revelation with the holy God living amongst His holy people in the ultimate holy place, the new Jerusalem come down from heaven.

> I saw no temple in the city, for its temple is the Lord God the Almighty and the Lamb. And the city has no need of sun or moon to shine on it, for the glory of God is its light, and its lamp is the Lamb. The nations will walk by its light, and the kings of the earth will bring their glory into it. Its gates will never be shut by day – and there will be no night there. People will bring into it the glory and the honour of the nations. But nothing unclean will enter it, nor anyone who practices abomination or falsehood, but only those who are written in the Lamb's book of life (Rev. 21:22-27).

A holy God among a holy people in a holy place – the enduring eschatological hope of the Scriptures, God's ultimate purpose for his world, not just in the far-off future but here and now and always.[35]

---

[35] As Christopher Rowland says, 'To be holy is one of the consequences of the new life in Christ which enabled the believer to enter that new relationship with God which the coming of Jesus Christ made possible' (J. Rogerson, C. Rowland and B. Lindars, *The Study and Use of the Bible* [Basingstoke: Marshall Pickering, 1988], 199).

Section B

OLD TESTAMENT

Chapter 3

PSALM 49: A PERSONAL ESCHATOLOGY

Philip S. Johnston

Psalm 49 answers the age-old riddle of an apparently pious person suffering oppression. The wisdom writer's rich persecutors cannot avoid the underworld at death, but he himself will be ransomed by God from Sheol. This indicates his faith in an alternative destiny, however undeveloped the concept. This interpretation of the psalm is defended against several recent proposals, and the linguistic evidence which has been cited to support a post-exilic date is found to be inconclusive. Thus Psalms 49 could express one strand of pre-exilic piety.

A positive view of life after death, in contrast to descent to Sheol, is usually seen as a late development in Israel. Even in the post-exilic era positive aspirations were tentative: some psalmists and sages possibly envisaged continued communion with God after death, though their comments have been interpreted otherwise, and some apocalyptists explored the notion of resurrection, though with uncertainty over its extent and importance. Since full discussion of the many texts and issues involved would be impossible in a single article, we will look at one key text, Psalm 49, and ask two questions in particular: (1) does it envisage post-mortem life with God at all, and (2) can it be clearly dated to the post-exilic period? Several verses of this psalm are notoriously difficult, so much so that at one point Kraus abandons attempts at a coherent translation.[1] Happily, however, the textual problems do not impinge significantly on our theme.

---

[1] It is interesting to note that several key 'eschatological' passages have notable textual difficulties, *e.g.* Jb. 19:25-27 and Is. 26:19. This suggests difficulties for early interpreters too.

Human Destiny in Psalm 49

The psalm opens in typical wisdom style:[2] its address in verses 2-3 is universal, to all peoples of the world, and explicitly inclusive, to rich and poor, to *běnē ʾādām* and *běnē ʾîš*. The latter terms are usually interpreted contrastively, as indicating low born and high born respectively.[3] This address is followed by a profusion of wisdom terms in verses 4-5: wisdom, meditation, understanding, proverb and riddle. Here the last term, *ḥîdāh* is the most important, indicating a riddle or puzzle which requires resolution. It is a riddle which the psalmist sets and then solves, to his satisfaction at least.[4]

This riddle is then presented in verses 6-7: it is the age-old problem of an apparently pious person in trouble and suffering oppression.[5] To this, two responses are given. The first, and longer by far, is enunciated in verses 8-10: no human can pay a ransom to avoid the underworld and live for ever. The MT of verses 8a and 9a reads: 'no man can ever ransom a brother . . . the ransom of their life is costly'.[6] The concept of ransom obviously comes from the legal world, and the MT might reflect the scenario where a wealthy individual pays to redeem an impecunious relative or, somewhat differently, where a victim's family allows a guilty party to pay a ransom instead of incurring the death penalty.[7] However, the text is usually emended to '*surely* no man can ransom *himself* . . . the ransom

---

[2]Verse numbers here follow the Hebrew text (one number higher than the English text). In English the RSV is cited unless otherwise indicated.

[3]This view has been questioned by some, *e.g.* N. P. Bratsiotis, ' ʾish, ʾishah', in G. J. Botterweck, H. Ringgren (eds.), *Theological Dictionary of the Old Testament*, Vol. 1 (Grand Rapids: Eerdmans, 2nd edn. 1977), 224.

[4]L. G. Perdue, 'The Riddles of Psalm 49', *JBL* 93 (1974), 533-542, locates the riddle primarily in verses 13 and 21, but this focuses on verbal parallels in an apparently refrain-like comment, at the expense of the bulk of the psalm. The second riddle in verses 8 and 16 merely gives the life and death context of wisdom.

[5]The term *ʿăqēbay* either means 'heels', giving 'the iniquity *at* my heels' (rather than '. . . *of* my heels'), or 'overreachers' (BDB), 'deceivers' (*cf.* yaʿăqōb), hence 'oppressors'. Either way, the sense of the line is clear.

[6]R. Rosenberg, 'The Concept of Biblical Sheol within the Context of Ancient Near Eastern Beliefs' (PhD dissertation, Harvard, 1981), 67f., suggests that ʾîš here means 'man of rank', as in the juxtaposed *běnē ʾādām* and *běnē ʾîš* (verse 3, Ps. 62:10; see above), and elsewhere (1 Sa. 26:15; 2 Sa. 16:18; 1 Ki. 2:2). But in no other text is ʾîš clearly 'man of rank', and in Ps. 49 itself *ʾādām'* indicates the rich (verses 13, 21), as well as *ʾîš* (also verse 17).

[7]*Cf.* Ex. 21:30: the owner of a lethally goring ox is spared death 'if a ransom is laid on him'.

of *his* life is costly'. This involves changing the opening word from *ʾāh* 'brother' to *ʾak* 'surely' (*cf.* verse 16), pointing the verb *pdh* as niphal instead of qal, and changing the suffix on *nepeš* to the singular.[8] While the two readings have different emphases, in both the point is stressed that human wealth is powerless to prolong life and to ransom people from *šaḥat* the pit. *šaḥat* is a well-known synonym of *šěʾôl* and occurs in similar contexts.[9]

This first response is further developed in verses 11-15. It opens with the observation that all die, whether foolish, like the unwelcome oppressors, or wise, presumably like the psalmist, and remain permanently in their graves (as the opening word of verse 12 is read by the ancient versions).[10] However, while acknowledging that death comes to all, the psalmist seems to have in view his wealthy opponents, since he adds that they leave to others their wealth, the object of their former trust (verse 7),[11] and he apparently contrasts their future lowly homes with their former real-estate capitalism (as verse 12b is usually interpreted). Human mortality mocks self-importance, verse 13. Verses 14-15 are the most textually difficult of the psalm – it is in verse 15b that Kraus abandons translation.[12] Yet the overall sense is largely undisputed: the destiny of the foolishly self-confident is Sheol. Here the psalmist clearly concentrates on the ungodly, and specifies their fate as the underworld.

---

[8]So *e.g.* A. A. Anderson, *Psalms (1-72)* (NCBC, London: Oliphants, 1972); P. C. Craigie, *Psalms 1-50* (WBC 19, Waco: Word, 1983); H.-J. Kraus, *Psalms 1-59* (Minneapolis: Augsburg, 1988). The idea that one person might want to ransom another from death is often discounted as unintelligible. Conversely, M. D. Goulder, *The Psalms of the Sons of Korah* (JSOTS 20, Sheffield: JSOT, 1882), argues for retaining *ʾāh* as the *lectio difficilior*.

[9]*Cf.* P. S. Johnston, *The Underworld and the Dead in the Old Testament* (PhD dissertation, Cambridge, 1993), § 1.5. *šaḥat* occurs 15 times in clear reference to the underworld (23 times in total).

[10]LXX, Syriac, Vulgate.

[11]BHS and others relocate verse 11b to follow verse 12b. This does not affect the interpretation.

[12]The last three of the five phrases are highly problematic. In the third phrase, the MT indicates vindication for the godly 'in the morning', the time of God's salvation (*cf.* C. Barth, *bôqer*, in *Theological Dictionary of the Old Testament*, Vol. 2, 2nd edn., Grand Rapids: Eerdmans, 1977, 226-228), but many scholars emend the whole phrase (*cf.* RSV, *etc.*). P. Bordreuil, 'mizzěbul lô: à propos de Psaume 49:15', in L. Eslinger, G. Taylor (eds.), *Ascribe to the Lord* (Fs. P. C. Craigie, JSOTS 67, Sheffield, JSOT, 1988), 93-98, reads the closing two words in MT as 'who is his prince?', a rhetorical cry of despair answered in verse 16.

I have argued elsewhere that there is a striking imbalance in the occurrences of the term *šĕʾôl* in the Hebrew Bible.[13] It is used predominantly (as in verse 15) of the fate awaiting the ungodly, a fate which the godly wish to avoid (as in verse 16), even if some like Job envisage it in their extremity of despair and abandonment by God. Peaceful death for the godly is never presented as descent to *šĕʾôl*. It is widely held by scholars that all ancient Semites envisaged descent on death to a gloomy underworld. Many Israelites may indeed have believed this, and it may be reflected in a few Old Testament verses,[14] but the widespread restriction of underworld terms to the ungodly in the canonical texts suggests at very least that the authors and/or editors viewed the underworld negatively.

This explains the psalmist's second response to his riddle, presented succinctly in verse 16. God will ransom him from *šĕʾôl* and will 'take' or 'receive' him. What humans are powerless to do, God will do for His faithful follower: God will provide for him an alternative destiny to the underworld. Ransom from *šĕʾôl* also occurs in a slightly different form in Hosea 13:14: 'Shall I ransom them from the power of Sheol (*yad-šĕʾôl*)? Shall I redeem them from death?' But there are difficulties in using this as an interpretative key to Psalm 49: the textual difficulty of the verse (with the versional variants echoed in 1 Cor. 15), the extensive use of image and metaphor throughout the chapter, and particularly the fact that Hosea 13 clearly refers to the *nation* of Israel. Ephraim has incurred guilt and died (verse 1)[15] – yet clearly Ephraim is still 'alive' and in-viting prophetic censure.

Some scholars interpret Psalm 49:16 as immediate rescue from immanent death without reference to permanent fate,[16] as Barth

---

[13]Johnston, *The Underworld and the Dead*, § 1; summarized in *idem*, '"Left in Hell?" Psalm 16, Sheol and the Holy One', in P. E. Satterthwaite *et al.* (eds.), *The Lord's Anointed* (Carlisle: Paternoster, 1995), 216-220.

[14]*E.g.* Ec. 9:10.

[15]J. Day, 'The development of belief in life after death in ancient Israel', in J. Barton, D. J. Reimer (eds.), *After the Exile* (Fs. R. Mason, Macon: Mercer U P, 1996), sees a notable irony here, on the basis that Hosea's audience, like the Ugaritans, considered Baal a dying and rising god. (I am endebted to Dr Day for an early copy of his article.)

[16]J. D. Pleins, 'Death and Endurance: Reassessing the Literary Structure and Theology of Psalm 49', *JSOT* 69 (1996), 19-27, argues this, though the chiastic structure he posits for the psalm (which is not altogether convincing) actually suggests the contrary, since the corresponding verse 10 describes a permanent destiny.

argued at length in a still influential work.[17] Barth developed Pedersen's view that Sheol is not so much a location for the dead as a force invading life and impinging on the living, and argued that the psalmists generally rejoiced in immediate deliverance from this power, but did not deny eventual consignment to the underworld. However, apart from the conceptual difficulties of Sheol as more a power than a place,[18] this view fails to do justice to Psalm 49 generally and to verse 16 specifically. Here the problem is not so much temporary oppression as an unjust order, and the final phrase of verse 16 implies more than preservation in life. To be sure, the same term, *yiqqāḥēnî*, occurs in Psalm 18:16 of immediate rescue ('He reached from on high, he took me'), but there physical rescue from immediate danger is explicit in the parallel lines ('he drew me out of many waters, he delivered me from my strong enemy . . .'). The context of Psalm 49 is quite different.

In a different vein, it is often noted that the same verb *lqḥ* is used of the distinctive fates of Enoch and Elijah,[19] and it is sometimes suggested that *lqḥ* has become a technical term for avoidance of death, for which the psalmist hoped here and possibly in Psalm 73:24 (*tiqqāḥēnî*). However, this is questionable: *lqḥ* is a common and semantically rich verb, its meaning here is quite straightforward, and it occurs for avoidance of death in so very few texts. Further, the psalmist may not necessarily have wished to avoid death in his conviction that God would keep him from the underworld.

The final verses of the psalm, verses 17-21, return to the theme that the wealthy cannot take their riches with them on death. Rather, they rejoin their ancestors, never again to see the light, verse 20. Out of context, this verse might seem to imply that everyone else, regardless of piety, goes to *šĕʾôl*. But following verses 17-19 the psalmist is probably referring to his enemies, whose predecessors he presumes to have been equally ungodly. (The expression 'to go to the generation of one's fathers' is reminiscent of two other biblical phrases, 'to be gathered to one's kin' and 'to sleep with one's fathers', though in the Hebrew Bible these are restricted to distinctive uses.)[20] Thus, verse 20 fits our interpretation of differentiated destinies.

---

[17]C. Barth, *Die Errettung vom Tode in den individuellen Klage – und Dankliedern des Alten Testamentes* (Zollikon: Evangelischer, 1947), 158-161.
[18]*Cf.* Johnston, *The Underworld and the Dead*, § 4.
[19]Gn. 5:24; 2 Ki. 2:3, 5, 9, 10.
[20]'To be gathered to one's kin': of patriarchs and early national leaders, mostly in the Pentateuch; 'to sleep with one's fathers': of kings of Israel and Judah who died peacefully; *cf.* Johnston, *The Underworld and the Dead*, § 5.

Finally, verse 21 echoes verse 13. In the MT, verse 13 reads 'man cannot abide' (*bal yālîn*), while verse 20 has 'man without understanding' (*lōʾ yābîn*). Many scholars posit an originally identical refrain, which has suffered in transmission, and emend one or other verse accordingly, usually the final one. However, the Hebrew expressions are nicely balanced, and the wisdom ending 'man without understanding', is certainly appropriate.[21]

Other Views

As is well-known, Goulder argues at length that the Psalms of Korah originated in the festival cult at Dan, and were later assumed by the Jerusalem cult with minimum adaptation.[22] In particular, Psalm 49 (along with Psalm 88) represented the nadir of the autumn festival liturgy. A Danite musician priest reassures worshippers not against the foolish rich but against foreign invaders, the supplanters (*ʿăqēbay*, verse 6). Of the two ransom verses, verse 8 is read without emendation as an indication that no prisoners will be taken,[23] and verse 16 as a declaration of temporal relief for king and community.[24]

However, few other scholars are convinced of this Danite connection. For instance, on the later group of Korahite psalms, Tate concludes that Goulder's view involves too much conjecture and too many forced readings, and does not tally with textual and archaeological evidence linking the Korahites with southern cities. Regarding Psalm 49 in particular, Alexander argues that Goulder's view fails to explain the wisdom nature of the psalm, and that the supposed warning to foreign nations is too allusive to be creditable.[25] Also, the psalm has no obvious military vocabulary for either

---

[21]P. R. Raabe, 'Deliberate Ambiguity in the Psalter', *JBL* 110 (1991), 213-227, accepts the MT, but also sees the refrain's last word as deliberately ambiguous, meaning 'perish' in verse 13 and 'are dumb' in verse 21.

[22]Goulder, *The Psalms of the Sons of Korah*.

[23]Goulder makes much of not emending the MT of Ps. 49, yet repoints elsewhere (*e.g.* Ps. 87:5).

[24]'It cannot but be a relief to be rid of the suggestion that the psalmist thought he would be taken, like Enoch and Elijah, direct to heaven; the whole passage makes perfect sense in line with normal Israelite concepts if we stick to the MT and assume a Danite context ' (192).

[25]M. E. Tate, *Psalms 51-100* (WBC 20, Dallas: Word, 1990), 356f.; T. D. Alexander, 'The Psalms and the Afterlife', *IBS* 9 (1987), 8f. Reviewers were also generally sceptical, *e.g.* R. J. Coggins, *ET* 95 (1983-84), 56; J. A. Galbraith, *CBQ* 47 (1985), 123f.

aggressors or defenders, and no rejoicing in victory as one might expect. For all its ingenuity, Goulder's view has failed to convince.

Craigie reads verse 16 as the foolish hope of the self-confident, who think that their privilege in life will also give them privilege in death. But this is unlikely, as Alexander again notes.[26] It would give little comfort to the righteous to know that they would share the same fate as their foes, and there is no textual hint that this is a false statement.

Smith argues that the last line of verse 12 alludes to the invocation of deceased ancestors. For Smith and others, veneration and consultation of the dead were not only widespread before the reforms of Hezekiah and Josiah, but were an accepted element in early eclectic and undogmatic Yahwism.[27] There is plenty of biblical evidence that necromancy was practised in Israel, both in the account of Saul at Endor and in the repeated prohibitions, though the argument that it was acceptable in early Yahwism depends on interpreting 1 Samuel 28 and all the relevant legal texts as retrojections from a later period. By contrast, there is scant textual evidence for the veneration of ancestors, or cult of the dead as it is often called. It amounts to the following: the curious reference in Deuteronomy 26:14 where the offerer of the triennial tithe avows that he has not offered any of it (literally) 'to/for a dead person', lĕmēt; the condemnation in Isaiah 57 of several illicit practices; and possibly the prophecy in Ezekiel 43 that the temple would no longer be defiled by royal corpses. Veneration of ancestors is also discerned behind other texts where explicit references have been removed by orthodox redactors, e.g.: the annual sacrifices of Elkanah and David's family; Absalom's erection of a pillar; Jehu's command to undertake for the dead Jezebel; the disputed qĕdôšîm 'holy ones' of Psalm 16:3; the condemnation of priests in Isaiah 28; prohibition of priestly contact with corpses; prophetic disapproval of new moon ceremonies.[28]

---

[26]Craigie, Psalms 1-50; Alexander, 'The Psalms and the Afterlife', 9.

[27]M. S. Smith, 'The Invocation of the Deceased Ancestors in Psalm 49:12c', JBL 112 (1993), 105-107. On early eclectic Yahwism cf. also K. Spronk, Beatific Afterlife in Ancient Israel and in the Ancient Near East (AOAT 219, Neukirchen-Vluyn: Neukirchener, 1986); T. J. Lewis, Cults of the Dead in Ancient Israel and Ugarit (HSM 39, Atlanta: Scholars, 1989); J. Tropper, Nekromantie (AOAT 223, Neukirchen-Vluyn: Neukirchener, 1989); M. S. Smith, The Early History of God (San Francisco: Harper & Row, 1990); E. Bloch-Smith, Judahite Burial Practices and Beliefs about the Dead (JSOTS 123, Sheffield: JSOT, 1992); R. Albertz, A History of Israelite Religion in the Old Testament Period, Vol. 1 (London: SCM, 1994).

[28]Cf. 1 Sa. 1:21; 2:19; 20:5f.; 2 Sa. 18:18; 2 Ki. 9:34; Nu. 19; Is. 1:13f.; Ho. 2:13; for detailed discussion see Johnston, The Underworld and the Dead, § 8.

However, apart from the tenuousness of many of the arguments regarding these texts, it is hard to see why zealous reformers intent on eradicating this practice would leave intact the vow of Deuteronomy 26:14 with its reference to food to/for a dead person. On the contrary, this implies that these grave offerings (whose precise nature and purpose remain undefined) were not seen as an abhorrent practice, even if inappropriate for the tithe. This in turn implies that those responsible for the text were not attacking a cult of the dead.

To return to Psalm 49:12, Smith makes four points: (1) the idiom for naming land is not *qrʾ bĕšēm* but *qrʾ*+ object + *bĕšēm*; (2) the commonly attested idiom *qrʾ bĕšēm* + object is a cultic one (as in the expression 'to call on the name of Yahweh'); (3) the Ugaritic cognate of *qrʾ* is used of invoking ancestors in KTU 1.161;[29] (4) mention of graves in the first line gives the context. Thus verse 12c 'refers to the practice of invoking names of deceased ancestors'. Presumably he would translate it: 'they summoned (ancestors) by their names onto the earth'.[30]

However, like many other arguments for reference to death cults, this is scarcely convincing. (1) Smith himself notes the wide syntactical variety regarding the naming of land. Thus there is hardly a common idiom, and verse 12c could well give a further variant. (2) The fact that *qrʾ bĕšēm* + the divine name is cultic does not determine other uses of *qrʾ bĕšēm*, nor does the use of *qrʾ* elsewhere. (3) The author of Psalm 49 is not concerned with illicit religious practice, and does not cite it in condemnation of the foolish rich. Rather, it is their confidence in wealth and power which he criticizes. The traditional interpretation of verse 12 fits this context, whereas Smith's proposal does not.

Date of Psalm 49

Psalm 49 is described unhesitatingly as post-exilic by many scholars,[31] for several reasons. (1) It is a commonplace in scholarly study that wisdom is a fairly late development in Israel, and that it came to fruition in the post-exilic era. And Psalm 49 is a parade example of a wisdom psalm. (2) The theme of post-mortem survival in two wisdom psalms, 49 and 73, confirms for many their attribution

---

[29]Smith incorrectly also lists *qrʾ* in Ps. 16:3-4.
[30]Smith, 'Invocation', 107. He does not actually provide a translation.
[31]*E.g.* Day, 'Development'.

to this period, since the concepts of resurrection and life after death are not traced to pre-exilic writings. (3) Several linguistic features are taken to indicate a late date.

However, while these arguments have some merit, none is conclusive. (1) A growing number of scholars accept that the roots of Israel's wisdom are ancient, and independent of the posited wisdom schools.[32] These views refer primarily to the sentence proverbs, but they also imply that other wisdom material could have emerged in the pre-exilic period. (2) While the concept of resurrection is widely seen as an exilic and post-exilic development, notably in Ezekiel 37, Isaiah 26 and Daniel 12, it is already at least hinted at in Hosea 6. Further, the concept of continued communion with God beyond death need not be linked conceptually with resurrection, and may emerge from a different theological matrix. (3) The linguistic evidence for a late date presented in detail by Schmitt is not as strong as it appears, since each point he makes can be questioned. His argument is outlined below.[33]

(a) Abstract plurals like *ḥokmôt* and *tĕbûnôt* (verse 4) occur more in later books, and are a mark of late wisdom literature. Elsewhere *ḥokmôt* only occurs three times and *tĕbûnôt* five times, mostly in wisdom books. *hāgût* in the same verse is another abstract noun indicative of lateness.[34] (a') But this is inconclusive. Abstract plurals of nouns indicating qualities certainly occur more frequently in late literature, but are not confined to it, *cf. dēʿôt* 'knowledge' in Hannah's Song, 1 Samuel 2:3, and *yĕšûʿôt* 'deliverance' in a royal thanksgiving psalm, Psalm 18:51 // 2 Samuel 22:51.[35] The predominance of abstract nouns (both singular and plural) in wisdom writings can be attributed to their subject matter and style as much as to their date.

(b) The description of the grave as a 'house for ever' (verse 12) only occurs elsewhere in Ecclesiastes 12:5. (b') However, as

---

[32]*Cf.* C. R. Fontaine, *Traditional Sayings in the Old Testament* (Sheffield: Sheffield Academic Press, 1982); C. Westermann, *Roots of Wisdom* (Edinburgh: T & T Clark, 1995). The role of schools has been thoroughly critiqued by S. Weeks, *Early Israelite Wisdom* (Oxford: Clarendon, 1994).

[33]A. Schmitt, *Entrückung - Aufnahme - Himmelfahrt* (Stuttgart: Katholisches Bibelwerk, 1973), 249-252.

[34]*ḥokmôt* Pr. 1:20; 9:1; 24:7 and *tĕbûnôt* Is. 40:14; Jb. 32:11; Ps. 78:72; Pr. 11:12; 28:16. For Schmitt, the *-ût* form of *hāgût* is late and its initial long *a* -vowel shows Aramaic influence.

[35]*Cf.* the list in B. K. Waltke, M. O'Connor, *An Introduction to Biblical Hebrew Syntax* (Winona Lake: Eisenbrauns, 1990), 121. They also note abstract plurals of state (youth, virginity, old age) and activity (prostitution, retribution).

Schmitt himself notes, there is widespread attestation of this idiom
from Sumerian literature onwards. So it is hardly an indication of the
lateness of Hebrew wisdom literature.

(c) Aramaic influence is evident in *ḥîdāh*(verse 5) and *yĕqār*
(verses 13, 21).[36] (c′) However, *ḥîdāh* also occurs in several narrative
accounts of Israel's past: Numbers 12 (vindication of Moses), Judges
14 (Samson's riddle, 8 times) and 1 Kings 10 (testing of Solomon).
yĕqār is more obviously a later term, occurring elsewhere only in
Esther (9 times), Job, Jeremiah, Ezekiel and Zechariah. But its use in
Jeremiah 20:5 (against Pashhur) and Ezekiel 22:25 (dated before 587),
both with the same meaning as in Psalm 49, suggests the term was
current before the exile. Of course, all these texts may have
undergone post-exilic reworking and updating of language, but this
argument would undermine all attempts to date texts by linguistic
development. By contrast, Goulder states categorically of Psalm 49:
'the late date is not evidenced by Aramaisms in the text'.[37]

(d) The absolute use of *ʾăḥērîm* 'others' (verse 11), is a late
development, seen also in Nehemiah, Ecclesiastes, Sirach and Daniel,
and influenced by Aramaic. (d′) While many instances of this
absolute use are late, it also occurs in the plural in the difficult Psalm
16:4 and in the singular in texts that are arguably early: the Book of
the Covenant, Samuel and Psalm 109.[38]

(e) *bwʾ* followed by *ʿad* is a late linguistic development,
witnessed at Qumran. (e′) However, one of the two other Old
Testament occurrences comes in the Book of the Covenant, so again
this expression is hardly indicative of date.[39]

To summarize: none of the three factors of genre, theology
and language proves a late date for Psalm 49. Of course, they do not

---

[36]Schmitt follows Wagner's study of Aramaic influence on late Hebrew. *Cf.* also
L. Koehler, W. Baumgartner *et al.*, *The Hebrew and Aramaic Lexicon of the Old
Testament* (Leiden: Brill, 1994-96).
[37]Goulder, *The Psalms of the Sons of Korah*, 183.
[38]Ex. 21:10; 22:4; 1 Sa. 17:30; 21:10; 2 Sa. 13:16; Ps. 109:8. Nothing precludes a pre-
exilic origin of Ps. 109 for H.-J. Kraus, *Psalmen, 2. Teilband* (BK XV/2,
Neukirchen-Vluyn: Neukirchener, 1961), 748 (this differs from the English
translation of the 5th edition: *Psalms 60-150* [Minneapolis: Augsburg, 1989], 760);
also L. C. Allen, *Psalms 101-150* (WBC 21, Waco: Word, 1987), 76. Other
occurrences: Ne. 5:5; Jb. 8:19; 31:8, 10; 34:24; Pr. 5:9; 25:9; Ec 7:2; Is. 42:8; 48:1;
65:22; Je. 6:12; 8:10; Ezk. 41:24; Dn. 11:4; 12:5. *Cf.* D. J. A. Clines (ed.), *Dictionary of
Classical Hebrew*, Vol. 1 (Sheffield: Sheffield Academic Press, 1993), 193.
[39]Ex. 22:8; Jos. 3:8. Schmitt also suggests that *ʿad-nēṣaḥ* (verse 20) is influenced by
bwʾ plus *ʿad*, since the usual form is *lānēṣaḥ*. But here it is hardly indicative of
date. More likely it is elegant variation, since *lānēṣaḥ* occurs in verse 10.

prove an early date either, and it is still quite possible that Psalm 49 is a late composition. But it is also potentially pre-exilic, and indicative of one strand of earlier piety.

Source of Concept

While there are obvious conceptual links between existence after death in communion with God on the one hand and resurrection on the other, it is important to distinguish between the two. The concepts are not inexorably linked, as is clearly demonstrated by the Egyptians' long-standing belief in the afterlife, without a developed notion of resurrection. Nevertheless, it is commonly argued that both are post-exilic developments resulting from contact with other civilizations and from the problems of the righteous suffering.

In particular, the faith of the psalmists in Psalms 49 and 73 (and possibly elsewhere) is seen as a step in post-exilic sapiential development. Day summarizes this literature as thesis, antithesis and synthesis: Proverbs largely presents the thesis of reward and judgment in this life; Job and Ecclesiastes the antithesis of the failure of retribution; and the wisdom psalms the synthesis of vindication after death.[40] While this summary of themes is certainly accurate, the Hegelian associations of the headings might suggest a developmental approach which cannot be demonstrated convincingly. On the contrary, there is much clearer linguistic evidence for a late date for Ecclesiastes than for the wisdom psalms, and the undoubtedly second-century Sirach reflects the view of the traditional 'thesis' rather than any development. Thus the wisdom psalms do not obviously come at the end of a period of development, and they could just as easily be early. There is ample evidence in Jewish and Christian history for the coexistence of divergent and even contra-dictory views over long periods, especially in matters eschatological.

There is little to suggest that the problem of individual retribution was only a post-exilic issue. The permanent loss of national sovereignty (such as it was) may have exacerbated the problem, since the prosperity of non-Yahwistic peoples was now writ large. But the problem is essentially presented as personal rather than national, and thus hardly dependent on political developments. And there are numerous indications in the historical books of arrogant and presumptuous foolish rich at all times of Israel's history. Thus it is equally possible to see the psalmist's conviction of ransom from death as a direct development from his own relationship with God

---

[40]Day, 'Development'.

and from his conviction that it would not be dissolved at death. In other words, his confidence that God would ransom him from Sheol owes more to theology than to history, more to his personal experience of Israel's covenant God than to the development of Israel's faith in response to the exile and to increased contact with other ancient religions. Though few of his contemporaries may have shared the writer's conviction, it is quite possible to see it as one genuine expression of pre-exilic personal eschatology.

Chapter 4

GOG AND MAGAG IN EZEKIEL'S ESCHATOLOGICAL VISION

Daniel I. Block

This essay seeks to interpret Ezekiel's oracle against Gog (chapters 38 - 39) within the context of his salvation oracles. It consists of three parts: (1) general observations in the light of which the Gog oracle should be interpreted; (2) general observations on the form and nature of the Gog oracle (generically it is best interpreted as a literary cartoon in eight frames); (3) a summary interpretation of the oracle. It concludes with brief reflections on the theological significance of the Gog oracle for Ezekiel's immediate audience and for his readers today.

Introduction

I had intended to include a general discussion of what is meant by the term 'eschatology', and a survey of biblical expressions generally thought to carry eschatological meaning. However, space constraints have forced me to move immediately into the eschatological hope of Ezekiel, and concentrate on the place of the Gog oracle in this prophet's vision of Israel's future. There is enough here to engage us. This essay will consist of three major parts: (1) general observations in the light of which the Gog oracle should be interpreted; (2) general observations on the form and nature of the Gog oracle; (3) a summary interpretation of the oracle as I see it. I shall conclude with brief reflections on the theological significance of the Gog oracle for Ezekiel's immediate audience and for his readers today.

General Observations on Ezekiel's Eschatology

Before discussing the Gog oracle itself, there are six observations on Ezekiel's eschatological messages as a whole which need our consideration.

First, although we tend to think of the eschaton as the end of human history as we know it, Ezekiel actually envisions two ἔσχατα, both involving the nation of Israel and/or Judah, one imminent, the other in the distant future. Most of the oracles of judgment in chapters 4–24 concern the end of the nation of Judah as Ezekiel and his contemporaries knew it. But eschatological language dominates only one oracle, the three-fold alarm of the sentry in 7:1-27.[1] The prophet's emotions are at a fever pitch as he announces the end of the nation with the six-fold repetition of the word קֵץ/הַקֵּץ, 'An end/the end!' (verses 2-3, 6),[2] and ominous references to הַיּוֹם, 'the day' (verses 7, 10, 12), and הָעֵת, 'the time' (verses 7, 12), which represent cryptic references to יוֹם יהוה, 'the day of Yahweh'. Ezekiel's emphasis on the event's imminence in this oracle[3] represents his answer to his contemporaries' dismissal of the notion of Yahweh's judgmental intervention in their history as a delusion (12:21-25) and/or as an irrelevant and remote eschatological event, having no bearing on the present generation (12:26-28).[4] But the end envisioned here is not a chronological end of time or the end of cosmic history; it is the end of a city's existence.

---

[1] The three alarms which crescendo with increasing intensity consist of verses 2aβ-4, 5-9, and 10-27 respectively.

[2] In this chapter LXX translates קֵץ as πέρας which, like ἔσχατος, may be used of both spatial extremity and chronological termination. ἔσχατος occurs six times in the LXX version of Ezekiel. In 35:5 it translates Hebrew קֵץ, 'end' (in the phrase קֵץ בְּעֵת עֲוֹן 'at the time of the punishment of the end'), which in this context refers to Jerusalem's imminent end. The remaining five occurrences are all found in the Gog oracle, where it is used spatially (for יַרְכְּתֵי צָפוֹן, 'the remotest part of the north' (38:6,15; 39:2), and temporally (for בְּאַחֲרִית הַשָּׁנִים, 'in the latter years'(38:8); בְּאַחֲרִית הַיָּמִים, 'in the latter days').

[3] Notice the language of imminence: בָּא/בָּאָה, 'It has come' (9 times in verses 1-12); עַתָּה, 'Now' (verses 3, 8); הִנֵּה, 'Behold, watch out!' (verses 5, 6, 10a, 10b); יָצְאָה, 'It has gone forth' (verse 10); הִגִּיעַ, 'It has arrived' (verse 12); מִקָּרֹב, 'shortly' (verse 8); and קָרוֹב, 'It is near' (verse 7).

[4] Cf. Y. Hoffmann, 'The Day of the Lord as a Concept and a Term in Prophetic Literature', ZAW 93 (1981), 46-47. Elsewhere Hoffmann argues that קָרוֹב יוֹם יהוה is a juristic technical phrase first coined by Zephaniah to emphasize the legal aspect of the day of Yahweh. It was primarily a day of judgment for the wicked Cf. 'The Root QRB as a Legal Term', JNSL 10 (1982), 70-73.

Whereas the judgment oracles in chapters 4–24 focus on Jerusalem's imminent eschaton, the restoration oracles of chapters 34–48 look beyond the judgment to the distant future, when the fortunes of the nation of Israel will turn around and the disastrous events of the imminent present will be reversed. Fragmentary messages of hope have indeed been sounded occasionally prior to the fall of Jerusalem to the Babylonians,[5] but the full development of these themes does not occur until the imminent eschaton arrives with the news that the city has fallen (33:21-22).

Second, the eschatological nature of Ezekiel's restoration oracles is not as obvious as scholars generally assume. Overtly eschatological language is rare in chapters 34–48. Indeed, if explicit technical vocabulary is a criterion for identifying an oracle as eschatological, then only the Gog oracle (38:1–39:29) qualifies, and even here this is uncertain. References to the day of Yahweh are absent altogether. The expression בַּיּוֹם הַהוּא, 'on that day', does indeed occur four times (38:10, 14, 18; 39:11), but in none of these instances does it bear the technical sense of יוֹם יהוה, 'the day of Yahweh'. The only possible eschatological signals are found in 38:8 and 38:16, which contain the phrases בְּאַחֲרִית הַשָּׁנִים, 'in the latter years', and בְּאַחֲרִית הַיָּמִים, 'in the latter days', respectively.[6] But these may arguably mean no more than 'in the course of time, in the future',[7] that is, when the conditions spelled out in 38:8 will have been fulfilled. Nowhere does the text suggest that the events envisioned 'pertain to the end of time'.

Third, Ezekiel's vision of Israel's future is founded upon the nation's ancient covenantal traditions[8] all of which involve eternal promises made by Yahweh to his covenant people. To *Abraham* Yahweh promised on oath a series of benefactions with universal[9]

---

[5] 11:16-21; 16:60-63; 17:22-24; 20:39-44.

[6] מִיָּמִים רַבִּים, 'after [literally "from"] many days', in verse 8 should probably also be included.

[7] Cf. H. Seebass, *TDOT* 1.210-212; E. Jenni, *THAT* 1.116-117. Compare Dn. 2:28 and 10:14, where 'in the latter days' functions as a technical term for the eschaton.

[8] For a helpful summary see D. L. Peterson, 'Eschatology (OT)', *ABD*, 2.575-579. For more detailed discussions concerning various aspects of Israel's eschatology see H.-P. Müller, *Ursprünge und Strukturen alttestamentlicher Eschatologie* (BZAW 109; Berlin: Alfred Töpelmann, 1969); H. D. Preuss (ed.), *Eschatologie im Alten Testament* (Wege der Forschung 480; Darmstadt: Wissenschaftliche Buchgesellschaft, 1978).

[9] E.g., Gn. 12:3, 'In you/your seed shall all the families of the earth (מִשְׁפְּחֹת הָאֲדָמָה) be blessed.' Cf. 18:18; 22:18; 26:4; 28:14.

and 'eternal' (עַד־עוֹלָם) implications: to be God to him and his descendants,[10] innumerable progeny,[11] and the land of Canaan.[12] At *Sinai* Yahweh entered into a covenant with the nation of Israel which promised for them a future of blessedness and prosperity.[13] To *David* and his descendants Yahweh promised eternal title to the throne of Israel.[14] Concomitant with this covenant with David was Yahweh's choice of *Zion* as his eternal dwelling place.[15] While Ezekiel's contemporaries had based their eternal security on these covenantal promises, the prophet himself had employed a variety of rhetorical strategies[16] to expose the illusory nature of their claims, predicting that Yahweh would abandon His temple,[17] the Davidic house would be removed from the throne,[18] Yahweh would leave His people,[19] and they would be removed from the land.[20] But the story could not

---

[10]Gn. 17:7-8; 26:3-4; *cf.* 12:3a.

[11]Like the dust of the earth, the sand on the seashore, and the stars of the sky. *Cf.* Gn. 13:16; 15:1-6; 16:10; 17:4-6; 22:17-18; 26:4, 24; 28:14.

[12]Gn. 12:7; 13:14-15, 17; 15:7-21; 26:3; 28:13; 35:12. *Cf.* Ps. 105:10 = 1 Ch. 16:17.

[13]Lv. 26:1-13; Dt. 28:1-14. Although the covenant curses warned against infidelity to the divine suzerain, the covenant held out the prospect of a renewal of the relationship if Israel would respond appropriately to their punishment. Lv. 26:40-45; Dt. 4:29-31; 29:29–30:20. The Sabbath is granted Israel as a symbol of the eternality of the covenant. Note the use of בְּרִית עוֹלָם, 'eternal covenant', in Ex. 31:16 and Lv. 24:8. David recognizes the eternality of this covenant in 2 Sa. 7:24, 26. The phrase gains popularity in the prophets. *Cf.* Is. 55:3; 61:8; Je. 32:40; 50:5; Ezk. 16:60; 37:26.

[14]2 Sa. 7:13, 16, 25, 29a, 29b (= 2 Ch. 17:12, 14, 23, 27a, 27b); *cf.* 1 Ki. 2:4; 8:25; 9:5; Ps. 89:4-5, 29-30, 37-38[3-4, 28-29, 36-37]; 132:10-12. *Cf.* the later description of this as a בְּרִית עוֹלָם, 'eternal covenant', in 2 Sa. 23:5.

[15]1 Ki. 8:12-21; Ps. 132:13-16; *cf.* Pss. 48; 68:16-19[15-18]; 78:68-71; 87. Also 1 Ki. 8:12-13.

[16](1) Legal addresses (רִיב): 14:12–15:8; 16:1-63; 20:1-44; 22:1-16; 23:1-49; (2) disputations: 11:1-12; 11:14-21; 12:21-25; 12:26-28; 18:1-32; 24:1-24; (3) figurative addresses (מְשָׁלִים): 19:1-14; 21:1-22[20:45–21:17]; 22:17-22; (4) laments: 19:1-14; (5) interpreted sign-acts: 4:1–5:17; 12:1-20; 21:23-32[18-27]; (6) watchman-type judgment speeches: 6:1-14; 7:1-27; 22:23-31; (7) vision reports: 8:1–10:22; 11:22-25.

[17]Ezk. 8–11.

[18]Ezk. 12:1-16; 17:1-21; 19:1-14. Jeremiah is even more emphatic announcing that Jehoiachin's/Coniah's descendants will never occupy the throne again (Je. 22:30).

[19]Ezk. 16; 23.

[20]It may be argued that all the oracles in chapters 4–24 are directed at one or more of the pillars on which the nation's immediate hopes rested. Promise of land (Abrahamic covenant): 4:1-3, 9-17; 5:5-15; 6:1-7; 7:1-27; 11:1-21; 12:17-20; 14:12-23; 15:1-8; 16:1-63; 21:6-22[1-17]; 21:23-32[18-27]; 22:1-31; 23:1-49; 24:1-15. Promise of covenant relationship (Sinaitic covenant): 3:16-21; 5:4, 16-17; 6:11-14; 14:1-23; 15:1-8; 16:1-60; 18:1-32; 20:1-44; 23:1-49; 33:1-20; 33:23-29. Promise of

end with the fall of Jerusalem. After all, Yahweh's promises were irrevocable and eternal.[21] When Jerusalem fell to Babylon the benefactions promised by those covenants had indeed been suspended, but the promises could not be annulled or permanently withdrawn. The deity–nation–land relationship had to be restored, and the Davidic ruler had to be reinstalled as king. These notions are at the heart of Ezekiel's eschatological hope.

Fourth, although the tone of Ezekiel's restoration oracles contrasts sharply with his earlier messages of judgment, familiar judgmental elements persist. The woe oracle against the leaders of Israel preceding the promise of a restored flock in 34:1-10 is reminiscent of the oracles against the false prophets and prophetesses in chapter 13. The oracle against Mount Seir/Edom before the promise of a restored land in 35:1-15 recalls the prophecies against the foreign nations in chapters 25–26. The lengthy Gog prophecy in chapters 38–39 shares many of these features as well.

Fifth, these extended salvation oracles provide further examples of what I refer to as typically Ezekielian resumptive exposition. Notions briefly introduced in the context of earlier judgment oracles[22] are picked up and expounded in great detail. There is no need to depreciate these fragments as later additions inserted under the influence of the fully developed oracles.[23] Not only had the covenant curses in Leviticus 26:40-45 held out the prospect of ultimate renewal after judgment;[24] the compassionate character of Yahweh and His fidelity to His covenant necessitated it.[25] Furthermore, Ezekiel's predecessor and contemporary, Jeremiah, envisioned just such an event within seventy years.[26] It is preferable,

---

dynasty (Davidic covenant): 12:1-16; 17:1-24; 19:1-14; 21:30-32[25-27]. Promise of residence in Zion: 7:20-24; 8:1-10:22; 11:22-25; 24:16-27.

[21]Just as Ezekiel's judgment oracles had sought to demolish the pillars upon which official orthodoxy based Jerusalem's/Judah's security, so the restoration oracles of chapters 34–48 seek deliberately to reconstruct those pillars: promise of land (Abrahamic covenant): 11:17; 22:42; 34:25-29; 35:1–36:15; 36:33-36; 38:1–39:20; 47:1–48:7, 23-29; promise of covenant relationship (Sinaitic covenant): 11:18-21; 16:60-63; 34:1-31; 36:16-32, 37-38; 37:1-14; 37:15-21; 37:25-28; 39:21-29; promise of dynasty (Davidic covenant): 17:22-24; 34:23-24; 37:22-25; promise of residence in Zion: 22:40-41; 37:26-27; 40:1–46:24; 48:8-22, 30-35.

[22]11:14-21; 16:53-63; 17:22-24; 20:39-44; 28:24-26.

[23]So also L. Boadt, 'The Function of the Salvation Oracles in Ezekiel 33 to 37', *HAR* 12 (1990), 3.

[24]*Cf.* also Dt. 29:29–30:10.

[25]*Cf.* Dt. 4:25-31.

[26]Je. 29:10-14, on which see G. Larsson, 'When did the Babylonian Captivity Begin?' *JTS* 18 (1967), 417-423. M. Fishbane has rightly maintained (*Biblical*

therefore, to interpret the earlier statements as pre-586 BC premonitions of Israel's final restoration.[27]

Sixth, Ezekiel's understanding of the sequence of events involved in Israel's restoration was conventional. It was not only based upon Israel's own perceptions of nationhood,[28] but also patterned after common ancient Near Eastern judgment-restoration traditions. Just as Ezekiel's portrayal of the sequence of human sin–divine wrath–divine abandonment–disaster/exile in his oracles of judgment followed established patterns,[29] so his structure of Israel's anticipated reconstruction finds numerous analogues in ancient literature. This structure typically included the following succession of motifs: (1) a change in the disposit-ion of the deity; (2) the appointment of a new ruler; (3) the reconstruction of the temple; (4) the return of the deity; (5) the regathering of the scattered population; (6) the estab-lishment of peace and prosperity.[30] For the prophet, and those responsible for collecting and arranging his oracles, the fateful

---

Interpretation in Ancient Israel [Oxford: Clarendon, 1985], 480) that this passage is not to be dismissed as an *ex eventu* prophecy: (1) *ex eventu* proclamations could afford to be more precise; (2) in Israel's Umwelt the figure seventy was a commonly accepted typological number for the duration of exile. *Cf.* R. Borger, *Die Inschriften Asarhaddons Knigs von Assyrien* (AfO Beiheft 9; Graz: E. Weidner, 1956), 65 (episode 15). On this text see D. D. Luckenbill, 'The Black Stone of Esarhaddon', *AJSL* 41 (1925), 167-168; J. Nougayrol, 'Textes hépatoscopiques d'époque ancienne conserveé au Museé du Louvre II', *RA* 40 (1946), 65. See also C. F. Whitley, 'The Term Seventy Years Captivity', *VT* 4 (1954), 60-72; A. Orr, 'The Seventy Years of Babylon', *VT* 6 (1956), 304-306; P. R. Ackroyd, 'The 'Seventy Year Period', *JNES* 17 (1958), 23-27; R. Borger, 'An Additional Remark on P. R. Ackroyd, *JNES* XVII, 23-27', *JNES* 18 (1959), 74; (3) the text fails to mention the reconstruction of the temple, an element that would certainly have been expected in an oracle after the fact.

[27]D. Baltzer ('Literarkritische und literarhistorische Anmerkungen zur Heilsprophetie im Ezechiel-Buch', *Ezekiel and His Book: Textual and Literary Criticism and Their Interrelation* [ed.] J. Lust [BETL 74; Leuven: Leuven University Press, 1986], 171), acknowledges that at least 11:14-21 dates to a time when the temple was still standing.

[28]Which demanded (1) the participation of the entire house of Israel; (2) the renewal of the relationship between people and deity; (3) the return of the population to the homeland; (4) the installation of an indigenous (Davidic) monarchy. *Cf.* D. I. Block, 'Nations', *ISBE* (rev. edn.), 3.492-495.

[29]*Cf.* D. Bodi, *The Book of Ezekiel and the Poem of Erra* (OBO 104; Freiburg/Göttingen: Universitätsverlag/Vandenhoeck & Ruprecht, 1991), 183-218.

[30]For details see my forthcoming SBL Seminar paper, 'The Absence of God in the Book of Ezekiel'; also my earlier discussion in *The Gods of the Nations: Studies in Ancient Near Eastern National Theology* (ETSMS 2; Winona Lake: Eisenbrauns, 1988), 133-148.

year of 586 BC did not mark the end, but the centre of the nation's history and Yahweh's dealing with her.[31]

In the light of these observations, the arrangement and shape of Ezekiel's salvation oracles are both logical and traditional. Generically his hopeful messages divide into two major blocks. In the first (chapters 34–39) the good news is proclaimed; in the second (chapters 40–48) the good news is envisioned. But in both the focus is on Yahweh's restorative actions, for the glory of His name, according to the following grand apologetic scheme:

1. Renewing Yahweh's role as divine shepherd/King of Israel (34:1-31)
2. Renewing Yahweh's land (35:1–36:15)
3. Renewing Yahweh's honour (36:16-38)
4. Renewing Yahweh's people (37:1-14)
5. Renewing Yahweh's covenant (37:15-28)
6. Renewing Yahweh's role as defender of His people (38:1–39:29)
7. Renewing Yahweh's presence among His people (40:1–46:24)
8. Renewing Yahweh's presence in the land (47:1–48:35)

It is within this cultural and literary context that the oracle against Gog in Ezekiel 38–39 must be interpreted, a matter to which we now turn.

The Nature and Design of the Gog Oracle

The boundaries of the Gog oracle are clearly defined by the word event formula in 38:1 and the signatory formula in 39:29. After the opening formula, which serves as a general heading for both chapters, the text divides into two remarkably symmetrical panels, consisting of 38:1-23 and 29:1-29. The intentionality of this symmetry is reflected in the close correspondence between the introductions of the two parts (38:1-4aα; 39:1-2aα) and their parity in length.[32] Although dramatic shifts in style and content and the insertion of numerous rhetorical formulae[33] create the impression of an extremely

---

[31]*Cf.* Baltzer, *Ezekiel and His Book*, 181.

[32]Panel A (38:2-23) consists of 365 words; panel B (39:1-29) 357 words.

[33]Most of these highlight this text as divine speech and/or emphasize the divine objective in the proclamation and the event: (1) new charges to the prophet to speak, which subdivide each of the major panels into two subsections (38:14; 39:17), yielding the following subsections: A[1] 38:2-13; A[2] 38:14-23; B[1] 39:1-16; B[2] 39:17-29; (2) the citation formula (38:3,14; 39:1,17); (3) the signatory formula, which may signal the conclusion of a paragraph (39:10, 20, 29), or function as rhetorical punctuation marks (38:18, 21; 39:5, 8, 13); (4) variations of the

complex oracle, chapters 38 and 39 function as a diptych, two leaves of a single document.

Whereas previous scholarship has concentrated on reconstructing the literary evolution of the Gog oracle,[34] I follow recent holistic approaches[35] in accepting the fundamental integrity

---

recognition formula, at the ends of paragraphs (38:16 [*cf.* the following citation formula]; 38:23 [the end of panel A]) or incorporated into the divine speeches (39:6, 7, 22, 28); (5) the logical particle, לָכֵן, 'Therefore' (38:14; 39:25), (6) time notices: וְהָיָה בַּיּוֹם הַהוּא, 'and it will happen in that day' (38:18; 39:11), מִיָּמִים רַבִּים, 'after many days', and בְּאַחֲרִית הַשָּׁנִים, 'in the latter years' (38:8), and בְּאַחֲרִית הַיָּמִים, 'in the latter days' (38:16) are chronological markers.

[34]Often these studies end by identifying an Ezekielian core, and attributing the rest to a series of interpretative additions (*Nachinterpretation*) by the 'School of Ezekiel'. W. Zimmerli's (*Ezekiel 2*, trans. J. D. Martin [Hermeneia; Philadelphia: Fortress, 1983], 296-299) reduction of the basic text to 38:1-9 (minus significant glosses), 39:1-5, 17-20, is more generous than some, but he ascribes the remainder to a series of interpretative expansions, each addition commenting on the pre-existent text. For evaluations of Zimmerli's treatment of these chapters see P. D. J. Scalise, *From Prophet's Word to Prophetic Book: A Study of Walther Zimmerli's Theory of 'Nachinterpretation'* (Yale University Ph.D. Dissertation. Ann Arbor: University Microfilms International, 1982), 114-134; M. S. Odell, '"Are You He of Whom I Spoke by My Servants the Prophets?" Ezekiel 38–39 and the Problem of History in the Neobabylonian Context' (Unpublished Ph.D. Dissertation. University of Pittsburgh, 1988), 1-42. Hossfeld (*Untersuchungen*, 402-508) limits the original core to 38:1-3a and 39:1b-5, the rest representing six stages of expansion: (1) 38:3b-9; (2) 39:17-20; (3) 38:10-16; 39:6-7, 21-22; (4) 38:17; 39:8-10; (5) 38:18-23; 39:11-13 (14-16?); (6) 39:23-29.

[35]M. C. Astour admits the oracle contains doublets and glosses which betray subsequent elaboration, but he argues 'the style and imagery of its basic parts are not different from those of the chapters which are generally accepted as genuine writings of Ezekiel' ('Ezekiel's Prophecy of Gog and the Cuthean Legend of Naram Sin', *JBL* 95 [1976)], 567). R. Hals (*Ezekiel* [FOTL; Grand Rapids: Eerdmans, 1989], 285) comments, 'The efforts of Zimmerli and Hossfeld here are welcome as speculative attempts of considerable heuristic value in enabling the discovery of even further complexities, but they are not at all convincing as actual literary reconstructions.' R. Klein (*Ezekiel: The Prophet and His Message* [SPOT; Columbia: University of South Carolina Press, 1988], 158) asserts that these chapters antedate 539 BC, and if such an early date can be accepted for all or part of the oracle, then the possibility remains that the prophet himself is responsible for the text. M. S. Odell ('Are You He of Whom I Spoke by My Servants the Prophets?') criticizes the work of previous form critics for severing the Gog oracle from the rest of the book of Ezekiel and artificially and arbitrarily divorcing prophecy, which represents a response to historical events, and theological reflection on prophecy, which is supposedly less tied to events. Contrast the approach of R. Ahroni ('The Gog Prophecy and the Book of Ezekiel', *HAR* 1 [1977], 1-27), who defends the unity of the oracle, particularly 38:1–39:24, but argues for a late, post-exilic date.

and coherence of chapters 38 and 39 as a literary whole.[36] With
respect to genre, ever since F. Hitzig first applied the term
'apocalyptic' to the prophecies of Ezekiel,[37] it has been fashionable to
interpret the Gog oracle as an example of this genre.[38] However,
recent work on apocalyptic literature raises doubts about the
propriety of this classification. It certainly does not fit the standard
definition of 'apocalyptic' offered by J. J. Collins:

> 'Apocalypse' is a genre of revelatory literature with a narrative
> framework, in which a revelation is mediated by an otherworldly
> being to a human recipient, disclosing a transcendent reality which
> is both temporal, insofar as it envisages eschatological salvation, and
> spatial insofar as it involves another, supernatural world.[39]

Beyond the issue of not fitting this definition of apocalyptic, we note
that many substantive and stylistic characteristics found in true
apocalypses are common in ordinary prophecy: conflict between
Yahweh and the enemies of Israel, the deliverance of his people,

---

[36]Though 39:25-29 may reflect later reflection, intentionally composed to
integrate the oracle with its broader present literary context.

[37]F. Hitzig, *Der Prophet Ezechiel* (KeH 8; Leipzig: Weidmann'sche Buchhandlung,
1847), xiv-xv.

[38]According to Ahroni (*HAR* 1 [1977], 11-13), its 'totally unrealistic and
imaginative' style, along with its hyperbole and fantasy, contrast sharply with
the historical roots and the realism of the rest of the book. Furthermore, the
cosmic dualism, represented by the conflict between Yahweh and Gog, the
obscurities, the symbolic language, the prominence of the number seven, the
enigmatic nature of the names of peoples, all point to an apocalyptic genre, and
the references to previous prophecy (38:17) and the expression, 'the navel of the
earth' (38:12), give supporting evidence for a late date. J. Becker ('Erwägungen
Zur Ezechielischen Frage', *Künder des Wortes: zur Theologie der Propheten*
[Würzburg: Echter Verlag, 1982], 137-149) interprets the entire book of Ezekiel as
a late pseudonynmous apocalyptic work.

[39]J. J. Collins, 'Towards the Morphology of a Genre', *Apocalypse: The Morphology
of a Genre*, Semeia 14 (Missoula: Scholars Press, 1979), 9. *Cf.* his preceding
paradigm of apocalyptic characteristics (pp. 5-9), which exposes the tenuous
nature of the links between Ezekiel 38–39 and other apocalyptic writings. See
also his fuller discussion of apocalyptic texts in the following essay of the same
volume, 'The Jewish Apocalypses', 21-59. According to P. D. Hanson ('Apocalyptic', *IDBSup*, 27; *cf. idem, The Dawn of Apocalyptic* [Philadelphia, 1975], for a
fuller study), apocalyptic involves a revelation given by God through a mediator
(usually an angel, but *cf.* Jesus Christ in Rev. 1:1-2) to a seer concerning future
events, expressed either in terms of a cosmic drama or elaborate symbolism. On
apocalyptic, see further D. S. Russell, *The Method and Message of Jewish Apocalyptic*
(OTL; Philadelphia: Westminster, 1964), 104-139; L. Morris, *Apocalyptic* (Grand
Rapids: Eerdmans, 1972); G. E. Ladd, 'Apocalyptic', *ISBE* (rev. edn.), 1.151-161.

Yahweh's sovereignty over the universe. Furthermore, the claim that this text transcends temporal and historical realities derives from inadequate attention to the social environment from which the prophecy derives and to which it speaks.[40] Expressions like 'after many days/years' (38:8) and 'in that day' (38:18; 39:11) thrust some elements of this prophecy into the distant future, and 38:18-23 introduces the notion of a cosmic shaking, but neither serves as a precursor to an ultimate eschatological salvation, nor a true consummation.[41] The focus remains on Israel's own salvation, which, like Ezekiel's previous restoration oracles results in the vindication of Yahweh's holiness, and the nation's recognition of Him. At issue is primarily the local problem: Gog and his hordes invading the land of Israel. The name Gog and the dominance of the number seven may be symbolic, but this is a far cry from the elaborate symbolism of Daniel or the New Testament book of Revelation. On these bases, the apocalyptic approach to the Gog oracle should be abandoned.

Some have interpreted the Gog oracle along the lines of Ezekiel's oracles against foreign nations in chapters 25–32. Having isolated 38:1-3a and 39:1b-5 as the original *Grundtext*, Hossfeld recognizes a structure similar to the first oracle against Egypt (29:1-6+) and Seir (35:1-4), and dates the prophecy prior to the oracles of chapter 32, which were delivered in 587-586 BC.[42] But this

---

[40]One of the primary criticisms levelled by Odell ('Are You He of Whom I Spoke?', 43-60) at many contemporary approaches.

[41]So also Hals, *Ezekiel*, 284, *contra* B. Childs ('The Enemy from the North and the Chaos Tradition', *JBL* 78 [1959], 187-198) and B. Batto (*Slaying the Dragon: Myth-making in the Biblical Tradition* [Louisville: Westminster/John Knox, 1992], 157-162), who characterizes the Gog oracle as 'proto-apocalyptic', a metahistorical portrayal of the cosmic conflict between Yahweh and chaos, symbolized by Gog.

[42]Hossfeld's text breaks down like this (*Untersuchungen*, 494-501):

Introduction (38:1-3a):

Word Event Formula	The word of Yahweh came to me as follows:
Address of the Prophet	Son of man,
Hostile Orientation Formula	Set your face toward Gog, prince of Meshech and Tubal,
Commissioning Formula	Prophesy against him and say,
Citation Formula	Thus has the Lord Yahweh declared:

The Message (39:1b-5a):

Challenge Formula	See, I am against you, O Gog, prince of Meshech and Tubal!
The Announcement	I shall turn you around, and drive you on, and draw you up

from the remotest parts of the north, and lead you to the mountains of Israel. I shall strike the bow from your left hand, and knock the arrows out of your right hand. On the mountains of Israel you will fall – you and all your hordes, and the peoples accompanying you – I shall hand you over as food to every kind of predatory bird, and every wild animal. On the open field you shall fall.

Conclusion (39:5b):

Conclusion of Divine Speech Formula	For I have spoken,
Signatory Formula	The declaration of the Lord Yahweh.

interpretation can be maintained only by disregarding the final shape of the text and ignoring its present placement at the heart of the restoration oracles.[43] Furthermore, an oracle against an enigmatic entity like Gog would be out of place in the context of the rest of the prophecies against the foreign nations, all of whom are Israel's immediate neighbours, and whose own history had touched Israel's at many points. The form critics' identification of the basic text may indeed be correct, but this does not mean the remainder is not authentically Ezekielian. Since Gog and his forces represent foreign nations in opposition to Yahweh, it is not surprising that this text displays many affinities with the former. But the differences in the final products are so pervasive, it is unwise to force the present oracle into that grid.

Although the general structure of the oracle proper (38:1–39:20) displays some resemblance to Ezekiel's judgment speeches, its complexity of style and content precludes formal classification on the basis of structure alone. The seven-fold occurrence of the recognition formula,[44] provides the most obvious clue to its genre and intention. The Gog pericope consists of a series of fragmentary proof-sayings which, when brought together in this fashion, result in a single powerful proof-oracle. Above all else, this complex divine speech expresses Yahweh's determination once and for all to reveal to the

---

M. Nobile ('Beziehung zwischen Ez 32,17-32 und der Gog-Perikope [Ez 38-39] im Lichte der Endredaktion', *Ezekiel and His Book,* 255-259) argues that the redactor of chapter 32 had the Gog oracle in front of him, and that the Gog-pericope appeared as the continuation and climax of the oracles against the foreign nations. In fact, the Gog oracle radicalizes the conflict between Yahweh and the nations. However, it was separated from the oracles against the nations because its fulfilment lies in the more remote future. Its placement before the Temple Vision (40–48) was determined by literary-liturgical considerations. he new temple cannot be described without first accounting for the basis of its construction, *viz.,* Yahweh's final victory over the cosmic forces of chaos (represented by the nations).

[43]Although the form and structure of the *Grundtext* bear some resemblance to 32:1-6+ and 35:1-4, the pronouncements in 25:1–26:6 show that the basic structure of Ezekiel's oracles against the foreign nations follows that of typical judgment speeches: accusation (introduced by יַעַן, 'because'), followed by the announcement of judgment (introduced with לָכֵן, 'therefore'). Furthermore, as Odell notes ('Are You He of Whom I Spoke?', 37), since chapter 32 announces the demise of Meshech and Tubal, it is unlikely they could have risen to greatness so quickly after the defeat announced here.

[44]38:16, 23; 39:6, 7, 22, 23, 28. This represents a denser concentration than anywhere else in the book. Two of these formulae occur in their simplest form (38:23; 39:6); the remainder vary greatly from the simple modification of Yahweh with 'the Holy One in Israel' in 39:7 to the elaborate additions in 39:23 and 39:28.

nations His holiness, and to His own people His covenant loyalty.[45]
Since both notions had appeared in an earlier fragment of theological
reflection at the end of the oracle against Tyre (28:25-26), and since so
many of the ideas raised there will be resumed and expanded here,[46]
the Gog pericope offers one more example of typically Ezekielian
resumptive exposition.[47]

For sheer vividness, imagery and hyperbole, this oracle has
few equals. These features alone caution against over-literalism in
interpretation. The intention of this text may be best appreciated if it
is approached as a satirical literary cartoon strip consisting of eight
frames. As the unit progresses, the images become increasingly
caricatured, climaxing in a bizarre picture of predatory birds and
wild animals seated around a table, gorging themselves on human
flesh (39:17-20). The sequence of events reflected in the frames may
be outlined as follows:

Panel A: The Defeat of Gog   (38:2-23)
Frame 1: The Conscription of Gog   (38:2-9)
Frame 2: The Motives of Gog   (38:10-13)
Frame 3: The Advance of Gog   (38:14-16)
Frame 4: The Judgment of Gog   (38:17-22)
Interpretative Conclusion   (38:23)

---

[45]The subject of the verb in the recognition formula shifts in the course of the
oracle, from the nations, in the first four and the sixth, to Israel in the fifth and
seventh. Significantly, nowhere is the divine aim declared to be Gog's
acknowledgment of Yahweh, which highlights his role as agent through whom
Yahweh achieves His goal, rather than the primary concern of his activity.

[46]The regathering of the nation (קִבֵּץ, cf. 38:8); the manifestation of Yahweh's
holiness (נִקְדַּשׁ , 38:16; 39:7, 25, 27); 'in the sight of the nations' (cf. 38:16); Israel
living securely in the land (יָשַׁב לָבֶטַח, cf. 38:8, 11; 39:26); Yahweh executing
judgments (עָשָׂה שְׁפָטִים, 28:26; עָשָׂה מִשְׁפָּטִים, 39:21); Israel recognizing Yahweh as their
God (cf. 39:21, 28).

[47]Whereas the earlier text had referred to the objects of Yahweh's judgment
vaguely as כָּל הַשָּׁאטִים אֹתָם מִסְּבִיבוֹתָם , 'all who scorn them (Israel) round about', these
are now identified specifically as Gog and his allies. The offence, expressed by
the verb שָׁאט, 'to scorn', is now described in detail as showing contempt for Israel
dwelling at peace within her own land, and taking advantage of her defenceless
state to satisfy their greed (38:10-14). But as exposition, the Gog oracle is not
slavishly bound to the antecedent fragment. Nor does it offer a phrase- by-phrase
commentary, nor adhere to western canons of logic and progression. The
demand for the latter in particular has led astray many interpreters, who, by
dissecting the text into a series of fragments, rob the oracle of its force.

Panel B: The Disposal of Gog	(39:1-29)
Frame 1: The Slaughter of Gog	(39:1-8)
Frame 2: The Spoiling of Gog	(39:9-10)
Frame 3: The Burial of Gog	(39:11-16)
Frame 4: The Devouring of Gog	(39:17-20)
Interpretative Conclusion	(39:21-29)

Many of these frames subdivide further on stylistic and substantive grounds into separate sub-sections. While each sub-unit has an identity and character of its own, they are thoroughly integrated to create a sequence of events whose total impact is much greater than the sum of its parts.

Summary Exposition

A detailed frame-by-frame exposition of the Gog oracle is not possible here. A summary interpretation of the key elements of each frame will, therefore, have to suffice.

Frame 1: The Conscription of Gog (38:2-9)

The first frame introduces the primary antagonist, Gog, prince, chief of Meshech and Tubal. There is no consensus on the interpretation of the name Gog, but this is not for lack of effort.[48] The most likely explanation derives Gog from Gyges, the name of the King of Lydia, mentioned in six inscriptions of Ashurbanipal (668-631 BC),[49] and known elsewhere for his invention of coinage.[50] Gog's homeland is

---

[48]Proposed explanations include: (1) a mythological 'locust giant', analogous to the scorpion man in the Gilgamesh Epic (*ANET*, 88; *cf.* Amos 7:1, which LXX read as *gzy*, 'locust' [H. Gressmann, *Der Messias*, FRLANT 6; Göttingen: Vandenhoeck & Ruprecht, 1929], 129, n. 1); (2) a personification of darkness (*cf.* Sumerian *gûg*, 'darkness' [P. Heinisch, *Das Buch Ezechiel übersetzt und erklärt* (HSAT 8; Bonn: P. Hanstein, 1923)], 183); (3) Gaga, a name that appears in EA 1:36-40, alongside Hanigalbat and Ugarit (W. F. Albright, 'Gog and Magog', *JBL* 43 [1924], 381-382); (4) Gaga, a deity mentioned in the Ugaritic sources (*cf.* K. H. Cuffey, *ABD*, 2.1056).

[49]See M. Cogan and H. Tadmor, 'Gyges and Ashurbanipal: A Study in Literary Tansmission', *Or* 46 (1977), 65, n. 1. The most important reference is found in *ARAB* 2.351-352.

[50]On his legendary reputation see Herodotus, *Histories*, 1.8-13. Some treat Gog as a dynastic name, referring in this context to his great grandson, Alyattes, under whom Lydia had once again become the dominant power in western Anatolia. J. L. Myres ('Gog and the Danger from the North in Ezekiel', *PEFQS* 64 [1932], 213-219) suggested this oracle was prompted by the 'Battle of the Eclipse' between Lydia and Media in 585 BC. *Cf.* more recently, I. M. Diakonoff, *Predystorija*

identified simply as 'the land of Magog'. Although both names may turn out to be artificial creations,[51] it seems best to interpret Magog as a contraction of an original *māt Gūgi*, 'land of Gog',[52] an allusion to the territory of Lydia in western Anatolia.[53] The first frame has Gog at the head of a powerful international alliance (קָהָל רַב) that includes four northern kingdoms: Meshek and Tubal (verses 2-3),[54] and Gomer and Beth-Togarmah (verse 6),[55] and three southern

---

armjanskogo naroda (*Protohistory of the Armenian People*) (Erevan, 1968), 179 (as cited by M. C. Astour, 'Ezekiel's Prophecy of Gog and the Cuthean Legend of Naram-Sin', *JBL* 95 [1976], 569-570).

[51]Many have seen in the names a cipher for Babylon: G. H. A. von Ewald, *Commentary on the Prophets of the Old Testament* (trans. J. F. Smith; London: Williams and Norgate, 1880), 192-193; Cooke, *Ezekiel* 480. J. Boehmer ('Wer ist Gog von Magog? Ein Beitrag zur Auslegung des Buches Ezechiel', *ZWT* 40 [1897], 321-355) saw in מגג a cryptogram for Babylon, a reverse kind of 'athbash' (*cf.* Jeremiah's שֵׁשַׁךְ, 'Sheshach' [25:26; 51:41], which, by replacing the first letter of the alphabet with the last, the second with the penultimate letter, *etc.*, yields בבל). Ezekiel's method is more complex. Replacing each letter in בבל by its successor yields גגמ, which, when reversed, produces מגג. Unfortunately, like all interpretations which see in the Gog oracle a message directed at Babylon, this understanding flies in the face of Ezekiel's consistent perception of the Babylonians as agents, not the enemies of God.

[52]So Astour, *JBL* 95 (1976), 569; E. Yamauchi, *Foes from the Northern Frontier* (Grand Rapids: Baker, 1982), 23. Josephus (*Ant.* 1.123, followed by Gressmann, *Der Messias*, 123-124) identified Magog with the Scythians: 'Magog founded the Magogians, thus named after him, but who by the Greeks are called Scythians.' A. van den Born ('Etudes sur quelques toponyms bibliques', *OTS* 10 [1954], 197-201; *idem*, *Ezechiël* [De Boeken van het Oude Testament; Roermond en Maaseik: J. J. Romen & Zonen, 1954], 223) assumes a scribal error for ארץ המגא, an ancient abbreviation for ארץ המגדן, 'the land of the Macedonian,' from which he deduces Gog to be a pseudonym for Alexander the Great. The name has no geographic or ethnographic analogues in ancient Near Eastern literature, though Albright (*JBL* 43 [1924], 383) proposed a blend with Manda, an abbreviation of Umman Manda, the common Mesopotamian designation for 'barbarian'.

[53]In Gn. 10:2 (= 1 Ch. 1:5) Magog is a personal name identifying the second son of Japheth and brother of Gomer, Madai, Javan, Tubal, Meshech and Tiras. LXX reads a personal name here as well, preparing the way for later writings in which Gog and Magog become a fixed pair of names of persons involved in the final eschatological battle. Rev. 20:8; *Sybilline Oracles* 3:319-320, 512; a fragment of the Targum *Pseudo-Jonathan* to the Pentateuch on Nu. 11:26 (*cf.* S. H. Levey, *The Messiah: An Aramaic Interpretation. The Messianic Exegesis of the Targum* [Cincinnati: Hebrew Union College Press, 1974], 105-107); fifth century Hebrew Apocalypse of *Enoch* 45:5.

[54]To be identified with Muški and Tabal respectively, two eastern Asia Minor kingdoms well-attested in Akkadian sources.

accomplices: Paras,[56] Cush (Ethiopia) and Put (Libya). The conjunction of Paras, Cush and Put here and elsewhere in the book[57]
suggests this triad derives from a traditional list of allies of Egypt.
But what is the significance of this alliance? Any answer to
the question must keep in mind three significant observations. First,
in contrast to the addressees in Ezekiel's oracles against the foreign
nations, the names listed all represent distant peoples, from the
fringes of Israelite geographic awareness. Second, the number of
allies totals seven, a prominent number in the Gog oracle as a
whole.[58] The number symbolizes totality, completeness,[59] raising the
conspiracy against Israel from a minor opportunistic incursion to a
universal conspiracy. Third, the names in Ezekiel's list form a
merismic pattern: Meshech, Tubal, Gomer and Beth Togarmah
represent the northern extreme of the world known to Israel; Paras,
Cush and Put the southern extreme, reinforcing the impression that
the entire world is ganging up on Israel.[60] At the head of this alliance

---

[55]To be identified with the Qimmiraia (Cimmerians) and Til-garimmu in
Akkadian sources. For a full discussion of these names see E. Yamauchi, *Foes
from the Northern Frontier*.

[56]Paras is best understood either as an alternative, perhaps Egyptian, spelling for
Pathros, 'Southland' (*cf.* Is. 11:11), or the name of power with strong links to Tyre
and Egypt (*cf.* Ezk. 27:10), to date unattested in extra-biblical records. *Cf.* Odell,
'Are You He of Whom I Spoke?', 103-106; *idem*, 'From Egypt to Meshech and
Tubal: The Extent of Rebellion Against Yahweh in Ezekiel 38–39', paper read to
the Society of Biblical Literature, November, 1989. The common identification of
Paras with Persia is unlikely not only because it is anachronistic, but also because
Ezekiel shows no interest whatsoever in Babylon's eastern neighbours. A later
insertion is ruled out because the presence of Persia in a list of subordinates to
Gog here and in 27:10 would have been quite unrealistic in any post 539 BC
situation.

[57]In 27:10 Paras, Lud (Lydia) and Put are military partners of Tyre; in 30:5 Cush,
Put and Lud are listed among allies of Egypt.

[58]Note the enemies' seven weapons (39:9), the seven years' worth of fuel these
provide (39:9), the seven months needed for the burial of the enemies' remains
(39:12). Ahroni (*HAR* 1 [1977], 17) also identifies seven sections in the
composition. Significantly the number of nations addressed in the collection of
oracles against the nations in chapters 25–32, and those who accompany Egypt in
Sheol in 37:16-32 also total seven. M. Nobile (*Ezekiel and His Book*, 256-257) sees
here evidence that the redactor of the latter text had the Gog pericope in front of
him.

[59]See M. H. Pope, *IDB* 4.294-295.

[60]Compare the use of similar rhetorical strategies in ancient Neo-Assyrian
sources, particularly the following boast of Sargon II: 'In the might and power of
the great gods, my lords, who sent forth my weapons, I cut down all of my foes
from Iatnana (Cyprus), which is in the sea of the setting sun, as far as the border
of Egypt and the land of the Mushki (Meshech), – the wide land of Amurru, the

Gog represents a formidable foe, able to attack whenever and wherever he pleases.

But how different is the appearance from the reality. Verses 4-6 are emphatic in affirming Yahweh's total control over the movements of Gog. This truth is announced in three short declarations: Yahweh will turn Gog around, put hooks in his jaws, and lead him out. Here the mysterious region beyond the Taurus mountains is portrayed as the lair from which Yahweh will lead Gog out like an animal on a leash. Verse 7 is cast as Yahweh's formal summons to Gog and the forces assembled to him, with Gog clearly in charge.[61] But Ezekiel's audience may have taken comfort in verse 8, which explains that the summoning[62] of Gog and his forces is not to be expected in the near future, but 'after many days', 'in later years'. Although LXX renders the latter expression with ἔσχατος, it is not clear that the end of time is in mind. The reference may be simply to a later time, when the historical phase of the exile is over and the new period of settlement in the land has arrived.

The rest of verse 8 offers further clarification of the timing of the summons for Gog. It will happen when the land itself will have recovered[63] from the destruction and slaughter of an invading army, and the population will have been regathered from many peoples of the diaspora and resettled securely[64] on the mountains of Israel. Since verse 8 functions as a shorthand version of Ezekiel's salvation

---

Hittite land in its entirety. . .' (ARAB 2 §54). Cf. §§82, 96, 97, 99, and §183 which uses the expression 'from Egypt to Mushki'. See the discussion by Odell, 'Are You He of Whom I Spoke?', 101-102; idem, 'From Egypt to Meshech and Tubal.' But Odell's thesis that Gog's campaign represents a rebellion against Nebuchadnezzar, incurring the wrath of Yahweh (just as Gyges' revolt against Ashurbanipal had incurred the wrath of Ashur), is unlikely because: (1) Nebuchadnezzar is entirely out of the picture in this oracle; (2) the Gog invasion is thrust into the distant future; and (3) the relationship between Ashurbanipal and Ashur is hardly parallel to Yahweh's relationship with Nebuchadnezzar.

[61]The meaning of the final clause in verse 7 is uncertain, but in the context מִשְׁמָר must carry a military nuance, presumably charging Gog with leadership over the vast forces allied with him by serving as their guardian.

[62]On פָּקַד = 'to summon, muster', in military contexts, see 23:21.

[63]On מְשׁוֹבֶבֶת, a polal feminine participle of שׁוּב, see W. L. Holladay, The Root šûb in the Old Testament with Particular Reference to its Usages in Covenantal Texts (Leiden: Brill, 1958), 106-107.

[64]The phrase יָשַׁב לָבֶטַח, which derives from Lv. 26:5b-6, serves as a minor key-word in the oracle (cf. verses 11,14; 39:26), describing the security offered by Yahweh when the blessings of the covenant are operative and the divine patron stands guard over them.

oracles,[65] Gog's invasion presupposes the fulfilment of the salvation oracles in chapters 34–37. Verse 9 spells out Yahweh's marching orders to Gog, instructing him to take all his assembled forces and attack the peaceful mountains of Israel like a furious storm cloud.

To summarize the opening frame, here Yahweh is portrayed as a general, mobilizing the forces of Gog and his allies for His own military agenda. Gog's invasion of the land represents a part of the calculated plan of Yahweh for His people. But this raises several questions. How can Gog, whom verses 3-6 had portrayed as the enemy of Yahweh, simultaneously play the role of Yahweh's agent? How can Yahweh employ foreign nations against His people, especially after He has re-established the eternal covenant relationship and restored the people to the land? In raising these questions this first frame sets the rhetorical agenda for the following frames of the prophecy against Gog.

Frame 2: The Motives of Gog (38:10-13)
A new citation formula signals the beginning of the second frame in which the focus shifts from Yahweh's initiative to the private motivations of Gog. 'Ideas' rise in his mind, and he devises evil schemes to bring calamity upon the unsuspecting land. Verse 11 emphasizes that the land is undefended, and its population undisturbed and secure. The text does not explain why the inhabitants of the mountains of Israel have taken no defensive precautions, but one may assume that they have finally put their confidence in Yahweh's promises of eternal peace and prosperity, as spelled out in the previous restoration oracles. Verse 12 offers additional information on the state of the nation: its ruins have been repopulated in fulfilment of 36:10, 33; the people are regathered from their dispersion among the nations; the population is prospering with abundant livestock and other movable goods, in fulfilment of 34:26-27; and her people live on top of the world.[66]

Apparently oblivious of Yahweh's hand, by his own confession Gog is motivated by a single passion: greed, the lust for loot and booty. But he is not alone in this. According to verse 13, Sheba, Dedan and the merchants of Tarshish have been watching Gog's activity with great interest. The reason for their interest may be

---

[65]Especially 36:1-15, addressed to the mountains of Israel and highlighting the restoration of its population, 36:24, 33-36 which speaks of regathering the people and rebuilding the ruins, and 34:25-29 which describes the scene of perfect peace and tranquillity.

[66]The interpretation of טַבּוּר as 'navel' is as ancient as LXX but should be abandoned. So also S. Talmon, *TDOT* 3.437-438.

guessed from their names: Sheba and Dedan represent merchant peoples (סֹחֲרִים) who conduct their trade via the overland routes across the Arabian Desert to the east of Israel, and Tarshish represents the maritime traders who control the Mediterranean route to the west. These traders' reaction to Gog's designs is expressed in the form of a series of rhetorical questions, but their motive is not entirely clear. Are they decent nations challenging Gog's greed, or are they wishing to capitalize on the opportunity themselves? Since their questions echo many of the expressions found in the previous verse, it seems Gog's greed is mirrored in their own covetousness. They too have their eyes on spoil, booty, silver, gold, livestock and other movable property. These merchants are vultures, hoping to take advantage of the spoils of this war.

Like the list of Gog's allies who come from the northern and southern extremes of the world known to Israel (verses 3-6), the names in verse 13 constitute a merismus, representing the nations who control the trading lanes of the world, from the far east to the far west. Taken together these two groups represent all four points of the compass. The entire world conspires against the unsuspecting and tranquil nation of Israel.

Frame 3: The Advance of Gog (38:14-16)

While the formulaic opening in verse 14 signals the commencement of the third frame, the introductory particle, לָכֵן, 'Therefore', intentionally draws a logical connection between this frame and the preceding: the arrogant advance of Gog is linked to the intentions of Yahweh. The most striking feature of this brief scene is the manner in which Gog's target is identified. Twice Yahweh refers to the people living securely as עַמִּי יִשְׂרָאֵל, 'my people Israel' (verses 14, 16), and once to the land as אַרְצִי, 'my land.' Since the normal deity–nation–land relationships are now operative, for Gog to attack this people and invade this land is to challenge their/its divine patron.

Verses 14b-16a highlight the opportunism of the invader. Precisely when Yahweh's people are enjoying their security in His land, Gog will emerge from his homeland in the far reaches of the north country. He and his vast host will sweep down on Yahweh's people on their horses and cover the land like a cloud. Employing an expanded version of the recognition formula, the prophet highlights His control over all these events. First, Gog's invasion is planned according to Yahweh's timetable, 'at the end of the years'.[67] Second,

---

[67]The expression assumes knowledge of verse 8, and reaffirms that the invasion of the land of Israel is not imminent, but pushed off into the distant future, after

Gog's invasion occurs at the overt instigation of Yahweh; he comes not merely with Yahweh's permissive will, but as His agent.[68] Third, Yahweh's purpose in bringing on the hordes of Gog is to convince the nations of His presence and His person.[69] In an ironical twist, Gog's opportunism *vis-à-vis* Israel is seized as an occasion to achieve Yahweh's own goals. In the mean time, this frame has also provided the answer to the first question raised by the first frame (verses 3-9): why would Yahweh bring Gog against His own people after the covenant relationships had been fully restored? Because an element in the divine agenda, the universal recognition of His person, remains unfulfilled.

Frame 4: The Judgment of Gog (38:17-22)

The fourth literary frame consists of two unequal parts, clearly distinguished in style and purpose (verse 17; verses 18-22). Reminiscent to the reader of John the Baptiser's query of Jesus, 'Are you the Coming One or are we to wait for someone else?'[70] Yahweh opens by posing a question to Gog whether or not he considers himself the fulfilment of earlier prophecies. Assuming this rhetorical question demanded a positive answer, in the past scholars have

---

Yahweh's people have been regathered from the diaspora, have settled in the land, the signs of His blessing have become evident, and they have begun to enjoy their peaceful and tranquil state.

[68]The formulaic declaration suggests to Ezekiel's audience that Yahweh is again carrying out His covenant threats against His people. The pronouncement עַל־אָרְצִי וַהֲבִאוֹתִיךָ, follows a conventional prophetic form, 'I will bring A against B.' Seven times in Kings the divine threat is announced by the prophets with מֵבִיא רָעָה עַל הַזֶּה, 'I will bring disaster upon B.' 1 Ki. 9:9 (upon Israel); 14:10 (upon Jeroboam); 21:21 (upon Ahab), 29 (upon Ahab's house); 2 Ki. 21:12 (upon Jerusalem and Judah); 22:16, 20 (upon this place, *viz.*, Jerusalem). The formula occurs fourteen times in Ezekiel. However, the influence of the covenantal threat (Lv. 26:25) is evident in the six-fold replacement of the general term for disaster (רָעָה) with חֶרֶב, 'sword' (5:17; 6:3; 11:8; 14:17; 29:8; 33:2), which also accounts for the use of חֶרֶב in verse 8 above. 14:21 lists 'my four severe judgments: sword, famine, wild animals, plague'. 14:22 has הָרָעָה. Ezekiel's historicizing tendency is evident in his substitution of real agents for 'sword' (7:24 [the most barbaric of nations]; 23:22 [Jerusalem's lovers]; 26:7 [Nebuchadnezzar upon Tyre]; 28:7 [strangers upon Tyre]), a rhetorical device to demonstrate that current events do in fact represent the fulfilment of Yahweh's covenant threats. See also Odell, 'Are You He of Whom I Spoke?', 116-121.

[69]That the unique form of the statement intentionally draws attention to the fact that Gog is not actually the agent through whom His holiness is manifested, but the locus of the revelation, is confirmed by the observation that wherever the concern is the revelation of Yahweh's holiness, it occurs in the midst of a people. So also Odell, 'Are You He of Whom I Spoke?', 132.

[70]Mt. 11:3 (*cf.* Lk. 7:19, 20).

devoted their energies to identifying which prophecies the question has in mind.[71] But in this regard they have been as misguided as Gog himself. There can be little doubt that Ezekiel's contemporaries would have identified Jeremiah's foe 'from the north', as Babylon under Nebuchadnezzar, especially since Jeremiah had explicitly made this identification himself (Je. 25:9). If Yahweh had actually directed this question to Gog himself, and if Gog had been aware of the earlier pronouncements concerning the 'foe from the north' by Israelite prophets, he would probably have answered in the affirmative. It would certainly have bolstered his ego if, apart from his personal greed, he could have claimed the role of Yahweh's agent, sent in to punish the Israelites, like Nebuchadnezzar before him. The question then feeds right in to Gog's ego-maniacal ambitions.

However, as the earlier frames have already demonstrated, Gog's self-understanding and Yahweh's perception of him are quite different. According to the first frame (verses 2-9) Yahweh alone brings Gog and his hordes on. Like a conqueror Himself, Yahweh will lead Gog in, dragging in his captives with hooks in their jaws. But according to the second frame (verses 10-13), Gog is totally oblivious of the fact that he is but a puppet on Yahweh's strings. He thinks he is campaigning against Israel of his own free will. Correspondingly, even if Gog would have answered this question positively, the correct answer is negative.[72] Gog is in fact not 'the foe from the north' of whom Jeremiah had spoken. His role is entirely different. He is not commissioned by Yahweh to serve as His agent of judgment. He and his troops are brought down from the mountains for a single purpose: that the holiness of Yahweh might be displayed in the sight of the nations.[73] Whatever havoc they hope to wreak on Yahweh's people they do of their own volition, and not at the command of God. This oracle, therefore, is not about unfulfilled prophecy, but about earlier prophecies illegitimately appropriated. Otherwise verses 18-23 become nonsensical. How could Yahweh announce in one breath that Gog is His agent, and in the next vent His wrath upon him with such fury?

In verses 18-23 the literary style and tone change dramatically, and the second person of direct address, used

---

[71]For a detailed discussion of this text see D. I. Block, 'Gog in Prophetic Tradition: A New Look at Ezekiel XXXVIII 17', *VT* 42 (1992), 152-172.
[72]So also Odell, 'Are You He of Whom I Spoke?', 122. There is no syntactic reason why this could not be the case. For a precise parallel to the present question see 2 Sa. 7:5, with which compare its unequivocal declarative counterpart in 1 Ch. 17:4.
[73]*Cf.* verses 16, 23; 39:6-7; also verses 22, 28.

throughout the preceding frames, gives way to the third person. For the first time the intensity of the opposition between Yahweh and Gog, announced in the opening challenge formula (verse 3), becomes apparent as Yahweh vents His fury toward Gog without restraint. The cause of the provocation is declared to be Gog's invasion of the land of Israel, an action that is now portrayed as his very own (cf. 39:2). But with the covenant relationship between Yahweh and His people fully restored, Yahweh cannot stand by idly. The divine patron of Israel must act.

Yahweh's emotional reaction to Gog's invasion is obvious as He explodes, heaping up expressions for anger unparalleled in the book, if not in the entire Old Testament. Fortunately for Israel, the wrath previously poured out on them will now fall upon their enemy. The firmness of Yahweh's resolve is reflected not only in the signatory formula, which interrupts the outburst, but the expressed motive for His utterance: 'I have spoken in my passion,' in verse 19a also leaves no doubt that the following threats arise out of His anger. The effects of Yahweh's fury are described in verses 19b-20. A massive earthquake will rock the land on which Gog has his sights, and reverberate throughout the earth, causing all living things to quake and levelling the landscape. With its epicentre in the land of Israel, the quake will bring down mountains and cliffs, symbols of divinely grounded stability, and crumble walls, symbols of strength fabricated by human hands. The force behind this cosmic upheaval is obliquely hinted at in the divine passive, 'they will be hurled down', and the addition of 'before me' at the beginning of the verse. The latter enhances the theophanic flavour of this frame, reminiscent of the quaking of the earth beneath the feet of the Israelites when Yahweh stepped down on Mount Sinai.[74]

Ezekiel's imagery in verses 19-20 is generally associated with Hebrew apocalyptic, and treated as a sign of the relative lateness of this composition.[75] However, the correlation between divine anger and cosmic collapse was widely recognized in Mesopotamia long before the exile of Judah. After listing a series of evils committed by the Babylonians, the annals of Esarhaddon describe the result:[76]

---

[74]Ex. 19. See also Jdg. 5:4-5; Is. 30:27-28; Hab. 3:3-7; Pss. 68:8-9[7-8]; 114.
[75]Zimmerli (*Ezekiel* 2, 313) comments, 'In comparison with the original Ezekiel oracle, the later apocalyptic style of verses 18-23 is unmistakable.' Similarly H. F. Fuhs, *Ezechiel II* (Neue Echter Bibel; Würzburg: Echter Verlag, 1988), 219.
[76]The various recensions of the account are gathered by Borger, *Asarhaddon* 13-14, episodes 5-6. *Cf.* also *ARAB* 2.250, §658.

Enlil (*i.e.*, Marduk) observed these. His heart fumed; his liver raged.
The Enlil of the gods, the lord of the lands plotted evil in order to
annihilate land and people. In the fury of his heart he determined to
destroy the land and to bring the people to ruin. An evil curse was
found upon his mouth. In the heavens and on the earth evil 'forces'
persisted. The symmetry (*mit-ḫur-tim*) [of the universe] collapsed.
The courses of the stars of Enlil, Anu, and Ea were disrupted and
augured evil. Their 'forces' were constantly changing. The *Araḫtu*
canal, a raging torrent, an angry stream, a swollen high tide like the
deluge itself, flooded the city, its residences, and its temples, and
transformed it into a wasteland.

Whereas in verses 19-20 Yahweh's involvement in the earthquake is
only obliquely alluded to, and the effects of His fury appear to fall
indiscriminately on all inhabitants of the globe, the impression
changes in verse 21 as Yahweh announces specifically the
summoning of the sword against Gog. In sharp contrast to the pre-
586 BC situation, in the future, when Israel, Yahweh's people, is
established in His land, alien invasion will excite His passions and
move Him to act in defence of both the land of Israel and its people.
Reminiscent of Gideon's war against the Midianites (Jdg. 7:22), when
Yahweh calls for the sword, the troops in the armies of Gog and his
allies will turn their weapons against each other.[77] But the sword is
not the only agent of death which Yahweh sends against Gog. Verse
22 catalogues three pairs of calamities: plague and bloodshed,
torrents of rain and hailstones, fire and burning sulphur.

   According to verse 22, these calamities represent the
execution of a divine sentence upon Gog and his hordes.[78] However,
verse 23, which offers an interpretative conclusion to the first panel,
also announces a three-fold revelatory purpose: to display Yahweh's
greatness (הִתְגַּדִּל), His holiness (הִתְקַדִּשׁ), and His person (נוֹדַעְתִּי) in
the sight of many nations.[79] While this declaration relates most
directly to the fourth frame, it summarizes Yahweh's intentions for
all the events of 'that day' (*cf.* verse 18), beginning with Yahweh's

---

[77]Compare the adaptation of the motif of the enemies of God's people destroying
themselves in Zechariah's eschatological battle (14:13).
[78]The niphal of שׁפט normally denotes 'to enter into judgment', or 'to commit to
trial' (17:20; 20:35-36), but in this case the guilt has already been established.
[79]The first two involve the only occurrences of these roots in the hithpael stem in
the book. These are examples *par excellence* of the estimative-declarative reflexive
use of the hithpael stem. *Cf. WO* §26.2f. The niphal of ידע , 'to make oneself
known', has occurred in earlier affirmations of Yahweh's self-disclosure in 20:5, 9
and 35:11.

conscription of Gog and ending with his annihilation. By rocking the earth and bringing down this far-flung military alliance in the full view of the nations, they will all acknowledge the truth that Israel had gained from her own judgment and subsequent restoration.

Frame 5: The Slaughter of Gog (39:1-8)

The introductory formulae in 39:1 echo 38:2, signalling the shift to the second panel of this complex oracle against Gog. The first frame of the second panel (the fifth over all) recapitulates some of the action of 38:19-23. However, the tone changes as the emphasis shifts from Yahweh's emotion to His actions against Gog. Except for two references to Gog's forces falling (verses 4, 5), and two recognition formulae (verses 6, 7), Yahweh is the subject of every verb in the frame.

As in 38:2, the challenge formula in 39:1b draws the lines in the conflict: Yahweh has set Himself in opposition to Gog. By a series of eight sharp, hard-hitting declarations, Yahweh outlines His strategy against the foe: He will turn Gog around, drive him on, lead him up from the remotest part of the north,[80] bring him to the mountains of Israel, knock his bow out of his left hand, force him to drop his arrows from his right hand, deliver his corpse as food for all the beasts and birds of prey, and torch the lands from which Gog and his allies have come.

While the effect of Yahweh's action is to neutralize Gog's offensive power completely, Yahweh will perform the ultimate indignity upon the corpses of Gog and his forces by leaving them on the mountains and in open fields for scavenging birds and mammals to devour. Not satisfied with the destruction of the armies of Gog, Yahweh will send fire against the lands from which Gog and his allies have come. The description of the inhabitants as 'secure' (לְבֶטַח) highlights the irony of the situation. Those who sought to take advantage of Israel's innocent and unsuspecting state now find that the long arm of Yahweh extends far beyond the borders of His own land to the ends of the earth.

The last line of verse 6 and verses 7-8 reiterate Yahweh's revelatory aims: the international recognition of His person and His character as the Holy One[81] in Israel. This revelation was necessary because it was precisely 'in Israel' that His reputation had previously

---

[80] As elsewhere in the book (1:4; 26:7; 32:30) צָפוֹן, 'north', is used in its normal directional sense, without mythological overtones.

[81] The strength of the latter determination is reflected in the three-fold occurrence of the root קדשׁ, referring twice to His holy name, which recalls 20:39 and 36:20-23. See also the end of this oracle (verse 29), and 43:7-8.

been defiled, leading to the nation's exile and creating mis-impressions in the foreigners' minds concerning His character (*cf.* 36:16-32). But those days are long past. The Gog debacle will demonstrate once and for all the holiness of Yahweh, not as a theological abstraction, but in action, as He stands to defend His people against the universal conspiracy of evil. The frame concludes with an emotional declaration of the inevitability of the coming event and irrevocability of the divine determination.

Frame 6: The Spoiling of Gog (39:9-10)
In verses 9-10 the attention shifts from Ezekiel's radically theocentric portrayal of Gog's demise to a graphic and earthy picture of human survivors mopping up after an enormous battle. Gog and God have had their day; for the first time the Israelites enter the picture. This frame may be the shortest of the series, but the imagery is vivid. The scene opens with the sight of the inhabitants of the cities of Israel, untouched by Gog's invading forces, emerging from their homes to dispose of the weapons of the annihilated foe. Ezekiel highlights the magnitude and intensity of the mopping-up operations with four special rhetorical elements: (1) the hendiadyc construction, 'they will burn and set on fire'; (2) cataloguing seven kinds of weapons to be burned; (3) citing the practical benefit the pile of weapons offered the Israelites – they provide firewood in a fuel-poor region; (4) recognizing the irony of the situation: the plunderers (*cf.* 38:12-13) have become the plundered, and vice versa. Those who had not raised a finger in their own defence may now divide the booty that has been delivered to their doorstep. The combination of these four elements creates a picture of utter and total destruction of the enemies' military hardware. Never again would these foes from the distant regions of the earth threaten God's people.

Frame 7: The Burial of Gog (39:11-16)
The opening date-notice marks the beginning of a new frame and reminds the prophet's audience of the chronological distance between the present and the events of the Gog oracle. Verses 11-13 focus on the activity of the Israelites, who go out *en masse* to bury the remains of Gog's armies. The corpses of the enemy strewn about 'the mountains of Israel' present the Israelites with a series of problems. First, since these are the bodies of Yahweh's enemies and the foes of his people, shall they be dignified with a proper burial, or left out in the open, exposed to scavenging animals and the elements? Second, given the massive numbers of the slain, which burial ground has room for all these bodies? Third, since the victims are all foreigners,

shall they be buried within the land of Israel, or deposited outside its borders to preserve the sanctity of the land? The aim of verses 11-13 is to answer these questions. Formally, these verses resemble an edict, issued by a superior to his servants, containing precise instructions for carrying out a mission. Each verse deals with a different aspect of the enterprise.

The answer to the first question is immediately obvious: yes, the remains of Yahweh's enemies must be buried in a mass burial site appointed by Yahweh 'in Israel', east of the sea, presumably the Mediterranean. The place is specifically identified as גֵּי הָעֹבְרִים, which is best treated as 'the valley of those who have passed on', that is deceased heroes,[82] referred to elsewhere as רְפָאִים.[83] When the corpses of Gog and his horde are gathered, the site will be renamed גֵּיא הֲמוֹן גּוֹג, 'the Valley of Hamon-Gog'. The name appears to play on גֵּי הִגֹּם, 'the valley of Hinnom', where the bodies of animals and criminals used to be burned.[84] From now on this place will serve as a permanent memorial to the destruction of the enemies of Yahweh and Israel.

Verses 12-13 describe the effects of the burial of Gog's remains. First, the land will be cultically purified. The observation that the process will take a full week of months, rather than the week of days prescribed in Numbers 19, speaks not only of the magnitude of the task, but also of the concern to render the land absolutely holy. Second, the enthusiasm of the people for the task, and the scrupulosity with which they bury the enemy will testify to their passion for the purity of the land and to their new-found security in Yahweh. Third, and most importantly, their actions will result in the public glorification of Yahweh. After all, the day of Gog is Yahweh's day.

---

[82]M. H. Pope (review of Spronk, *Beatific Afterlife*, UF 19 [1987], 462) describes the עֹבְרִים as 'those who cross over the boundary separating them from the living so that from the viewpoint of the living they "go over" rather than "come over".'

[83]So S. Ribichini and P. Xella, '"La valle dei passanti" (Ezechiele 39:11)', UF 12 (1980), 434-447; K. Spronk, *Beatific Afterlife in Ancient Israel and in the Ancient Near East* (AOAT; Neukirchen-Vluyn: Neukirchener Verlag, 1986), 229-230; M. H. Pope, 'Notes on the Rephaim Texts from Ugarit', in M. de Jong Ellis (ed.), *Essays on the Ancient Near East in Memory of Jacob Joel Finkelstein* (MCAAS 19; Hamden: Archon, 1977), 173-175. Though Ezekiel is not averse to speaking about the residents of the netherworld (*cf.* הַגִּבּוֹרִים, 'the mighty men', 32:27), for reasons unknown he avoids the term רְפָאִים. Perhaps it bore too many pagan associations, or was too closely tied to the cult of the dead.

[84]*Cf.* Zimmerli, *Ezekiel 2*, 316-317.

Verses 14-16 expand on the theme raised in verse 12, highlighting how the absolute purification of the land is achieved. A standing commission shall be appointed to supervise the burial of Gog's remains. These men shall pass up and down the length of the land for seven months, inspecting every corner for remnants of the vanquished warriors. Whenever the inspectors discover so much as a bone of the enemy on the surface of the ground, they are to mark the spot with a sign-post. Finally, sextons shall follow the supervisors, and transport the bones to the Valley of Hamon Gog to be buried.

The reiteration of the name of the site as Hamonah in verse 16 constitutes the punch line of the frame.[85] Although critical scholars in the past have tended to delete וְגַם שֵׁם עִיר הֲמוֹנָה, 'actually Hamonah is a city name', as a gloss,[86] or emended it to yield a better sense,[87] the statement performs an emphatic function. Whether the clause was added at the oral stage, or at the time of transcription, it offers an additional clue to the riddle: where are all these bodies to be buried? The answer, in a city called Hamonah.[88] Based on Ezekiel's use of הֲמוֹנָה elsewhere, the 'Valley of Hamon-Gog' speaks of the tumultuous pomp of Gog and his hordes, and recalls the usage of the term in previous oracles against foreign nations, especially the final oracle against Egypt.[89] But the association of the term with Jerusalem in three earlier judgment oracles is especially instructive. The present form is linked assonantally with 7:12-14, where הֲמוֹנָה had functioned

---

[85]See M. S. Odell, 'The City of Hamonah in Ezekiel 39:11-16: The Tumultuous City of Jerusalem', *CBQ* 56 (1994), 479-489.

[86]*BHS*; Zimmerli, *Ezekiel 2*, 293; even generally conservative D. Barthélemy *et al.* (eds.), *Preliminary and Interim Report on the Hebrew Old Testament Text Project*, Vol. 5, *Prophetical Books II: Ezekiel, Daniel, Twelve Minor Prophets* (New York: United Bible Societies, 1980), 130. For an explanation of how the gloss might have appeared in the text see L. C. Allen, *Ezekiel 20-48* (WBC 29; Dallas: Word, 1990), 202.

[87]*REB*, 'no more will be heard of that great horde', is based on Driver's proposed emendation ('Linguistic and Textual Problems: Ezekiel', *Bib* [1938], 5-87): שֶׁמַע הֲמוֹנָ֑ יִ וְגָמַר.

[88]Syntactically the P-S structure, with P indefinite relative to S, signals a non-circumstantial verbless clause of classification (*cf.* F. I. Andersen, *The Hebrew Verbless Clause in the Pentateuch* [JBLMS 14; Nashville: Abingdon, 1970], 42-46). Gn. 28:19 reverses the sequence of common and proper nouns: לוּז שֵׁם־הָעִיר לָרִאשֹׁנָה וְאוּלָם, 'but actually the name of the city was previously Luz'. The addition of the adverbial modifier, מִיֹּום, the addition of גַם, and the absence of the article on עִיר distinguish this statement from the final declaration of this book (48:35), call for a different interpretation.

[89]*Cf.* Hossfeld, *Untersuchungen*, 472-473; Bodi, *Ezekiel and the Poem of Erra*, 119-120.

as a shorthand expression for all of Jerusalem's riotous and rebellious behaviour.[90] According to 5:7, Jerusalem's הֲמוֹן, expressed in a refusal to follow the covenant demands and all kinds of abominations, had exceeded the tumult of all the surrounding nations. Some of these nations appear in 23:40-42, bringing their own base and boisterous ways right into the city of Jerusalem, at her invitation. Here too Hamonah stands for Jerusalem. But as in 23:4 and 48:35, Ezekiel uses a symbolic name, highlighting a particular characteristic of the place. In the present context Hamonah's primary function is to memorialize the demise of Israel's last and greatest enemy. However, by association it also memorializes the transformation of the city, and with it the nation. The people who had once superseded the pagan nations with their tumultuous arrogance and rebellion now impress the world with their scrupulous adherence to the will of Yahweh. Once the city (and the entire land) has been purged of every vestige of defilement, the stage is set for Yahweh to return (43:1-7) and replace the retrospective name for a new forward looking (מִיּוֹם) one. Hamonah is gone; 'Yahweh is there!' (48:35)

The seventh frame concludes by reiterating that the primary concern in all this human activity is the cleansing of the land. Yahweh is not satisfied with having defeated Gog and his allies; so long as their corpses are visible, the land remains unclean. A totally restored covenant relationship demands a God with a holy name, a holy people and a holy land.

Frame 8: The Devouring of Gog (39:17-20)

The placement of the scene described in the final frame in this sequence of literary caricatures after the burial of Gog creates certain logical and logistical problems, but the reader is reminded that this is a literary cartoon, and realism has been sacrificed for rhetorical effect. Indeed, as the oracle has progressed the scenes have become increasingly bizarre, climaxing here in a spectacle more fantastic than all. Like political caricatures, this frame is not to be interpreted as prophetic literary photography, but as an impressionistic literary sketch.

The entire frame is cast in the form of an official invitation to special guests to attend a grand banquet hosted by Yahweh. The style may be formal, almost poetic, but the imagery is grotesque, as the prophet invites all kinds of carnivorous and scavenging creatures to

---

[90]While the oracle is directed against the land as a whole, the activities described in the text are basically urban, and the city is specifically mentioned in verses 15 and 23.

an enormous banquet that he has prepared for them. His picture
recalls other prophetic texts, in which an overwhelming victory is
followed by a *zeba* meal.[91] Ezekiel's designation of this banquet as a
zeba classifies it as a ritual event,[92] but the normal image of a *zeba* is
caricatured by altering all the roles. In place of a human worshipper
slaughtering animals in the presence of Yahweh, Yahweh slaughters
humans for the sake of animals, who gather from all over the world
for this gigantic celebration (זֶבַח גָּדוֹל) on the mountains of Israel. The
battlefield has been transformed into a huge sacrificial table. In place
of the flesh of rams, male goats, bulls and fatlings of Bashan, this
table is spread with an abundance of flesh, fat and blood of 'heroic
figures' and princes of the earth. Verses 19-20 paint a picture of
unrestrained gluttony at Yahweh's table, concluding with a reminder
of the true sacrificial victims: all the participants in the previous
battle against Yahweh, including the horses. The literary image
sketched here must have been shocking for a person as sensitive to
cultic matters as Ezekiel, but how the priestly prophet reacted to this
horrifying image we may only speculate.

The Final Word (verses 21-29)
Although scholars tend to dismiss verses 21-29 as a series of late
editorial additions,[93] verses 21-24 and 25-29 are best viewed as two

---

[91]*Cf.* Is. 34:6-8 and especially Zp. 1:7 with which this banquet displays
remarkable affinities. These banquets are reminiscent of two divinely hosted *dbḥ*
meals referred to in Ugaritic texts:

UT 51 iii:17-22 (*ANET*, 132):
> For two kinds of banquets (*dbḥm*) Baal hates,
> Three the Rider of the clouds:
> A banquet (*dbḥ*) of shamefulness,
> A banquet (*dbḥ*) of baseness,
> And a banquet (*dbḥ*) of a handmaid's lewdness.

Krt A:73-79 (*ANET*, 143):
> Go up to the top of the tower;
> Climb to the top of the wall;
> Lift up your hands to heaven,
> Sacrifice (*dbḥ*) to Bull, your father El;
> Cause Baal to come down with your sacrifice (*dbḥ*);
> The son of Dagan with your game.

[92]The word could apply to burnt (עוֹלָה), peace (שְׁלָמִים), grain (מִנְחָה), purification
(חַטָּאת), and reparation (אָשָׁם) offerings.

[93]For a summary of recent approaches and a more detailed analysis of this text
see D. I. Block, 'Gog and the Pouring Out of the Spirit: Reflections on Ezekiel
XXXIX 21-29', *VT* 37 (1987), 257-261.

halves of a whole, displaying remarkable structural balance and symmetry, as the following synopsis illustrates:

Topic	39: 21-14	39:25-29
A The Actions of Yahweh	21a	25
B The Response of the Objects of his Action	21b	26-27
B' The Recognition Formula(tied to Israel's exile)	22-23a	28
A' The Hiding of Yahweh's Face	23b-24	29

In addition to their parallel structures, each segment is organized internally on a chiastic pattern. Both begin and end with descriptions of the divine action, between which are sandwiched the humans' responses.[94] Each ends with a reference to Yahweh hiding His face, a notion that is otherwise foreign to the book. But in content the two parts diverge, exhibiting a relationship to each other as that of 'a dialectic of action and response'.[95] The first describes Yahweh's action of judgment in response to Israel's rebellion; the second His salvific activity on her behalf, and the response this evokes in the nation. In the first recognition formula, the nations primarily recognize Yahweh; in the second Israel does so. In effect, even if not in style, verses 20-29 perform the same function in relation to chapter 39 as 38:23 had served in relation to chapter 38. Each represents a summary statement of Yahweh's designs in handling His people.

In verses 21-24 the prophet describes the impact of Yahweh's judgmental activity: the nations will experience the justice and power of Yahweh. However, recognizing that Ezekiel's primary audience consists of fellow exiles, and it is their transformation that he seeks, the prophet interrupts his observation concerning the nations with a modified version of the recognition formula to announce the implications for Israel of the victory over the military hordes: from that day and onwards they will acknowledge Yahweh. The defeat of Gog would mark a turning point in the nation's history. Although the statement considers the Gog debacle an event in the distant future (*cf.* 38:8, 16), it apparently does not occur at the end of time. Rather it signals the beginning of a new era, which will be characterized by Israel's recognition of Yahweh and the full realization of covenant relationship.

From the perspective of the battle of Gog, the events described in verses 23-24 are in the distant past. The people of Israel have returned to their land and have lived securely in it for many

---

[94]H. van dyke Parunak (*Structural Studies in Ezekiel* [Ph.D. Dissertation, Harvard University; Ann Arbor: University Microfilms, 1983], 506) recognizes the following pattern: A (verses 22-24), B (verses 25-27), A' (verses 28-29).
[95]Thus Odell, 'Are You He of Whom I Spoke?', 151.

years. Now, after the defeat of Gog, the nations will realize that all
the events preceding this restoration had in fact fulfilled the laws of
divine justice. Because of the nation's perversion (עָוֹן), covenantal
infidelity (מָעַל), defiling sacrilege (טֻמְאָה) and covenant betrayal
(פֶּשַׁע), the Israelites had been exiled from their land. Witnessing
Yahweh's harsh treatment of His people, the nations had concluded
that Yahweh was either incompetent to defend His people against
Nebuchadnezzar, or He had gone back on His own covenant
commitment to them. Because neither of these explanations was true,
His reputation had been profaned. Now they realize that Israel had
brought this fate on herself. Their wickedness had provoked Him to
hide His face and deliver them into the hands of their enemies. As it
turns out, the devastation of Jerusalem and the exile of Judah's
population was neither a function of the superior military strength of
the Babylonian forces, nor a reflection of Marduk's superiority over
Yahweh. This was the result of Yahweh's own deliberate action
against His own people. Accordingly, the glory of Yahweh will be
established when the nations recognize the justice of Yahweh's
dealings with His own people in the past and His dealings with them
in the present.

Having highlighted the justice of Yahweh in His judgmental
actions, in verses 25-29 Ezekiel's focus turns to the impact of
Yahweh's saving activity. Fortunately for Israel, the judgment could
not be the last word. The same covenant which had warned the
nation of the consequences of persistent apostasy also declared that
Yahweh would not abandon His people for ever. He had promised
He would not forget His covenant with His people.[96] By now the
connection with Gog has disappeared completely. This is a message
for Israel – the Israel of Ezekiel's own day. The divine speech opens
abruptly with עַתָּה, 'Now', snatching the hearers' attention away
from the distant utopian future, and bringing them to the very real
needs of the present. The interest is no longer in 'the latter years'
(38:7), or 'the latter days' (38:16), but on today; not in 'that day'
(38:10, 14, 18, 19; 39:8, 11), or 'from that day and onward' (39:22), but
now. Ezekiel ends this remarkable oracle with a glorious word of
grace for a despairing people, wondering how and when all the
events described in the previous six chapters might be fulfilled.

Verse 25 is thematic, announcing that Yahweh's mercy[97] and
passion (קִנְאָה) will win out over His wrath as He restores the
fortunes of Jacob. In verses 26-27 Ezekiel expands on these two ideas.

---

[96]Lv. 26:44-46; cf. Dt. 4:30-31.
[97]The verb רחם occurs only here in the book.

Far from being a source of pride at having been selected as the objects of divine compassion, Israel's experience of grace will lead to a recognition of their own unworthiness. The prophet, speaking for Yahweh, then elaborates on the notion of publicly vindicating Yahweh's holy reputation. Yahweh's actions toward His people, both punitive and salvific, are played out before the world-wide audience. Verse 28 describes the effect of this action on the nations in one final recognition formula, greatly elaborated to highlight the covenantal aspect of this new day of grace. At the heart of the international awareness this time is not only the knowledge of Yahweh, but also the recognition of Israel as His covenant people. They will realize that it was as their covenant Lord that He had sent them off into exile among them. And it is as covenant Lord that Yahweh brings them back to their own land – every one of them!

The oracle concludes with one more surprising twist, as Ezekiel transforms what had been for him a stereotypical threat of judgment, 'I will pour out my wrath', into a glorious gospel message, 'I will pour out my Spirit.' While the idiom בְ רוּחִי וְנָתַתִּי, 'I will put my spirit in . . . ', in 36:27 had associated the divine action with the rebirth/revitalization of Israel,[98] the divine Spirit poured out upon the nation serves as a sign and seal of the covenant, Yahweh's mark of ownership.[99] This accounts for His intervention on behalf of His people against Gog before the latter may so much as touch them.

Conclusion

By way of summary, Ezekiel's aim in proclaiming this remarkable oracle of Gog and his hordes has been to provide his audience with specific and concrete proof that Yahweh meant exactly what He said. The oracle looks forward to a time when the promises of restoration found in chapters 34–37 have been realized and Israel is prospering and secure in her land in the latter days (38:6,16). Into this pacific and tranquil land Yahweh deliberately brings these hordes from the north (38:49), who imagine themselves to be operating of their own free will (38:10-13). However, like Pharaoh of Egypt in Exodus 7–14, Gog is an agent called to fulfil the revelatory purposes of Yahweh. That purpose has two dimensions: to declare the greatness, holiness and

---

[98]Cf. Ezekiel's fuller exposition of this notion in 37:1-14. For discussion of the Spirit as divine animating agency see D. I. Block, 'The Prophet of the Spirit: The Use of *rwḥ* in the Book of Ezekiel', *JETS* 32 (1989), 34-41.
[99]Cf. Block, *ibid.*, 46-48.

glory of Yahweh's person, on the one hand,[100] and the firmness of
His commitment to His people, on the other.[101] The defence of this
people, who did not need so much as to lift a sword, vindicates His
great name while at the same time confirming His word. The
presence of the Spirit of Yahweh poured out upon the returned exiles
guarantees that He would never leave any of the house of Israel at
the mercy of her enemies, and that He would never hide His face
from them, as the contemporaries of Ezekiel had just witnessed. In
short, Gog becomes the agent through whom Yahweh declares
concretely that the tragedy of 586 BC will never be repeated.

In declaring this word concerning Gog, Ezekiel calls upon all
who read it to recognize five themes: First, Yahweh is the unrivalled
Lord of human history. He raises up nations; He puts them down.
Their activities are always subservient to His agenda. Second,
Yahweh's reputation is linked to the status and well-being of His
people. So long as they are mired in bondage and subservience to
alien powers His holiness and glory stand in question. Third,
Yahweh keeps His covenant. He does not forget the commitments He
has made to His people and will not abandon the faithful in their
hour of need. As a seal of His commitment He pours out His Spirit
upon them. Fourth, above all else, Yahweh is a God of grace and
mercy, who reaches out to those who have rebelled against Him and
offers not only forgiveness, but the full benefits of covenant
relationship. Finally, this oracle reminds us that for the believer the
experience of divine grace is a humbling experience. Far from feeding
egotistical ambitions and a misguided thirst for self-esteem, or from
blinding one to one's sinful past, it evokes in the recipient intense
feelings of unworthiness.

---

[100] 38:16, 23; 39:7, 13, 21, 25, 27.
[101] 38:14-16; 39:7, 22-29.

Section C

NEW TESTAMENT

Chapter 5

'LET THE READER UNDERSTAND': TEMPLE AND ESCHATOLOGY IN MARK[1]

Kent E. Brower

Mark's eschatology is centred on Jesus and His death, which is linked to the temple. Opposition to God's kingdom leads to the passion narrative; the passion narrative leads to the destruction of the temple. Since God's judgment was inaugurated on the temple system in the death of Jesus, its fate was sealed. This, however, is not the culmination of things ('the End'). For Mark, the very destruction of the Temple is confirmation that God's purposes are now centred in Jesus and the new people of God. These purposes are being accomplished and vindication will follow. In the face of an attenuated End, Jesus' words to his disciples are still vital: 'What I say to you, I say to all: Keep awake' (13:37).

Introduction

Eschatology is a notoriously slippery word for which a bewildering variety of definitions confronts us. All of them, however, have the thread of τέλος running through them. In that light, perhaps no harm can be done by adding one more broad definition, namely, 'the direction and goal of God's active covenant faithfulness in and for His created order.' This essay is an attempt to make some contribution to understanding how Mark saw this action. Four preliminary points need to be made.

[1] Thanks are offered to the Warden of St Deiniol's Library, Harwarden, for a two-week residential scholarship in support of this research.

First, this essay takes a text-centred, narrative-critical approach to the Gospel of Mark.[2] Narrative approaches to the gospels have been shown to be particularly illuminating in uncovering a level of meaning which may have been obscured through other approaches.[3] Stylistic features in Mark itself encourage a narrative-critical approach[4] with an obvious instance in the text cited in our title: 13:14, 'Let the reader understand'.[5]

Perhaps this approach may clarify some aspects of Mark's eschatology[6] which, in turn, may inform and even correct some modern notions, some of which seem to have a rather tenuous relationship with New Testament eschatology.

But what of the sociological context of Mark's readers? Several scholars have drawn attention to the importance of 'story' in biblical studies.[7] All groups of people, including the early Christians, have a

---

[2]See Stephen H. Smith, *A Lion with Wings: A Narrative Critical Approach to Mark's Gospel* (The Biblical Seminar 38; Sheffield: SAP, 1996) for a comprehensive survey and bibliography of scholars who have used this method to good effect as well as to see Smith's own contribution. Smith gives a timely reminder that our conclusions will be those of 'a contemporary, print-conscious readership, and not those of a first-century oral-conscious community hearing the text for the first time' (33). See also Mark Powell, *What is Narrative Criticism? A New Approach to the Bible* (London: SPCK, 1993).

[3]See T. J. Geddert's illuminating *Watchwords: Mark 13 in Markan Eschatology* (JSNTSS 26; Sheffield: JSOT, 1989). See also K. E. Brower, *The Old Testament in the Markan Passion Narrative* (Unpublished Ph.D. Thesis, The University of Manchester, 1978), 'Mark 9:1 Seeing the Kingdom in Power', *JSNT* 6 (1980), 17-41, and 'Elijah in the Markan Passion Narrative', *JSNT* 18 (1983), 85-101. A controlled reading of the gospel, which takes the intention of the implied author seriously as a first-century document addressed to his implied readers, also in the first century allows modern readers to hear the same message and apply it to their own lives today.

[4]See, for example, Joanna Dewey, *Markan Public Debate: Literary Technique, Concentric Structure and Theology in Mark 2:1–3:6* (SBLDS 48; Chico: Scholars, 1980) and the wealth of examples given by Smith.

[5]Some scholars think this narrator's note is another way of saying, 'let the scriptures be fulfilled' and thereby draws attention to Daniel as the interpretative key to chapter 13. See Smith, 30, n. 43. But important though Daniel is as background to this passage and other Markan texts, this is not persuasive. See M. A. Beavis, *Mark's Audience: The Literary and Social Setting of Mark 4:11-12* (JSNTSS 33; Sheffield: JSOT, 1989), 40, who supports the view taken here.

[6]See G. B. Caird and L. D. Hurst, *New Testament Theology* (Oxford: Clarendon, 1994) as an example of bringing a variety of witnesses to the table for discussion. Mark is one of those witnesses.

[7]See, for example, D. Rhoades and D. Michie, *Mark as Story: An Introduction to the Narrative of a Gospel* (Philadelphia: Fortress, 1982); W. G. Kelber, *Mark's Story of Jesus* (Philadelphia: Fortress, 1979) and N. T. Wright, *The New Testament and the*

story, a history which they hold as the common thread of their identity. Stories are coherent and need to be read or heard as a whole. Although there is considerable evidence that Mark was originally written to be read in an oral performance,[8] this essay will not focus on the notion of 'story', nor on 'orality'. For our purposes, the important point is the need to hear and read Mark as a connected and coherent whole.[9]

Second, the approach taken here is non-technical. It will simply attempt to read afresh the communication of the 'implied author' (that is, the author as revealed within the text) to the 'implied readers' (that is, to the readers as they seem to be envisaged by the implied author). Such an approach does not depend upon accurate identification of the actual author nor precise determination of the first readers or the destination of the gospel. Nor does this approach depend upon tracing the pre-history of the text or determining the historicity of the events within the text. But neither does this approach ignore the historical setting. References to characters or events in the text, therefore, are primarily to their description in the text.

Third, this essay assumes that Mark tells the story of Jesus for more than antiquarian interests. There are many indications that Mark, by telling the story of Jesus and His disciples in the face of opposition, wishes to encourage his readers, confirming to them that vindication will come if they are faithful in proclaiming God's purposes, the gospel, in word and deed (see 8:34-38; 10:29; 14:9).

Fourth, this essay has a rather limited scope, namely, the place of the temple in Mark's eschatology. Clearly, a full discussion of Markan eschatology would require attention to a much wider range of topics, not least the vast subjects of the kingdom of God and the Son of Man. If eschatology is rather more narrowly defined as the

---

People of God. Christian Origins and the Question of God 1 (London: SPCK, 1992, reprinted with corrections, 1993).

[8]See W. G. Kelber, *The Oral and the Written Gospel* (Philadelphia: Fortress, 1983) and T. Haverley, *Oral Tradition Literature and the Composition of Mark's Gospel* (Unpublished Ph.D. Thesis, The University of Edinburgh, 1983).

[9]In our anxiety to avoid making Mark into a modern author working with a laptop, it is important not to diminish the quality and character of his achievement. See B. L. Mack, *A Myth of Innocence* (Philadelphia: Fortress, 1988), 321: 'In modern critical parlance, Mark's Gospel is a very richly textured story. Its most distinctive feature is the complexity of what critics call intertextuality. . . . It was created by effort, intellectual effort, and it is marked by conscious authorial intention. Mark was a scholar. A reader of texts and a writer of texts.' Although many of Mack's conclusions are fanciful, his observation on the text of Mark is valuable.

doctrine of last things, with 'last things' being understood as wholly future and usually apocalyptically conceived events at the end of time,[10] then chapter 13 is the natural starting point. But that is not the definition of eschatology used here. Chapter 13, whatever its origin – Jesus, unknown tradent, Mark himself – has a temple setting in Mark's narrative which should be taken seriously. Chapter 13 will, therefore, be considered only as one contribution to Mark's eschatology.

Mark, Jerusalem and the Temple

Jerusalem as a city is of little significance to Mark; before holy week, it is mentioned by name only six times, two of which describe the point of origin of scribes (3:27; 7:1), two further times in the third passion prediction (10:32, 33), once to describe the origin of people who came to be baptized by John (1:5) and once as the home of part of the multitude who followed Jesus (3:8). Before holy week, Jesus' ministry is centred on the Sea of Galilee and its surrounding cities and territories. Even in holy week, Jerusalem is important primarily because of the temple and the religious establishment. Mark is very conscious of the importance of the temple as the locus of the holy God's dwelling amongst His people, the centre of the sacrificial system and the national shrine.[11] For Mark, Jerusalem, the temple and the religious establishment are inseparable; they are also the subject of his critique.

Although there are rare glimpses that this is not the entire picture, the sense of conflict with Jerusalem is never far from the surface as the narrative progresses. In 3:22, it is scribes from Jerusalem who accuse Jesus of being possessed by Beelzebul. The debate over purity is again with scribes from Jerusalem (7:1). Then, when Jesus begins His journey to Jerusalem from Caesarea Philippi, Mark identifies the opponents of Jesus more specifically in two of the three passion predictions, 8:31 and 10:3. In these, Mark specifically names the chief priests, scribes and elders as those who would be instrumental in Jesus' death. Mark also has subtle ways of indicating

---

[10]Whether Mark and his readers expected the end of the space–time universe can be doubted. See N. T. Wright (*Jesus and the Victory of God. Christian Origins and the Question of God 2* [London: SPCK, 1996], 345), who states that 'there was no reason whatsoever for them [Jesus and other first century Jews] to be thinking about the end of the space–time universe'. If Wright and others are right, a whole plethora of modern 'Late, Great Planet Earth' notions are called into question.
[11]See Wright, *Jesus and the Victory*, 406-412.

his critique of the temple system. The first reference to Jerusalem (1:5) has 'all the people of Jerusalem' (but presumably not the temple authorities or the Pharisees) coming to be baptized for the forgiveness of sins. Hints of conflict to come already appear, for this baptism was completely outside the established provisions for forgiveness of sins within the temple sacrificial system.[12]

The conflict, of course, is wider than simply with those from Jerusalem. Modern scholarship has given us a far clearer picture of second-temple Judaism in general and the historical Pharisees in particular than we had even twenty-five years ago.[13] Thankfully, gone from scholarly discussion is the caricature of a hidebound, legalistic and bankrupt Judaism and a hypocritical Pharisaism which, unfortunately, still exist in all too much of popular Christian preaching. But a narrative reading of the gospel cannot ignore the Markan picture of a rapidly deteriorating relationship between Jesus and the Pharisees which comes to a head early in the narrative. The Pharisees consider Jesus to be blasphemous, pronouncing forgiveness of sins, once again outside the prescribed means of grace; perhaps the Herodians already perceive Him as a danger to the temple establishment. By 3:6, the Pharisees have already conspired with the Herodians to destroy Jesus. By chapter four, the Pharisees and other 'insiders' including His natural family, are already outside of Jesus' circle (see 3:31). Initially, the conflict with the Pharisees has nothing overtly to do with the temple authorities; they are simply joining forces with the Herodians in a common cause. Even so, at this stage, they seem to be strange bed-fellows. Mark makes two other links between the Pharisees and these persons before the passion narrative itself: in 8:15, he warns against the leaven of the Pharisees and of Herod, and in 12:13, the Pharisees and the Herodians are in the temple looking for a way to trap Jesus. Thus, by the time we reach holy week, we are not surprised when the complicity of the Pharisees with the temple authorities is exposed as they act at the behest of the religious establishment, the chief priests and the scribes. Once we

---

[12]See R. L. Webb, *John the Baptizer and Prophet: A Socio-Historical Study* (JSNTSS 62; Sheffield: SAP, 1991) and Wright, *Jesus and the Victory*, 160-162. The conflict may involve some rural/urban, Galilee/ Judaea aspects, but attempts to reduce it to them are simplistic.

[13]In the last two decades, a renewed interest in the historical Jesus (see Wright, *Jesus and the Victory*, chap. 3, 83-124) has been matched by the application of text-centred approaches to the gospels. Although this paper focuses on Mark's eschatology, his message is very close to that of the historical Jesus as shown in the work of the 'Third Questers'. See also Ben Witherington III, *The Jesus Quest: The Third Quest for the Jew of Nazareth* (Downers Grove: IVP, 1995).

recall the fact that Herod's major achievement and, perhaps, the source of his claim to be the rightful occupant of the throne of David was the temple he was building, this puzzling collaboration between the Pharisees and the Herodians becomes clearer.[14] It is also important to note, however, that the Pharisees are not named as part of the condemnation of Jesus, although historically they formed part of the συνέδριον. Rather, the temple establishment, the high priest, the chief priests and the scribes deliver Jesus to Pilate.

When Jesus has finished His teaching in the temple but before the final act of the drama, the passion narrative itself, He offers a major piece of teaching to His disciples specifically concerning the fate of the temple. The temple embodies the religious establishment, the whole sacrificial system, the means and centre of purity and holiness, the hopes and aspirations of the people of God.[15] But if Jesus were to announce that God's promises for His people were already being fulfilled in His message and activity (1:15-16) and were to invite people to enter the new covenant community (1:16ff; 3:13; 14:24), apart from the temple system, then conflict with the temple authorities would be inevitable. Unless Israel itself recognized who He was and joined the new people of God, the beginning of the good news would inevitably end in the passion narrative and ultimately, in the destruction of the temple. That is precisely what we find in Mark's narrative.[16]

---

[14]See W. Horbury, 'Herod's Temple and "Herod's Days"', in W. Horbury (ed.), *Templum Amicitiae* (JSNTSS 48; Sheffield: JSOT, 1991), 147, who suggests that 'this aspect of Herodian kingship [Herodian messianism] deserves further consideration among the antecedents of the Christ cult'. See also Wright, *Jesus and the Victory, passim.*

[15]The temple frequently is a cypher for the religious authorities, not unlike the statement sometimes heard in the UK, 'The Palace has announced . . .' referring, of course, to an announcement by an official speaking on behalf of Her Majesty.

[16]See P. G. Bolt, 'Mark 13: An Apocalyptic Precursor to the Passion Narrative', *Reformed Theological Review* 54 (1995), 10.32. Bolt argues that the wider context of Mark 13 does not have an anti-temple theme, but only an anti-religious authorities theme. Bolt is, of course, correct in what he affirms. But there is an underlying and implicit anti-temple motif shown by setting of 11:1–13:3 in the temple or its environs. It comes to explicit expression in 13:2. Bolt minimizes the importance of the setting and 13:2. Nor can one ignore the fact that Jewish nationalism, the temple and Judaism were intertwined in the second temple period in such a way that it is virtually impossible to discuss the temple authorities without including the temple itself. The destruction of the temple itself was directly related to the nationalistic direction of Judaism, which ended in the Jewish War of AD 66. Mark saw (or anticipated) this event as more than a mere political curiosity and, as Wright, *Jesus and the Victory*, 362, states, 'Jesus

The End of the Beginning: ΝΑΟΣ and Passion Narrative

Scholars have long noted that Mark uses two different words for temple but does not use them interchangeably. Before the passion narrative, the term used is ἱερόν, referring to the whole temple complex without reference to any specific part of the temple. When he uses ναός, it seems fairly clear that Mark thinks of the inner sanctuary of the temple.

ναός occurs three times in the passion narrative, all closely connected. The first occurs on the lips of Jesus' accusers in their testimony against Jesus; the second in 15:29 is on the lips of the παραπορευόμενοι; the final occurrence is used by the narrator in the death scene. The choice seems to be deliberate and significant. In the passion narrative, Mark focuses on the inner sanctuary. Mark's passion narrative is replete with echoes and allusions to the Old Testament; there is little doubt that the Old Testament gives significance to the sanctuary.[17] The inner sanctuary was the holy of holies, the locus of God's dwelling amongst His people and the central focus of worship. Although there appears to be a wide variety of views about the sanctity of the actual temple in second-temple Judaism, G. I. Davies suggests 'belief in the divine presence in the second-temple was much more widespread than is commonly allowed'.[18] The temple, then, was intimately connected with the purposes of God for His people. Against this background, Mark's critique begins to show how he understands the unfolding of God's new purposes.

The Accusation

'We heard him saying "I will destroy this ναός made with hands and after three days I will build another not made with hands" '(14:58).

There are a number of interesting aspects to the accusation against Jesus in 14:55-61. First, Mark seems to be at pains to state that the testimony against Jesus was borne by false witness against Him: ἐψευδομαρτύρουν κατ᾽ αὐτοῦ. But in precisely what way is the witness against Jesus false? Crucially, the Markan Jesus does not deny the

---

staked his reputation on his prediction of the Temple's fall within a generation; if and when it fell, he would thereby be vindicated.'

[17]See W. R. Telford, 'More Fruit from the Withered Tree: Temple and Fig-Tree in Mark from a Graeco-Roman Perspective', *Templum Amicitiae*, 264-304, who reminds us of the Graeco-Roman context as well.

[18]G. I. Davies, 'The Presence of God in the Second Temple and Rabbinic Doctrine', *Templum Amicitiae*, 33.

accusations.[19] As noted earlier, Jesus has already been in conflict with the temple establishment, culminating in their expressed desire to have Him arrested (12:12). Then, he has given an extensive sketch of the prospects for the people of God and the vindication of the Son of Man in the context of predicting the dire fate of the temple. Such strident critique of the temple, of course, was as old as the prophets: the Markan Jesus had plenty of precedent in Jeremiah. Some sects of second-temple Judaism were even prepared to withdraw completely from the temple until it could be properly purified and return to the holy place fit for God's dwelling which was its intended purpose.[20]

We must, therefore, return to the question again: in what way is this witness false? R. E. Brown summarizes the scholarly suggestions in his monumental *The Death of the Messiah*.[21] First, the witness is false because the witnesses themselves could not agree precisely on what Jesus said. This suggestion may be technically correct but, according to Mark, Jesus' teaching and action give rise to just such a widely held view, at least according to 15:29. Second, Jesus did not say anything like this at all, or at least, He only said part of the statement; thus, χειροποίητον...ἀχειροποίητον is inauthentic. Third, the witnesses completely misunderstood Jesus' words. The misunderstanding could have been the emphasis that Jesus himself (note the emphatic ἐγώ) would destroy the ναός. Or, alternatively it could have been the bald statement, 'I will destroy this temple and after three days will build it again,' which was false, to which Mark added, from the Jesus tradition, the corrective χειροποίητον . . . ἀχειροποίητον; in short, χειροποίητον . . . ἀχειροποίητον is authentic Jesus material. Brown is not fully satisfied with any of these solutions, but at this point in Mark's passion narrative simply thinks that 'in 14:58 the readers are meant to see the depth of the hostility toward Jesus in such false testimony that make him appear like an apocalyptic fanatic'.[22] Clearly, hostility to Jesus is building to a

---

[19]Since there are a number of echos from Isaiah in the passion narrative, this could be little more than a deliberate allusion to the silence of the Isaianic lamb (Is. 53:7). But that is probably not a sufficient explanation.

[20]See J. P. M. Sweet, 'A Temple not made with Hands', *Templum Amicitiae*, 384, who notes that 'at Qumran, there was opposition not to the present Temple but to the present priesthood, and it is clear that they did not see their House of Holiness as a total and permanent replacement for the Temple.'

[21]R. E. Brown, *The Death of the Messiah* (New York/London: Doubleday/Geoffrey Chapman, 1994), 444-454.

[22]*Ibid.*, 453.

crescendo (14:1, 10-11). Aspects of the narrative itself show that it has reached the final stage in the opposition to Jesus.[23]

Brown's conclusion about mounting hostility is correct as far as it goes. But does it go far enough? It may also repay us to revisit his first suggestion, namely, that the witnesses were the problem, to see if it could be nuanced slightly differently. A dominant theme elsewhere in the passion narrative is the portrayal of Jesus as a righteous sufferer.[24] If this motif is also influential here, Mark may be noting that the witnesses are false, not because of the content of their testimony, but because they are testifying against Jesus. Jesus, as righteous sufferer, would inevitably suffer the accusations of false witnesses. Even if what they say is true (when interpreted correctly), those who oppose Jesus are false accusers by definition. If this is so, then the irony is that false witnesses who oppose Jesus actually bear true testimony (see also 1:24; 3:11 and elsewhere throughout the gospel).[25] The Markan Jesus does expect that the ναός will be destroyed and rebuilt. Mark confirms this by having Jesus remain silent before His accusers, just as He is silent before Pilate in 15:5.

But if the accusation is not false, in what sense does Mark consider it to be true? Heretofore in this narrative, it could be argued that the general critique of the temple is true, but the specific details as given and understood by the many who bear false witness were not. Mark is therefore introducing another nuance to the teaching of Jesus Himself, especially with this first use of ναός and the introduction of the χειροποίητον . . . ἀχειροποίητον contrast (see Acts 7:58). The critique of the temple ναός should not be understood primarily in physical terms. It points, rather, to the underlying purpose of the ναός as the dwelling place of God amongst His people. Mark confirms that the point is not primarily physical by the inter-play between διὰ τριῶν ἡμερῶν and χειροποίητον . . . ἀχειροποίητον. This was no ordinary human activity. It was an action beyond the bounds of human possibility – destruction and rebuilding, all in three days and without hands.

---

[23]While not decisive in themselves, the imperfect verbs ἐζήτουν (verse 55) and ἐψευδομαρτύρουν (verse 56) suggest the possibility that verse 55 may reflect the long standing policy of the Sanhedrin against Jesus (Mk. 3:6; 11:18; 14:1) as well as a clear indication of present activity. (See C. S. Emden, 'St Mark's Use of the Imperfect Tense', *ExpT* 65 [1953/4], 146-149).

[24]See Donald Juel, *Messiah and Temple* (SBLDS 31; Missoula: Scholars Press, 1977).

[25]Is it worth observing that the demons' confession of Jesus as 'the Holy One of God' and 'the Son of God' in 1:24 and 3:11 occur in narrative contexts very close to the call of the disciples, the foundation of the new covenant community?

The Mockery

'And those who passed by derided him, wagging their heads, and saying, "Aha! You who would destroy the ναός and build it in three days, save yourself and come down from the cross!"' (15:29-30).

Mark's next use of ναός occurs on the lips of the passers-by in 15:29. Their mockery is a variation of the accusation in 14:58. The scene and the words are full of irony, a technique put to masterful use by Mark, especially in his passion narrative.[26] The irony here is found in the fact that those who mock think that they are actually holding Jesus' manifestly false words (as they think) up to ridicule, while Mark and his readers know the words to be true in a way which the actors in the drama cannot comprehend. The mob mocks perhaps because they have been stirred up by the chief priests (15:11). The chief priests and scribes mock because they have long ago decided that Jesus was to be opposed, a dangerous blasphemer who uttered preposterous words. In their view, the crucifixion was the final proof of Jesus' folly. But Mark's readers know that nothing is as it seems to Jesus' opponents in the passion narrative.

The crucifixion scene is replete with images available to the perceptive reader. The important righteous sufferer motif, already noted earlier in the passion narrative, lies behind 15:22-24. Equally impressive is the range of descriptions and titles for Jesus contained in this section. All of them, on the story level, are points of mockery, but at the level of Mark and his readers, they are points of high irony and profound meaning. Mark's readers know that Jesus is indeed 'The King of the Jews' (15:26), that precisely by staying on the cross and giving His life, He is actually saving it (15:30, see 8:35) and that His power to save others is demonstrated in the cross itself (15:31). He is indeed 'the Messiah, the King of Israel' (15:32a) and in the crowning irony of all, the religious leaders ask to see so that they might believe at the precise moment when they are seeing, but failing to believe (15:32b).

This concentration of images in the crucifixion scene is important for Mark. But for our rather more limited purposes, the key aspect of the mockery centres around the ναός. Both the passers-by and the chief priest and scribes mock the seeming inability of Jesus to fulfil His own words concerning the ναός. Indeed, closer examination shows just how closely tied to the temple charge the whole crucifixion really was in Mark's view.

The tradition is unanimous that Jesus was not crucified alone. But is this fact sufficient explanation of Mark's inclusion of the others in his story? According to 15:27, He was crucified between two

---

[26]See Smith, *A Lion with Wings*, chap. 6 for a full discussion.

λησταὶ who then join Jesus' opponents in mocking Him (15:32c). At that point they disappear from Mark's narrative, presumably because they have no further part to play in the story, in contrast to Luke 23:39-43 and John 19:18, 32, both of whom use Jesus' fellow victims for a further purpose.

The three times that λησταὶ is used by Mark are all connected with the temple. In 11:17, Jesus states that the temple has become a 'den of λησταὶ', alluding to Jeremiah 7:11. At His arrest He asks, 'Have you come out as against a ληστὴν?' (14:48). Now, He is crucified between two λησταὶ, the references to whom bracket the mockery centred on the temple in the crucifixion scene (15:27, 32b). But what does Mark intend his readers to understand by this?

Translators have not done modern readers any favours by rendering the word λησταὶ as 'robbers' or 'thieves'. Neither of these English words convey the fact that the term λησταὶ was usually associated with violence. Almost certainly by the time of Mark's readers, it would have been more closely attached to the notion of 'revolutionary', itself perhaps sufficient reason for Luke to use the more general and politically neutral κακοῦργος instead.

One must exercise care here. According to Brown, although the term referred to violent men anytime in the first century, there is no evidence of λησταὶ connoting a 'revolutionary' in Jesus' time. That period, he argues, was a time of relative peace in Judaea without hard evidence of revolutionary activity. And, 'if we follow Josephus closely, even in the revolutionary period, decades after Jesus' lifetime, λησταὶ are a wider class of violent men of different types and motivations'.[27]

But can one go further? Others, like Wright, read the evidence differently. In the period before Jesus, for example, in the hills lived brigands whom Herod the Great destroyed. These λησταὶ, according to Wright, were revolutionaries whose nationalistic hopes were centred on the temple.[28] Wright admits that this does not necessarily mean that there were revolutionaries in the temple in Jesus' day. As Brown has shown, such a conclusion could well be anachronistic. But, for Wright, 'the point has to do with ideology: the temple had become, in Jesus' day as in Jeremiah's, the talisman of nationalist violence, the guarantee that YHWH would act for Israel and defend her against her enemies.'[29]

---

[27]Brown, *The Death of the Messiah*, 686-688.
[28]See Joel Marcus, 'The Jewish War and the *Sitz im Leben* of Mark', *JBL* 111 (1992), 441-462, who argues that Mark arose in a context much more closely related to the Jewish War than the traditional Roman provenance would suggest.
[29]Wright, *Jesus and the Victory*, 420.

Wright's argument for this point is cumulative and persuasive. However, for our purposes, the issue is whether or not, in Mark's view, Jesus was being accused of holding these nationalistic views (almost certainly wrongly, in Mark's understanding) and whether Mark's readers would have understood λῃσταὶ as a term including, if not pointing to, violent revolutionaries (again almost certainly, 'Yes'). Although Wright overstates the case when he says 'crucifixion was the punishment reserved, not for thieves or swindlers, but for revolutionaries',[30] crucifixion was an instrument of state terror predominantly used against the lower classes, 'slaves, violent criminals and unruly elements in rebellious provinces, not least in Judaea'. [31]

Mark's point in the link of λῃσταὶ and the mockery, thus, become clearer. Jesus is crucified as a λῃστής. His arrest, the accusation, the *titulus* on the cross and the mockery all point in this direction. As far as His religious and political opponents are concerned, He is crucified as a man of (potential?) violence against the temple. But, for Mark and his readers, this is a completely false impression of who He was. His critique of the temple was precisely in line with the prophetic recalling of the temple to its intended purpose, namely, as the dwelling of the holy God in the midst of His holy people. Instead of seeing the temple as the centre of a nationalistic revolution against Rome (a den of λῃσταὶ), He wanted nothing to do with violent revolution. The mockery of the crucified λῃστής was thus very similar to that of the scribes and the chief priests – to them He was also a failed visionary. For Jesus and for Mark's readers, however, the revolution which was centred on the temple was of a completely different order. And the death scene itself would show the true meaning of Jesus' altogether more radical temple critique.

The Fulfilment

'And the curtain of the ναός was torn in two, from top to bottom. And when the centurion, who stood facing him, saw that he thus breathed his last, he said, "Truly this man was the Son of God!"' (15:38-39).

There can be little doubt that the death scene is the climax of Mark's narrative. The darkness at noon, the cry of dereliction, the Elijah misunderstanding, and the death cry lead the whole narrative to its

---

[30]*Ibid.*, 420.
[31]M. Hengel, *The Cross of the Son of God* (ET; London: SCM, 1986, reprint of *Crucifixion*, 1977), 179. Hengel, 178, states: 'Crucifixion was and remained a political and military punishment.'

pinnacle, the confession of the centurion.[32] Each aspect is full of significance for Mark and his readers. But Mark includes one other event. At the precise moment at which Jesus breathed His last, the καταπέτασμα τοῦ ναοῦ is torn in two from top to bottom.

In Mark, the centurion's confession depends directly on the way Jesus breathed His last; strictly speaking, the story does not need the rending of the veil to work. When such information is nevertheless included, it often is a good indication of its significance.[33] Careful narrative analysis of the scene shows that the 'darkness at noon' over the whole land (τῆς γῆς) cannot be other than God's action in judgment on the world. Similarly, the rending of the veil can only be attributable to God. Together they form an *inclusio* around the whole dramatic sequence in which God's action is clearly demonstrated. To the onlookers of 15:29-32, of course, Jesus' death confirms their belief that He is a false prophet and a deluded ληστής. 'But the reader knows differently. . . Rather than being absent from the death scene, God's action is observable from start to finish. . . Things are not as they appear on the surface.'[34]

If judgment is the underlying motif behind the darkness at noon, it is almost as certain to be the theme in 15:38.[35] But what does Mark intend his readers to understand by this judgment? An atomistic exegesis of 15:34 may suggest that the cry of dereliction was God's judgment in abandoning Jesus. Much more convincing is the view that the whole death scene is one of the vindication of Jesus through suffering and death, not unlike the vindication of the 'one like a son of man' from Daniel 7. This view is confirmed by the use of ἐσχίσθη in 15:38: 'By the violent rending (σχίζειν) God responds vigorously, not only to vindicate Jesus whom God has not forsaken, but also to express anger at the chief priests and Sanhedrin who decreed such a death for God's Son.'[36] There is again an irony in all this, for those who earlier had been told that they would see the Son of Man in judgment (14:62) and who had mockingly wished to 'see and believe' (15:32), were now experiencing precisely that judgment

---

[32]See Smith, *A Lion with Wings*, 91.

[33]Both Matthew and Luke include the incident, but they put it to slightly different use. In Matthew, the rending of the καταπέτασμα τοῦ ναοῦ is one of the phenomena he includes, but probably not the one(s) which give(s) rise to the centurion's confession; for Luke, reference to the event precedes the death cry and is tied to the darkness at noon. Thus, in Luke the centurion's declaration of Jesus' innocence is related to the entire death scene, not to one of its parts. John does not consider it necessary to mention the rending of the veil.

[34]Brower, 'Elijah in the Markan Passion Narrative', 94.

[35]See Brown, *The Death of the Messiah*, 1099-1102.

[36]*Ibid.*, 1100.

in the obvious rending of the veil. Judgment was being exercised by God on the very heart of the temple by opening the ναός, perhaps confirming the purpose of the temple for all nations (see 11:17).

Mark's picture of God's judgment is just as severe as that of Jeremiah and Ezekiel. The rending of the veil from top to bottom symbolized the belief that the present temple system was being rendered obsolete by Jesus' death. For Mark, the death of Jesus marks the end of the beginning of the gospel about Jesus Christ.

The End and the Beginning

Many an inkjet cartridge has been emptied on translating and interpreting the centurion's confession, ἀληθῶς οὗτος ὁ ἄνθρωπος Υἱὸς Θεοῦ ἦν. What did the centurion say: 'a son of God' or 'the Son of God'? That debate cannot be settled simply by choosing your grammarian. And what did he mean when he said it? Fortunately, neither of those two points need detain us, since we are not primarily concerned with the historical level. At the level of the implied author and implied readers, however, this is the true confession: Jesus is Son of God most clearly as He breathes His last and the temple veil is torn from top to bottom.

For Mark, this is the eschatological nodal point, decisive in the direction and goal of God's good purposes for His created order.[37] This is the point to which the narrative has built. The accusation in 14:58 stated that 'in three days I will build another'. Mark highlights this three-day scheme: Jesus crucified on 'the day of Preparation, that is, the day before the Sabbath' (15:42), followed by the note in 16:1, 'And when the Sabbath was past', and concluded by 'very early in the morning, on the first day of the week . . . when the sun had risen' (16:2). The basis for the scheme was laid earlier, of course, in the three-fold passion predictions of 8:31; 9:31 and 10:33, where Jesus states three times that 'after three days he will rise'. There is, therefore, more than a hint that Mark sees 'the other ναός ἀχειροποίητον' connected with the death and resurrection of Jesus; the rending of the καταπέτασμα τοῦ ναοῦ in two from top to bottom symbolizes the end of the ναός; the building of the other ἀχειροποίητον is fulfilled through the death–resurrection and the

---

[37]See G. R. Beasley-Murray, 'Resurrection and Parousia of the Son of Man', *TynB* 42 (1991), 303, 'the death–resurrection of Jesus is the fundamental eschatological act of God. . . . An important function of the gospels is to make it clear that the acts and the words of Jesus were as truly eschatological as his death and resurrection. . . .'

reconstitution of His disciple band as the foundation of the new covenant community (see 14:24). No wonder that Mark ties the confession so closely to the rending of the temple veil by God: the judgment on the temple involves both the ending of the old nationalistic notion of the temple's place in God's purposes and the concentration of God's good purposes in His Son who is now to be the locus of the destiny of God's people.[38]

This reading of the passion narrative is supported by an obvious literary *inclusio* of Mark 1:1 and 15:39. Mark begins his narrative with the phrase, 'the beginning of the good news about Jesus Christ, the Son of God' (1:1) and draws the narrative to its climax with the centurion's confession, 'truly this was the Son of God' (15:39). But this *inclusio* cannot simply be accepted without further support. The well-known textual difficulty of 1:1 continues to spark interest[39] and it cannot be taken for granted that Mark actually included the phrase 'son of God' in his original composition.[40]

It is possible, however, to think of the *inclusio* more broadly in terms of the introductory section (1:1-15) and the climax and dénouement (15:38–16:8). Mark has echoes of some themes from the introduction in the concluding section. In 1:9-11, after Jesus' baptism, God's action is shown through the rending asunder of the heavens and the voice from heaven which announces that 'this is my son, the beloved one, in whom I am well pleased'. In 15:38-39, God is again in action, rending (same word) the temple veil from top to bottom, when Jesus finishes His mission and purpose by following the will of His father to death (14:36). This time, however, the confession is not the prospective announcement by God stating Jesus' being and mission, but the retrospective confirmation that Jesus has been precisely the Son of God in the whole gospel story and supremely so in the death scene. Jesus was never more truly Son of God than when He died.

Surrounding that comparison are a number of subsidiary themes. According to 1:15, Jesus came announcing the good news of the kingdom of God; in 15:43, Joseph of Arimathea is described as 'looking for the kingdom of God'. He is obviously a 'true Israelite', one who has 'seen and believed' in contrast to the other leaders; they also saw but failed to believe. To see the kingdom of God coming in

---

[38]Development of this theme would include a careful discussion of the corporate aspects of the 'Son of Man', a topic beyond the scope of this essay.

[39]See P. M. Head, 'A Text-Critical Study of Mark 1:1, "The Beginning of the Gospel of Jesus Christ"', *TS* 37 (1991), 621-629.

[40]One suspects, as Caird and Hurst, *New Testament Theology*, 168, n. 63 observe, that 'the answer is ultimately theological, not textual'.

power (see 9:1) cannot be divorced from the death of Jesus.[41] 'Galilee' is the location of Jesus' first proclamation and calling of the disciples (1:16ff.); it is also the place where the scattered disciple band will be reconstituted as promised by Jesus in 14:28 and fulfilled in the words of the young man in the empty tomb (16:7). There the narrative concludes in its well-known open-ended fashion. Mark and his readers, of course, know that the story continues.

For Mark, the passion narrative, in which Jesus shapes a new people of God from those who respond to His call, is the end of the beginning. God's purposes were being achieved by Jesus in a new and radical way. It is also the beginning of the end. In the death of His messiah, the Son of God, God's judgment was inaugurated on the temple system. With judgment on the ναός, it could only be a matter of time before there would not be 'one stone upon another' in, the ἱερόν.

The Beginning of the End: The ʹIEPON and the Fall of Jerusalem

Jerusalem and the temple, the locus of the holy God's dwelling in the midst of His holy people, dominate the narrative from 8:31 onwards, initially through the anticipation of Jesus' fate outlined in the numerous predictions of and allusions to His passion, as well as His call to cross-bearing discipleship. But the sustained focus on the temple begins in 11:1. Jesus enters the temple from Bethany on the Mount of Olives (11:12) and leaves the temple to announce its fate in explicit terms from the Mount of Olives opposite the temple (13:3).[42] Within this section Mark engages the temple in three inter-locking themes.

The Prophetic Representative Action in the ʹIEPON: (10:46 –11:26)
This section begins with the healing of Bartimaeus.[43] Blindness and sight are, of course, metaphors used by Mark to contrast two kinds of seeing, one with understanding and the other without. Bartimaeus, whose plea to the Son of David is answered by the restoration of his sight, understands enough to join Jesus 'on his way' into Jerusalem.

---

[41]See Brower, 'Mark 9:1 Seeing the kingdom in Power'.

[42]Several scholars have drawn attention to the significance of the Mount of Olives as an allusion to Zc. 14:4-5. See recently, for example, Wright, *Jesus and the Victory*, 344, who states, 'this can hardly be accidental'.

[43]The healing itself marks the conclusion to Jesus' teaching on discipleship, introduced by the two-stage healing of the blind man in Bethsaida (8:22-26).

The emphasis of Son of David is picked up in the immediately following entry to Jerusalem and further elaborated in Jesus' teaching to the throng in 12:35-37. The entry itself has a number of remarkable features. There are messianic overtones which, nevertheless are very restrained, non-violent and non-nationalistic. Jesus clearly is the Son of David, but not precisely as expected.

The entry is followed by the statement that Jesus 'went into the temple; and when he had looked around at everything, as it was already late, he went out to Bethany with the Twelve'(11:11). Mark alone makes this apparently casual observation. But is it merely a redundant note, as Matthew seems to think? Perhaps not. This anti-climactic statement certainly minimizes any sense of 'triumphal entry'. Yes, Jesus was the Son of David, but His entry to the temple was at once more profound than, and different from, simply the arrival of the Son of David. Identification of Jesus as Son of David was not wrong,[44] it was just inadequate. Second, Jesus 'looked around at everything'. Geddert has drawn attention to the fact that Jeremiah 7:11, used later in 11:17, reads 'Has this house, which is called by my name, become a den of robbers in your eyes? Behold, I myself have seen it, says the Lord.' Geddert's question, 'Does Mark suggest that Jesus was able to see from the divine perspective . . . and that readers are called to do the same?'[45] must be answered with a clear 'Yes'.

But the central text is the fig-tree/temple/fig-tree episode. Telford's general conclusion to his careful analysis of this episode is compelling: the cursing of the fig-tree signifies that the entry to Jerusalem and the temple story should not be understood as a Messianic purification, but as a visitation in judgment upon the temple.[46]

There may be more to Mark's story, however. Clues come through a wider reading of the Old Testament background to Jesus' words in 11:15b-17. As Wright has pointed out, Jeremiah 7 is followed by Jeremiah 8:11-13, in which God says 'there are no grapes on the vine, nor figs on the fig tree; even the leaves are withered, and what I gave them has passed away from them.' The cursing of the fig-tree is intimately connected to the 'sorrowful Jeremianic demonstration that Israel, and the temple, are under judgment.'[47] The

[44]*Contra* W. R. Telford, *The Barren Temple and the Withered Tree* (JSNTSS1; Sheffield: JSOT, 1980), 262.
[45]Geddert, *Watchwords*, 129.
[46]Telford, *The Barren Temple*, 261. It is, however, scarcely judgment upon the 'Jewish people' as Telford states.
[47]Wright, *Jesus and the Victory*, 422.

whole episode, therefore, may be understood as 'an acted parable of judgment'[48] or, perhaps even better, as a prophetic representative act in which the Markan Jesus not only predicts but symbolically effects the prediction of judgment.[49] Similarly, Isaiah 56:7 is part of a remarkable passage in which God welcomes to Himself those, such as eunuchs, who ordinarily are excluded from His people (56:3-8). It is, however, immediately followed by a passage which is scathing in its denunciation of corrupt leaders (56:9–57:13). God welcomes; corrupt leaders are excluded (57:21). This, then, is no mere cleansing of the temple. Mark sees it as a judgment on the temple whose leaders have distorted its intended purpose as the house of prayer for all nations. Instead of welcoming the foreigners, they have made it into 'a den of λῃστῶν'. Echoing Jeremiah's strident criticism of the temple, through the juxtapositioning of the cursing of the fig-tree with the allusion to two highly charged Old Testament texts and contexts, the Markan Jesus prophetically enacts the fate of the temple.[50] The message to the chief priests and the scribes was clear; their response was to seek a way to destroy Him (11:18).

Mark occasionally uses the fulfilment of one prediction to show that another will also be fulfilled. In the trial scene, for example, while Jesus is being mocked as a false prophet, His prediction about Peter's denial (14:30) is coming true to the letter (14:53-72). The same occurs here. On their exit from Jerusalem, the disciples note that the cursed barren fig-tree has actually withered. Mark's readers, like the disciples, remember (11:21). Then Jesus follows with an apparently unconnected statement about mountain removal. But this too, points directly to the temple.

> The Temple, known to the Jewish people as 'the mountain of the house' or 'this mountain' was not to be elevated, as expected, but cast down. . . . The Temple was to be removed in the lifetime of the Markan community and Mark prepares his readers for it. Its demise is suggested proleptically in the rending of the veil following Jesus' death (15:38).[51]

---

[48]*Ibid.*, 416.
[49]See the last supper for another example of a prophetic representative act, 14:22-25.
[50]See Juel, *Messiah and Temple*, 135.
[51]Telford, *The Barren Temple*, 119.

Teaching in the ' IEPON: 11:27–12:44

The fig-tree/temple/fig-tree complex is followed by a block of teaching deliberately set in the temple. This setting gives it cohesion and significance. The whole section is pervaded by a growing sense of conflict with the temple establishment who queue up, one after another, to confront Jesus. They are now either explicitly linked as a united opposition (see 12:13) or, as in the case of the Sadducees, an aristocratic, conservative group probably linked with the chief priests and likely very content with the temple *status quo*.[52] Thus, we have chief priests, scribes, elders, Pharisees, Herodians and Sadducees all in opposition to Jesus. As a final but minor touch, Mark has Jesus sitting κατέναντι the treasury (12:41), just as he sits κατέναντι the temple in 13:3 to teach His disciples. Jesus Himself is at His combative best.

A series of six questions, including four 'royal riddles'[53] follows. The riddles serve to validate Jesus' action in the temple. The first riddle (11:27-33) questions the source of Jesus' authority and, hence, His right to act as He does. Readers will know that Jesus' authority comes from God: He was anointed by the Spirit as God's servant for His mission and purpose, and was confirmed as God's 'beloved son' by the voice from heaven, all at His baptism. Readers also remember that Jesus has already exercised His έξουσία in teaching, healing, exorcisms (1:22, 27) and, most controversially, in forgiving sins. This, according to the scribes, is the prerogative of God; hence, they accuse Jesus of blaspheming (2:7-10). Jesus has also given έξουσία to His disciples (3:15; 6:7). His action of judgment in the temple, therefore, was done, not primarily because He is the Son of David, but under the authority of God, a point which His opponents refuse to acknowledge, but could not deny.

Wright's interpretation of the parable of the wicked tenants and the second riddle (12:1-12) is particularly helpful. In sum,

> the prophetic story of the rejected servants climaxes in the rejected son; he, however, is the messianic stone which, rejected by the builders, takes the chief place in the building. Those who oppose him find their regime (and their temple) destroyed, while his kingdom will be established. . . . The whole picture serves as a

---

[52]See Wright, *The New Testament and the People of God*, 210-212.
[53]Wright, *Jesus and the Victory*, 394, 510. Wright places the riddles firmly in the life and ministry of Jesus, partly because he thinks that Mark would have no need to tone down statements about Jesus' messiahship. Be that as it may, the riddles and the questions have a narrative and geographical setting which enhance Mark's link of temple and eschatology.

further, and richer, explanation of what Jesus had been doing in the
temple and why.[54]

For Mark, this also points forward, not only to the passion narrative,
but also to chapter 13.

On the surface, the 'Caesar or God' riddle (12:13-17) may
seem to help Mark's readers understand their appropriate
relationship to the state. But his setting of the story in the temple
points elsewhere. The question is brought by the Pharisees and the
Herodians at the behest of the chief priests, scribes and elders (12:13)
as part of their opposition in an attempt to entrap Jesus in either an
impious or revolutionary statement. The very possession of a coin
with the emperor's image by the pious confirms the hypocrisy which
Mark notes. Equally, however, the entry to Jerusalem and the
prophetic representative act in the temple have already shown that
Jesus is not about violent revolution, which would be Caesar's way,
just as surely as would be the comfortable acquiescence of the
Herodians to the current state of affairs. Although not all of Wright's
discussion here is convincing, his conclusion that this response
'protests against Jewish *compromises with the pagans*'[55] which had
become the *modus operandus* of the temple establishment is surely
correct.

In the final riddle (12:35-37), the Markan Jesus cites Psalm 110
to show that the Son of David/Messiah identity is inadequate. 'Jesus
implies that he has gained his authority over the temple not merely
as David's son but, more particularly, as David's lord.'[56] He is not the
messiah of popular expectation, whether the victor over the enemy or
the restorer of the temple. In fact, the restorer has already come and
His work is complete (9:12). Rather, the activity in the temple must be
understood in the broader terms of Mark's eschatology centred in the
good news of God in Jesus Christ, Son of God (1:1; 15:39).[57]

---

[54]Wright, *Jesus and the Victory*, 501.

[55]*Ibid.*, 506.

[56]*Ibid.*, 509.

[57]There may also be other reasons why Psalm 110 is used here. In the passion
narrative, the Psalm is again cited at 14:62. There it: 'could well co-ordinate with
the idea of a new Temple not made with hands comprised of the members of the
new covenant community headed by Jesus (14:24, 28) instead of the old, bankrupt leadership. In that case, the eternal priesthood symbolized by the order of
Melchizedek, an order 'not made with hands' will replace the present earthly
order, an order, 'made with hands'. The old Temple, headed by the high priest
who questions Jesus, ends in the judgement of the Son of Man and is replaced by
the new Temple whose high priest is after the order of Melchizedek', (Brower,
OT, 382). But if this is Mark's intention, it is not immediately obvious.

The two questions addressed to Jesus confirm Him as the authoritative interpreter of the Scriptures. When the Sadducees come to test Him (12:18-27), He confounds them by telling them that they know neither the Scriptures nor the power of God (12:24). Their failure to accept the resurrection was merely a symptom of their captivity to the *status quo* and so, they are quite wrong (12:27). The second question (12:28-34) is even more important. A scribe asks for Jesus' opinion of the great commandments. Jesus summarizes them with the *Shema* of Deuteronomy 6:4 and the call to love of neighbour from Leviticus 19:18. The scribe, commending Jesus for His answer, then repeats the summary and adds that these two commandments count for much more than all burnt offerings and sacrifices. Jesus said to the scribe, 'You are not far from the kingdom of God.'

The sequence is remarkable. Heretofore in Mark the scribes have been painted almost entirely in hostile hues. But that is not Mark's whole picture. Hostility to Jesus and His message that the kingdom of God has arrived is the only reason for condemnation. Those who see and believe are inside the kingdom; those who see, but fail to perceive, put themselves outside. Mark commends those who earnestly seek the kingdom.[58] Here, and only in Mark, this scribe has penetrated to the heart of God's call of His holy people and the sole basis for Jesus' announcement of the kingdom. The significance of his response cannot be overestimated. To say *in the temple and following Jesus' prophetic representative action in the temple*, that these commandments given by Jesus are more than all the burnt offerings and sacrifices brings the whole sequence to its point. These two commandments, the heart of second-temple Jewish piety, are at the centre of Jesus' kingdom Torah, but because the kingdom has arrived, the teaching has a much more radical and daring conclusion. The centre of God's good purposes was to be found in the inward, in-the-heart Torah promised by Jeremiah and Ezekiel. That time had arrived: the purpose and goal to which the temple pointed, but which had not been grasped, was now being proclaimed and effected in Jesus Himself.[59]

No wonder that Mark tells us, 'And after that no one dared ask him any question' (12:34b). All that remains of the temple teaching is a warning against covenant unrighteousness disguised as

---

[58]Even the rich young man of 10:17-31 is treated kindly, although he fails at the decisive point – the full commitment to following Jesus which would make him an insider. Joseph of Arimathea, 'a respected member of the council' (βουλευτής), is commended as one seeking the kingdom of God (15:43).

[59]Wright, *Jesus and the Victory*, 566.

piety (12:38-40) and a dramatic illustration of the contrast between partial and total commitment (12:41-44).

The Temple and the End: Chapter 13

Mark 13 has always attracted attention,[60] not least because it points decidedly to the future. As already seen, however, it is part of a bigger section and in that context makes its contribution to Markan eschatology, not in isolation from it.

Mark gives some hints which show how he intends his readers to understand this section. First, this is still discipleship-teaching. An *inclusio* of 13:5 'and Jesus began to say to them', with 13:37 'and what I say to you I say to all', shows that Mark has his implied readers in view.[61] Jesus speaks of events which have not yet occurred in the life of His disciples, but which have already occurred (or are about to occur) in the lives of Mark's readers. This has implications for interpretation; as Brown laconically observes, 'detectable comprehensibility to a 1st-century audience is an important (even if not sufficient) guide to interpretation'.[62] Second, as R. H. Lightfoot showed almost fifty years ago,[63] the chapter is linked with the following passion narrative through a variety of continuing motifs. Thus, chapter 13 '. . . is the logical ending of the story and intimately related both to the main narrative and to the passion and resurrection of Jesus'.[64] Third, and obviously, this chapter concerns the fate of the temple. Scholars have debated the issue of just how much of the chapter relates to the temple.[65] That debate cannot be entered here. In light of the first two hints, however, I concur with Geddert's judgment that 'Mark 13 is an anti-temple speech; it is not a speech introduced by a few unimportant references to the temple and then proceeding with total disregard for the temple and its fate.'[66]

---

[60]Earlier studies sought to establish the unity of the so-called 'Little Apocalypse'. See, for example, G. R. Beasley-Murray, *Jesus and the Future: An Examination of the Criticism of the Eschatological Discourse, Mark 13 with Special reference to the Little Apocalypse Theory* (London: Macmillan, 1954), and David Wenham, *The Rediscovery of Jesus' Eschatological Discourse: Gospel Perspectives 4* (Sheffield: JSOT, 1984).

[61]The teaching is for his readers, just like the call to cross-bearing in 8:34-38 extended beyond the historical first disciples. But here, the teaching is even more clearly directed to the readers.

[62]Brown, *The Death of the Messiah*, 1113.

[63]In *The Gospel Message of St. Mark* (Oxford: Oxford University Press, 1950), 48-59.

[64]Geddert, *Watchwords*, 192.

[65]But see Bolt who thinks the reference to the temple in 13:3 is incidental.

[66]Geddert, *Watchwords*, 146.

Jesus does not easily reach the point of predicting temple destruction. Mark shows Jesus calling all of Israel to join the restoration movement (1:38; 2:17; 8:34) and to become part of the new people of God (3:35; 6:7-13; 10:23-31) because God's purposes for His world have entered a new and decisive stage (1:14-15), which will come to fruition (4:10-34). But Mark also shows resistance almost from the beginning. As the narrative progresses, it becomes increasingly clear that the opposition is not from the crowds but from the temple establishment. Finally, and, as Brown notes, 'only when faced with obdurate irreformability does Jesus say (13:1-2) that not one stone will be left on another from the wonderfully built temple'.[67] Implacable opposition to Jesus leads to the passion narrative; the passion narrative leads to the destruction of the temple. Once the ναός is redundant because it is replaced by the crucified and risen Christ and His covenant community, and in the face of opposition to God's kingdom inaugurated in Jesus, the temple's fate is sealed. 'For Mark, the destruction of the Temple represented both the natural political outcome of the Jewish refusal to follow Christ and the divine censure of that refusal.'[68]

If we take seriously, as I think we must, the central place the temple has occupied throughout Mark's story, then chapter 13 becomes less difficult. Here the work of the 'Third Questers' casts some illumination on Mark's picture of Jesus, with Wright's work particularly insightful.[69] Wright shows that the apocalyptic imagery used in chapter 13 needs to be understood without the 'crass literalism' which has so often distorted its meaning and purpose. It is the normal Jewish language used to draw out the significance of major socio-political events.[70] If this is so, then attention must be focused on the meaning of the events under discussion (in this case, the destruction of the temple), rather than the apocalyptic phenomena used to indicate significance.

Throughout his Gospel, Mark has refocused the central Jewish hopes of restoration and deliverance by God on to Jesus and His people, thus bringing 'the story of Israel to its appointed climax'.[71] That story has ultimate significance. Chapter 13 highlights the defeat of

---

[67]Brown, *The Death of the Messiah*, 456.
[68]Paula Fredriksen, *From Jesus to Christ: The Origins of the New Testament Images of Jesus* (New Haven: Yale, 1988), 50.
[69]See Wright, *Jesus and the Victory*, especially 339-368, as well as the overall direction of his two major works.
[70]*Ibid.*, 361.
[71]*Ibid.*, 362-363, his italics.

the real enemies of God and the vindication of the true people of God in the coming vindication of the Son of Man.

This, however, is only the beginning of the new world order; it is not the culmination of all things ('the End'). But, contrary to the opinion of many exegetes, Mark is not specifically addressing that issue.[72] In fact, as Geddert notes, 'Mark has presented the material in such a way that the relationship between the destruction of the temple and the End of the age is left completely uncertain'.[73] Furthermore, Mark is actually opposed to any form of sign-seeking:[74] not only is it impossible to state the time of the End, any such speculation is not to be believed (verses 6, 21-23).[75] Rather, Mark's purpose is far more pastoral than predictive. Mark's concern for his first readers is 'to teach them how to live as faithful disciples without knowing when the End will come'.[76] Mark 13:32-37, far from being detached from the narrative, shows that the point of chapter 13 is to encourage 'discipleship and mission, discerning ears and eyes to detect God at work, and unfailing confidence that the kingdom, still hidden, is destined to be revealed'.[77]

But what about Mark's modern readers for whom the destruction of the temple is little more than a piece of ancient history and for whom the End has long seemed delayed? Are there signs in Mark about the *timing* of the End to which we ought to be paying attention? The answer must be 'No!' But he does have a message in his gospel which may have relevance even for those facing the millennium. Mark pays such careful attention to the relationship between the temple and the End because the very destruction of the temple is confirmation that God's good purposes are now centred in Jesus and the new people of God. These purposes are being accomplished and vindication of His people will also be accomplished: the End will be found in the climax of God's good purposes in Christ.

---

[72]Bolt, for example, argues that Mark 13 finds fulfilment in the passion and exaltation of Jesus. Bolt is probably right to see 'this generation'(13:30; see also 9:1) as pointing to events in the narrative itself. But there is a future element in chapter 13 which extends beyond the immediately following passion narrative, but which does not extend indefinitely into the future. Hence, those who hold that the primary referent in this chapter is to the destruction of the temple give greater coherence to the narrative as a whole.

[73]Geddert, *Watchwords*, 230.

[74]*Ibid.*, 29-58

[75]B. Witherington III, *Jesus, Paul and the End of the World: A Comparative Study in New Testament Eschatology*, (Downers Grove: IVP, 1992), 42.

[76]Geddert, *Watchwords*, 109.

[77]*Ibid.*, 255

Summary and Conclusion

What is the story behind the story? The conflict between Jesus and the temple establishment is merely the backdrop to Mark's implicit eschatology. This conflict brought God's judgment on the very heart of the temple system through the death of the messiah, the Son of God. But this judgment also carried with it the conviction that God's purposes for the temple would be realized through Jesus and His new covenant community. In light of the new irrelevance of the temple, it could only then be a matter of time before there would not be 'one stone upon another'. This had already been anticipated earlier in Mark's narrative. Jesus' entire time in Jerusalem was spent in conflict with the temple authorities. The initiation of judgment on the temple system, symbolized by the prophetic representative action in 11:15-17, was sustained through the teaching in the temple, culminating in the affirmation of the great commandments and the critique of burnt offering and sacrifices. The Olivet Discourse predicted the end of the temple complex itself. That historical event has (or would have) cosmic significance, for it would be the vindication of the Son of Man and His beleaguered followers. They were encouraged to keep awake and to focus on the mission of proclaiming the gospel, even if they could not know when God's ultimate good purposes would finally be realized.

What does this story tell us about Mark's eschatology? First, Mark's focus on Jesus is unremitting. He is the embodiment of God's eschatological purposes, promised by the prophets and realized in the new covenant community with the promised in-the-heart Torah. His incarnation is the eschatological nodal point. Second, Mark believes that God's purposes were being opposed by the temple authorities who, despite repeated calls by Jesus, refuse to enter the new people of God, preferring to continue down the path to inevitable destruction. Faced with the disaster of the Jewish War (impending or actual), Mark shows that even calamity is within the bigger picture of God's ultimate purposes. Third, Mark reminds his readers that, although the temple's destruction is the beginning of the End and the vindication of the beleaguered people of God, the culmination of all things is completely beyond prediction. In the face of an attenuated End, Jesus' words to His disciples are still vital: 'What I say to you, I say to all: Keep awake!' (13:37).

Chapter 6

THE DESTRUCTION OF THE TEMPLE AND THE RELATIVIZATION OF THE OLD COVENANT:
Mark 13:31 and Matthew 5:18

Crispin H. T. Fletcher-Louis

In this essay it is argued that the principal reference of 'heaven and earth' is the temple-centred cosmology of second-temple Judaism which included the belief that the temple is heaven and earth in microcosm. Mark 13 and Matthew 5:18 refer, then, to the destruction of the temple as a passing away of an old cosmology and also, in the latter case, to the establishment during Jesus' ministry and at His death and resurrection of a new temple cosmology – a new heaven and earth.

In the synoptic gospels there are two references to the passing away of heaven and earth. First, at Mark 13:31 (Mt. 24:35 and Lk. 21:33) Jesus predicts that 'heaven and earth will pass away, but my words will not pass away'. There is no substantial difference between the first three gospels in this saying. Secondly, Matthew and Luke both relate a similar saying: Matthew 5:18, '. . . until heaven and earth pass away not one jot or tittle will pass away from the Law; until all has happened'; Luke 16:17, 'It is easier for heaven and earth to pass away than for one tittle to fall from the Law.' The context of the first (Mark 13:31) is that of the Markan eschatological discourse, whilst that of the second is unclear at Luke 16:17 and certainly that of Jesus' attitude towards the Torah at Matthew 5:18. Until recently there was little cause for disagreement over the meaning of the first. However, both Matthew 5:17 and Luke 16:17 have been intensely debated and belong to passages about which there is still a good deal of scholarly disagreement and uncertainty.

In another context I will deal with Luke 16:17.[1] Instead, it is my aim here to propose a new interpretation of Mark 13:31 (and parallels) and Matthew 5:18. In brief I propose that by 'heaven and earth' is meant the Jerusalem temple and the Torah constitution at the centre of which the former stands. Neither saying envisages the collapse of the space–time universe (as has been understood by modern interpretation). Both refer to the imminent end to the social, religious and economic structure of Israel's covenant relationship with God with the attendant destruction of the temple.

The Two Gospel Sayings

The First Saying (Mark 13:31)
Mark 13:31 (Mt. 24:35) comes at the climax of Jesus' eschatological prophecy; Mark 13:2-37 (Mt. 24:2-44). The occasion for the whole chapter is a prediction of the destruction of the temple in AD 70, which leads to an account in Mark 13:3-23 (Mt. 24:3-26) of the tumultuous social and political upheavals in the years of revolt which preceded that catastrophe. The orthodoxy of twentieth-century scholarship has read the vivid description of cosmic disturbances and the coming of the Son of Man in the latter half of this chapter (Mk. 13:24-37; Mt. 24:29-44) as a prediction of the end of the world, what, it is assumed, Matthew calls the 'parousia'. This 'end-of-the-world' was evidently closely associated with the destruction of Jerusalem which would immediately precede it. Thus, within Mark 13:24-37 (Mt. 24:29-44) the description of the passing away of heaven and earth at Mark 13:31 (Mt. 24:35) is read as an unequivocal statement of the end of history, when the material empirical world will cease to exist.

This reading of the latter half of the chapter as a whole and this verse in particular then creates an infamous problem in the history of early Christianity: this cosmic melt-down has not yet actually happened. The problem is acute because the previous verse promises that 'this generation will not pass away until all these things happen' (Mk. 13:30 and Mt. 24:34). That generation could possibly be that of the evangelists, but is more naturally that of Jesus Himself. Either way, this prophecy was not fulfilled and twentieth-century scholars have been left to explore the social and religious

---

[1] In a forthcoming study I intend to show that Lk. 16:17 has a similar sense to my interpretation of Mt. 5:18 because it, like Matthew's verse, is set in the context where the identity, privileges and cosmic ideology of the Jerusalem temple have been appropriated by the Jesus community.

implications of the so-called 'delay of the parousia' for the history of earliest Christianity.

In the case of Mark, writing before the destruction of Jerusalem, historically this failure can be explained simply as a result of false prophecy. Yet for Matthew, who, it is normally assumed, writes after AD 70, it is difficult to understand his insistence that the end would take place 'immediately' (εὐθέω, verse 29) after the tribulation of the years AD 66-70 (described in verses 15-26), since that end-of-the-world did not actually take place 'immediately' after the destruction of Jerusalem.

In recent decades an attempt to circumvent the delay in the parousia problem has been pursued by George B. Caird and his two pupils Marcus Borg and N. T. Wright.[2] Their approach, which is represented now in its most thoroughgoing form in the first two volumes of Wright's *Christian Origins and the Question of God*,[3] understands Mark 13 in its entirety as a prediction of the destruction of Jerusalem and the world-wide cataclysmic events of the years AD 66-70. This rereading is, in turn, reliant on a reappraisal of apocalyptic eschatological language generally, which, it is argued, should not be viewed as a literal description of the space–time universe, but, rather, a metaphorical account of events *within* history, which thereby invests those events with their appropriate theological meaning. That the language of Mark 13:24 (Mt. 24:29), in particular, should refer to historical political events is consistent with the use of similar imagery in the Old Testament where there is a marked 'tendency to mythologize historical episodes to reveal their transcendent meaning'.[4]

Obviously this approach is to be welcomed if it solves the historical and literary problem of the so-called 'delay of the parousia'. Caird and his followers are right to pay closer attention to the reference to socio-political realities in Jewish and Christian

---

[2] G. B. Caird, *Jesus and the Jewish Nation* (The Ethel M. Wood Lecture delivered before the University of London on 9 March 1965; University of London: Athlone Press, 1965), 20-22; M. Borg, *Conflict, Holiness and Politics in the Teachings of Jesus* (Studies in the Bible and Early Christianity 5; New York & Toronto: Edwin Mellen Press, 1984), 209-227. For nineteenth-century commentators who adopted a similar position see *e.g.* A. Plummer, *A Critical and Exegetical Commentary on the Gospel according to St. Luke* (ICC; Edinburgh: T. & T. Clark, 1896), 485 on Lk. 21:32.

[3] *The New Testament and the People of God* (London: SPCK, 1992), 280-299 and *Jesus and the Victory of God* (London: SPCK, 1996), 361-368.

[4] The words are those of Frank Moore Cross, *Canaanite Myth and Hebrew Epic* (Cambridge, Mass.: Harvard University Press, 1973), 144. For Mk. 13:24 *cf.* esp. Is. 13:10; 34:4; Ezk. 32:7; Joel 2:10, 30-31; 3:15; Am. 8:9. *Cf.* generally *e.g.* Is. 51:9-11; Je. 4:23-28.

apocalyptic language. It remains to be seen whether their approach, in particular the dangerously reductionist understanding of apocalyptic language, does full justice to all the data, both Jewish and Christian.

There are a couple of weaknesses in this new reading. In particular Mark 13:31 presents something of a thorn in the flesh of the Caird school. In his new book on Jesus, Wright's reading of Mark's thirteenth chapter is intelligible, and in the main persuasive, up to 13:30-32. However, his attempt to grapple with 13:31 significantly weakens his case.[5] His reading is not entirely clear. He seems to take these words, on analogy with Isaiah 40:8 ('the grass withers, the flower fades, but the word of our God shall stand for ever'), as an affirmation of the security of the prophetic word.[6] That is just possible, but in the present context, which has been dominated by the imagery of cosmic conflagration, however metaphorical that imagery may be, it is difficult to imagine that the language of 13:31 should not refer specifically to what has preceded. In that case, Wright would have to argue that Mark 13:31 also refers to the destruction of Jerusalem in AD 70. Yet about that literary connection he is significantly silent. Perhaps, given the difficulty of reading 'heaven and earth shall pass away' as a reference to the events of AD 70, he has chosen to avoid the obvious. However, given the clearly climactic nature of the whole discourse, his own claim, that '[t]his is like saying "Truly, truly, I say to you", only magnified to the furthest degree', is unpersuasive.[7]

To the tradition of interpretation in which Borg and Wright stand, it has also been objected that Mark 13:24-27 does not explicitly refer to the destruction of Jerusalem or the temple:[8] whilst their

---

[5]Mark 13:31 is conspicuously absent from the discussion in R. T. France, *Jesus and the Old Testament. His Application of Old Testament Passages to Himself and His Mission* (London: The Tyndale Press, 1971), 227-239; Borg's *Conflict*, and his 'An Orthodoxy Reconsidered: The "End-of-the-World Jesus"', in L. D. Hurst and N. T. Wright (eds.), *The Glory of Christ in the New Testament: Studies in Christology in Memory of George Bradford Caird* (Oxford: Oxford University Press, 1987), 207-217.

[6]Wright, *Jesus and the Victory*, 364-365.

[7]In Wright's favour is the fact that nowhere do the Jewish texts supply a close parallel to Mark 13:31 which could be taken to demand the end of the space–time universe. At *1 Enoch* 90:16 'the first heaven shall depart and pass away', but there is no reference to the earth: history, albeit a utopian one, is assumed to follow (90:17).

[8]See *e.g.* D. Wenham, ' "This Generation Will Not Pass . . ." A Study of Jesus' Future Expectation in Mark 13', in H. H. Rowden (ed.), *Christ the Lord: Studies in*

approach may well be right to read Mark 13:14-23 as a build-up which expects, but does not itself provide, the actual description of the destruction of the Jerusalem temple, it is not entirely clear how Mark 13:24-31 provides that temple-focused climax. Even when the metaphorical language of Old Testament political historiography is granted, it is not clear why Mark 13:24-31 need, at any point, refer specifically to Jerusalem and temple, rather than the Mediterranean-wide turmoil of the years AD 66-73.

It is not our purpose to critique the basic thrust of this AD 70/temple-centred reading. I believe that here Caird, Borg and Wright are on the right lines. Rather, in what follows I hope that a modest *re*mythologizing of the language of the synoptic eschatological discourse will tighten-up weaknesses in their argument, in particular with respect to Mark 13:31 (Mt. 24:35).

Mark 13:31 also has one interpretative difficulty of its own. The second half of the two-part verse refers to the promise that Jesus' words will not pass away. Which words are meant: the words of the discourse, or the totality of Jesus' teaching? If there is here a promise that Jesus' prophecy begun at Mark 13:2 will not fail, then the language is a little odd: we might have expected οἱ δὲ λόγοι μου (or even οἱ δὲ λόγοι οὗτοι) οὐ μὴ ἐκλείψουσιν ('my words [or 'these words'] will not fail'). There is no verbal allusion to Isaiah 40:8 LXX, which might have been expected, had the force of that text been in mind. There is not, in any case, any cosmic scope in that Old Testament text. If, on the other hand, there is here a promise that Jesus' teaching as a whole will endure the collapse of the space–time universe, then one has to wonder what role it will have beyond the end of history when His teaching quite clearly prescribes the lifestyle of the people of God *within* history.

Given that Mark 13:31 contrasts the passing away of heaven and earth with the endurance of Jesus' words, there is a clear similarity, particularly to the Matthean form of the Q saying at Matthew 5:18 (Lk. 16:17). Not surprisingly, we find that problems of the former recur in the latter, to which we now turn.

The second saying (Matthew 5:18)

Matthew 5:18 is part of the Matthean heading (5:17-20) to Jesus' teaching on the Torah at 5:21–7:27. These four verses are full of exegetical questions and interpretative difficulties: not the least of which is the apparently absolute denial of any change or relativization of the Torah implied by Jesus' words in verse 18. As

---

Christology Presented to Donald Guthrie (Leicester: Inter-Varsity Press, 1982), 127-150, esp. 139, criticizing R. T. France, *Jesus and the Old Testament*, 227-239.

this verse is normally understood, the expression 'until heaven and earth pass away' is meant either as a euphemistic 'never' or as a reference to the cosmic melt-down which we have already described. Either way, the (probably Jewish–Christian) author of this verse and the compiler of Matthew assumed that the Torah remained valid in its entirety (ἰῶτα ἕν ἤ μία κεραία οὐ μὴ παρέλθῃ, 'one jot or tittle will not pass away') both during Jesus' ministry and throughout the subsequent history of the church.

Not only does this clearly fly in the face of the policy of other early Christian leaders such as Paul, Stephen and the author of Mark (see esp. Mk. 7:1-23), it also creates a problem within the immediate Matthean context, since it is widely assumed that some kind of relativization of the Torah is involved in the third (5:31-32), fourth (5:33-37), fifth (5:38-42) and sixth (5:43-48) of the 'antitheses'.

Matthew 5:18 would appear to deny that any of the details of the Torah can become redundant ('pass away'). The issue, it should be noted, is not the Torah's *annulment*, for which the previous verse has used the verb καταλύω, but its *relativization*, for which the verb παρέρχομαι is used. Whilst there is indisputably no antagonistic sense of annulment of the Torah in 5:21-48,[9] the latter four 'antitheses' *do* envisage that, at the very least, there is an appropriate passing away in the sense of obsolescence to some of the Torah's provisions. The Torah's provisions for the appropriate implementation of divorce (Dt. 24:1-4),[10] the saying of oaths (Lv. 22:17-25; Nu. 6; 15:1-10; 30; Dt. 23:21-23; *cf.* 11QTemple 53:9–54:7),[11] the laws of retribution (Ex. 21:24; Lv. 24:20; Dt. 19:21) and vengeance against one's enemies (*e.g.* Dt. 25:17-19) are now to be disregarded. One conclusion cannot be avoided: in this teaching-material there is the *passing away* of many of the Torah's jots and tittles.[12]

---

[9]W. D. Davies and D. C. Allison, *A Critical and Exegetical Commentary on the Gospel of Saint Matthew* (ICC; Edinburgh: T. & T. Clark, 1988), 1. 507-509.

[10]The issue is highly complicated, but Mt. 19:3-9 at least understands what the Old Testament allowed to no longer be relevant.

[11]For the Old Testament's commandment that oaths be said, see Ex. 22:10; Nu. 5:19-22.

[12]It is a weakness of much of the discussion to date, and the position represented by recent commentaries, especially that of Davies and Allison, that only two options – conformity to Torah (albeit with radicalization) and (antagonistic) contradiction – are offered as ways of understanding the relationship between Jesus' teaching and Torah. A third way, otherwise explored by, for example, John Meier, *Law and History in Matthew's Gospel* (AnBib 71; Rome, 1976), which emphasizes the controlling salvation-historical paradigm, deserves greater attention.

In the recent history of interpretation there has been much reflection on whether there is any history of religions precedent for a messianic Torah in which some of the details of the law no longer apply. W. D. Davies has collected some rabbinic evidence for this expectation, but it is mostly late and of meagre volume.[13] Matthew 5:18 has therefore been widely compared with a common Jewish view of the law as eternal and unchanging.[14] However, in the light of recent work on the Temple Scroll from Qumran (11QTS) there is at least one very important pre-Christian parallel to the belief that in the eschaton some laws of the old Torah would become obsolete. In his recent monograph of the temple Scroll Michael Wise has ably demonstrated that the hermeneutical key to the writing of the Temple Scroll is the construction of an eschatological Torah. As such, laws pertaining to Israel outside the Land in a state of exile are deemed no longer relevant to the eschatological conditions of the people of the renewed covenant, and are therefore omitted.[15] This Torah envisages no more sexual immorality (Dt. 23:18-19), divorce or polygamy (Dt. 24:1-4; 25:5-10, *cf.* 57:17-19 and CD 4:12–5:2), no more borrowing or lending, no more slavery (Dt. 15:8-18; 23:16-17; 24:7); no foreigners (Dt. 14:28-29; 15:1-7; 23:20-21; 24:14-15, 17-23; 26:1-11, 12-15), and no more wicked men (Dt. 19:1-13; 24:7; 25:1-3, 11-12, *cf.* 4QpPs 37 ii 6-7; *Pss. Sol.* 17:27). All the laws which pertain to, or even touch on, these pre-eschatological realities are thus deemed redundant. The importance of the Temple Scroll has been noted by W. D. Davies and D. C. Allison in their recent commentary, though they are now *wrong* to insist that this text does not 'call into question . . . the perpetuity of the Mosaic Law'.[16] On the contrary, it does precisely that. In Matthean terms, the Temple Scroll describes an (eschatological) time when many of the jots and tittles have passed away from the Torah.

In the context of second temple eschatological expectations, Matthew 5:21-48 now makes perfect sense as not only a radicalization of Torah, but also a relativization of contents which the Jesus

---

[13]*Torah in the Messianic Age and/or the Age to Come* (JBLMS 8; Philadelphia, 1952); *Setting of the Sermon on the Mount* (Cambridge: Cambridge University Press, 1964), 109-190.

[14]*Cf. e.g. Exod. Rab.* 6:1; *Lev. Rab.* 19:2; *Bar.* 4:1; *Wis.* 18:4; 4 Ezra 9:37.

[15]See esp. Michael Owen Wise, *A Critical Study of the Temple Scroll from Cave 11* (The Oriental Institute of the University of Chicago; Studies in Ancient Oriental Civilisation 49; Chicago, 1990), 161-175. See p. 188 for the similarity to Matthew's gospel. Also his 'The Eschatological Vision of the Temple Scroll', *JNES* 49 (1990), 155-172.

[16]*Matthew*, 492, *cf.* 493, n. 28.

movement, on analogy with the Essenes behind the Temple Scroll, deemed inappropriate for the perfection of Israelite nature and society. In this light, Matthew 5:21-48 might appear to represent one kind of Jewish Christianity – a dispensationalist one – and Matthew 5:18 another kind – a conservative (pharisaic-rabbinic?) one. As such, the latter hardly functions very well as part of a heading for the former.

Furthermore, it is not clear what role Matthew 5:18d 'until all has happened' (ἕως ἂν πάντα γένηται) has, if verse 18b-c does indeed intend an absolute denial of the possibility of the relativization of the Torah. These last four words, which stand in a clear parallelism to verse 18b's 'until heaven and earth pass away' (ἕως ἂν παρέλθη ὁ οὐρανὸς καὶ ἡ γῆς), seem to qualify that absolute denial; envisaging a time when, because all has happened (or been accomplished), it will in fact be possible for a jot or tittle to pass from the Torah. If, however, we insist that the passing away of heaven and earth has to refer to the cessation of the space–time universe then this clause would be almost unique to Matthew's gospel, indeed for the whole of the New Testament, in referring to a period after the cessation of history during which it will be possible, nevertheless, to discuss meaningfully which parts of the Torah are retained and which allowed to fall away. The only possible parallel to this thought is the saying at Matthew 24:35, where Jesus' words are said to remain for ever, whilst heaven and earth will pass away. It is this saying, however, which is itself presently open to reinterpretation.

Furthermore, if verse 18d were simply a repetition of 18b, reiterating a reference to the cessation of the space–time universe, then we would have a case of unnecessary redundancy in an otherwise carefully crafted and nuanced passage. Attempts to avoid the redundancy are unconvincing and actually point in another direction for the meaning of verse 18c-d. For example, Davies and Allison defend the text against the charge of redundancy on the grounds that verse 18d 'introduces the idea, absent from the preceding ἕως clause, of God's prophetic promises and redemptive purposes (*cf.* the mention of 'prophets' in verse 17 and the prophetic use of πληρόω)'.[17] However, this point itself undermines their insistence that verse 18c-d refers to the collapse of history, since throughout Matthew the prophetic promises are said to be fulfilled here and now *within history in the ministry, death and resurrection of Jesus.*[18]

---

[17]*Matthew*, 495.
[18]2:15, 17-18, 23; 4:14-16; 8:17; 12:17-21; 13:14-15, 35; 21:4-5; 27:9-10, *cf.* 2:5-6; 3:3; 10:35; 11:10; 21:42; 22:44; 24:30; 26:64.

One other widely adopted strategy designed to avoid the problematic verse 18d is what has been called the 'ethical explanation'.[19] According to this view, verse 18d refers to the fulfilment of the law as it has been redefined by Jesus, supremely, that is, by the statement that in the command to love God and one's neighbour all the Torah and the prophets are summed up. However, this view is unwarranted on a number of grounds. It relies on a translation of γένηται as 'accomplished' (rather than 'happen'), for which there is no linguistic support.[20] Secondly, the 'jot and tittle' demand that we have here a reference to the Torah legislation in all its details.[21] In general, this solution fails to appreciate the Torah-specific concerns of early Christianity in general and Matthew's gospel in particular.

I submit that the problem is insurmountable whilst 5:18b is taken to refer to a collapse of the space–time universe. Consequently, in anticipation of our own solution to the problem we should consider favourably the minority interpretation which has explored the possibility that the passing away of heaven and earth refers figuratively to events within history.

Though the possibility is rejected in his recent commentary,[22] in 1962 W. D. Davies suggested that the happening of all things is a reference to the 'figurative' passing away of heaven and earth at Jesus' death and resurrection.[23] This approach has been explored in greatest detail by John P. Meier and there are a number of considerations to recommend it.[24] First, if the eschatological turning point is taken to be the death and resurrection, after which time the entirety of the Torah is no longer applicable, then this would accord well with the dispensational approach to mission according to which the message is confined to Israel during Jesus' ministry (Mt. 10:5; 15:24) and after His resurrection the command is given to evangelize

---

[19]E.g. W. Trilling, *Das wahre Israel: Studien zur Theologie des Matthäus-Evangeliums* (StANT 10; 3rd edn., Munich, 1964), 169-170; U. Luz, *Matthew 1-7* (Minneapolis: Fortress Press, 1989), 266.

[20]See Meier, *Law and History*, 53-54 who adds (p. 54, n. 39) that '. . . to make *panta* mean "all the just demands of the Law," which in turn means "the law of love," is to make too many demands on one simple and vague word'.

[21]Davies and Allison, *Matthew*, 1.495, n. 37.

[22]*Matthew*, 1. 494-495.

[23]*Christian Origins and Judaism* (London: Darton, Longmann & Todd, 1962), 31-66.

[24]J. P. Meier, *Law and History* and *The Vision of Matthew: Christ, Church and Morality in the First Gospel* (New York: Paulist, 1978), 222-264. See also R. G. Hamerton-Kelly, 'Attitudes to the Law in Matthew's Gospel: A Discussion of Matthew 5:18', *BR* 17 (1972), 19-32.

all nations (28:18-20).[25] Secondly, elsewhere amongst early Christians
– Paul in particular – the relativization of the Torah is associated with
the death and resurrection of Jesus (Rom. 3:21-28; 7:4; Gal. 2:19).
Thirdly, all four gospels regard the death and resurrection of Jesus as
an eschatological event.[26] Already in Mark the darkening of the
whole earth at the sixth hour; the rending of the temple veil as Jesus
breathed His last; the application of Old Testament 'Day of the Lord'
prophecies from deutero-Zechariah and the parallelism between
Mark 13 and the passion, interpret the death and resurrection as
eschato- logical events. In Matthew this interpretation is accentuated
in a specifically cosmological direction by the addition of the
description of an earthquake at the crucifixion and the raising of the
dead from their tombs (Mt. 27:51b-53). Finally, that by all these
events Matthew understands at least a figurative reference to the
passing away of heaven and earth might be suggested by the fact that
at 28:11 one of the guards from the tomb went to the chief priests and
reported to them ἄπαντα τὰ γενόμενα ('all that had happened'). The
language in this peculiarly Matthean verse is remarkably similar to
the πάντα γένηται of Matthew 5:18d. It now becomes clear that the
purpose of this last clause of 5:18 is to specify the passing away of
heaven and earth as a specifically Christological focused event within
imminent history.

Whilst this approach has much to be recommended, in its
present formulation it suffers, broadly speaking, from two
deficiencies.[27] First, Davies and Allison have objected that 'Matthew
nowhere explicitly relates changes in the Torah to Jesus' passion and
resurrection. . . '[28] This point can be overstated since it is possible that
(a) Matthew 28:18-20 envisages a mission to the nations in which the

[25]See esp. Meier, *Law and History*, 25-29.
[26]See esp. D. C. Allison, *The End of the Ages has Come: An Early Interpretation of the Passion and Resurrection of Jesus* (Philadelphia: Fortress, 1985).
[27]For what follows see Davies and Allison, *Matthew*, I. 494-495. Criticisms from Phillip Segal, *The Halakah of Jesus of Nazareth according to the Gospel of Matthew* (Lanham: University Press of America, 1986), 22, are really beside the point. From 2 Cor. 5:17 it is clear that some early Christians thought that by virtue of the arrival of the Messiah, heaven and earth had undergone an eschatological transformation. Guelich, *The Sermon on the Mount* (Waco: Word, 1982), 146, objects to Meier's interpretation on the grounds that the fulfilment quotations, which it may be argued underlie 5:18d, refer to Jesus' life and ministry in Matthew, not to the death and resurrection. However, the connection between Jesus' death and resurrection and 5:18d via the fulfilment of Old Testament prophecy, which *is in fact* present at 26:54, 56; 27:9-10, need only be a subsidiary point in the argument.
[28]Davies and Allison, *Matthew*, 494, n. 33.

identity markers which constitute the Torah no longer pertain, but
have been replaced by Baptism in the Father, Son and Holy Spirit and
Jesus' teaching in the gospel, and that (b) the Lord's supper (Mt.
26:26-30), and that which it symbolically represents, is intended to
replace the temple cult as the means of atonement. Yet, Davies and
Allison are right that the relativization of the details of the Torah are
not explicitly related to Jesus' death and resurrection in Matthew.
Rather the Matthean teaching which seems to relativize the Torah
(5:21-48, *cf.* 12:1-8; 19:1-9) pertains to the situation in the ministry.[29]
Unless the intention is heavily allegorical and Matthew's readers had
no thought for the life of Jesus, only their own community situation,
then the Torah's relativization is not strictly analogous to the
dispensational difference between mission to Israel before death/
resurrection and to the nations after that event.[30] The relativization of
the Torah during the ministry would imply that already, before the
death and resurrection, it would be true to say that for Matthew
'heaven and earth' have passed, or are in the process of passing
away.

The second objection, which takes us to the heart of this
study, is the modern inability to conceive of Jesus' death and
resurrection as the passing away of heaven and earth. Even though
Dale Allison has made a good case for an eschatological
interpretation of the passion, he has gone beyond many and himself
falls short of the passion narrative as *the* event which could be
described in the language used at Matthew 5:18b. Whilst there are
earthly cosmic disturbances at the crucifixion, it is not clear how they
could be described as the 'passing away of heaven and earth'. Even
Meier himself assumes that at Matthew 24:35 there is a reference to
the 'catastrophic events in the cosmos at the end of human history'.
There is then, for him, a clear conflict of intention between the two,
otherwise very similar verses, Matthew 5:18 and 24:35. Although he
sees an intimate linguistic and redactional relationship between these
two verses, Meier can only attempt an unconvincing cover-up of the
obvious inconsistency which his 'end-of-the-world' reading of the
latter creates.[31]

But Meier's approach is not to be discarded. It has the
unquestionable strength of its salvation-historical and Christo-

---

[29]*Cf. ibid.*, 494, n. 33; '. . . the "fulfilment" of 5:17-20, a passage which after all
introduces the rest of Mt. 5, is more naturally interpreted as referring to the
teaching of the earthly Jesus rather than to salvific events at the end of the
ministry'.
[30]*Pace* Meier, *e.g. Vision*, 234.
[31]Meier, *Law and History*, 62-63.

logically focused conceptual framework. When we have examined the shape of the dominant second temple cosmology we will be in a position to return to refine this approach in a way which, I think, will satisfy its detractors.

The Temple as the Cosmos in Miniature

It used to be thought that second temple Judaism was free from mythology. It was also thought that apocalyptic, whence the language of 'heaven and earth passing away', was a social and religious phenomenon which developed outside and in opposition to the theology of the temple cult.[32] Both these positions now seem unlikely; there was a lively, if distinctively Jewish mythology, which was in fact centred on the temple cult.[33] Apocalyptic, which was closely bound up with that mythology, is increasingly seen as priestly and cult-centred.[34]

The implications of the appreciation of Judaism's temple-centred mythology for the description of its histories and theologies, including that of early Christianity, are far reaching.[35] That

---

[32]See esp. P. D. Hanson, *The Dawn of Apocalyptic* (Philadelphia: Westminster, 1973).

[33]See *e.g.* R. Patai, *Man and Temple: In Ancient Jewish Myth and Ritual* (London: Thomas Nelson and Sons, 1947); J. Z. Smith, 'Earth and Gods', in *Map is not Territory* (SJLA 23; Leiden: Brill, 1978), 104-128; Jon D. Levenson, *Sinai and Zion: An Entry into the Jewish Bible* (Minneapolis: Winston, 1985), esp. 102-184; *idem*, *Creation and the Persistence of Evil: The Jewish Drama of Divine Omnipotence* (San Francisco: Harper & Row, 1988), 73-99; John Day, *God's Conflict with the Dragon* (University of Cambridge Oriental Publications 35; Cambridge: Cambridge University Press, 1985) on the *Chaoskampf* and Tabernacles; Margaret Barker, *The Gate of Heaven: The History and Symbolism of the Temple in Jerusalem* (London: SPCK, 1991); Ben F. Meyer, 'The Temple at the Navel of the Earth', *Christus Faber: The Master-builder and the House of God* (Allison Park, Penn.: Pickwick Publications, 1992), 217-279 and most recently C. T. R. Hayward, *The Jewish Temple: A Non-Biblical Sourcebook* (London & New York: Routledge, 1996). For an overview of an approach to apocalyptic as temple centred see the present author's 'The High Priest as Divine Mediator in the Hebrew Bible: Dan 7:13 as a Test Case', *Society of Biblical Literature 1997 Seminar Papers* (Atlanta: Scholars Press, 1997).

[34]We should note, for example, Martha Himmelfarb, *Ascent to Heaven in Jewish and Christian Apocalypses* (Oxford: Oxford University Press, 1993), 14-46; David Bryan, *Cosmos, Chaos and the Kosher Mentality* (JSPS 12; Sheffield: Sheffield Academic Press, 1995); Stephen L. Cook, *Prophecy and Apocalypticism: The Postexilic Social Setting* (Minneapolis: Fortress, 1995).

[35]The work of Barker, *Gate of Heaven* and *The Great Angel: A Study of Israel's Second God* (London: SPCK, 1992) and Meyer, 'Navel of the Earth', is a start.

mythology thought of the temple as the point at which the creation had taken place and around which it now revolved – the Navel of the Earth (*Jub.* 8:19; *1 Enoch* 26:1, *cf.* Ezk. 38:12); the meeting point of heaven and earth – the Gate of Heaven. As such the temple cult exists in a mythological space and time, closely identified with both Eden and the future 'eschatological' paradise.

Most importantly of all for our purposes was the belief that the temple was regarded as the 'epitome of the world, a concentrated form of its essence, a miniature of the cosmos'.[36] The temple was far more than the point at which heaven and earth met.[37] Rather, it was thought to correspond to, represent, or, in some sense, to be 'heaven and earth' in its totality. The idea is readily grasped if its three-fold structure, the sanctuary (supremely the Holy of Holies), the inner and outer courts, are allowed to correspond to heaven, earth and sea respectively. In the words of *Num. Rab.* 13:19;

> The Court surrounds the temple just as the sea surrounds the world.

For Josephus the original pre-temple tabernacle was similarly divided into three parts, two of which were 'approachable and open to all'. Moses thereby 'signifies the earth and the sea, since these two are accessible to all; but the third portion he reserved for God alone, because heaven is inaccessible to men' (*Ant.* 3:181, *cf.* 3:123).[38]

Josephus and the *midrash rabbah* to Numbers are post-second temple authors and where any notice has been taken of their temple cosmology it has sometimes been assumed to be a post-biblical development, and therefore of minor importance.[39] Though this symbolism might not be out of place in the wider Greco-Roman world, there is no reason to think that here Josephus or, over half a millennium later, the rabbis are accommodating to a pagan ideology.[40] In fact, there is now a clamorous chorus of Old

---

[36]Levenson, *Zion*, 138, *cf. Creation*, 73-99; Patai, *Temple*, 105-138; Beate Ego, *Im Himmel wie auf Erden* (WUNT 2.34; Tübingen: Mohr-Siebeck, 1989), 20-23; Meyer, 'Navel of the Earth', 231.

[37]As Wright, *Jesus and the Victory*, 205.

[38]The tripartite division of the temple, which was already by the first century expanded to a seven-fold division (*cf.* Josephus *War* 1:26 with *m. Kelim* 1:8) appears to have been closely related to three and seven storied cosmologies familiar to students of apocalyptic literature (*e.g.* 1 Enoch 14:8-18; Apoc. Abr. 19:4).

[39]See *e.g.* Craig R. Koester, *The Dwelling of God: The Tabernacle in the Old Testament, Intertestamental Jewish Literature, and the New Testament* (CBQMS 22; Washington DC: The Catholic Biblical Association of America, 1989), 61.

[40]This is rightly perceived by Holladay, *Theios Aner in Hellenistic-Judaism: A Critique of the Use of This Category in New Testament Christology* (SBLDS 40;

Testament/Hebrew Bible scholars who have welcomed the presence
of the belief in the temple-as-microcosm throughout Israel's canonical
scriptures.

With respect to the post-exilic Priestly material (P), Joseph
Blenkinsopp argued in a 1976 article that the writer of P has
structured his material in order to establish a set of literary and
linguistic correspondences between creation (Gn. 1) and the tabernacle (Ex. 25–40).[41] In a similar vein P. J. Kearney has argued that in
Exodus 25–31, where in seven speeches each beginning with the
words 'And the *Lord* spoke to Moses, saying . . .' (Ex. 25:1–30:10;
30:11-16; 30:16-21; 30:22-33; 30:34-38; 31:1-11; 31:12-17), God gives
Moses His blueprint for the tabernacle, there is a deliberate
correspondence to the seven days of creation in Genesis 1.[42]
Obviously, this means that creation has its home in the liturgy of the
cult and the tabernacle is a mini-cosmos.[43]

A similar picture emerges from the literature of the exile and
early post-exilic literature. Susan Niditch has convincingly demonstrated that the same ideology permeates the vision of the new
temple community in Ezekiel 40–48. She creatively draws on
comparative religion material and concludes: 'On one level, Ezekiel's
vision *is* the building, *is* the cosmos, as the mandala in each of its
orders is the cosmos.' The importance of temple mythology for first
and second Zechariah is well-known, and Eibert J. C. Tigchellar has
now suggested that, like Exodus 25–31, the visions of Zechariah 1–8
are structured to conform to the sequence in Genesis 1.[44]

Jon D. Levenson, who further supplies clear proof for the
roots of this mythology in the architecture of the solomonic temple,
has gathered up much of the wider biblical material in a
thoroughgoing demonstration of its importance for biblical

Missoula, Mont.: Scholars Press, 1977), 86-89; Levenson, *Creation*, 96. In Acts 7:48-
50 it is the *hellenist* Stephen who attacks this cosmic mythology and in *b. Sukk.*
51b and *b. B. Bat.* 4a the cosmopolitan Herod has to be dissuaded from
destroying its architectural representation in his temple rebuilding project.

[41]'The Structure of P', *CBQ* 38 (1976), 275-292 (esp. 275-283).

[42]'Creation and Liturgy: The P Redaction of Exodus 25–40', *ZAW* 89 (1977), 375-
387.

[43]For the reception of Kearney's argument, which can be developed much
further, see, *e.g.*, Moshe Weinfeld, 'Sabbath, Temple and the Enthronement of the
Lord, The Problem of the *Sitz-im-Leben* of Gen. 1:1–2:3', in A. Caquot and M.
Delcor (eds.), *Mélanges bibliques et orientaux en l'honneur de M. Henri Cazelles*
(AOAT 212; Neukirchen-Vluyn: Neukirchener Verlag, 1981), 501-511; Levenson,
Creation, 82-83.

[44]*Prophets of Old and the Day of the End: Zechariah, the Book of Watchers and
Apocalyptic* (OS 35; Leiden: Brill, 1996), 18-19, 38, 45.

theology.[45] From our fragmentary knowledge of Israel's various calendars, it is clear that the two principal New Year festivals, in Tishri and Nisan were associated with the dedication of the sanctuary (1 Ki. 8:2; *cf.* 2 Ch. 7:9; 1 Ki. 12:32-33; Ezr. 3:1-6) and the erection of the tabernacle (Ex. 40:2, 17) respectively.[46] In its earliest history this temple mythology has to be understood in the context of ancient Near Eastern mythology related to kingship, the divine conflict with the forces of Chaos and foundation of temple/city. That the cosmic temple mythology should have made an impact on Israelite religion is to be expected, since this was always part of the mythological *lingua franca* of the ancient Near East.[47] Perhaps its simplest biblical example is Psalm 78:69 where we read:

> He built his sanctuary like the high heavens, like the earth, which he has founded for ever.

On the basis of detailed points of correspondence between biblical texts and ancient Near Eastern parallels, Levenson raises the 'tantalising possibility that "heaven and earth"... in the Hebrew Bible may, on occasion, be an appellation of Jerusalem or its temple.'[48] His case is particularly strong for a text such as Isaiah 65:17-18 where the new heavens and earth are related to the restoration of Jerusalem:

> For I am about to create new heavens and a new earth; the former things shall not be remembered or come to mind. But be glad and rejoice for ever in what I am creating; for I am about to create Jerusalem as a joy . . . [49]

Needless to say, this possibility is of enormous significance for our two New Testament texts.

In the light of this Old Testament material, the presence of the wider temple mythology throughout post-biblical literature and

---

[45]*Zion*, 111-176; *Creation*, 78-99. In both volumes Levenson explores the wider ideological and theological issues at stake in the history of the modern suppression of this Old Testament mythology.
[46]For tabernacles/Day of Atonement and New Creation see *Jub.* 5:10-19, esp. 5:18 referring to Lv. 16:34 and 11QTS 29:9 at the end of a description of the sacrifices for tabernacles.
[47]For examples of ancient Near Eastern parallels to the temple as microcosm motif see Victor (Avidgor) Hurowitz, *I Have Built You an Exalted House: Temple Building in the Bible in Light of Mesopotamian and Northwest Semitic Writings* (JSOTS 115; Sheffield: Sheffield Academic Press, 1992), 335-337.
[48]*Creation*, 90.
[49]*Ibid.*, 90-91: Levenson compares the use of the expression 'heaven and earth' at Gn. 14:19.

its temple-as-microcosm component is unsurprising. Indeed, I would go so far as to say that this ideology was as axiomatic for late second-temple theology as is a concept such as covenant which we now recognize to be everywhere assumed even when not explicit.

Despite scholarly neglect we do find that this mythology is everywhere present in the post-biblical literature. C. T. R. Hayward has demonstrated that it is at least implicit in the fiftieth chapter of the Hebrew Sirach and is made explicit by the Greek translator ben Sirach.[50] He has persuasively argued that, from the same period, the establishment of a temple at Leontopolis in the first half of the second century BC was bound up with the renewal of the cosmos.[51] Ben Zion Wacholder has suggested that the peculiarly cubic architecture of the Temple Scroll found at Qumran, which he correlates closely with the cosmology of the early Enoch literature, reflects a similar conceptual world. The 'future sanctuary prescribed in the scroll seems to have been designed to correspond to the renewal of the heaven and the earth at the end of days'.[52] Certainly at one point in the Temple Scroll there is an unequivocal identification of the creation of the sanctuary as the day of creation.[53]

Both Josephus and Philo explore at some length the cosmic symbolism of the tabernacle/temple and its paraphernalia (Philo *Mos* 2:71-145; Josephus *Ant.* 3:123, 179- 187).[54] Both agree that the woven work of the tabernacle and the temple veil are made from four materials symbolizing the four elements – earth, water, air and fire (*War* 5:212-213; *Ant.* 3:138-134; *Quaestiones in Exodum* 2:85, cf. *Mos.* 2:88). Both regard the seven lamps as symbolic of the planets (*Mos*

---

[50]*Temple*, 38-84, esp. 79-80.

[51]'The Jewish Temple at Leontopolis: A Reconsideration', *JJS* 33 (1982), 429-443 (esp. 436-437).

[52]*The Dawn of Qumran* (Cincinnati: Hebrew Union College Press, 1983), 40, cf. 33-40. Cf. Margaret Barker, 'The Temple Measurements and the Solar Calendar', in George J. Brooke (ed.), *Temple Scroll Studies. Papers presented at the International Symposium on the Temple Scroll, Manchester, December 1987* (JSPS, 7; Sheffield: JSOT Press, 1989), 63-66.

[53]11QT 29:9: [. . .'ד יום הבריה אשר אברא אני את מקדשׁי', '. . . until the day of creation, when I will create my Temple'. In his *editio princeps* Y. Yadin first adopted the reading יום הברכה, though he later conceded the possibility of reading הבריה which is now universally accepted. See Yadin, *The Temple Scroll*, 3 vols. (Jerusalem: Israel Exploration Society, 1983), 2. 129, 354-355.

[54]At *War* 4:324 Josephus refers to the priests who lead 'the cosmic worship' (τῆς κοσμικῆς θρησκείας). For the later suppression of this cosmic temple mythology, as evinced by the magical text *Sefer Yesira* see Peter Hayman, 'Some Observations on Sefer Yesira: (2) The Temple at the Centre of the Universe', *JJS* 37 (1986), 176-182.

2:103; *War* 5:146, 217). Both consider the high priest's garments to be yet another extended cosmic metaphor (*Mos.* 2:117-126, 133-135, 143; *Ant.* 3:180, 183-187). In addition to the points of agreement, each has his own peculiar points of symbolic interpretation. So, for example, for Philo the pomegranates and flowers on the bottom of the high priest's garments symbolize earth and water; the bells the harmonious alliance of the two (*Mos.* 119-121). For Josephus the pomegranates and bells represent lightning and thunder (*War* 5:231; *Ant.* 3:184). It is clear that in the main Philo's cosmological interpretation of the sanctuary is that of mainstream Judaism, since at various points he adds his own more allegorical and rarefied geometric and numerical interpretations (*Mos.* 2:80, 84, 98f., 101-105, 127f.).[55]

Besides the passage in *Numbers Rabbah* this understanding of the temple is recurrent in rabbinic literature even though so much energy after AD 135 had been directed towards creating a world-view – a cosmology – which could give Judaism meaning in the absence of the temple.[56] Before its fall, the temple, of course, lay at the heart of Jewish practice and belief. Given its tangible presence in the national consciousness, nourished through Scripture, daily prayer and festivals, it is worth recalling the talmudic tradition that the inner walls of the temple had been constructed so as to look like the waves of the sea (*b. Sukk.* 51b, *b. B. Bat.* 4a).[57]

---

[55]For the place of these texts in the wider context of Philo's thought see Hayward, *Temple*, 108-141.

[56]See J. Z. Smith, 'Earth and Gods', 104-128; Schäfer, 'Tempel und Schöpfung. Zur Interpretation einiger Heiligtumstraditionen in der rabbischen Literatur', *Studien zur Geschichte und Theologie des rabbinischen Judentums* (AGJU 15; Leiden: Brill, 1978), 122-133. See esp. *Pesiq. R.* 5:3 (on Nu. 7:1); *Pesiq. Rab. Kah.* 1:4-5, 21:5; Rabbi Jacob ben Assi in Midrash Tanhuma *Peqûdê* 2 (Levenson, *Creation*, 170, n. 77). Cf. *Pirqe R. El.* 3 (edn.: Friedlander, 17-18) as the climax of the narrative of creation. At *Pesiqta Rabbati* 7:4 (*cf. Gen. Rab.* 3:9; Tanhuma Buber, *naso* 24) the first day of the temple's service (Nu. 7:12) is regarded as the first day of creation. For the tradition assigned to the tanna Rabbi Pinhas ben Ya'ir see Patai, *Temple*, 108 and see texts cited by Ego, *Im Himmel*, 21, n. 15. Note also *b. Ber.* 55a ('Rav said: "Bezalel knew the letters by which heaven and earth were created"'); *b. Shabb.* 87b; Sifra *schemini*, 43 (Schäfer, 'Schöpfung', 131-132); *Midrash Tadshe*, ch. 2 (in Adolph Jellinek [ed.], *Bet ha-Midrasch* [Jerusalem: Warhmann, 3rd edn. 1967], 2:164-167).

[57]The ocean symbolism of the temple walls appears to have influenced the famous early mystical tradition concerning four who entered *pardes* (*b. Hag.* 14b). Cf. David J. Halperin, *The Faces of the Chariot: Early Jewish Responses to Ezekiel's Vision* (TSAJ 16; Tübingen: Mohr-Siebeck, 1988), 194-210, who supplies parallel Hekhalot texts.

The implications of this mythology for Mark 13:31 (Mt. 24:35) hardly need comment.[58] Within the broader sweep of the temple focus throughout this eschatological chapter and the specific time reference in the preceding verse (Mk. 13:30; Mt. 24:34), Jesus' promise that 'heaven and earth' will pass away makes best sense, not as a collapse of the space–time universe, as has been so often understood, but as a collapse of a *mythical* space–time universe which is embodied in the Jerusalem temple. Mark 13:31 therefore provides a neat *inclusio* with the reference to the destruction of the temple at the beginning of the chapter (Mk. 13:2). It provides *the* definitive statement that the expected destruction which has been anticipated, in particular from Mark 13:14 onwards, has now arrived. Of course, as a summary statement it picks up the language of 13:24-25 which now makes perfect sense in the context of the detailed correspondences between the temple and structures of the cosmos.

In this history of religions context, the claim by Caird, Borg and Wright that Mark 13 is entirely concerned with the destruction of the Jerusalem temple makes excellent sense. However, their reading is properly located not simply in a particular understanding of Old Testament and apocalyptic metaphor but a broader temple mythology. It is to this mythology which texts such as Jeremiah 4:23-28 and *2 Baruch* 10:6-19, to which Borg and Wright appeal, properly belong.

The extent and importance of this mythology could be appreciated only with a fuller and more detailed examination of the data. In particular, I suspect, that reference to the social anthropology undertaken by the likes of Peter Berger and Mary Douglas would clarify the relationship between the temple cult and Jewish cosmology. Clearly the mythology assumes a mutual dependence between the structure and stability of heaven and earth and Israel's Torah constitution. The one is contingent upon the other. The connection is clearly made in a number of primary texts which would merit further attention.[59]

---

[58]For its presence elsewhere in the New Testament see perhaps Heb. 12:25-29 in context.

[59]For the interdependence of (temple-centred) Torah and cosmology see *e.g.* *Jubilees* (esp. 1:29; 2:17ff., 30; 6:18; 12:25-27; 16:27; 23:18f.; 33:10-14; Pseudo-Philo's *Biblical Antiquities* 11:3; 15:6; 23:10; 32:7.

The Passing Away of Heaven and Earth and the
Relativization of the Torah (Mt. 5:18)

In the light of the Jewish background and our rereading of Mark 13:31, we are now in a position to consider in more detail a possible solution to the problematic use of the expression at Matthew 5:18d. There are, I suggest, three interlocking referents in the expression 'until heaven and earth pass away' at 5:18d: (1) the destruction of the Jerusalem temple in AD 70 confirming the obsolescence of the Old Covenant; (2) Jesus' death and resurrection confirming the institution of the New Covenant and its messianic Torah; (3) Jesus' life, ministry and teaching as the embodiment of the new creation and the setting-up of the messianic Torah which His new community follows.

The first of these referents, the destruction of the temple in AD 70, is unproblematic.[60] With the destruction of the Jewish cult the keeping of the Torah in all its details became impossible. The non-Christian Jews who attempted a rebuilding of the Jewish nation state and temple in AD 132-135 and those who later still composed the Mishnah believed that the Torah was not for ever obsolete; it was worth, against the evidence, maintaining a belief in the temple-centred Torah. However, from a Christian perspective the destruction of the temple would naturally be regarded as a definitive relativization of the Torah. The temple and the covenantal obligations which it administered, and the total vision of the world ('heaven and earth') which it expressed, had ceased to exist. It seems now that when the close parallel to Matthew 5:18 at 24:35 refers to the passing away of heaven and earth and endurance of Jesus' words, the first of the three referents in the former text is to the forefront. With the temple cult gone, Jewish Christians should not feel its loss since they still had Jesus' teaching.

But this first referent itself raises a question. Given that the temple represented not simply a focus of teaching, but much more the means of individual and social atonement and maintenance of cosmic structure, what enabled the early Christians to sit lightly to its loss by comparison to the framers of the Mishnah? Did they have something more than Jesus' teaching (Mt. 24:35b) which rendered the loss of the temple insignificant?

Certainly they did, and the second of the two referents at Matthew 5:18, the death and resurrection of the Messiah Jesus, lies at the heart of the early Christian belief that the temple cosmology has

---

[60]For this interpretation of 5:18 see A. Feuillet, 'La synthèse eschatolo-gique de Saint Matthieu', *RB* 57 (1950), 62-91, 180-211.

been fulfilled and replaced (with concomitant relativization of the Torah) in the Lord and Saviour.

We have already assessed the evidence discussed by W. D. Davies and John P. Meier for the crucifixion and resurrection as a passing away of heaven and earth at Matthew 5:18. We have seen that the main problem with their interpretation was the lack of any clear indication that the cosmic disturbances surrounding the crucifixion could be regarded as themselves the *passing away of heaven and earth*. However, in the light of our discussion of the cosmic temple mythology, that lacuna is readily filled. First, it is widely believed that the rending of the temple veil (Mt. 27:51a) symbolizes the destruction of the temple itself.[61] That, of course, as we have just seen, would mean the inability to keep the Torah in all, if not most, of its details. If the temple's destruction is symbolized and if the temple embodies heaven and earth, then a Jewish (Christian) reader of the synoptic crucifixion scene would naturally assume that at this point there is insinuated the passing away of heaven and earth.

Secondly, even if the rending of the veil does not intend an allusion to the temple's destruction, only the entry of Jesus' spirit into the Holy of Holies and the establishing of a new relationship between God and man, that is, between heaven and earth, then the veil-rending presents the reader with another reason to discern the passing away of heaven and earth. Both Philo and Josephus agree (*War* 5:212-213; *Ant.* 3:138-144; *Quaest. Exod.* 2:85, *cf. Mos* 2:88) that the veil, in its fourfold constituent parts 'typified the universe':

> For the scarlet seemed emblematic of fire, the fine linen of the earth, the blue of the air, and the purple of the sea; the comparison in two cases being suggested by their colour, and in that of the fine linen and purple by their origin, as the one is produced by the earth and the other by the sea. On this tapestry was portrayed a panorama of the heavens, the signs of the Zodiac excepted (Josephus, *War* 5:212-213).

In that case, the destructive rending of the temple veil itself signifies the passing away of heaven and earth. Since this happens at exactly the same moment as Jesus breathes His last, there is clearly some

---

[61]See already Pseudo-Clementine *Recognitions* 1:41; *Lives of the Prophets* (C. C. Torrey [ed.], *The Lives of the Prophets: Greek text and translation* [Philadelphia: JBL Monograph Series 1]).

correlation between Jesus' death and the passing away of heaven and earth.[62]

I submit that, when read in the light of the contemporary temple mythology, one of the only two substantial objections to the Davies–Meier reading of Matthew 5:18 with reference to the cross and resurrection is removed. For all three synoptics this was the decisive moment at which heaven and earth passed away (and were recreated at resurrection).

The other objection to the Davies–Meier reading of Matthew 5:18 was the fact that the strongest indications of a Matthean relativization of the Torah refer not to the period after the death and resurrection, but the period of the ministry: already in the Sermon on the Mount some jots and tittles have passed away. Matthew 5:18 therefore demands that there also be some reference to new creation within the life and ministry of Jesus, rather than solely at the cross and resurrection.

We are thus led to consider the third referent in Matthew 5:18b; the creation of a new heaven and earth during His ministry. This phenomenon has received little attention in Matthean scholarship. It deserves far more attention than the present juncture allows. In the present context a number of preliminary considerations are pertinent.[63]

First, Davies and Allison have recently adopted the minority position of commentators which reads Matthew's opening words 'Βίβλος γενέσεως. . . ' (Mt. 1:1) as a title for the whole gospel recalling the title of the first book of the Hebrew Bible and the words at Genesis 2:4 and 5:1. As such, they argue, it should be translated 'the book of the genesis' or '. . . of the new creation'.[64] Though their arguments have not been universally accepted,[65] they rightly compare other passages in which Matthew associates Jesus' birth and

---

[62]The literary connection suggests a set of correspondences between Jesus, the temple and the cosmos, the foundation of which is to be found in the P account of creation and tabernacle, and which I will explore elsewhere.

[63]Beside a thoroughgoing demonstration of the importance of new creation for Matthew's theology, further study would demonstrate the temple context of four of Matthew's five other 'heaven and earth' references (5:34-35; 11:25; 16:19; 18:18-19), the other being 28:18.

[64]Davies and Allison, *Matthew*, 1. 150-153.

[65]Their suggestion is dismissed by G. Stanton, 'Matthew: Βίβλος, εὐαγγέλιον, or βίος?', in F. V. Segbroeck, C. M. Tuckett, G. Van Belle and J. Verkeydon (eds.), *The Four Gospels*, 3 vols. (Festschrift for Frans Neirynck; Leuven: Leuven University Press, 1992), 2.1187-1202 on the grounds that the thought is lacking elsewhere in Matthew.

ministry with the new creation.[66] Among these, the way in which
Jesus is associated with the king of creation who rules over the
chaotic waters (8:23-27, *cf.* Gn. 1:1-2) itself deserves to be placed in the
wider context of Israelite temple and divine kingship mythology.[67] In
the context of our discussion, Davies and Allison's comparison with
the reference back to the paradisal conditions in Matthew 19:3-9 is
particularly important. There the Matthean relativization of Old
Testament divorce law, which is seen as contingent upon Israel's
hardness of heart, is explicitly related, to the new creation in
accordance with that which was initially intended. Thus Torah is
contingent upon both protology and eschatology.

This latter passage could readily fall under the rubric, 'as
heaven and earth pass away the details of the Torah will fall away'
(Mt. 5:18). Here cosmology is firmly rooted in anthropology and
soteriology. But is there any evidence that this was more than a
possible connection between two, otherwise widely separated
passages? Is there any evidence that the relativization of the Torah at
Matthew 5:21-48, which 5:18 introduces, was also understood in
relation to the creation of a new heaven and new earth during Jesus'
ministry? The parallel to Matthew 19:3-9 at 5:31-32 omits reference to
Genesis 1 and 2 and so might be thought to count against any
connection between Matthew's Torah hermeneutic and any putative
realized eschatology. However, given the thrust of our history of
religions and exegetical argument thus far, I suggest that Matthew
has created his Sermon on the Mount with an interpretative
framework, hitherto ignored, as explicit in its correlation of new
creation and Torah relativization as that at Matthew 19:3-9.

When wrestling with Matthew 5:17-20 commentators rarely
relate Jesus' words to the immediately preceding material in 5:13-16.
They concentrate solely on the so-called 'antitheses' which follow
(5:21-48) and the rest of the Sermon (6:1-7:27). Furthermore, when
trying to make sense of the structure of the Sermon as a whole, 5:13-
16 is relegated to being a 'transitional passage' without any
important relationship to any of what follows. Reading 5:18 as I
suggest, the place of 5:13-16 in the immediate context becomes clear.

---

[66]Davies and Allison, *Matthew*, 1.153. See also W. D. Davies, 'The Jewish Sources
of Matthew's Messianism', in J. H. Charlesworth (ed.), *The Messiah: Developments
in Earliest Judaism and Christianity* (Minneapolis: Fortress Press, 1992), 494-511
(esp. 496-498).
[67]*Cf. e.g.* Ps. 89:25 with 89:10. See rightly T. D. N. Mettinger, *In Search of God: The
Meaning and Message of the Everlasting Names* (Philadelphia: Fortress Press, 1988),
112-113.

There is a significant opinion among commentators that 5:14 is meant to evoke Zion/Jerusalem ideology in general and the interest in Jerusalem as a light to the world in particular. The image of a city set on a hill as a light to the world evokes Old Testament descriptions of Israel's capital (Is. 2:2-4; 42:6; 49:6; Mi. 4:1-3) which are themselves taken up in post-biblical literature (*Sib. Or.* 5:420-423; *cf.* Rev. 21:10-11) and the rabbis (*Gen. Rab.* 59:5; *Pesiq. R.* 20:7).[68] Some are sceptical as to this symbolism.[69] But it is entirely consistent with the salt saying in the previous verse which evokes the temple sacrifices (*cf.* Lv. 2:13; Ezk. 43:24; *Jub.* 21:11; 11Qtemple 20). These were also meant to have an atoning and healing purpose for the whole earth (*cf.* 5:13 τῆς γῆς). The Jerusalem/temple focus is also fitting given the allusion to the covenantal blessings (and curses) at the end of Deuteronomy (28:1-14, *cf.* 27:15-28, 68; 29) in Matthew 5:3-12.[70] In Deuteronomy these blessings and curses were to be pronounced on Mount Gerizim and Mount Ebal. However, Deuteronomy 31:9-13 stipulates that the Deuteronomic Law, of which they are a part, was to be recited septennially at the feast of booths, which was celebrated at Jerusalem in the second temple period (*m. Sotah* 7:8).

Immediately after 5:17-20 Matthew chooses for the first of Jesus' six *halakhic* pronouncements one which contains an overtly temple-focused illustration (5:23-24). If Matthew 5:13-16 as a whole has in mind the creation of the people of God as the New or True Jerusalem, then a reference in 5:18 to the old (temple-centred) Jerusalem passing away is entirely natural. There is then an implicit sense of both newness and fulfilment in 5:13-16, which corresponds to these two themes in 5:17-18.

Furthermore, the imagery of the city set on a hill in 5:14 now chimes in with the last passage in the Sermon on the Mount at 7:24-27. There, there is no explicit mention of a hill; rather a house built on a rock is set over against a house built on sand. However, given the set of mythological images which surround the view of the temple as

---

[68]These are explored in full by K. M. Campbell, 'The New Jerusalem in Matthew 5:14', *SJT* 31 (1978), 335-336, who cites Is. 14:32; 60:1-3, 19; Mi. 4:6f.; Tob. 13:9-11; *Sib. Or.* 5:249f.; 5:420-423; 3:787; *Gen. Rab.* 59:5 and more generally Is. 2:2-5; 42, 49, 54 and 60. To his passages should be added Josephus' description of Jerusalem and its temple at *War* 5:67, 208, 222-223; *Ant.* 15:393. *Cf.* Meyer, 'Navel of the Earth', 261. For the restoration of paradisal light and the temple cult, see *e.g.* C. T. R. Hayward, 'The Figure of Adam in Pseudo-Philo's Biblical Antiquities', *JSJ* 23 (1992), 11-14. For the creation of light in the temple in rabbinic literature see Schäfer, 'Schöpfung', 128-129.

[69]*E.g.* Luz, *Matthew*, 251, *cf.* Davies and Allison, *Matthew*, 1.475 for hesitation.

[70]See N. T. Wright, *The New Testament and the People of God*, 386-388.

cosmos, there is in this passage a clear evocation of a similar Zion theology. N. T. Wright has now, rightly I believe, pointed out that a parable about a house built on a rock evokes the temple, which is widely described simply as a (or God's) 'house'.[71] The warning that a house built on sand will fall under the tempest of the elements therefore looks forward to the destruction of the Jerusalem temple in AD 70 which is the principal focus of Matthew 24.

Wright's reading is substantially reinforced by the temple mythology from the Old Testament through to the rabbis. As the point at which creation took place, Zion is inviolable against the forces of Chaos, represented archetypally by the flood waters which God had overcome in Genesis 1:1.[72] Zion is a temple city built on the same foundation stone which God, and then David (*y. Sanh.* 29a; *b. Sukk.* 53b; *b. Mak.* 11a) had used to still the waters of Chaos. As such she is able to withstand the 'thunder and earthquake . . . whirlwind and tempest' (Is. 29:6 in context of 28:14–29:10, *cf. e.g.* Pss. 24; 46). Whilst Israel is set on her 'Rock, the mountain of the *Lord*', the *Lord* destroys 'with a cloudburst and tempest and hailstones' the enemies of His people (Is. 30:29-30).[73] Whilst commentators regularly compare Matthew 7:24-27 with the flood account of Genesis 6–9, that passage itself is part of this larger mythology. In the biblical account, the ark in which Noah and his family were protected was related to the tabernacle.[74]

Of course, in the context of the gospel Jesus is *reusing* this temple mythology. The house no longer stands for the Jerusalem temple. It is individuated to the wise follower of Jesus who hears and follows His teaching (7:24). In the allusion to the future destruction of the Jerusalem temple – the 'passing away of heaven and earth' – Matthew's Jesus follows the prophetic model of subversive remythologizing set by, for example, Ezekiel 13:9-16:

> My hand will be against the prophets who see false visions and utter lying divinations. . . . Because in truth they have misled my people, saying, 'Peace,' when there is no peace; and because, when the people build a wall, these prophets smear whitewash on it. . . . There

---

[71]Wright, *Jesus and the Victory*, 292, 334. *Cf. The New Testament and the People of God*, 387, n. 59.
[72]Of the storm passages regularly cited by commentators to Mt. 7:24-27, Is. 28:16-17; 29:6 are clearly part of the temple mythology tradition.
[73]*Cf. Sib. Or.* 3:685-692; 1QH 3:14f. with 3:1f.
[74]See *e.g.* Claus Westermann, *Genesis 1-11: A Commentary* (London: SPCK, 1984), 421 on Genesis 6:16; Joseph Blenkinsopp, 'Structure of P', 283-286. *Cf. e.g.* Hayward, *Temple*, 52 on *Ben Sira* 50:7.

will be a deluge of rain, great hailstones will fall, and a stormy wind will break out . . . there shall be a deluge of rain, and hailstones of wrath to destroy it (*cf.* Je. 7:3ff.).

Read in this way Matthew 7:24-27 creates a neat *inclusio* with 5:13-16 around the rest of the Sermon on the Mount.[75] These two scenes evoke two of the most fundamental components of the temple mythos; the creation of the primal light and the construction of the cosmic mountain.[76] They thus provide the hermeneutical lens through which the whole of the Sermon is to be read: this *halakah* is that of the new creation – its adherents belong to a new temple constitution, a new heaven and a new earth. Follow Jesus' words and the prerogatives of Jerusalem and the temple are yours.[77] Ignore them and you will go the same way that Ezekiel's opponents went in 587 BC.

   This *inclusio* thus provides an essential hermeneutical key to the interpretation of the whole Sermon. The *halakah* which it lays out is that of the new temple community for whom there is already dawning a new heaven and a new earth. The details of the Torah of the old covenant are thus in part relativized. The creation of the new community is understood in clearly cosmological terms and the (new) Torah is regarded as contingent upon that ecclesiologically focused cosmology.

   I submit that the difficulties presented by the two variants of the same 'heaven and earth passing away' saying have now been substantially resolved. It must be admitted that new questions have been thrown up. What is the relationship between the three layers of meaning we have discerned at Matthew 5:18? Where else in Matthew do we find such a confluence of ecclesiology, Christology, cosmology and Torah ideology and what is the wider Jewish background to such thought? To an exploration of these and other questions I will return elsewhere.

---

[75]The beatitudes (blessings) of Mt. 5:3-12 are coupled with the curses of Mt. 23:13-36.

[76]Reading *e.g.* Schäfer, 'Schöpfung', 125-129; Levenson, *Zion*, 132-136 one cannot fail to appreciate the symbolism of this *inclusio*.

[77]The logic is consistent with the return to paradise in Mt. 19:3-9. It is also, I would suggest, the key to understanding Mt. 12:1-8.

Chapter 7

TRANSCENDING IMMINENCE: THE GORDIAN KNOT OF PAULINE ESCHATOLOGY

Ben Witherington, III

The axiom of New Testament scholarship, that Paul started out with expectations of Christ's imminent return only to change his mind after 'delay', disappointment and maturity, deserves to be challenged. References to the Lord's nearness often mean his spatial proximity among believers, not a temporal closeness. Paul, like his Lord, from whom he drew much imagery on this subject, did not work from a timetable but attempted both to moderate expectation (Thessalonians) and to stimulate it (Corinthians). For Paul, the certainty of what awaits matters more than the timing of it, and therefore scholars have to reckon with his combination of possible imminence and definite return.

It is, by now, old news that Paul's letters are filled with ideas and phrases that fall in one way or another under the rubric of eschatology. No scholar I know of would deny that Paul offers various remarks on the future of the world and of believers, and on the role that Christ will play in those end-time events. Nor is there really any debate that Paul also speaks in terms of some eschatological events as having already transpired. In particular, Paul's labelling of Christ's resurrection as not an isolated phenomenon within history, but rather the first-fruits of the general eschatological resurrection of God's people (1 Cor. 15:20), makes quite clear that Paul in a very real sense believed 'the future is now'.[1]

This, however, leaves the question: what is the relationship between the eschatological 'already' and the eschatological 'not yet'?

---

[1] See my discussion of this entire matter in *Jesus, Paul, and the End of the World* (Downers Grove: IVP, 1992).

One common way of framing an answer to this question has been to speak of a tension between imminence and delay.[2] Whatever the merits of this sort of conceptual framework for analysing other early Jewish and Christian documents that contain eschatological and apocalyptic remarks, I am convinced there are several problems with this entire way of framing the question if the subject is Pauline eschatology. The problems will be enumerated here and then expounded on as this essay develops.

First, when one encounters the language of eschatological imminence one must determine whether Paul is speaking of spatial or temporal nearness. It cannot be simply assumed that temporal nearness is meant. Secondly, when temporal nearness is the subject, one must be able to determine whether Paul is reflecting or correcting eschatological views of a certain imminence of the return of Christ. Thirdly, when the language of temporal nearness is used and Paul's own views are the issue, the question becomes whether Paul is referring to the mere possibility of the nearness of the end or of Christ's return, or whether he is asserting the definite nearness of such events. If it is simply the real possibility of such events on the near horizon, then we certainly cannot frame the discussion in terms of imminence and delay. The term 'delay' implies that an event or series of events is overdue or late; it implies that there is a certain time-schedule which has not been met. I submit that Paul had no such set timetable in his head, which he then later in life had to readjust when Christ didn't appear in the period when he wrote his earlier letters. Fourthly, I submit that when Paul spoke of this matter of end-times and end-timing he drew on the Jesus material both in terms of his specific remarks and in terms of his imagery, and this indebtedness, rather than a more general indebtedness to early Jewish apocalyptic and eschatological thinking, best explains his views. In short, I think the eschatological analyses of A. Schweitzer should no longer determine the way the discussions of Paul's eschatology (or for that matter Jesus' eschatology) should be framed.[3]

Textual Red Herrings

A classic example of a text which has often been taken to refer to the temporal nearness of Christ, but which in fact in all likelihood refers to the spatial nearness of the Lord, is found in Philippians 4:5-6. The

---

[2]See for instance C. L. Holman, *Till Jesus Comes: Origins of Christian Apocalyptic Expectation* (Peabody: Hendrickson, 1996).
[3]See my discussion in *Jesus, Paul and the End of the World*, 20ff.

term ἐγγύς can of course refer to nearness in time or space, but words only have particular meanings in particular contexts, and it is important in this case not to divorce Philippians 4:5 from Philippians 4:6. What we have in these verses is probably a Pauline echoing of the language of the Psalms. In particular, Psalm 145:18-19 would seem to lie in the background here, and that text reads: 'The Lord is near to those who call upon Him.' This may be compared to Paul's words: 'The Lord is near. Do not be anxious, but in all things pray and petition, with thanksgiving making your requests known to God.' One may also want to compare Psalm 34:17-18, which speaks of calling on the name of the Lord and then adds that 'the Lord is near to those who call upon Him'. Psalm 119:151 may also be considered on this issue.[4] The context of Paul's exhortation here is that he is offering concluding remarks which include final exhortations, prayer reminders and a benediction (verse 7). This larger context where comfort and final exhortations (rejoice, do not worry) are in order supports the conclusion that here spatial not temporal nearness is meant. What could be more comforting or more a motivation to prayer than the reminder of the psalmist that the Lord is near and thus will hear those who call upon Him? In this case, Paul is talking about the imminence of the Transcendent One, not the imminence of a transforming time.

There are other texts with temporal terms that I would suggest are also red herrings, though for different reasons. For instance, consider 1 Corinthians 7:29 and 31. Here the subject is how Christians will or should behave during the rest of the time until the end comes. Notice that in verse 31 Paul indicates that the present form of this world is *already* passing away.[5] In other words, he is referring to a process already set in motion, not one about to begin or on the near horizon. The most crucial event in the eschatological timetable has already taken place, namely the Christ event, and it has relativized the *schema* of this world and the significance of all worldly relationships. One can no longer place ultimate value or faith in the things of this world.[6] This brings us back to 1 Corinthians 7:29. Should the key term συνεσταλμένος be translated short or shortened? In view of verse 31, the latter translation would make perfectly good

---

[4]See my *Friendship and Finances in Philippi* (Valley Forge: Trinity Press, 1994), 112-113.

[5]Notice too in Rom. 13:11-14 that Paul has in mind an eschatological process already set in motion by the Christ event, not some time that is about to break in or some impending distress.

[6]See my discussion in *Women in the Earliest Churches* (Cambridge: Cambridge University Press, 1988), 34ff. and the notes there.

sense and comport well with the notion that something has already happened that has changed the world.

From a grammatical point of view as well, συνεσταλμένος surely should be seen as a participle not an adjective, and this too points to the translation 'shortened'. The word is used in nautical contexts to speak of a sail being shortened because of something that has already happened, namely a change in the weather. Paul, if you will, is speaking of the fact that there has already been a change in the eschatological weather. That the time has been shortened means one must reckon with the possible imminence of the end and so be prepared. The most crucial event which prepares for that end has already transpired. But precisely because Paul does not know any specifics about the timing, he can speak only of shortening, not shortness of time. Here Paul offers an ethic grounded in the 'already' of what Christ has done, but given added urgency by the possible imminence of Christ's return.[7]

Our third text that should not be the victim of an overly 'enthusiastic' imminence reading is 1 Thessalonians 4:15. Here Paul is talking about the fate of those believers who have died in the Lord, and those who are alive on earth when the Lord returns. What is usually not recognized in the exegesis of this text is that Paul is dealing with two relative unknowns, not one. Paul not only does not know when the Lord will return, he also does not know exactly when he will die. He believes that the Lord could return in his lifetime. He also believes that he could die before the Lord returns, as other Christians had already done (*cf.* Phil. 1:19-26). In these circumstances, there is in fact only one category in which Paul could place himself when speaking of the Lord's return – with the living. If Paul did not know the timing of Christ's return or of his own death with any precision, he could not say 'but we who will die before the Lord returns . . .' He had to put the matter just as he does. In short, one cannot conclude that 1 Thessalonians 4:15 clearly means that Paul thought the Lord would definitely return during his lifetime. Possible imminence had to be conjured with, but certain imminence is not affirmed here. Thus in this text we cannot even talk about a tension between imminence and 'delay'. Only something that does not arrive according to an already known and precise schedule could be said to be delayed.

---

[7] See B. Winter's essay in this volume for another angle on this problematic text.

Over-realized Eschatology and Paul's Converts

It is seldom mentioned, but in fact two kinds of over-realized eschatology are possible. There is first the sort that Paul is trying to correct in 1 Thessalonians 4–5, and there is secondly the sort he is dealing with in 1 Corinthians. In the former case, Paul is trying to make clear that the Thessalonians have misunderstood him if they thought that he said the Lord's return was necessarily just around the corner. In response to this sort of temporally oriented over-realized eschatology, Paul offers words of caution and eschatological reserve. In the latter case, over-realized eschatology in fact amounts to overly spiritualized eschatology, with the assumption that the Corinthians already had in the Spirit all there was to salvation. Paul satirizes this position when he says to the Corinthians, 'Already you have all you want! Already you have become rich! Quite apart from us you have become kings!' And then he adds somewhat forlornly, 'I wish that you had become kings, so that we might be kings with you' (1 Cor. 4:8). To this sort of eschatological error, Paul holds out the clear prospect of a future resurrection body for the believer (1 Cor. 15). Life in the Spirit was not all there was to Pauline eschatology.

By listening to C. Morris' humorous reconstruction of 'Epistles to the Apostle', we get a glimpse of the kind of things the Thessalonians might have written to Paul on the basis of their misreading of his earlier preaching. In one letter we hear:

My dear Paul:

The followers of Jesus in this city are in receipt of your letter which was read out in church a month ago and which appears to confirm a widely held view that our Lord will be returning in glory at any moment to take believers such as my humble self back with him to heaven. Being a hard-headed businessman I took your words with the utmost seriousness. To prepare myself and my family for the Day of the Lord, I sold my business at a knock-down price and gave the proceeds to the poor – and that, let me add, was a tidy sum, but I assume we won't need cash in heaven!

So here I am with my bags packed, my property disposed of, and myself, my wife, and my children taking it in shifts to scan the skies for something unusual to appear. In fact every time I hear a trumpet, I nearly jump out of my skin! And what has happened? Nothing.

I can't help feeling that I've been made to look an utter fool in the eyes of my friends and business acquaintances. They all think I've gone stark raving mad. Meanwhile, the man who bought my business, far from suffering the catastrophe of the wicked, is making a handsome profit and living in my house, which is one of the finest in the city. He is allowing us to camp at the bottom of my, or rather, his garden, with passersby leaning over the fence gaping at us and making offensive remarks. Not a pleasant predicament for a former mayor to be in. Not that earthly honors matter, of course. But one has one's legitimate pride. Would you kindly tell me what to do next?

Paphlos,
(formerly Managing Director Paphlos Importers Limited)[8]

Of course, this is written with tongue firmly in cheek, but in fact it makes the point very well that Paul's audiences from time to time and from place to place often misunderstood what Paul was trying to say about eschatological matters. Possible imminence is a hard concept to distinguish from definite imminence, and Paul may well have not always made nice clear distinctions in his initial preaching. Furthermore, if, as is likely, Paul's converts in Thessalonica were mainly Gentiles, it is hardly likely that they would have had much experience in interpreting sermons filled with eschatological remarks. Graeco-Roman religion placed no real emphasis on the possible 'end of the world' or related matters. Indeed, what eschatology they did have to reckon with was Imperial eschatology, involving the deification of the Emperor and the propaganda about his conveying of divine benefits.[9] The point which is most crucial for us is that the eschatology of Paul's converts which the apostle is correcting must not be too readily or rapidly predicated of the apostle himself.[10]

If Paul must offer eschatological nuancing and reserve to the Thessalonians (see esp. 2 Thes. 2), to the Corinthians Paul must stress both the reality and the temporality of future eschatology, something about which the Thessalonians apparently had no doubts. As various

---

[8]C. Morris, *Epistles to the Apostle: Tarsus Please Forward* (Nashville: Abingdon, 1976), 13ff.

[9]See my discussion in *Conflict and Community in Corinth* (Grand Rapids: Eerdmans, 1995), 295ff.

[10]One of the more horrific experiences a teacher can have is to take up his students' notebooks spontaneously and read what they thought he was saying. It is a sobering activity to say the least.

scholars continue to remind us, Paul's letters are *ad hoc* in character, dealing with specific situations, and these subjects are largely determined by the needs of the moment. These letters are not compendiums of Paul's random thoughts on given subjects. It is thus; more than a little tricky to tease out a more fully orbed picture of what Paul thought on a complex subject like eschatology. Nevertheless, we may take it as unlikely that Paul said anything on this subject purely for effect. In other words, something of his real views on eschatology are revealed in these letters. We are not dealing with mere sophistic rhetoric, 'full of sound and fury [but] signifying nothing'.

Notice how at the very outset of 1 Corinthians Paul stresses the necessity for the Corinthians to be prepared for the Day of the Lord. 1 Corinthians 1:7 says pointedly that the Corinthians are waiting for the revealing of the Lord Jesus Christ.[11] We have already mentioned the eschatological remarks in the midst of Paul's practical teaching in 1 Corinthians 7, but one could equally well point to brief asides like 'Do you not know that the saints will judge the world?. . . Do you not know that we are to judge angels?' (1 Cor. 6:2-3), which make very clear that Paul believes the Corinthians are guilty of not viewing things with one eye on the eschatological not-yet. This is also clear from remarks like Paul's statement that 'we' are the ones 'on whom the ends of the ages have come. So if you think you are standing, watch out that you do not fall' (1 Cor. 10:11-12).

Most importantly, we have 1 Corinthians 15 where not only the fact of the resurrection and the nature of the resurrection body are discussed, but even a cursory outline of future events that will transpire when the Lord returns is presented (15:22-28). Paul surely takes the time to do this because too many Corinthians were clueless or had not adequately come to grips with the fact that there would indeed be more eschatological events, and that future reality should effect how believers act and behave before the parousia. Paul's words are carefully chosen and meant to convey the notion that there were definite things yet to transpire in God's plan for His people who were being conformed to the image of Christ.[12] His eschatology must not

---

[11]To both the Thessalonians and the Corinthians Paul must say 'Wait and be prepared', but for different reasons. The Corinthians are not looking for, or at least are not prepared for the coming, and the Thessalonians are overly eager and as a result are not doing all the things they ought to be doing while waiting for the return. They are to be busy, not busybodies (see *e.g.* 1 Thes. 5:14; 2 Thes. 3:6-13). The Corinthians need to stop doing things that indicate they think there will never be a future coming and with it final judgment.

[12]Lest we think Paul, like the Corinthians, was guilty of overly spiritualizing matters eschatological, it is most unlikely that in 1 Cor. 15:44 when Paul refers to

be confused or fused with either of the errors of 'imminence' of which the Thessalonians or the Corinthians were guilty.

Paul and the Eminent One

Here we must reflect briefly about Paul's own eschatology. We have already accepted that it is quite impossible to avoid the conclusion that Paul believed it was possible that the Lord might return soon. Paul's temporal remarks simply cannot be spiritualized to the extent that the tension between the temporal 'already and not yet' is eliminated. Yet we have stressed that this tension should not be described as one between imminence and delay. That formulation in both its halves has to do with the future whether sooner or later, whereas Paul formulates the matter by talking about eschatological events that have already happened in the past and those which have not yet come to pass.

1 Thessalonians 5:2-11 has long been a text which produces controversy. Here Paul describes the Day of the Lord as something which comes 'like a thief in the night'. We can gather from verse 3 (when they say 'There is peace and security', then *sudden destruction will come upon them, as labour pains come upon a pregnant woman . . .*) that the force of the metaphor and the analogies drawn to make its meaning plain is that this day will come suddenly and at an unexpected time. The metaphor suggests that for the unbeliever it will indeed amount to destruction, like a thief breaking into the house of the unsuspecting and unprepared and destroying everything. For the believer as well, the timing of the event is unknown. The difference is that the believer is prepared and therefore the event, while still sudden, is not unexpected. Thus Paul adds, 'But you beloved are not in darkness for that day to surprise you like a thief for you are all children of light . . .'(verse 4).

Preparedness is urged by Paul, and this exhortation is not banal, not because Paul had or could tell his converts the parousia was necessarily imminent, but because he could stress the certainty of Christ's parousia happening, coupled with its possible imminence

---

a spiritual body he means a body made out of Spirit. It is far more likely that he is contrasting two kinds of physical bodies – one empowered by a natural life principle; one totally empowered and enlivened by the Holy Spirit. In any event, it may also be noted that D. B. Martin, *The Corinthian Body* (New Haven: Yale, 1995), 104ff. has shown that many persons in the Greco-Roman world did not see 'spirit' as a non-material category at all, but rather a more refined sort of substance.

(possible, precisely because Paul did not know the timing of the event). It is significant that verse 2 suggests that Paul had already taught the Thessalonians about the issues of times and seasons and how Christ's coming would be like a thief in the night. This is not new information for the audience, it is a reiteration and expansion upon what the apostle had already said. It suggests that Paul had already cautioned them against theological forecasting about Christ's return.

It is interesting that if there were a problem about what was perceived by some converts to be the 'delay' of Christ's return, it is already in evidence in what many scholars would see as Paul's earliest letter, a letter written within about two decades of Christ's death. There is no need to dispute the suggestion that some early converts perceived things in this way and indeed believed in the return of Christ as something definitely on the near horizon. It is crucial, however, to say that this is a misreading of Paul's own view, as 1 Thessalonians 4–5 makes evident.

Already in 1 Thessalonians Paul is cautioning eschatological reserve and damping down any eagerness for forecasting. This teaching of eschatological reserve is not a phenomenon that arose late in the first century to compensate for a worry about 'delay' that developed amongst the earliest Christians as the first generation and the apostles died out. It would appear that in the case of the apostle himself, the 'thief in the night' concept caused the apostle to reckon with the possibility of either living until the Lord returned or dying before then (cf. 2 Cor. 5:6-10; Phil. 1:21-26). This did not amount to a change in his eschatology, between 1 and 2 Corinthians, but rather a simple spinning out of the implication of the 'thief in the night' idea which is found already in 1 Thessalonians in the early 50s.[13]

Several texts in Romans deserve our consideration at this point, because they too reflect this tension between already and not yet, and even between eschatological reserve and caution coupled with a belief in possible imminence. Working backwards through

---

[13]Here is not the place to get into a long argument about the authenticity of 2 Thessalonians, but the point I would stress is that, if Paul always believed that the Lord's return was certain, but only possibly imminent, he could also have definitely conjured with the possibility of a certain series of preliminary eschatological events such as we find discussed in 2 Thessalonians 2. In this regard he would not be any different from Jesus in his teaching about the messianic woes or preliminary events (see Mk. 13), or other early Jews who were convinced that a series of events would precede the coming of the messiah (cf. e.g. 4 Ezra, the 'parables' in 1 Enoch, and especially Daniel 6–7 itself where the beastly empires and emperors rule before the human and humane figure comes to establish dominion on the earth).

Romans we come to Romans 16:20 first. This verse involves a word of encouragement that evil will not prevail for ever, and more to the point, there is a stress on how much greater God's power is than Satan's. In a oxymoronic and ironic phrase, Paul speaks of the God of peace crushing Satan under the feet of the Christian audience. The debate has always been about the phrase ἐν τάχει. Does it mean 'soon' or does it mean 'suddenly' or 'quickly'? If 1 Thessalonians 5 is any guide, it would seem logical, and it is lexically perfectly feasible, to translate the phrase 'suddenly' or 'quickly'. As various grammarians have emphasized, the phrase is an adverbial one and so under normal circumstances it ought to indicate the *manner* or way in which something is done, rather than the timing.[14]

There is, however, another way of reading this text. If we do conclude that the phrase ἐν τάχει means 'soon', then perhaps the emphasis should be placed on the phrase 'under *your* feet'. The context here is frankly not very eschatological. Paul is encouraging them to avoid evil and do good, and urging them to deal with those who cause dissensions and offences. In other words, Paul is dealing with local problems in the somewhat divided Roman church. Notice that Paul does not say that God will soon crush or place Satan under Christ's feet (*cf.* 1 Cor. 15:24-25). It is thus quite possible that Paul is using eschatological language here to describe God's near incursion into the situation to deal with the dissensions and problems amongst Roman Christians. Paul sees those problems as generated by the Prince of Darkness. If this interpretation is correct, then the text says nothing and implies nothing about the return of Christ at all, much less the timing of such an event. Paul believes Christians are already in the eschatological age. It is then to be expected that he will characterize social difficulties and their solutions in the church in eschatological terms, such as we find in Romans 16:20.

The eschatological basis and framework of all of Paul's practical advice is seen clearly when we turn to Romans 12–13. At 12:2 Paul stresses that Christians are not to be conformed to the world, the form of which is after all passing away, but rather be transformed by the Holy Spirit which produces the renewal of the Christian mind, heart, will, emotions, habits. The transformation of the mind allows clear Christian judgments about what is the will of God and what is not.

Christians also know, since they have the eschatological Spirit of God in their lives, that they are living in the eschatological

---

[14]See the discussion in my *Jesus, Paul and the End of the World*, 31ff. and the notes there.

age. If asked what time it was, Paul would have replied happily, 'It is the eschatological age, and God's present people are those upon whom the ends of all previous ages have come to fruition and completion.' This leads us to a brief discussion of Romans 13:11-14.

Notice firstly that Paul is reminding the audience about what time *it already is*, not what time it will soon be. The time already is the time to wake up. Because of the possible nearness of the conclusion of God's salvation plan, one must be awake or alert. What then are we to make of the use of the term 'the day', dramatically contrasted with 'the night'? It would appear that Paul is talking about two ages, one that is passing away, and one that is dawning. This 'day' is said to be ἤνγικεν. The perfect tense of the verb ἐγγίζω requires careful translation. Notice that this verb in this tense is often used in the gospels to describe the coming of the kingdom (Mt. 3:2; 4:17; 10:7; Mk. 1:15). The two basic options of translation are 'has come' or 'is at hand/near'. As W. R. Hutton has shown, the most natural translation of this key verb in the perfect tense is either ' has come' or 'is at hand'.[15] In Romans 13 itself, bearing in mind that Paul has said that it is already time to wake up, it would seem likely that Paul means not merely that the day is near, but rather that the first rays of dawn have already arrived – the day is here or at hand. This conclusion seems especially probable since Paul speaks of his converts already being 'sons of light', which is a Semitic idiom for being a product of a particular era or age. A person cannot be a product of an age that does not yet exist! Thus 'the day has arrived' and so it is time to wake up and get to work. This is why G. B. Caird can rightly stress that Paul is not balancing imminence and delay, but rather already and not yet. He stresses that 'the statement that the night is almost over and the day is breaking follows hard on a vast missionary programme which involves conversion of the whole Gentile world and of all Israel'.[16] I would submit that this kind of juxtaposition is possible in Pauline thought if the imminence of the parousia is only seen as possible, not certain.

If, as most scholars still think, Philippians is one of Paul's later letters, it is in order to point out that Paul's fervency about the idea of Christ's return has in no way been tempered, nor has it waned. Philippians 1:6, 10 makes it quite clear that Paul is still looking forward to that day, and 3:20 speaks of the eager expectation of Christ the Saviour's return from heaven to earth. Of course, the amount of time Paul spends discussing eschatological matters is

---

[15]W. R. Hutton, 'The Kingdom of God has Come', *ET* 64 (1952-53), 89-91.

[16]G. B. Caird, *Paul's Letters from Prison* (Oxford: Oxford University Press, 1976), 22.

largely determined by the questions and problems the congregation was raising. What we see no sign of, interestingly enough, is a trend from the earlier to the later letters where Paul is increasingly wrestling with the problem of delay, or increasingly downplaying future eschatology. What we do find, especially in the prison letters, is an increasing reckoning by the apostle with the possibility that he may die soon and so probably before the Lord returns. Yet at the same time as the remarks in Philippians 1:18-26, we also see the eager expectation of 1:6, 10 and 3:20. This is so because in fact, for Paul, the timing of his own impending death has become less of an unknown as time has passed than the timing of the parousia, which was always incalculable. J. C. Beker astutely observes:

> Paul's Christian hope is a matter of prophecy, [but] not a matter of prediction. The incalculability of this hope is for Paul one of its essential marks . . . . Paul emphasizes the unexpected, suddenness and surprising character of the final theophany (1 Thess. 5.2-10) . . . . Thus the delay of the parousia is not a theological concern for Paul. It is not an embarrassment for him; it does not compel him to shift the center of his attention from apocalyptic imminence to a form of realized eschatology.[17]

Perhaps in the end the Gordian knot of Pauline eschatology is not so difficult to unravel after all. The key is jettisoning the paradigm imminence–delay, and talking instead of already and not yet, as Paul himself does. Fervency comes from confidence in the certainty of and, to a lesser degree, from the possible imminence of Christ's return.

Ad Fontes

It is more than a little possible that what was distinctive about Paul's eschatology was not uniquely Pauline in character. Indeed I would suggest that Paul in his eschatological remarks is in various ways and to a significant degree simply expounding upon early Jewish Christian ideas. In particular, I believe that an indebtedness to the Jesus tradition can be demonstrated in matters eschatological, but there is also indebtedness to very early Jewish Christian ways of speaking about eschatological matters.[18]

---

[17]J. C. Beker, *Paul's Apocalyptic Gospel* (Philadelphia: Fortress Press, 1982), 48-49.
[18]Though it has become fashionable in some of those scholarly circles where Q is given an especial importance (for example in the Jesus Seminar) to suggest that Jesus' originally non-eschatological teaching has been 'eschatologized' by

On the latter front, one can point to 1 Corinthians 16:22 where we find the *marana tha* utterance. What this surely suggests is that: (1) there was a fervent hope among the earliest Jewish Christians who spoke Aramaic, which is to say probably the earliest Jerusalem Jewish Christian community, that the Lord would return and possibly soon, and (2) this event was regularly a subject of prayer. Indeed so regularly had it become an element of prayer in early Christian worship that the Aramaic phrase became a liturgical formula that Paul and others felt important to convey to their largely non-Aramaic-speaking converts. It is clear not only from this text, but also from texts like Galatians 4:5-6 and Romans 8:15, that Paul was in touch with the worship life of earliest Jewish Christians as they adored Christ and prayed as He taught them to pray. This small, but important window of Aramaic phrases in Paul's letters allows us to see that he was in contact with the thinking of the earliest Christians about God and the return of Christ.

If we turn, however, to the actual echoes of the Jesus tradition in Paul's own eschatological teaching, a good deal could in fact be said, but we must content ourselves with a few cursory remarks. Firstly, we must ask about the origin of the 'thief in the night' metaphor used of the coming of the Day of the Lord and here I would suggest that Paul reflects an indebtedness to the Q saying found in Luke 12:39/Matthew 24:43. Notice, as J. Fitzmyer stresses, that nothing is said in this saying about the thief being delayed, it is simply that the time of the burglary is unknown.[19] Even if one takes Luke 12:40 to be a secondary expansion of the saying,[20] verse 39 still speaks about watchfulness because someone is coming at an unknown time, an hour when he is least expected. It would appear that this teaching of Jesus had a wider impact than just on Paul, for we also find echoes of it in Revelation 3:3 and 16:15 and in 2 Peter 3:10 as well. In each case the metaphor is taken to allude to the

---

'Matthew' and also by Paul (*cf.* the recent offering by Robert Funk entitled *Honest to Jesus* [San Francisco: Harper, 1996]), however, this neglects the importance of the Markan apocalypse found in Mk. 13, as well as the eschatological character of various of Jesus' parables. Here I am using eschatological in the narrower sense of teaching about the future final events that are yet to transpire. A much stronger case can be made for Luke's having toned down or historicized the eschatological teachings of Jesus, than for the opposite suggestion of eschatologizing a non-eschatological body of Jesus' teachings. See the introduction to my *The Acts of the Apostles: a Socio-Rhetorical Commentary* (Grand Rapids: Eerdmans, 1997), and the Excursus on Lukan eschatology within the commentary.
[19]J. Fitzmyer, *The Gospel of Luke X-XXIV* (New York: Doubleday, 1985), 986.
[20]I have disputed this in *Jesus, Paul, and the End of the World*, 46ff.

coming Day of the Lord at an unexpected and indeed unknown time. Notice how the *Gospel of Thomas* redirects the tradition in a non-eschatological direction to refer to the breaking into the believer's life of the 'world' (*Thomas* 21:3; *cf.* 103).

There are in fact other hints in the eschatological discourse found in 1 Thessalonians 4:13–5:11 that Paul is drawing on and amplifying the Jesus tradition. For example, we may point to the reference to a word of the Lord at 4:15, which reference, when compared to texts like 1 Corinthians 7:10 and 25, suggests not an utterance of the risen Lord to Paul, but a drawing on the words of the earthly Jesus. We may also wish to point to the extensive work of D. Wenham establishing a considerable pattern of dependence of Paul's teaching, including his eschatological teaching, on the Jesus tradition.[21]

It is true, of course, that Paul is not simply a tradent, but one may well wonder whether a saying like Mark 13:32 was known to Paul and influenced how he couched the entire discussion of the matter of the timing of Christ's return. Mark 13:32, found in the middle of an eschatological discourse which discusses both preliminary events and then afterwards the return of the Son of Man (without specifying the temporal relationship of the former and the latter in any specific way), suggests that other early Christians than Paul were familiar with the notion that the timing of the second coming was unknown, indeed even unknown to Jesus, an idea that it is hardly believable the early church would have invented.

I submit that if in fact Jesus did profess ignorance of the timing of the coming of the Son of Man, and this was widely known, one would then have to explain why a notion of the 'delay' of the parousia would have ever arisen in the first place, especially in the first three or four decades after Christ's death. I would suggest that in fact such an idea did not really arise during that period! Not 'imminence and delay', but rather 'already and not yet' were the terms in which the eschatological discussion was couched in earliest Christianity.

It is probable that when the notion of possible imminence did begin to fade in the latter third of the first century after the first

---

[21]See in the first place his essay 'Paul and the Synoptic Apocalypse', in *Gospel Perspectives: Studies of the History and Tradition in the Four Gospels*, Vol. 2 (Sheffield: JSOT Press, 1981), 345-375 and more recently his *Paul: Follower of Jesus or Founder of Christianity?* (Grand Rapids: Eerdmans, 1995). One may also wish to consult on this topic J. D. G. Dunn, 'Jesus Tradition in Paul', in B. Chilton and C. A. Evans (eds.), *Studying the Historical Jesus: Evaluations of the State of Current Research* (Leiden: Brill, 1994), 155-178.

generation had largely died out, there were some moves not mainly to speak of delay, but rather to de-eschatologize or historicize the Jesus tradition and other early Jewish Christian traditions. This process continued on unabated well into the second century and was challenged by both orthodox and heterodox groups, for example by the Montanist movement in Asia Minor. What that movement attested to was the loss of eschatological focus and fervency in the early church.

We may be able to see the beginnings of rationalization or the philosophizing about the non-appearance of the second coming in a text like 2 Peter 3:8-15, and here perhaps, at the end of the first century, or some would say in the first years of the second century, we may begin to talk about a tendency to speak about the issue of slowness. What is striking about this text, however, is how very different it is from what we find in Paul's letter or in the synoptic gospels. The eschatological tune has been transposed into a rather different key. 'One year is as a 1000 years' sounds very different from 'we who are left, who are alive when the Lord returns'. What has been lost is the vivid sense of possible imminence, though the certainty about the coming is still evident.

Paul in his letters transcended the issue of imminence by focusing primarily on what was already true, on those eschatological events which had already transpired. As P. Achtemeier has recently put the matter when asking whether there was a generative centre to Paul's theology: 'I think there is, and I take it to be the conviction that Jesus rose from the dead, and that God was the one who brought it about.'[22] For Paul the Pharisee, resurrection could never be seen as an isolated event in the midst of history. Rather it had to be seen as the beginning of the end. Precisely because Paul was convinced that Christ had died and was raised, he was convinced that the eschatological age was already in progress. Paul's certainty about what had already transpired, led to confidence and expectancy about what was yet to happen. Paul could not talk about the delay of the eschatological age or the delay of the coming of the kingdom of God or the delay in the coming of the messiah, precisely because he believed all of those things had already happened or begun. If he had spoken of delay, it would have had to be about the delay of the completion of an age or process already set in motion. But Paul's confidence in God was such that, in view of God's having already acted in Christ, Paul did not see it as mere wishful thinking to talk

---

[22]P. Achtemeier, 'The Continuing Quest for the Coherence in St. Paul', in E. H. Lovering, Jr. and J. L. Sumney (eds.), *Theology and Ethics in Paul and his Interpreters* (Nashville: Abingdon, 1996), 132-145, here 138.

about the possible imminence of the end of the eschatological age. Yet he preferred to place the emphasis on what God had already done in Christ, using what was yet to come as an additional rather than the primary sanction for his exhortations (*cf. e.g.* 1 Cor. 15:50-58 to Rom. 13:11-14).

The naturalist John Muir once suggested that we normally look at life as if from the reverse side of a tapestry, and what we see is loose ends, dangling knots and the like. I would suggest that this is the point of view from which too many scholars have viewed Pauline eschatology. Muir goes on to say that occasionally the light shines through the tapestry and we look beyond the knots and loose ends and get a glimpse of a beautiful well-woven larger design. Schweitzer trained us well in this century to focus like a laser beam on the language of imminence in the New Testament. Perhaps it is time to observe the eschatological tapestry from a different point of view. Perhaps in the end we will discover that what we have often viewed as a knotty problem or a threadbare argument is in fact a well-woven fabric of already and not yet rather than unravelling ideas about certainty of imminence followed by worries about delay.

Chapter 8

REVELATION'S ASSEMBLY INSTRUCTIONS

Alan Garrow

Revelation claims to tell the story of 'what must soon take place' (1:1,19; 4:1; 22:6). However, despite many centuries of scholarly analysis, Revelation's presentation of the sequence of future events has appeared confused and confusing. This essay summarizes a piece of recent research which claims to have overcome these long-standing structural difficulties. It suggests that the structure of Revelation is analogous to that of a flat-pack piece of furniture. When the different functions of each section of text are identified, then it is possible to see how the whole text works together to present a six-part serial narrative, which contains a coherent account of 'what must soon take place'.

Revelation gives every appearance of providing a rich resource for students of New Testament eschatology. The reader's expectation that the book will reveal the sequence of events that lead to the End is initially established by the title of the whole book; 'The revelation of Jesus Christ which God gave him to show his servants what must soon take place'(1:1). This title is reinforced in 1:19. The main vision cycle then opens with a repetition of the promise to show John, 'what must take place after this'(4:1), and closes by reflecting that this promise has been kept; 'the God of the spirit of the prophets has sent his angel to show his servants what must soon take place' (22:6). However, despite all these clear indications of the function of the text, John's record of the sequence of future events is notoriously obscure. John Sweet expresses the problem thus:

> The purpose of the revelation is to show his servants what must soon take place . . . But the scenes and events which John goes on to

describe are repetitive and jump back and forth in time; as they stand they cannot be made to fit a linear time-scale.[1]

The majority of commentators attempt to overcome the problem of John's jagged and repetitive time-line by suggesting that the events of the End are recapitulated.[2] However, these approaches tend to force obstinate verses into the proposed scheme, or simply leave them out altogether. Fiorenza is fair when she concludes that:

> Previous attempts to explain the sequence of visions or the total composition of Revelation either by linear or cyclic understandings of time have not succeeded in presenting a convincing inter-pretation.[3]

The aim of this essay is to point towards a way of understanding the structure of Revelation that discloses a coherent account of 'what must soon take place'. If this may be achieved, then Revelation may actually become the invaluable resource for students of New Testament eschatology that it has always, tantalizingly, promised to be.

My approach to the structure of Revelation is built on two foundational hypotheses. The first, and simpler of the two, is that the story of 'what must soon take place' is contained within the Lamb's scroll of Revelation 5:1.

It has already been noted that Revelation 1:1 sets up the general expectation that the text will reveal 'what must soon take place'. This expectation is then focused on the main vision cycle in Revelation 4:1. However, no action actually takes place on earth until after the scroll of 5:1 is given to the Lamb by the One on the throne. This suggests that the scroll is the container of the revelatory information that the text claims to divulge. This expectation is reinforced by the universal attention that is paid to the One on the throne, the Lamb and the scroll that it holds through the course of chapter five. In 5:11 the four living creatures, twenty-four elders and myriad upon myriad of angels focus on these two central characters and one central object. In 5:13 everything in heaven, earth and under the earth have their attention focused in this direction. The central

[1]J. Sweet, *Revelation* (London: SCM and TPI, 2nd edn. 1990), 58.
[2]G. R. Beasley-Murray, *The Book of Revelation* (London: Oliphants, 1978), 30; A. Y. Collins, *Crisis and Catharsis* (Philadelphia: Westminster Press, 1984), 111-112; Sweet, *Revelation*, 44; G. B. Caird, *The Revelation of St. John the Divine* (London: A. & C. Black, 2nd edn. 1984), 104-106; J. M. Court, *Revelation* (Sheffield: JSOT Press, 1994), 85.
[3]E. S. Fiorenza, *The Book of Revelation: Justice and Judgment* (Philadelphia: Fortress Press, 1985), 46.

importance of the Lamb's scroll is then sustained into chapter six as the Lamb starts to break its seals and the revelatory process is set in train. I therefore agree with Richard Bauckham when he states that, 'the content of the scroll is "what must soon take place".'[4]

The second, and more complex, hypothesis is that, while the story of 'what must soon take place' is contained within the Lamb's scroll, not all of Revelation 6:1–22:5 (from the beginning of the unsealing of the scroll to the close of the main vision cycle), directly reveals these contents. Rather, different sections of 6:1–22:5 perform different functions with respect to the revelation of the scroll's contents. If these different functions may be identified, then text that directly reveals the contents of the scroll may be separated from, and seen in right relation to, text with an ancillary role with respect to the revelation of the scroll's contents.

This approach to the structure of Revelation is similar to the way in which a Do-It-Yourself enthusiast might approach a flat-pack bedside cabinet. In order to assemble a flat-pack piece of furniture it is necessary to lay all the pieces on the floor and establish what function is performed by each piece. When these different functions have been identified, then the pieces may be placed in correct relation to one another to present a useful, raised horizontal surface at about bed height. Not every piece will have the function of providing the table-top, some will have an ancillary, supporting function. In the same way, I suggest, not all of Revelation 6:1–22:5 has the function of directly revealing the contents of the Lamb's scroll. Rather, some sections have functions which support the presentation of the scroll's contents. These supporting roles are no less vital than the sides of the bedside cabinet, but if they are confused with the contents of the scroll itself, then the kind of difficulty with which we are familiar when it comes to the interpretation of Revelation may be expected.

Supporting Text

The investigation of the function of each section of text within 6:1–22:5 begins with an analysis of sections of text with ancillary functions with respect to the revelation of the contents of the Lamb's scroll.

---

[4] R. Bauckham, *The Climax of Prophecy* (Edinburgh: T. & T. Clark, 1993), 263.

Foreshadowing Text

I suggest that a large proportion of 6:1–11:14 has the function of foreshadowing the contents of the Lamb's scroll. Foreshadowing is the literary device by which an author creates partial uncertainty (suspense) about 'what will happen'.[5] For example, the soothsayer in _Julius Caesar_ warns Caesar to, 'Beware the Ides of March', thus making the audience certain that something bad will happen on March 15, while maintaining partial uncertainty about exactly what will happen. In the context of Revelation, I suggest that 6:1-17; 7:9-17; 8:1–9:21 and 11:1-13, all create partial uncertainty regarding the contents of the scroll by foreshadowing those contents before they are directly revealed.

The visions that accompany the breaking of the first six seals of the Lamb's scroll (6:1-21) may be seen as foreshadowings of the contents of the scroll for the following reasons. First, as Bauckham observes, 'Most [commentators] think that the contents are progressively revealed as the Lamb opens the seven seals (6:1–8:1). But it would be a very odd scroll to which this could happen. Normally all the seals would have to be broken before the scroll could be opened.'[6] Just as it is not possible to open a door that is held shut by seven bolts until all have been drawn, so a scroll sealed with seven seals cannot be opened and read until all the seals have been broken.

The content of the visions that accompany the breaking of the seals also suggests that they are foreshadowings. The four riders present a classic foreshadowing image in that they are called out by each of the four living creatures who 'stand around the throne on each side of the throne'(4:6). In the imagination of the hearers, therefore, they may be expected to travel in four different directions – to the four corners of the earth – to call the world to repentance by warning its inhabitants of what will happen once the contents of the scroll are finally divulged. The violence, conquest and disaster which they prophesy by their actions is realized in the events of chapter sixteen when the kings of the east destroy Rome. The fifth and sixth seal vision also look forward to events that are recorded later in the text. The fifth vision looks forward to the completion of the number of martyrs, something which may be expected to happen under the reign of the beast who conquers the saints (13:7). The sixth seal vision looks forward to the final cataclysm which is spelt out in very similar terms towards the end of the text in Revelation 20:11-15.

---

[5] S. Chatham, _Story and Discourse: Narrative Structure in Fiction and Film_ (London: Cornell, 1978), 48, 59-60.
[6] Bauckham, _Climax_, 249-250.

Revelation 6:1-17 therefore provides a kind of 'table of contents' of the whole scroll. It intimates the kind of events that are likely to be contained in the scroll, but it does not provide the full and ordered story-line that the original hearers would have been waiting for. Such a story-line might be expected to follow the pattern common to many apocalypses: persecution, followed by the punishment of the persecutors, followed by the salvation of the persecuted.[7]

By Revelation 6:17, therefore, the scroll is held shut by only one seal. The natural question for the original hearers at this point is, If these disasters are about to happen soon, then what will happen to God's faithful people? Revelation 7:1-17 answers this question by depicting God's faithful people before and after the final judgment. As Sweet puts it, 'The scene [7:1-8] is not part of the sixth unsealing; it relates to the present time, while 7:9-17 belongs to the Age to Come.'[8] By showing the faithful ones sealed in the present and then depicting them as they will be seen at the end of the story, the faithful hearers' spiritual security is assured throughout all that is to follow. A by-product of this assurance is partial information about events that are contingent upon the opening of the scroll. As G. B. Caird says, 7:9-17 is, 'in almost every detail an anticipation of the joys of the celestial city'.[9] That is to say that 7:9-17 foreshadows events that will be described in full when the contents of the scroll of final things are directly revealed.

In Revelation 8:1 the action returns to the process of unsealing the scroll. As the seventh seal is finally broken (8:1), the original hearers would have expected that now, at last, the contents of the scroll would be revealed. Instead they are greeted by seven trumpeters. That the trumpet visions of 8:2–9:21; 11:14 are a further set of foreshadowings of the scroll's contents is indicated by four factors. First, trumpets were a common means of announcement in ancient and biblical cultures.

Second, the seven trumpets have a strong parallel in the account of the fall of Jericho recorded in Joshua 6. Caird notes, '[John] must have had this story (the fall of Jericho) in mind when he wrote [the trumpet series].'[10] This parallel is significant in that trumpets were blown on the six days prior to the day when the great blast was sounded and the walls of Jericho actually fell. In the same way Revelation's first six trumpets lead up to the final and all-important seventh trumpet (11:15; *cf*.10:7).

---

[7]Collins, *Crisis and Catharsis*, 111-112.
[8]Sweet, *Revelation*, 147.
[9]Caird, *Revelation*, 102.
[10]*Ibid.*, 108.

Third, there is an undisputed correlation between the three woes of 8:13; 9:12; 11:14 and the last three trumpets, to the extent that the woes are the trumpets. 'Woe' in the New Testament always points towards some future disaster, rather than describing a present one. This connection between woes and trumpets is significant in that the second woe/sixth trumpet closes in 11:14. This implies that all that is contained within 9:12–11:13 is part of the foreshadowing sixth trumpet vision. This conclusion is reinforced by the announcement of the angel in 10:6, 7, 'There will be no more delay, but in the days when the seventh angel is to blow his trumpet, the mystery of God will be fulfilled, as he announced to his servants the prophets.' This implies that there has been delay in revealing the mystery of God up until this point in the narrative, and that this delay will continue until the seventh trumpet is blown in 11:15.

Fourth, that which is foreshadowed by the trumpet visions is directly revealed later in the text. There is a strong, and often noted, correlation between the trumpet visions and the execution of the bowl judgments in Revelation 16:1-21. This can be seen using an adaptation of C. Rowland's table:[11]

Trumpets	Bowls
8:7: hail and fire mixed with blood; third of earth burnt up.	16:2: evil sores appear on those with mark of Beast.
8:8-9: third of *sea* creatures die after burning mountain into sea and latter is turned into *blood*.	16:3: *sea* becomes *blood* and every living thing in thrown it dies.
8:10-11: third of *water* made bitter after star falls from heaven; people die from drinking water	16:4: *rivers and springs* become blood.
8:12: third of *sun* does not shine nor do moon or stars.	16:8-9: humans scorched by *sun*.
9:1-6: air polluted by smoke from abyss after star falls from heaven. Locusts harm humans. Humanity tormented by insects with stings.	16:10: darkness over kingdom of the Beast.
9:13ff.: third of humanity killed after the release of the angels bound at the *Euphrates*.	16:12: *Euphrates* dried up to prepare a way for the kings of the east.

---

[11]Chris Rowland, *Revelation* (London: Epworth, 1993), 82. See also the similar table in J. Lambrecht (ed.), *L'Apocalypse Johannique et L'Apocalyptique dans le Nouveau Testament* (Louvain: Gemblot, 1980), 89-90.

In conclusion, the trumpet visions of Revelation 8:2–9:21; 11:14 foreshadow the contents of the Lamb's scroll by partially announcing the bowl judgments of 16:1-21.

Within the sixth trumpet two further foreshadowings of the content of the Lamb's scroll are presented. First, there are the aborted seven thunders. Thunder announces theophany in Exodus 19 and so, like the trumpet visions, the thunders may be expected to provide further foreshadowings of the scroll's contents. However, the sealing up of the thunders is used instead to indicate that a further set of seven foreshadowing visions need not be endured before the actual contents of the Lamb's scroll are fully revealed. Instead, the hearers are assured, 'There will be no more delay, but in the days when the seventh angel is to blow his trumpet, the mystery of God will be fulfilled, as he announced to his servants the prophets' (10:6, 7).

The second foreshadowing within the sixth trumpet has more substantial contents. Before the seventh trumpet is blown, John draws out the suspense a little longer by introducing the so-called 'little' scroll. The function of this scroll has been the subject of recent debate. In his *Climax of Prophecy* Richard Bauckham argues that the Lamb's scroll and the 'little' scroll are identical. Hence, when the contents of the little scroll are divulged in 11:1-13, then a direct revelation of the content of the Lamb's scroll is provided, albeit '*in nuce*'.[12] This position presents a number of difficulties. These include the place of the little scroll within the foreshadowing sixth trumpet, and the promise of the angel in 10:6, 7 that the point at which delay will cease is after the seventh trumpet has been blown (11:15).[13]

Apart from the location of the little scroll within the second woe/sixth trumpet another point suggests that the content of the little scroll foreshadows the content of the Lamb's scroll, rather than directly reveals it. In contrast to Bauckham's position, I suggest that the purpose of the little scroll is to show how John's revelatory experience is consistent with the visions of the ancient prophets, at the same time as surpassing their insights. The text achieves this by presenting John in the guise of an Old Testament prophet such as Ezekiel and Daniel (*cf*. Rev. 10:8-11 with Ezk. 2:8–3:3). He then paraphrases their prophecies of the End (11:1-13) in a way that partially announces the contents of the Lamb's scroll. By presenting the ancient prophecies as merely foreshadowing the revelation of

---

[12]Bauckham, *Climax*, 266. In this line of argument Bauckham follows F. D. Mazzaferri, *The Genre of the Book of Revelation: from a source critical perspective* (Berlin and New York: de Gruyter, 1989), 267-269.
[13]A detailed refutation of Bauckham's position (*Climax*, 243-257) may be found in A. J. P. Garrow, *Revelation* (London: Routledge, 1997), 26-32.

Jesus Christ, the text is able to show how John's revelation is superior to those of the past, at the same time as being validated by them.

The foreshadowing function of the little scroll is supported by the strong correlation between the events described in 11:1-13 and those recorded in greater detail in 12:1–14:5; 16:19.

For example, the spiritual protection of God's people is similarly described in both passages: In 11:1 this security is described in terms of the measuring of the temple;[14] in 12:6 security is symbolized by the woman's flight to the desert.[15] In both cases this period of security lasts for 1,260 days (11:3 and 12:6). This period of security coincides with the length of Gentile supremacy in both passages: in 11:2 the Gentiles trample the city for forty-two months; in 13:5 the Beast reigns for the same period described in the same terms. Further, in 11:7 the beast rises from the Abyss to kill the witnesses; in 13:7 the saints are conquered by the beast who rises from the sea.[16] The number and detail of the parallels between these two passages mean that it is hard to imagine that they could be referring to different events. I therefore conclude that 11:1-13 foreshadows 12:1–14:5; 16:19.

In summary, the seal visions provide an overall table of contents of later events. The vision of the fate of the faithful in 7:9-17 looks forward to the final bliss of God's faithful people (21:1-8). The trumpet visions (8:2–9:21; 11:14) then foreshadow the bowl judgments (16:1-21). The contents of the little scroll (11:1-13) foreshadow 12:1–14:5; 16:19.[17]

Serializing Text

Revelation was designed to be read aloud to an assembled congregation (1:3, 11).[18] As it is a lengthy text, it would be more conveniently handled if read in separate instalments. Having entertained the hypothesis of serial performance, it is possible to consider where breaks in the narrative might occur. The location of breaks in performed serial narratives is strongly influenced by two universal features of this genre. First, the author must draw the audience back for following instalments. Second, the author controls

---

[14]*Cf.* Caird, *Revelation*, 130-131.

[15]*Cf. ibid.*, 151.

[16]Further correspondences between these two passages are considered in Garrow, *Revelation*, 32.

[17]See Garrow, *Revelation*, for a diagrammatic presentation of these foreshadowings.

[18]Bauckham, *Climax*, 3; Collins, *Crisis and Catharsis*, 144; D. L. Barr, 'The Apocalypse of John as Oral Enactment', *Interpretation* 40 (1986), 243.

where a particular instalment closes. These two factors combine to create the need for, and the means of creating, cliff-hanging instalment endings.

If breaks in performed serial narratives commonly occur at points of heightened suspense, so as to create cliff-hanging instalment endings, then two points in Revelation are ideally arranged so as to create this effect: just after the breaking of the seventh seal and just after the blowing of the seventh trumpet. In both cases suspense grows through each successive vision until the hearer is led to believe that as the last seal is broken, or the last trumpet is blown, then the mystery of 'what must soon take place' is just about to be revealed.

A comparison of the verses around these two points in the narrative reveals a striking set of similarities between them. In turn these similarities may be found at three other points in the text. Table 1 (on page 196) sets out a summary of these common features.[19]

The instalment theory accounts for the function of a further set of sections within Revelation 6:1–22:5. Opening formulae that indicate a progressive revelation of the heavenly things occur at the beginning of each instalment (4:1; 8:1; 11:19; 15:5; 19:11a). Also, there are closing formulae at the end of each instalment (7:9–8:1; 11:15-18; 14:6–15:4; 19:6-10; 22:6-21). These include a picture of the final outcome of the story, a hymn and a reference to the Eucharist,[20] as well as a high point of suspense. In the later instalments suspense is created by announcements of 'what will happen'. For example, in 14:6–15:8 announcing angels, reapers of harvest first-fruits and angels poised with bowls of judgment are used to create suspense regarding what will happen in the following instalments. Similarly, voices announce the marriage of the Lamb at the end of the fifth instalment (19:6-10), but this is not revealed until the next performance (21:18).

Reviewing and Interpreting Text

A third ancillary function, with respect to the revelation of the contents of the Lamb's scroll, is performed by sections of text that review and interpret the contents of the scroll after they have been divulged. Text with this function is straightforwardly indicated by the presence of an interpreting angel. Such angels appear in 17:1 and 21:9[21] and explain, in the course of 17:1-18 and 21:9–22:5,

---

[19]A detailed analysis of the eight break characteristics may be found in Garrow, *Revelation*, 35-53.

[20]See D. L. Barr, 'Apocalypse', *Interpretation* 40 (1986), 254.

[21]C. H. Giblin, *The Book of Revelation: The open book of prophecy* (Collegeville: Liturgical Press, 1991), 159, 196.

	3:22	8:1 (re-opening at 8:1)	11:18	15:4	19:10
Suspense at end of instalment	Must wait for description of what must soon take place.	Must wait for scroll's contents (now unsealed).	Must wait for scroll's contents, (no more announcements).	Must wait for bowls to be emptied.	Must wait for Harmageddon and messianic supper.
Use of 'anoigo'	4:1 After this I looked, and there in heaven a door stood open.	8:1 When the Lamb opened seventh seal...	11:19 Then God's temple in heaven was opened. …	15:5 After this … the temple of the tent of witness in heaven was opened.	19:11 Then I saw heaven opened,
Action derived from heaven	4:1ff	8:1ff	11:19ff	15:5ff	19:11ff
Signs of the coming of God (cf. Exodus 19)	4:5 Lightning, rumblings, thunder.	8:5 Thunder, rumblings, lightning, earthquake.	11:19 Lightning, rumblings, thunder, earthquake, hail.	15:8 Smoke fills the temple.	19:11 The messianic rider arrives.
Closing hymn	2:7,11,17,29; 3:6,13,22.	7:15-17.	11:17-18	15:3-4	19:6-8
Final outcome picture	2:7,10,17,26-28; 3:5,12, 21.	7:9-17	11:15-18	15:2-4	19:6-9
Eucharistic reference	2:7,17; 3:20	7:16	11:17	14:14-20	19:7,9
Length: (1:1-3:22) 1,811 words	(4:1-8:1) 1,620 words	(8:1-11:18) 1,728 words	(11:19-15:4) 1,729 words	(15:5-19:10) 2,055 words	(19:11-22:21) 1,728 words

Table 1: *Criteria for the identification of breaks between instalments*, from A. J. P. Garrow, *Revelation* (London: Routledge, 1997).

the immediately preceding visions (16:1-21 and 19:11–21:8 respectively). The extended hymn recorded in 18:1–19:5 also looks back to the vision of the fall of Babylon seen in the vision of 16:1-21.

Story-telling Text

The function of every section of text within 6:1–22:5 is now accounted for, with the exception of 12:1–14:5; 15:6–16:21; 19:11b–21:8. However, the rest of the text points towards these sections by way of foreshadowing, announcement or interpretative review.[22] This structural arrangement suggests that these three passages reveal the most important information provided by Revelation; the contents of the Lamb's scroll, the story of 'what must soon take place'.

Further investigation of these three passages reveals that, when placed end to end, the characters and events that they depict follow a logical and coherent event-line: the faithful are persecuted by the dragon, beast and second beast in 12:1–13:18. This persecution results in the exultation of the martyrs, after the pattern of Christ, who join the army of heaven depicted in 14:1-5. In the next section of story-telling text, 15:6–16:21 (interpreted by 17:1-18), some persecutors are punished in the fall of 'Babylon'.

In the final section of story-telling text, 19:11–21:8, the heavenly army of martyrs sweeps down behind the judging and punishing Messiah. As a result, the persecuting second beast, the beast and Satan are each destroyed – in reverse order to their original appearance. Ultimately the persecuted but faithful people of God are rewarded, first by a messianic age of one thousand years, and, after the final judgment, by the bliss of full communion with God and the Lamb in the new heaven and new earth.[23]

Conclusion

The aim of this essay has been to point towards a way of under-standing the structure of Revelation that discloses a coherent account of 'what must soon take place'. This aim has been achieved inasmuch as the function of the different sections of text within Revelation 6:1–22:5 have been shown to work together to present 12:1–14:5; 15:6–16:21 and 19:11b–21:8 as the direct revelation of the 'what must soon take place' as contained within the Lamb's scroll.

---

[22]See Garrow, *Revelation* for a diagrammatic presentation of this information.
[23]A fuller attempt to describe and interpret the sequence of events depicted in 12:1–14:5; 15:6– 6:21; 19:11b–21:8 may be found in Garrow, *Revelation*, 80-123.

However, this is not to say that Revelation has now become an entirely transparent resource for students of New Testament eschatology. For this to be the case, further work must be done to identify the precise meaning and significance of the various characters and actions that are symbolically represented in these three focal passages of Revelation. If this may be achieved, then it should be possible to understand John's view of eschatology, as recorded in Revelation, with a more useful clarity than has previously been possible.

Chapter 9

NEW TESTAMENT TEACHING ON HELL

E. Earle Ellis

In Memoriam *John W. Wenham*

Of three views advocated in the patristic church, universal salvation is excluded by Scripture. But is the 'everlasting punishment' of the wicked an unending process of suffering or an extinction of their being that has an everlasting effect? The former view, reflecting the influence of Platonic philosophy, was present in early Judaism. But the latter better accords with the biblical teaching on the nature of man as mortal and of death as the wages of sin. Immortal being is God's gift only to those who belong to Jesus Christ.

One's understanding of the biblical teaching on the destiny of those outside Christ will probably be governed by the answer given to three antecedent biblical questions. Is man by nature mortal or immortal? Is he both an individual and a corporate being or an individual only? Is death as 'the wages of sin' (Rom. 6:23) an extinction of being or is it continuing existence in separation from God? For this topic, as for others, biblical anthropology is an essential presupposition for understanding biblical eschatology.

Patristic Writers

Since the early centuries of the church three views on the destiny of the wicked have been advocated,[1] views that may be termed (1)

---

[1]*Cf.* E. H. Plumptre, 'Eschatology', in W. Smith and H. Wace (eds.), *Dictionary of Christian Biography*, 4 vols. (London, 1877-87), II, 189-196. For a classification of

universal salvation, (2) everlasting punishment as a process, *i.e.* of
suffering or torment, and (3) everlasting punishment as an effect, *i.e.*
of extinction or annihilation. In the patristic church, Origen (*c.* AD
185-254) was the primary representative of the first view and
Augustine (AD 354-430) of the second. Ignatius (*c.* AD 35-110), Justin
Martyr (*c.* AD 100-165), Arnobius (d. 303-330) and Athanasius (*c.* AD
296-373) are prominent examples of conditional immortality, that is,
immortality given only to those in Christ, and of its corollary, a
punishment that is everlasting in its effect, *i.e.* an extinction of being.

In an early writing,[2] Origen expresses the view that all things
will ultimately be brought into subjection to God (1 Cor. 15:25) by
being 'restored' (ἀποκατάστασις, *cf.* Acts 3:21) to perfection with the
resultant salvation of every person, *i.e.* universalism.[3] He builds his
theory not only on the principles of 'the free will of man and the
goodness of God' (Kelly) but also on the views of the Greek philosophical schools,[4] including the assumption of a Platonic body/soul
dualism in which the soul is either immortal or destined for immortality with God.[5]

---

early Christian writers, see E. Petavel, *The Problem of Immortality* (London, 1892),
495f.

[2]*On First Principles* (= περὶ ἀρχῶν = *De principiis*) 1, 6, 1-4. This work was written
during Origen's Alexandrian period, *i.e.* before AD 231. *Cf.* J. Quasten, *Patrology*, 3
vols. (Westminster, MD, 1983), II, 57.

[3]For a critique *cf.* Petavel, *Problem*, 277-312. A view similar to Origen's may be
reflected in K. Barth, *Christ and Adam: Man and Humanity in Romans 5* (New York,
1957); critiqued by R. Bultmann, 'Adam and Christ according to Romans 5', in W.
Klassen and G. F. Snyder (eds.), *Current Issues in New Testament Interpretation. FS
O. Piper* (New York 1962) 143-165. For a contemporary advocate of universal
salvation *cf.* J. Moltmann, 'The End of Everything is God. Has Belief in Hell had
its Day?' *ExpT* 108 (1996-97), 263f.; *idem*, *The Coming of God* (London, 1996), 235-
255: '. . . Christ's death on the cross [is] the foundation for universal salvation'
(254). But where is that in the Scriptures? From a biblical perspective any view
of universal salvation founders (1) on the many judgment texts that exclude such
an interpretation (*e.g.* Is. 66:22f.; Dn. 12:2; Mt. 12:31f.; 25:46; 2 Thes. 1:6-9), (2) on
the facts that the term 'all' may mean, *e.g.* 'all kinds' (*cf.* Rom. 11:32) and not
necessarily 'every individual', and (3) that 'to reconcile' (ἀποκαταλλάξαι,
ἱλάσκεσθαι) an enemy, *i.e.* to remove the enmity, is accomplished for believers by
the death of Christ (Col. 1:20) and for unbelievers by their own death. *Cf.* H.
Bavinck, *Our Reasonable Faith* (Grand Rapids, 3rd edn. 1978), 358f.; G. C.
Berkouwer, *The Work of Christ* (Grand Rapids: Eerdmans 1965), 256-260; L.
Morris, *The Apostolic Preaching of the Cross* (London: Tyndale Press, 1955), 125-
133; J. R. W. Stott, *The Cross of Christ* (Leicester: IVP, 1986), 197-202.

[4]*Cf.* H. Chadwick, *Origen: Contra Celsum* (Cambridge, 1980), x-xiii; A. Harnack,
History of Dogma, 7 vols. in 4 (1894; New York, 4th edn. 1961), II, 377ff.

[5]Origen, *Contra Celsum* 7, 32. *Cf.* J. N. D. Kelly, *Early Christian Doctrines* (London,
2nd edn. 1960), 469-474, esp. 473f. Athenagoras (*de res.* 13, 1) appears to be the

Augustine, appealing largely to Matthew 25:41-46 and opposing Origen's interpretation, argues that the destiny of the wicked is an everlasting process of suffering of both body and soul.[6] He bases his argument on an initial assumption, following the Platonists, that the human soul is immortal by nature. As a previous adherent of Manicheism and then of Platonism, he regarded neo-Platonism as the philosophy closest to Christianity.[7] With his great influence the Augustinian view became dominant throughout the western church.

The view designated conditional immortality, with its corollary, the annihilation of the wicked, is represented by a number of patristic writers.[8] Since this fact is perhaps less well known, a few quotations may be useful. Ignatius, who regarded union with Christ as 'the medicine of immortality' (φάρμακον ἀθανασίας),[9] writes that 'if

---

first Christian writer to describe man as made up of an 'immortal soul' (ἐκ ψυχῆς ἀθανάτου) and a body. Cf. L. W. Bernard, *Athenagoras* (Paris, 1972), 124f. Before he was converted, Athenagoras had been a philosopher supporting Middle Platonism (37-51). Cf. also *Epistle to Diognetus* 6:7f. (? c. AD 200).

[6] Augustine, *City of God* 21, 1, 1–21, 27, end. Augustine simply asserts that the soul was created immortal (6, 12, middle). However, he had predecessors, *e.g.* Tertullian (*de anima* 4; 22), who disagrees with Plato's view that the soul is pre-existent, but none the less accepts this Greek philosopher's conception of its immortality and 'the substance which [man] derived from God himself' (*ab ipso deo traxit*, *Adv. Marcion* 2, 5, middle) with the consequence, apparently, that the wicked will suffer for ever (*cf.* Tertullian, *de spectaculis* 30). *Cf.* Petavel, *Problem*, 250f.

[7] Augustine, *City of God*, 8, 5, beginning. *Cf.* R. A. Markus, 'Augustine', in A. H. Armstrong (ed.), *The Cambridge History of Later Greek and Early Medieval Philosophy* (Cambridge, 1970), 342-346, 359ff.; E. de Pressensé, 'Augustinus', *DCB* 1 (1877), 217.

[8] Especially the earlier writers. *Cf.* further E. W. Fudge, *The Fire that Consumes* (Houston, 1989), 313-342; Petavel, *Problem*, 229-245; H. Constable, *The Duration and Nature of Future Punishment* (Boston, c. 1890), 237-326, esp. 325; E. White, *Life in Christ* (London, 1878), 416-425. Pace W. V. Crockett, 'The Metaphorical View', in W. Crockett (ed.), *Four Views on Hell* (Grand Rapids, 1992), 65f. Patristic writers cannot be said to favour the Augustinian view of everlasting torment because they use biblical phrases like 'everlasting punishment' (2 *Clem.* 6:7; *Martyr. Polycarp* 11:2; *cf.* Mt. 25:46), 'everlasting fire' and 'fire that is never quenched' (*Martyr. Polycarp* 11:2; 2:3; *cf.* Jude 7; Mk. 9:47f. = Is. 66:24). After all, it is precisely the meaning of these phrases that is the question at issue.

[9] Ignatius, *ad Eph.* 20, 2: 'Assemble yourselves in one faith and one (ἐνί) Jesus Christ . . ., breaking one bread, which (ὅ) is the medicine of immortality, the antidote that we should not die but live forever (διὰ παντός) in Jesus Christ.' *Cf.* J. B. Lightfoot, *The Apostolic Fathers*, 3 vols. in 5 (London, 1885), II, i, 87: 'The ὅ may refer to the whole preceding clause . . . or to the ἄρτος alone . . . [but] the latter is more probable . . . .' If so, it is no more sacramentalist than Jn. 6:51-58; Mt. 26:26

[God] were to imitate us according to how we act, we would no longer exist' (μιμήσηται καθὰ πράσσομεν, οὐκέτι ἐσμέν).[10] He implies that God's judgment would mean the destruction of our being.

Justin Martyr is more explicit:

> A destruction (κατάλυσιν) of the whole cosmos, in order that (ἵνα) evil angels, demons and men may no longer exist (μηκέτι ὦσι), God delays to make because of the seed of the Christians (*Apology* 7:1).

> Those who appear worthy of God never die. But others are punished (αἱ κολάζονται) as long as God wills them to exist and to be punished. Whatever things are or ever shall be, besides God, these things have a perishable nature (φύσιν φθαρτήν). . . . For this reason souls (ψυχαί) both are punished and die (*Dialogue with Trypho* 5:3ff).[11]

Irenaeus is equally explicit on man's mortality and his attainment of immortality only in Christ:

> And [God] laid down for [Adam] certain conditions: so that, if he kept the command of God, then he would always remain as he was, that is, immortal; but if he did not, he would become mortal, melting

---

parr. It is not the eucharistic element but the corporate union with Jesus, which the element symbolizes, that assures immortality. *Cf.* W. R. Schoedel, *Ignatius of Antioch* (Philadelphia, 1985), 97ff.; A. D. Nock, 'Liturgical Notes', *JTS* 30 (1929), 391ff.; P. N. Anderson, *The Christology of the Fourth Gospel* (WUNT 2/78) (Valley Forge, PA, 1997), 119-127: 'When the phrases, "medicine of immortality" and "the antidote which wards off death" [in Ignatius, *ad Eph.* 20, 2], are considered in their context, it is clear that the central issue is one of corporate unity and solidarity. . .'. '[The] "medicine of immortality" refers not to the breaking of a loaf but the breaking of *one loaf* (*cf.* the clear connection to 1 Cor. 11:16 [10:16]). . .'. 1 *Clem.* 35:1f. similarly describes 'life in immortality', 120 (ζωὴ ἐν ἀθανασίᾳ) as a gift of God to believers.

[10]Ignatius, *ad Mag.* 10:1. The apodosis clause in a condition contrary to fact is only occasionally in the present tense (*cf.* Mk. 9:42) and often drops the ἄν. *Cf.* F. Blass, A. Debrunner, R. W. Funk, *A Greek-English Lexicon of the New Testament* (Chicago, 1957), 523; A. T. Robertson, *A Grammar of the Greek New Testament in the Light of Historical Research* (London, 1914), 1014.

[11]In *Dialogue* 5:1 those who regard the soul as immortal are called Platonists. Justin, *Dial.* 80:4, identifies as heretics 'those who say there is no resurrection of the dead but that when they die, their souls are taken up into heaven'. Justin's pupil, Tatian (*Address to the Greeks* 13:1), also argues that the soul is mortal. *Cf.* J. Pelikan, *The Shape of Death* (Nashville, 1961), 11-29.

into the earth, whence his frame had been taken (*Demonstration of the Apostolic Preaching* 15).[12]

How can he be immortal, who in his mortal nature did not obey his Maker? (*Against Heresies* 3, 20, 2).[13]

[Souls and spirits] had a beginning . . . and endure as long as God wills that they should have an existence and continuance. . . . [God] imparts continuance forever and ever (*in saeculum saeculi*) on those who are saved (*Against Heresies* 2, 34, 3).

'[But] they shall wish that they had been burned with fire' (*cf.* Isaiah 9:5) [is said of] those who believe not on Him. . . . [For] those who after Christ's appearing believed not on Him, there is a vengeance without pardon in the judgment (*Demonstration of the Apostolic Preaching* 56).

Theophilus of Antioch (*c.* AD 190), speaks similarly:

Man was neither mortal nor immortal by nature. . . but was able to receive both (δεκτικὸν ἀμφοτέρων). If he [kept] . . .the command of God, he would receive immortality as a re- ward from Him and would become [like] God, but if he . . . [disobeyed] God, he would be responsible for his own death. . . . Everyone who performs [God's commands] can be saved and, attaining to the resurrection, can 'inherit imperishability' (ἀφθαρσίαν) (*ad Autolycum* 2, 27).[14]

At the end of the third or the beginning of the fourth century, Arnobius, one of the last early apologists, presents a view of conditional immortality similar to these second-century writers. He

---

[12]Translation of Pelikan, *Shape*, 104. *Cf.* L. M. Froidevaux (ed.), *Irénée de Lyon, Démonstration de la Prédication apostolique, Source Chrétienne* 62 (Paris, 1971), 54; J. A. Robinson, *St. Irenaeus. The Demonstration of the Apostolic Preaching* (London, 1920), 83. *Cf.* Gn. 3:19. But see Irenaeus, *Against Heresies*, 2, 34, 2: 'Nevertheless [souls] endure and extend their existence into a length of ages (*in longitudinem saecularum*) in accordance with the will of God their creator.'
[13]Otherwise: G. Wingren, *Man and the Incarnation. A Study in the Biblical Theology of Irenaeus* (Philadelphia, 1959), 204-207, who is quite misleading on this question.
[14]*Cf.* R. M. Grant (ed.), *Theophilus of Antioch, Ad Autolycum* (Oxford, 1970), 69ff. *Cf.* Mt. 19:17, 25; Phil. 3:11; Heb. 11:35; 1 Cor. 15:50, 53.

observes rightly that God has no obligation or necessity to save anyone[15] and writes:

> [The death] that is seen by the eyes is only a separation of soul from body, not the last end – annihilation: this I say is man's real death, when souls which know not God shall be consumed in a long pro-tracted torment with raging fire . . . (*Against the Pagans* 2, 14, end).

> The souls of men are of a neutral character . . . subject to the law of death, and are of little strength and that perishable. They are gifted with immortality if they rest their hope . . . on God Supreme who alone has power to grant such [blessings] (*Against the Pagans* 2, 53, middle).

Arnobius has been criticized as 'an immature Christian'; unjustifiably since we have no knowledge of his thought apart from his treatise against the pagans. In any case, he is only one among a number of mostly earlier Christian writers who espoused conditional immortality, that is, immortality only for the righteous in Christ. Athanasius' essay *On the Incarnation of the Word*[16] sounds remarkably like these earlier writers:[17]

---

[15]Arnobius, *Against the Pagans* 2, 64, end. *Cf.* W. H. C. Frend, 'Arnobius', in N. G. L. Hammond and H. H. Scullard (eds.), *Oxford Classical Dictionary* (Oxford, 3rd edn. 1970), 122, who thinks that Arnobius 'shows little trace of Christian theology': but see H. Brice and H. Campbell, 'Arnobius', in A. Roberts and J. Donaldson (eds.), *The Ante-Nicene Fathers*, 10 vols. (Grand Rapids, 1951; *c.* 1885), VI, 409f.; H. C. G. Moule, 'Arnobius', in *DCB* I (1877), 167ff. However, Arnobius shows a knowledge of the apostolic writings, defends them, perhaps the Gospels, against pagan criticism (1, 54-58), cites at least one text verbatim (2, 6, end; 1 Cor. 3:19) and alludes to other biblical passages. But he makes little use of Scripture for his argument, probably because his 'vast range of learning' (Brice, *Arnobius*, 408) is focused on a scathing critique of paganism in terms of its own views and practices.

[16]The translations are dependent in part on those of R. W. Thomson (ed.), *Athanasius, Contra Gentes and De Incarnatione* (Oxford, 1971), 142-185, esp. 184f., 274-277; A Religious of the Community of St. Mary the Virgin [Penelope Lawson] (tr.), *St. Athanasius, On the Incarnation* (London, 3rd edn. 1953), 29f., 96. *Cf.* also C. Kannengiesser (ed.), *Athanase D'Alexandrie. Sur l'incarnation du Verbe*, *SC* 199 (Paris, 1973), 276-279, 340f., 468f.

[17]Some regard him as inconsistent on this issue since Athanasius, *Against the Pagans* 32-33, speaks of the soul as 'immortal' (ἀθάνατος). But, like Irenaeus, he may mean no more than that the soul does not die with the body. See above, note 12. Otherwise: A. Roberts (ed.), 'St. Athanasius: Select Works and Letters', in P. Schaff and H. Wace (eds.), *Nicene and Post-Nicene Fathers*, 14 vols. (New York, 1890-1900), IV, 32ff.

For the transgression of the commandment was making [men] turn back again according to their nature; and as they had at the beginning come into being out of non-existence, so were they now on the way to returning, through corruption, to non-existence (εἰς τὸ μὴ εἶναι) again. If having then a nature not to exist (τὸ μὴ εἶναι), they were called into existence by the presence (παρουσία) and mercy of the Word, it followed that. . .because they turned to [evil] things that have no being (εἰς τὰ οὐκ ὄντα), they also were deprived of everlasting existence (τοῦ εἶναι ἀεί). . . . For indeed man is by nature mortal in that he was created from nothing (de incar. 4, 20-26).

[As Christians] according to the mortality of the body we are dissolved (διαλυόμεθα) only for the time that God has ordained for each in order that we may be able 'to obtain a better resurrection' [Heb. 11:35] (de incar. 21, 5ff.).

Athanasius concludes his treatise with a reference to Christ's second coming when He will bestow on believers 'resurrection and incorruptibility' (τὴν ἀνάστασιν καὶ τὴν ἀφθαρσίαν) and will assign those who have done evil to 'everlasting fire and outer darkness' (πῦρ αἰώνιον καὶ σκότος ἐξώτερον; 56, 14-18). In the light of his earlier comments that man apart from Christ is on his way back to non-existence, he appears to view the divine fire of judgment as accomplishing and climaxing that effect:

Thus joined to [the saints] in the fellowship of life (τῇ ἀγωγῇ τῆς συζήσεως), one may escape the danger that threatens sinners and the fire [that comes] on them at the day of judgement . . . . (de incar. 57, 16f.).

Both Arnobius and Athanasius build their arguments more on philosophical than on biblical foundations. Although they presuppose from their Greek philosophical background a body/soul dualism, they do not from that infer the 'soul's' immortality, but only that its life extends in some way beyond that of the body.

Intertestamental Evidence

Among the intertestamental writings of Judaism are the Qumran texts, the Old Testament Apocrypha and some pseudepigraphal apocalyptic writings; the last are less easy to date and are largely post-first-century in origin or include post-first-century Christian interpolations.[18] Like the patristic literature and the Apocryphal New Testament, these documents also reflect one or other of the two viewpoints, *i.e.* everlasting suffering[19] and annihilation.[20] Also, like the patristic writers, they exhibit in part a body/soul dualism rooted in Platonic philosophy.[21] The Qumran texts, like the Sadducees[22] and the Old Testament,[23] speak of the whole man as mortal[24] and as perishing at death, and, like the Old Testament, they also affirm his resurrection at the last Day.[25] In this respect they are closer to biblical

---

[18]The only Jewish apocalyptic pseudepigrapha that can be dated with confidence before the first century AD are parts of *1 Enoch*. Fragments of the 11 manuscripts of *1 Enoch* appear at Qumran from the first (1-36), third (72-82), fourth (83-90) and fifth (91-108) sections of the Ethiopic text. There are no fragments from the section, the Book of Parables (1 *Enoch* 37-71). *Cf.* J. T. Milik (ed.), *The Books of Enoch: Aramaic Fragments of Qumran Cave 4* (Oxford, 1976), 5ff., *passim*; M. A. Knibb, *The Ethiopic Book of Enoch*, 2 vols. (Oxford, 1978), II, 6-15. See below, n.40.

[19]Judith (16:17), apparently alone among the Old Testament Apocrypha, expresses this view, *i.e.* that 'in the day of judgment' God will take vengeance on Gentiles who attack his people, 'giving fire and worms to their flesh and they shall cry in consciousness forever' (ἐν αἰσθήσει ἕως αἰῶνος). *Cf.* also 4 *Macc.* 12:12; perhaps 9:9. See below, note 39.

[20]*E.g. 1 Enoch* 98:10: 'You are ready for the day of destruction. And do not hope that you will live . . .; rather you will go and die, . . .' (Knibb); *cf.* 90:25ff.; 97:1. Also 4Q418 69:7f.: 'Those who seek the truth will rise for the judgment. . . . All the crazy at heart will be annihilated, and the sons of iniquity will be found no more' (Martinez).

[21]In first-century Judaism Philo and the Pharisees believed that 'the soul' was immortal. *Cf.* Philo, *opificio mundi* 135: Man 'was created at once mortal and immortal, mortal with respect to his body and immortal with respect to his mind'; Josephus, *Ant.* 18, 14; *idem, War* 2, 162f.: 'The Pharisees [say]. . . every soul is imperishable' (ἄφθαρτον) . . . and those of the wicked are punished with an everlasting vengeance' (αἰδίῳ τιμωρίᾳ); R. Meyer, 'φαρισαῖος', *TDNT* 9 (1974), 21; *idem, Hellenistisches in der rabbinischen Anthropologie* (Stuttgart, 1937). *Cf.* R. Hammer (ed.), *Sifre* (New Haven, CT, 1986), 307: '. . . man, whose soul is from heaven and whose body is from the earth' (Sifre 306 on Dt. 32:2).

[22]*Cf.* Acts 23:8; Josephus, *War* 2, 8, 11-14; *Ant.* 18, 16; (H. L. Strack and P. Billerbeck, *Kommentar zum Neuen Testament*, 4 vols. (München, 1922-28), I, 885f. (on Mt. 22:23); E. Schürer, *The History of the Jewish People in the Age of Jesus Christ*, 3 vols. in 4 (Edinburgh, 1973-87), II, 391f.; II, 411. The Sadducees were under Hellenistic influences and on this question were more Epicurean than Old Testament. *Cf.* Josephus, *Ant.* 10, 277f. with 13, 173 and *idem, War* 2, 164f.; Mishnah, *Sanhedrin* 10:1; R. Meyer, 'Σαδδουκαῖος', *TDNT* 7 (1971), 46f.

[23]*E.g.* Pss. 6:5; 115:17; see below, n. 30.

[24]*Cf.* 1QS11:20-22; 1QH 3:24; 10:3; 12:25-31; D. Flusser, 'The Dead Sea Sect and Pre-Pauline Christianity', in C. Rabin and Y. Yadin (eds.), *Aspects of the Dead Sea Scrolls* (Jerusalem, 1958), 262, *cf.* 254, 257; M. Mansoor, *The Thanksgiving Hymns* (Leiden, 1961), 84-89.

perspectives, both Old Testament[26] and New Testament.[27] But neither the Qumran writings nor the Old Testament Apocrypha, nor the largely post-first-century Jewish apocalyptic[28] and rabbinic writings are of central importance; they are neither appealed to nor (with one exception) cited by the New Testament. And it is, I think, a fundamental error in method to interpret the New Testament primarily from Jewish apocrypha and pseudepigrapha or (as the History of Religions school did) from the views of the surrounding paganism, even from pagan views that had infiltrated sectors of Judaism.

More important than views of the different Jewish parties is the teaching of canonical Scripture which, rightly understood, is for biblical Christianity the infallible revelation of God from which all Christian doctrine must be vetted. The issue for evangelicals, then, is one of biblical interpretation, and to that question we may now turn.

Old Testament Witness

The primary background for understanding the New Testament's teaching on the punishment of the wicked is the background to which it appeals. That is the Old Testament Scriptures which were received as canonical authority by first-century Judaism[29] and which, with the possible exception of Esther, were identical with the Old Testament canon received by Protestants and Jews today.

The Old Testament displays distinct conceptions of death as the punishment for sin.[30] It depicts the death state and sphere, *i.e.* שְׁאוֹל (Sheol = ᾅδες, Hades), as a kind of mass grave, six feet under,

[25]4Q418 69:7f. ('Sapiental Work A'); 4Q521 12 ('Messianic Apocalypse'); 1QH 3:19-22; 6:29f., 34; *cf.* 4:21f.; 11:12; 18:25-29; J. H. Charlesworth, 'Toward a Taxonomy of Resurrection Texts (1QH, 4Q521, Luke, and the Fourth Gospel)', *NTS* 44, forthcoming; E. Puech, 'Messianism, Resurrection, and Eschatology at Qumran and in the New Testament', in E. Ulrich and J. VanderKam (eds.), *The Community of the Renewed Covenant* (Notre Dame, IN, 1994), 235-256, esp. 246-253; M. Black, *The Scrolls and Christian Origins* (London, 1961), 142, 190f. Otherwise: H. Ringgren, *The Faith of Qumran* (1963; New York, 2nd edn. 1995), 148-151.
[26]See below, notes 33-37, 42, 44-51.
[27]See below, notes 82, 83. For the rabbinical writings see below, note 39.
[28]*Pace* K. S. Harmon, 'The Case against Conditionalism', in N. de M. S. Cameron, *Universalism and the Doctrine of Hell* (Carlisle, 1992), 193-224.
[29]*Cf.* E. E. Ellis, *The Old Testament in Early Christianity* (WUNT 54), (Tübingen, 1991), 36-50; R. Beckwith, *The Old Testament Canon of the New Testament Church* (London, 1985), 274-323; S. Z. Leiman, *The Canonization of Hebrew Scriptures* (Hamden, CT, 1976), 131f., 135.
[30]*E.g.* Gn. 2:17; 3:17ff.; Ezk. 18:4.

over which God has power to deliver by resurrection, but with which He has no relationship (Is. 14; Ezk. 31–32).[31] Despite some metaphorical and symbolic scenes of conversation among the maggots,[32] the Scripture represents the departure into Sheol as the end of individual being, a returning to the common earth[33] and 'virtual annihilation'.[34] While one may continue to 'live' in one's name or progeny,[35] viewed as a corporate extension of one's own soul,[36] there is no longer any personal life or being. The 'spirit [that] returns to God who gave it' (Ec. 12:7) is not, as Platonists read it, a part of the individual's personality, much less his essential ego, but rather the 'spirit of life' (Gn. 7:22; cf. 2:7) that God grants and, at death, takes back (e.g. Jb. 34:14f.). Man's end is 'like water spilt on the ground which cannot be gathered up again' (2 Sa. 14:14). Death levels him with all other dying life: man and beast, righteous and wicked, wise and foolish.[37] Sheol is then both the natural end of all mortal creatures and also God's judgment on the disobedient Adamic race.

Anthropologically, the Old Testament views the human 'personality [as] . . . an animated body, not (like the Greek) . . . [as] an incarnated soul'.[38] It knows no body/soul dualism and has no Platonic conception of an immortal soul with an after-death experience different from the body. Under the influence of Greek mythology and philosophy, this changes later in the thought of some Pharisaic rabbinic tradition,[39] of Jewish[40] and Christian apocalyptic

---

[31]E.g. Jb. 7:9; Pss. 6:5; 30:9. Cf. E. E. Ellis, 'Life', in J. D. Douglas (ed.), The New Bible Dictionary (Leicester: IVP, 2nd edn. 1982), 697-701, esp. 698; N. J. Tromp, Primitive Conceptions of Death and the Nether World in the Old Testament (Rome, 1969), 129-140; J. Pedersen, Israel: Its Life and Culture, 4 vols. in 2, (Copenhagen, 1959), I, 460-470.

[32]Ezk. 31–32; Is. 14:4-11; cf. Lk. 16:19-31.

[33]Gn. 3:19; 25:8; 37:35; Dt. 31:16; Jb. 3:13ff.; 10:9; 17:13-16; Pss. 6:5; 49:12; 144:4; 146:4; Ec. 2:14; 3:19ff.; 9:10; 12:7.

[34]A. R. Johnson, The Vitality of the Individual in the Thought of Ancient Israel (Cardiff, 1949), 93. Cf. Ellis, 'Life', 697f.

[35]Ps. 72:17; Is. 66:22.

[36]Cf. Pedersen, Israel, I, 254ff.

[37]Ec. 3:19ff.

[38]H. W. Robinson, The Christian Doctrine of Man (Edinburgh, 3rd edn. 1947), 27.

[39]Cf. Meyer, Hellenistisches 25-32, 44-69; (note 21); the texts cited in Billerbeck (note 22), II, 222-234 (on Lk. 16:19-31); IV, 1016-1165. All in all, the rabbinic literature affirms an extended judgment of the unrighteous in Gehenna, followed by their annihilation. Cf. e.g. Mishnah, Eduyoth 2:10; Tosefta Sanhedrin 13:4: 'The Israelites. . . and Gentiles who sinned go down to Gehenna and are judged there. . . . And, after twelve months their souls perish, their bodies are burned, Gehenna absorbs them, and they are turned into dust under the feet of the righteous, as it is written. . . (Mal. 4:3).' Cf. F. Weber, Jüdische Theologie auf Grund des Talmud und

pseudepigrapha[41] and of some patristic literature. Here the real, immaterial personality, the soul, continues after the physical body dissolves into dust. The Old Testament, however, views man as a unity and pictures the whole person as going into the grave.[42] What then is the hope of the godly and the special judgment of the wicked? The Old Testament hope is the resurrection of the whole person from Sheol. Contrary to a widespread scholarly tradition,[43] a resurrection hope was not a late-appearing conception, since it is found in pre-Exodus Egypt (J. H. Breasted; A. H. Sayce)[44] and

---

verwandter Schriften (Hildesheim, 1975; based on 2nd edn. 1897), 390-398: 'Therefore, by God's judgment, the nations (*Völkerwelt*) will be delivered to annihilation through the fire of *Gehenna*. In this way the earth, henceforth in the sole possession of Israel and freed from the ungodly, can be renewed and become the abode of everlasting life' (398).

[40]Apart from parts of *1 Enoch* the Jewish apocalyptic pseudepigrapha are very probably post-first century. In any case they and early Christian pseudepigrapha contain views of body/soul anthropology and of the after-death state of the wicked that are heavily influenced by pagan Greek philosophical and mythological conceptions. *Cf.* R. J. Bauckham, 'Early Jewish Visions of Hell', *JTS* 41 (1990), 335-385; M. Himmelfarb, *Tours of Hell* (Philadelphia, 1983); A. Dieterich, *Nekyia: Beiträge zur Erklärung der neuentdeckten Petrusapokalypse* (Stuttgart, 1969; based on 2nd edn. 1913). See above, note 18.

[41]ÆFN1 Everlasting torment of the wicked is reflected in, *e.g.* the Ascension of Is. 1:3; 10:8ff. (perhaps) and the Ethiopic Apocalypse of pseudo-Peter 7-10. (Further, *cf.* Himmelfarb [note 40], 8-40; A. K. Turner, *The History of Hell* [New York, 1993], 83-88). One of several 'Apocalypses' of pseudo-Peter, it may be dated to the later second century if it is the 'Apocalypse of Peter' commented on by Clement of Alexandria (*cf.* Eusebius, HE 6, 14, 1) and mentioned in the Muratorian Canon; but see D. J. Theron, *Evidence of Tradition* (Grand Rapids, 1959), 113n (on the Muratorian Canon). On the other hand, the apocryphal *Acts of Paul* 8, 3, 24-27, and *Acts of Peter* (Vercel.) 17, middle, apparently assign the wicked to annihilation.

[42]Pss. 30:3; 33:19; 88:3; 89:48. See above, note 33. *Cf.* Ellis (note 31), 697f.; W. Eichrodt, *Theology of the Old Testament*, 2 vols. (London, 5th edn. 1967), II, 214f.

[43]*E.g.* Schürer, *Jewish People*, II, 391f., 411; G. von Rad, *Old Testament Theology*, 2 vols. (London, 1975), I, 405ff.; II, 350. This tradition appears to rest in part on reading Old Testament texts with philosophical preconceptions of the ego's survival of death (*e.g.* von Rad, I, 405ff. on Ps. 73:23-28) and, in part, on a nineteenth-century evolutionary pattern applied to Old Testament thought in which 'resurrection' was placed late on the scale. Consequently, where 'resurrection' was admitted, the texts were dated late; where the texts were dated early, a 'resurrection' exegesis of them was rejected. It was the merit of Michael Dahood to show the historical and exegetical fallacy of the pattern. See below, note 46.

[44]*Cf.* J. H. Breasted, *A History of Egypt from the Earliest Times* (New York, 2nd edn. 1909); *idem, Development of Religion and Thought in Ancient Egypt* (New York, 3rd edn. 1959), 55-61, 288ff.; A. H. Sayce, *The Religions of Ancient Egypt and Babylonia*

may have been appropriated from there and reformulated under inspiration by Israel's prophets.[45] In Egypt, it underlay the careful embalming practice, the placing of grain in the tomb and even the burial of Pharaoh's ship alongside the tomb so that in a future resurrection he could use it again to sail the Nile.

In the Psalms, some of which are among the most ancient Old Testament literature, the hope of resurrection is repeatedly expressed, as Michael Dahood, Derek Kidner and others have argued.[46] The resurrection also, according to Jesus,[47] underlies God's Exodus declaration that He is the God of dead Abraham, a declaration implicitly affirming that He would resurrect Abraham, since '[God] is not the God of the dead.'[48] Paul voices the same thought when he teaches that 'if the dead are not raised, . . . those who have fallen asleep in Christ have ceased to exist' (ἀπώλοντο, perished, 1 Cor. 15:18) and, in Romans 4:17, where he equates the resurrection of the dead with the calling of non-being into being.[49] In the Old Testament, resurrection is implicitly affirmed throughout in

---

(Edinburgh, 1902), 170: '. . . the doctrine of the resurrection of the body became an integral part of the Osirian faith'.

[45]It was apparently also present elsewhere in the ancient Near East. *Cf.* E. B. Smick, 'The Bearing of New Philological Data on the Subjects of the Resurrection and Immortality in the Old Testament', *WTJ* 31 (1968-69), 12-21, who concludes that 'some notion of resurrection from the dead was a part of [pre-Abrahamic] Sumerian mythology' (21).

[46]D. Kidner, *Psalms*, 2 vols. (London, 1975), I, 74, 86, 90; II, 263, 466f. *Cf.* Pss. 16:9ff. (Acts 2:26f.); 17:15; 49:12, 14f.; 73:23-27; 139:18; M. Dahood, *Psalms*, 3 vols. (Garden City, NY, 1970), I, 106, *passim*. From a careful study of the relationship of the biblical Psalms to North West Semitic data (and of their differences from the psalms of Qumran), Dahood concluded not only that the biblical Psalter was pre-Exilic (III, xxxiv - xxxvii) but also that these ancient Psalms contain 'a deep and steady belief in resurrection and immortality' for the righteous (III, xli - lii; *cf.* I, xxxvi). Although his exegesis can be faulted in some respects, Dahood's method and analysis were sound and appear to mark a permanent advance in the research. *Cf.* Tromp (note 31), 124 (on Is. 26:19), 184 (on Ps. 3:6); Smick 'Bearing', 12-21. Otherwise: H. J. Kraus, *Psalms*, 2 vols. (Minneapolis, 1988), II, 91ff., 517, who rejects any expectation of resurrection from Sheol in these Psalms and, following G. von Rad, interprets Ps. 73:24 to anticipate an after-death communion with God in 'a completely different realm of life' (I, 93). But this contradicts all Old Testament depictions of death and Sheol and appears to import Platonic conceptions into the text.

[47]*Cf.* Lk. 20:27-40, esp. 37f. par; E. E. Ellis, *The Gospel of Luke* (Grand Rapids, 7th edn. 1996), 234-237.

[48]Mt. 22:32 par.

[49]*Cf.* E. Käsemann, *Romans* (Grand Rapids, 4th edn. 1980), 123: '. . . the resurrection of the dead [in Rom 4:17] . . . deserves to be called a creation out of nothing and presents the eschatological repetition of the first creation.'

God's power to deliver one from Sheol, but it is explicitly expressed as God's purpose in comparatively few passages in Job, Psalms, Isaiah and Daniel.[50] Equally, a resurrection, *i.e.* resuscitation of the wicked, raised for punishment, is present explicitly only in Daniel and perhaps Isaiah.[51] For the Old Testament, then, the assurance of future life does not lie in the idea that some part of the individual survives death, but in the firm hope that God will raise from death those in covenant relationship with Him.

New Testament Teaching

The New Testament teaching on the punishment of those outside Christ rests upon and arises from the Old Testament teaching on the nature of man and the nature of death. The Scriptures, both Old and New Testament, represent individual personality as a complex and totally mortal monism, a unity that can be viewed from different perspectives, but that cannot be broken into separately existing parts.[52]   The biblical view is compatible with an outer/inner distinction[53] or even a matter/thought or matter/will distinction, as long as both aspects are recognized as mortal and as a part of the present fallen creation and thus subject to the natural death process. But it is incompatible with an anthropological dualism in which one part, *i.e.* the soul or spirit, is considered to have immunity from the processes of the present natural order and thus to be exempt from death, *i.e.* from a cessation of existence. This kind of dualism[54] has

---

[50]*E.g.* Job 19:26; Pss. 16:8-11; 49:14f.; Is. 25:8; 26:19; Ezk. 37; Dn. 12:2. *Cf.* J. Baldwin, *Daniel* (Leicester: IVP, 1978), 204f. *Cf.* also Jon. 2:1-10 with Mt. 12:40.

[51]Dn. 12:2; Is. 66:24, expounded and applied by Jesus to His hearers re the unquenchable fire of the final judgment (Mk. 9:42-48). It is clearly taught in the New Testament, *e.g.* Jn. 5:28-29; Acts 24:15; 2 Cor. 5:3, 10; Heb. 11:35; *cf.* Phil. 3:11 (ἐξανάστασις); Rev. 20:5f. *Cf.* E. E. Ellis, 'II Corinthians v. 1-10 in Pauline Eschatology', *NTS* 6 (1959-60), 211-224, esp. 219-222.

[52]This may be illustrated by Jesus' interchange with the Scripture scholar at Mk. 12:30-33: 'You shall love the Lord your God with your whole heart and. . . soul and. . . mind (διανοίας) and strength' (ἰσχύός); and the scribe replied, 'Well said, teacher, . . . , [for] to love Him with one's whole heart and. . . understanding (συνέσεως) and. . . strength. . . is much more than burnt offerings. . . .' It is clear that the whole person from the perspective of his inner-self is meant and that the variation in terminology is a matter of indifference. See below, note 53.

[53]*Cf.* E. E. Ellis, 'Sōma in 1 Corinthians', *Interpretation* 44 (1990), 132-144: 'Like the Old Testament and unlike a Platonic body/soul or body/spirit dualism, both the inward and outward aspects of the person refer to physical being' (135).

[54]It is reflected in the philosophically oriented work of J. W. Cooper, *Body, Soul, and Life Everlasting* (Grand Rapids, 1989), and it seems to underlie R. H. Gundry's

departed from a biblical understanding to a conception rooted in Platonic philosophy, a reading of the New Testament with glasses ground in Athens, resulting in a reconceptualization and redefinition of all the New Testament terms and concepts used for the punishment of the unrighteous. It thereby excludes *a priori* the meaning (in an active sense) of extinction of being, *i.e.* annihilation, or (in a reflexive or passive sense) of cessation of being.

The New Testament is quite clear about immortality: only God 'has immortality' (ἀθανασία, 1 Tim. 6:16). It states that among mankind only those in Christ will 'put on immortality', and they will do so individually only at their bodily resurrection at the second coming, *i.e.* parousia of Christ (*e.g.* 1 Cor. 15:22f., 52, 53f.). Paul teaches that this transformation effects the conquest and defeat of death, which is the punishment for sin (1 Cor. 15:54-57; *cf.* Rom. 5:12, 18f.; 6:23). The New Testament similarly applies and restricts other terms, like 'everlasting life' or just 'life'[55] to those in Christ. In this context one may now examine the New Testament terms and concepts used for the ultimate punishment of the wicked.[56]

In the New Testament, hell is the translation of two terms, *Hades* (ᾅδες = Sheol), which, with one possible exception, continues the Old Testament meaning of 'the grave',[57] and *Gehenna* (γέεννα = גֵּיא הִנֹּם *gehinnom*). For the purposes of this essay, hell ordinarily refers to *Gehenna*.[58] It is used by Jesus in His exposition of Isaiah 66:24 (Mk. 9:42-48), an eschatological context that very probably refers to the Day of final judgment. It is depicted in terms of the garbage dump in the valley of Hinnom on the south side of Jerusalem, 'where their worm does not die and the fire is not quenched' (Is. 66:24).[59] Although hell cannot be equated with the analogy, it is represented

---

Soma in Biblical Theology (Grand Rapids, 2nd edn. 1987), esp. 159f. But see A. Köberle, 'Das griechische und das biblische Verständnis von Seele', *Theologische Beiträge* 14 (1983), 133-142.

[55]*E.g.* Mt. 19:29; 25:46; Lk. 10:25; Jn. 3:15f.; Acts 13:46ff.; Rom. 2:7. On 'life' *cf.* Mt. 7:14; Jn. 5:29; Acts 11:18; 2 Cor. 5:4; 1 Pet. 3:7.

[56]The meaning of terms and phrases is not the whole of exegesis, but it is the essential starting point from which any sound exegesis must proceed.

[57]Mt. 11:23 (= Lk. 10:15 [Capernaum]); 16:18 (gates of death); Acts 2:27, 31 (Ps. 16:10f.); 1 Cor. 15:55 אָ2, Aᶜ (Ho. 13:14); Rev. 1:18; 6:8; 20:13f. (death and the grave). Lk. 16:23: 'He was buried in Hades' (א* lat Mcion). Here the scene is similar to Is. 14:9ff., but it is closer to later Greek apocalyptic/mythological perceptions in the picture of bodily torment. See below, note 78.

[58]The term occurs 12 times in the New Testament, all but one (Jas. 3:6) in the teaching of Jesus. *Cf.* Mt. 5:22, 29f.; 10:28; 18:9; 23:15, 33.

[59]*Cf.* 2 Ki. 23:10. For rabbinic and Jewish apocalyptic pseudepigraphic views *cf.* Billerbeck (note 22), IV, 1029-1118; Bauckham, 'Early Jewish', 382-385.

by it as the ultimate end, an end as outcast, refuse, suffering (for those thrown out there alive) and decay. As hell is used elsewhere by Jesus, it ordinarily has similar connotations of God's final punishment of the wicked on the last Day of this age. As such it seems to presuppose, *e.g.* in Matthew 23:15, 33, a resurrection, that is, resuscitation of the unrighteous for judgment.

The New Testament uses analogies other than the Jerusalem dump for the punishment of the wicked on the last Day.[60] John the Baptist and Jesus compare that punishment to a number of non-human objects: burned-up chaff or tree or weeds or branch (Mt. 3:12; 7:19; 13:40; Jn. 15:6); a destroyed house, bad fish discarded, an uprooted plant, a chopped down tree (Mt. 7:27; 13:48; 15:13; Lk. 13:7). Jesus also uses human analogies: The unrepentant unbelievers on the Day of judgment, *i.e.* at the coming of the Son of Man, will be like those drowned in the flood, and those burned up at Sodom, and Lot's wife reduced to salt (Lk. 17:27, 29, 32). They will be like wicked tenants destroyed, the rejecter ground to powder, the evil servant cut to pieces (Mt. 21:41, 44; 24:51); like the Galileans killed by Pilate, those killed by a falling tower, rebels slain (Lk. 13:2, 4; 19:14, 27). On these analogies the punishment of the wicked will be a life-destroying act with a permanent and unrecallable effect.

The destiny of the wicked is also compared by Jesus to a process of punishment: a debtor held in prison, those thrown out of the house into darkness and weeping (Mt. 8:12; 22:13; 25:30). But it is not said that the process is without end.

Nouns, other than hell, that describe the destiny of unbelievers also may involve a process such as an undefined vengeance (ἐκδίκησις),[61] or punishment (κόλασις, τιμωρία),[62] or divine wrath (ὀργή).[63] Perhaps 'fire' might be included here, but the purpose and effect of fire is either to purge and refine or, in this context, to destroy utterly although pain may accompany the disintegration.[64]

Other nouns for the judgment of the unrighteous connote obliteration. They include annihilation (ἀπώλεια),[65] destruction

---

[60]See below, Appendix.

[61]Lk. 18:7f.; 2 Thes. 1:8; Heb. 10:30f.

[62]Mt. 25:46; Heb. 10:9.

[63]Mt. 3:7; Jn. 3:36; Rom. 1:18; 2:5, 8; 3:5; 5:9; 9:22; Eph. 2:3; 5:6; Col. 3:6; 1 Thes. 1:10 (2:16); 5:9; Rev. 6:17; 11:18; 16:19; 19:15.

[64]Mt. 5:22; 13:42, 50; 25:41; Mk. 9:47f.; Lk. 17:29f.; 2 Thes. 1:8; Heb. 10:27; 2 Pet. 3:7; Rev. 11:5; 18:8; 19:20; 20:9f., 14f.; 21:8.

[65]Mt. 7:13; Jn. 17:12; Acts 8:20; Rom. 9:22ff.; Phil. 1:28; 3:19; 2 Thes. 2:3; 1 Tim. 6:9; Heb. 10:39; 2 Pet. 2:1.

(ὄλεθρος),[66] death (θάνατος),[67] end (τέλος),[68] disintegration (φθόρα).[69] Verbs used in this context can also have a connotation either of process[70] or of end of being.[71] Of course, for all of these terms one can find an instance where the meaning, annihilation, does not apply. Augustinians, with their presupposition that the individual's essential being cannot cease to exist, present such an instance and suppose that it can be applied to the biblical contexts. But if asked what Greek or Hebrew term would connote annihilation, they offer none, at least none that appear in Scripture. They have decided the question by their presupposition and will be persuaded by no linguistic nor exegetical argument.

New Testament texts on the destiny or punishment of the wicked often have an accompanying adjective, everlasting or age-lasting (αἰώνιος). The term αἰώνιος should not be translated 'eternal' because that word has philosophical connotations, a contrast of time with eternity, that has no place in Scripture. The Bible presents man totally as a temporal creature whom God relates to, in both salvation and judgment, totally in time and history, this age and the age to come.[72] For the wicked, Scripture speaks of an everlasting sin (ἁμάρτημα, Mk. 3:39), everlasting punishment (κόλασις, Mt. 25:46), everlasting judgment (κρίμα, κρίσις, Heb. 6:8; Mk. 3:25A), everlasting fire (πῦρ, Mt. 18:8; 25:41; Jude 7), and everlasting destruction (ὄλεθρος, 2 Thes. 1:9).

For the destiny of the righteous, the New Testament uses the same adjective: everlasting judgment (κρίμα, Heb. 6:2).[73] Cf. everlasting salvation (σωτηρία, Heb. 5:9), ever- lasting redemption

---

[66]1 Thes. 5:3; 2 Thes. 1:9 (1 Tim. 6:9).

[67]Rom. 1:32; 6:21ff.; 7:5; 8:6; 1 Cor. 15:21f.; 15:56; 2 Cor. 2:16; 7:10; Jas. 1:15; 5:20; 1 Jn. 5:16; Rev. (2:11); (20:6); 20:14; 21:8.

[68]Rom. 6:21f.; 2 Cor. 11:15; Phil. 3:19; 1 Pet. 4:17.

[69]Gal. 6:8; 2 Pet. 1:4; 2:12.

[70]E.g. (torment): βασανίζειν (Mk. 5:7f.; cf. 1:24); (Rev. 14:10); (20:10); φθείρειν, διαφθείρειν, καταφθείρειν (disintegrate): 1 Cor 3:17; (2 Cor. 4:16); Rev. 11:18; 2 Pet. 2:12; ἐσθίειν (eat, consume): Heb. 10:26f.; κολάζειν (punish: 2 Pet. 2:9).

[71]E.g. ἀποθνήσκειν (die, be dead): cf. Jn. 8:24; Lk. 20:36; Jn. 11:26; ἀπόλλυναι (perish, dissolve, come to an end, lose): Mt. 10:28, 39; 16:25; Lk. 13:3; 17:27, 29; 20:16; Jn. 12:25; Rom. 2:12; 1 Cor. 10:10f.; 15:18; (2 Thes. 2:10); (Heb. 1:11); (Jas. 4:12); 2 Pet 3:5ff.; Jude 5-7; (ἐψ)ὀλοθρεύειν (cut off, destroy): Acts 3:23; Heb. 11:28.

[72]Cf. O. Cullmann, Christ and Time (London, 1952); idem, Salvation in History (London, 1967).

[73]F. Delitzsch, Commentary on the Epistle to the Hebrews, 2 vols. (Edinburgh, 1868), I, 272: 'κρίμα αἰώνιον is the final judgment, deciding forever the blessedness of the righteous and the damnation of the wicked (Acts xxiv.25)'. That is, it is a one-time point action with an everlasting effect.

(λύτρωσις, Heb. 9:12), everlasting life (ζωή, Mt. 25:46). In Matthew 25:46 Jesus places together both the destiny of the righteous and that of the cursed:

> Then they will go away into everlasting punishment (κόλασιν), but the righteous into everlasting life.

The two destinies are represented as co-extensive, but they leave two questions unexplained. (1) What is the punishment? (2) Are the two destinies everlasting processes of 'everlasting living' and 'everlasting punishing' or are they point actions, a one-time dispensing of life and dispensing of punishment that have an everlasting effect? On the second question, similar texts help us to understand that the latter alternative is the proper interpretation of Matthew at 25:46. When Jude 7 refers to Sodom undergoing the judgment of 'everlasting fire' it does not mean that Sodom is ever burning, but that the effect of the burning lasts for ever. When Hebrews speaks of 'an everlasting salvation' (σωτηρία αἰωνία, 5:9) or 'an everlasting redemption' (αἰωνία λύτρωσις, 9:12) accomplished by the sacrifice of Christ 'once for all' (ἐφάπαξ 9:12; cf. 7:27; 10:10), it is clear that it does not mean an everlasting process of saving or redeeming, but rather a one-time act of salvation and redemption that has an everlasting effect. The same is true of the expression 'everlasting judgment' (κρίμα αἰωνιον) in Hebrews 6:2. As Delitzsch pointed out long ago, the phrase refers to the final judgment at Christ's second appearing (Heb. 9:28) that decides for ever the blessedness of the righteous and the damnation of the wicked.[74]

Only one passage in the New Testament speaks of a punishment of 'everlasting torment', and it refers to the punishment of non-human figures, 'the devil, . . . the beast and the false prophet' (Rev. 20:10), in a vision-revelation full of highly symbolic scenes. If the passage is taken literally, it appears to contradict the teaching at Hebrews 2:14 that Jesus will destroy (καταργεῖν) the Devil.

The most important and frequent terms for the punishment of sin are death (θάνατος) and destruction or annihilation (ἀπώλεια) and their corresponding verbs.[75] How did this kind of language come to be understood by the later patristic and the medieval church to imply everlasting suffering? The change very probably came about, as Harnack argued, from the fusion of the gospel with Platonic philosophy,[76] especially by the Alexandrian school of Clement and

---

[74]See above, note 73.
[75]See above, notes 65, 67, 71.
[76]Harnack, *Outlines of the History of Dogma* (Boston, 1957), 155.

Origen, which resulted in 'the transformation of the ecclesiastical tradition into a philosophy of religion'.[77] This fusion promoted in the church a dualistic Platonic anthropology that shifted the Christian hope and the judgment of God from the parousia of Christ and the resurrection of the dead to the departure of the soul to heaven or hell at death.[78] Probably influenced also by the Gnostics, it redefined redemption from a redemption of matter to a redemption from matter. With its acceptance of the philosophical dogma of the immortal soul, it paved the road to the doctrine of universal salvation (Origen) or of an everlasting dualism of good and evil (Augustine), the kingdom of God above and the continuing hell below.[79]

Conclusion

The New Testament's teaching of resurrection to immortality as God's gift only to those belonging to Jesus Christ[80] defines its understanding both of salvation in Christ and of God's judgment on those outside Christ. In the case of the latter, it represents, as a good number of writers have recognized,[81] a judgment effecting the

---

[77]Harnack, *History of Dogma*, 7 vols. in 4 (New York 1961; based on 3rd edn. 1894), II, 319-380. *Cf.* Eusebius, *Historia Ecclesiastica* 6, 37, 1; S. R. C. Lilla, *Clement of Alexandria* (Oxford, 1971), 15, 173-181, 229.

[78]In some Jewish pseudepigrapha (Bauckham) and rabbinic writings (Billerbeck) the punishment of *Gehenna* ('hell') begins already in Hades ('hell') before the resurrection, as it does in the parable told by Jesus, the rich man and Lazarus (Lk. 16:19-31). *Cf.* Bauckham, 'Early Jewish Visions', 384f.; Billerbeck, *Kommentar*, IV, 1023-1026. Jesus uses a well-known story as an illustration, however, not to give a preview of life after death. *Cf.* Ellis, *Luke*, 201-206. See n. 57 above.

[79]*Pace* Henri Blocher, 'Everlasting Punishment and the Problem of Evil', in Cameron, *Universalism*, 283-312, who makes the intriguing argument that those in hell no longer sin and that their cries are only in recognition and remorse that they had earlier rejected God. But as an Augustinian-Calvinist, Blocher should recognize that if their remorse is a 'godly sorrow' it is the product of the Holy Spirit in His work of redemption; if only a remorse that they were caught and judged, that remorse continues to be sin.

[80]Jn. 5:28f.; 1 Cor. 15:22f., 53ff.; 2 Tim. 1:10; *cf.* Mt. 25:46; Mk. 10:30 par; Jn. 6:40; Rom. 2:7; 6:23; 1 Pet. 1:4.

[81]*Cf.* B. F. C. Atkinson, *Life and Immortality* (Taunton, UK, *c.* 1968); D. L. Edwards and John Stott, *Evangelical Essentials* (Downers Grove, IL, 1988), 312-329 (John Stott); Michael Green, *Evangelism Through the Local Church* (London, 1990), 69f.; H. E. Guillebaud, *The Righteous Judge* (Taunton, UK, 1964); P. E. Hughes, *The True Image* (Grand Rapids, 1989), 398-407; C. Pinnock, 'The Destruction of the Finally Impenitent', *CTR* 4 (1989-90), 243-259; J. W. Wenham, 'The Case for Conditional Immortality', in Cameron, *Universalism*, 161-191. *Cf.* also the literature cited by J. L. Garrett, *Systematic Theology*, 2 vols. (Grand Rapids, 1995), II, 786-807.

annihilation of their being. This judgment will be God's act on the last Day of this age when the 'just and unjust',[82] the living and the dead raised to life, will stand before Jesus Christ to receive His verdict, 'each according to what he has done in the (natural, Adamic) body'.[83] For the impenitent it will involve 'weeping and gnashing of teeth',[84] a sense of loss and pain proportionate to God's just recompense to each,[85] and it will culminate in 'the second death'[86] in the 'lake of fire',[87] an utter destruction and extinction of existence.[88] 'Judgment Day' will be a sombre, awesome and universally panoramic occasion, in which all mankind and the hosts of angels and archangels will see and will recognize God to be 'both righteous and the One who counts righteous' those who have faith in Jesus who, as a propitiation, bore their 'everlasting punishment' on the cross of Calvary.[89]

God's last word is not judgment, but salvation. It is the magnificent biblical teaching of resurrection to immortality[90] and everlasting life in 'a new heavens and a new earth'.[91] At that wonderful time the whole of God's creation will be in perfect harmony and the former 'Silent Planet'[92] will resonate with God's praise and prospects. And all evil in God's universe, including all evil creatures, will have passed into nothingness and 'shall not be remembered, nor come into mind' anymore.[93]

---

[82]Acts 24:15; cf. Lk. 13:28f.; Jn. 5:28f.; Heb. 9:27.

[83]2 Cor. 5:10; cf. Mt. 25:31-46; Rev. 20:11-15; 21:5-8.

[84]Mt. 8:11f.; cf. 22:13f.; 24:51 Q; 25:14, 30; Lk. 19:11, 27; Rev. 18:9f.

[85]Lk. 12:40, 46ff.

[86]Rev. 2:11; 20:6, 14; 21:8.

[87]Rev. 20:10-15; cf. Mt. 5:22; 13:40-43, 49f.; Mk. 9:47f. par.; Jn. 15:6; Heb. 10:26f.; 2 Pet. 3:7-13.

[88]Mt. 7:13f.; 2 Thes. 1:7ff.

[89]Is. 53:4-12; Lk. 23:33; Rom. 3:25f.; 1 Pet. 2:24.

[90]1 Cor. 15:53ff.

[91]2 Pet. 3:13; cf. Is. 65:17; 66:22.

[92]Cf. C. S. Lewis, Out of the Silent Planet (London, 1938).

[93]Is. 65:17; cf. 2 Pet. 3:13; Rev. 21:4.

APPENDIX

New Testament Terms Used for the Fate of Unbelievers

I. Verbs

ἀποθνήσκειν = מוּת (die, be dead): *cf.* Jn. 8:24; Lk. 20:36; Jn. 11:26.

ἀπόλλυναι = אָבַד (perish, lose, dissolve, destroy, come to an end):
Mt. 10:28, 39; 16:25; Lk. 13:3; 17:27, 29; 20:16; Jn. 12:25; Rom. 2:12;
1 Cor. 10:10f.; 15:18; (2 Thes. 2:10); (Heb. 1:11); (Jas. 4:12); 2 Pet.
3:5ff.; Jude 5-7.

βασανίζειν (torment): (Mk. 5:7f.; *cf.* 1:24); (Rev. 14:10); (20:10).

διαφθείρειν = שָׁחַת (disintegrate): (2 Cor. 4:16); Rev. 11:18.

ἐσθίειν (eat, consume): Heb. 10:26f.

(ἐξ) ὀλεθρεύειν = כָּרַת, שָׁדַד (destroy) (cut off, destroy): Acts 3:23; Heb. 11:28.

καταργεῖν (abolish, waste, destroy): 2 Thes. 2:8; 2 Tim. 1:10; Heb. 2:14.

καταφθείρειν (disintegrate): 2 Pet. 2:12.

κολάζειν (punish): 2 Pet. 2:9.

φθείρειν (disintegrate, corrupt): 1 Cor. 3:17.

II. Nouns

ἀπώλεια = אָבַד (destruction, annihilation, ruin):
Mt. 7:13; Jn. 17:12; Acts 8:20; Rom. 9:22ff.; Phil 1:28; 3:19; 2 Thes. 2:3; 1 Tim. 6:9;
Heb. 10:39; 2 Pet. 2:1; 3:7, 16.

ἐκδίκησις (vengeance, recompense): Lk. 18:7f.; 2 Thes. 1:8; Heb. 10:30f.

ὄλεθρος (destruction, death): 1 Thes. 5:3; 2 Thes. 1:9; (1 Tim. 6:9).

γέεννα = גֵּיא הִנֹּם (hell): Mt. 5:22, 29, 30; 10:28; 23:15, 33; Mk. 9:47f. (Is. 66:24);
Jas. 3:6.

κόλασις = מִכְשׁוֹל (punishment, a cutting off): Mt. 25:46.

ὀργή = אַף (wrath [of God]): Mt. 3:7; Jn. 3:36; Rom. 1:18; 2:5, 8; 3:5; 5:9; 9:22; Eph.
2:3; 5:6; Col. 3:6; 1 Thes. 1:10; (2:16); 5:9; Rev. 6:17; 11:18; 16:19; 19:15.

θάνατος = מוּת (death): Rom. 1:32; 6:21ff.; 7:5; 8:6; 1 Cor. 15:21f.; 15:56; 2 Cor.
2:16; 7:10; Jas. 1:15; 1 Jn. 5:16; Rev. (2:11); (20:6); 20:14; 21:8.

πῦρ = אֵשׁ (fire): Mt. 5:22; 13:42, 50; 25:41; Mk. 9:47f.; Lk. 17:29f.; 2 Thes. 1:8; Heb.
10:27; 2 Pet. 3:7; Rev. 11:5; 18:8; 19:20; 20:9f., 14f.; 21:8.

τέλος = כָּלָה (end): Rom. 6:21f.; 2 Cor. 11:15; Phil. 3:19; 1 Pet. 4:17.

τιμωρία (punishment): Heb. 10:9.

φθόρα = שָׁחַת (disintegration, decay): Gal. 6:8; 2 Pet. 1:4; 2:12.

III. Adjectives

αἰώνιος – αἰών = עוֹלָם (everlasting, age-lasting) cf. eternal.

Modifying:

A.   ἁμάρτημα (sin): Mk. 3:39 κρίμα (judgment): Heb. 6:8.
ὄλεθρος (destruction): 2 Thes. 1:9.
κόλασις (punishment): Mt. 25:46 κρίσις (judgment): Mk. 3:29A.
πῦρ (fire): Mt. 18:8; 25:41; Jude 7.

B. Compare

1. Ps. 24:7 (everlasting temple doors and gates); Dt.' 35:15 (everlasting hills); 1 Sa. 27:8 (everlasting nations); 1 Ch. 15:2 (everlasting levitical priesthood); Pr. 22:28 (everlasting landmark). Rom. 16:25; 2 Tim. 1:9; Tit. 1:2 (everlasting times, χρόνοι).

2. Mt. 25:46 (everlasting life); Heb. 5:9 (everlasting salvation); 6:2 (everlasting judgment); 9:12 (everlasting redemption).
    Process or Effect?

IV. Analogies

A. Inanimate Objects

1. Burned up chaff (Mt. 3:12), weeds (Mt. 13:40), tree (Mt. 7:19), branch (Jn. 15:6).
2. Uprooted plant (Mt. 15:13), chopped down tree (Lk. 13:7), bad fish thrown away (Mt. 13:48).
3. House destroyed by hurricane (Mt. 7:27).

B. Human Life

1. Wicked tenants destroyed (Mt. 21:41).
2. Rejecter ground to powder (Mt. 21:44).
3. Evil servant cut to pieces (Mt. 24:51).
4. Galileans killed by Pilate (Lk. 13:2).
5. Men killed by falling tower (Lk. 13:4).
6. Those drowned in the flood (Lk. 17:27).
7. Those burned up at Sodom (Lk. 17:29; Jude 7).
8. Lot's wife turned to salt (Lk. 17:32).
9. Rebels slain (Lk. 19:14, 27).
10. Debtor's kept in prison (Mt. 5:26; 18:34f.).
11. Those thrown out of party into darkness (Mt. 22:13) Cf. Mt. 8:12.
12. Worthless servant thrown out of house into the dark (Mt. 25:30).

Chapter 10

THE DURATION OF DIVINE JUDGMENT IN THE NEW TESTAMENT

Peter M. Head

This essay discusses some New Testament passages which address the subject of the duration of divine judgment. Attention in Jesus' teaching is given to: (1) His use of the terminology of Gehenna (e.g. Mk. 9:42-48) in the context of the allusion to Isaiah 6:24; (2) the implications of His appeal to the inhabitants of Sodom and Gomorrah; and (3) Matthew 25:31-46. Paul's discussion in 2 Thessalonians 1:5-10 is also discussed, with particular attention to the notion of 'eternal destruction'. The essay closes with some brief and general comments on the language of judgment in the Apocalypse.

Introduction

This brief paper springs from a dialogue with the paper of Earle Ellis and is intended as a basic response. The thrust of the piece is to question whether recent attempts to limit the duration of divine judgment, in support of either annihilation or conditional immortality, have done justice to New Testament teaching on the subject.

Few could doubt that the topic of hell, and especially its traditional formulation as involving 'eternal conscious punishment' is clearly on the evangelical agenda. Some might trace this to 1988, when John Stott's position was drawn out in discussion with David Edwards in *Essentials*: 'I also believe that the ultimate annihilation of the wicked should at least be accepted as a legitimate, biblically founded alternative to their eternal conscious torment.'[1] From an-

---

[1] D. L. Edwards and J. Stott, *Essentials: A Liberal-Evangelical Dialogue* (London: Hodder & Stoughton, 1988), 320.

other perspective, questions concerning the traditional view have been associated with British evangelicals closely associated with the Tyndale Fellowship since its inception (note the studied ambiguity of the UCCF doctrinal statement at this point). John Wenham, for example, had abandoned the traditional view following discussions with Basil Atkinson in Cambridge in the 1930s: 'for more than fifty years I have believed the Bible to teach the ultimate destruction of the lost, but I have hesitated to declare myself in print'.[2]

Numerous problems with the traditional view have been highlighted in recent years (although relatively few of them escaped the attention of Augustine, Calvin, Edwards and Warfield). Crucial among them are some general theological problems concerning: the continuing existence of the wicked in punishment is inconsistent with God's love (how can He leave them unreconciled and sentence to a sadistic punishment?), God's justice (how can an infinite punishment be deserved for finite sins?) and God's ultimate victory (how can God be all in all if there remains an eternal hell?). Two more specific problems are also often raised. First, it is often said that the traditional view depends on Greek philosophical ideas, foreign to the Bible, of the immortality of the soul. Second, it is often suggested that the language of destruction, so widespread in both Old Testament and New Testament, is not taken sufficiently seriously in the traditional view, which mistakes the eternal consequences of God's annihilating judgment with its eternal duration. It is with this subject that this essay is particularly interested. In this context we must be thankful for a renewed call for faithfulness to Scripture as the agent for reforming evangelical traditions.

Jesus' Teaching

In Mark 9:42-48, Jesus urges His listeners that hell (or *Gehenna* – the word is used in verses 43, 45, 47) should be treated with such extreme seriousness that any steps should be taken in this life to avoid it because what you do in this life determines your future destiny:

---

[2]J. W. Wenham, 'The Case for Conditional Immortality' in N. M. de S. Cameron (ed.), *Universalism and the Doctrine of Hell: Papers Presented at the Fourth Edinburgh Conference on Christian Dogmatics, 1991* (Carlisle: Paternoster, 1992), 161-191 (quotation from 190; note the earlier comments re Stott, F. F. Bruce, P. E. Hughes and E. M. B. Green on 166f.). Basil F. C. Atkinson, *Life and Immortality: An Examination of the Nature and Meaning of Life and Death as they are revealed in the Scriptures* (privately published; Taunton: Phoenix Press, no date).

> And if your eye causes you to stumble, tear it out; it is better for you to enter the kingdom of God with one eye than to have two eyes and to be thrown into hell (*Gehenna*), where their worm never dies, and the fire is never quenched (9:47f.).

Gehenna is presented as diametrically opposed to 'life': it is better to enter life than to go to *Gehenna*. The interest for us is both in Jesus' use of the term *Gehenna* and in His description of it as involving unquenchable fire (verses 43 and 48) and deathless worms (verse 48). It is common practice, both in scholarly and less technical works, to associate the description of *Gehenna* with the supposedly contemporary garbage dump in the valley of Hinnom. This association often leads scholars to emphasize the destructive aspects of the judgment here depicted: fire burns until the object is completely consumed. Two particular problems may be noted in connection with this approach. First, there is no convincing evidence in the primary sources for the existence of a fiery rubbish dump in this location (in any case, a thorough investigation would be appreciated). Secondly, the significant background to this passage more probably lies in Jesus' allusion to Isaiah 66:24.

Isaiah 66:24 closes the book of Isaiah with a stark promise of judgment against those who rebel against the Lord (*cf.* verses 66:3f., 6, 17). In 66:22f. there is a positive promise of salvation: all flesh coming to worship the Lord in an enduring manner (from one month to the next, from week to week), or with most commentators (*e.g.* Whybray, Westermann, Young), in everlasting worship. But those who worship are said in verse 24 to go forth and observe the dead bodies of those judged by the Lord, who are in a state of eternal death and destruction: 'their worm shall not die, their fire shall not be quenched'. The point of this language seems to be to stress the permanence of the experience of judgment. The worm and fire relate to the bodies of rebellious men: their destructive, distasteful activity continues eternally as an abhorrence to 'all flesh' (that is, those saved at the end).

Is it possible that the recent emphasis on the completeness of the destruction is an over-reaction? Certainly Jewish thought, relating Isaiah 66:24 to passages of judgment promised in the valley of Hinnom (*e.g.* Jeremiah 7:32; 19:6f.), related *Gehenna* to the place of eternal punishment. The language of *Gehenna*, chosen by Jesus, echoes this tradition and suggests a durative aspect to the unquenchable fire and continuing destructive activity of the worm. A thorough study of the influence of Isaiah 66:24 within second temple Judaism would also be a useful (and large) research project. Some clear examples in which

Isaiah 66:24 functions to support statements of eternal duration for judgment include:

> Judith 16:17: 'Woe to the nations that rise up against my people! The Lord Almighty will take vengeance on them in the day of judgement; fire and worms he will give to their flesh; they shall weep in pain for ever.'

> 1 Enoch 27:2ab-3: 'This accursed valley is for those accursed forever; here will gather together all (those) accursed ones, those who speak with their mouth unbecoming words against the Lord and utter hard words concerning his glory. Here shall they be gathered together, and here shall be their judgement, in the last days. There will be upon them the spectacle of the righteous judgement, in the presence of the righteous forever. The merciful will bless the Lord of Glory, the Eternal King, all the day.'

> Cf. 1 Enoch 54:1-6: a deep valley burning with fire where kings and rulers were to be imprisoned with iron chains, cast into 'the abyss of complete condemnation'.

In the *Sibylline Oracles* I.103, *Gehenna* is associated with 'terrible, raging, undying fire'; in II.292 *Gehenna* is associated with God's terrible judgments; it is described (paradoxically) as a place of darkness, it is the place of punishment for the wicked angels (the Watchers; *cf. 1 Enoch* 10:13; 18:11) and extended to sinful humanity (*cf. 1 Enoch* 90:23f.).[3]

That death, and even destructive judgment, did not imply for Jesus the cessation of existence, is also confirmed by His appeal to the inhabitants of Sodom and Gomorrah. Clearly the destructive judgment of these cities does function elsewhere in the Bible as a paradigm for God's judgment, emphasizing the destructive nature of that judgment (Gn. 19; *cf.* Is. 1:9; 13:19f.; Jer. 50:40; Jude 7; 2 Pet. 2:6). But the Isaiah paradigm exists alongside Jesus' assumption of a continued existence for the inhabitants of Sodom and Gomorrah who face a future resurrection to judgment (Mt. 10:15; 11:23f.). If the destructive judgment exercised upon Sodom and Gomorrah is

---

[3]As a place of judgment (4 Ezra 7.36: furnace of Gehenna); cf. Ass. Moses 10.10; 2 Clem 17.7 re judgment, after citing Is. 66:24 ('their worm shall not die . . . ') those who denied Jesus are 'punished with grievous torments in unquenchable fire'; 1QS 2: Satanic men were cursed: 'be damned in the shadowy place of everlasting fire!' See Geza Vermes (ed.), Dead Sea Scrolls (Sheffield: Sheffield Academic Press, 4th edn. 1995), 63.

compatible with some form of continued existence, then the language of extinction and destruction can be used to refer to a judgment through which existence continues (*cf.* esp. 2 Pet. 2:4-10: kept under punishment until the day of judgment, verse 9).

Another passage of crucial importance is Matthew 25:31-46. Here Jesus, building on the teaching of Daniel 12:2, pictures the separation of humanity in judgment. Those who are blessed by God, who have aided the mission of the Messiah by supporting His missionaries, are granted a kingdom which involves eternal life. Those who are cursed are sent away from the King's presence (verse 41: 'depart from me') into the 'eternal fire' which had been prepared for the Devil and his angels, these go into a punishment – the Judge sentences them to be punished for their wickedness in rejecting His missionaries. This punishment is eternal, like the fire of verse 41: 'these will go away into eternal punishment, but the righteous into eternal life' (verse 46). The main issue raised here is the meaning of the word rendered 'eternal'. Since it is used to describe both the life and the punishment, the traditional view is that the blessing and the judgment are co-temporal, that is this relates to an existence in the new order which does not end ('eternal', although it can denote something that pertains to the quality of the life to come, never includes the thought that this should end).

Paul's Teaching

Paul does not really say a great deal on this subject. The passage which most clearly addresses the subject is 2 Thessalonians 1:5-10. Here, in a context of trial and persecution, Paul writes to believers that their faith and perseverance have been used by Paul as an example to encourage other churches (verse 4). In verse 5 Paul introduces (rather abruptly) the idea that the righteousness of God's judgment is shown in the very situation of faithful perseverance in the midst of persecution and opposition because God's purpose is that they might be counted worthy of the kingdom of God.

Paul then moves on in verse 6 to assert that God's justice is demonstrated in His punishment of those who oppose the gospel. At the return of Jesus (verse 7, remember Mt. 25), His people will be granted rest, but those who oppose the gospel will experience God's retributive justice. Specifically, in verse 9 this involves a two-fold punishment: eternal destruction, and exclusion from God's presence. The key term is ὄλεθρος (rendered 'destruction' in RSV and NIV here) and used in three other places in the New Testament with the general meaning of 'destruction' or 'ruin' (1 Cor. 5:5; 1 Thes. 5:3; 1 Tim. 6:9; BAGD[4] also suggests 'death' but this does not seem necessary).

The only other place where these two terms are used together is in the Greek version of the Old Testament in 4 *Maccabees* where 'eternal destruction' is used in parallel with 'eternal torment by fire' and 'intense and eternal fire and tortures, and these throughout all time will never let you go'.

4 *Maccabees* 9:9 (in a manner somewhat parallel to 2 Thes. 1) relates the defiance of the seven youths; torture meant nothing because 'we, through this severe suffering and endurance, shall have the prize of virtue and shall be with God, for whom we suffer' (verse 8). But the tyrant (Antiochus IV) would deservedly undergo from the divine justice eternal torment by fire (ὑπὸ τῆς θείας δίκης αἰώνιον βάσανον διὰ πυρός), suggesting a continual judgment, with torment and fire (*cf.* 13:15). In 10:15 the same thing is described (by the fourth brother) as 'the eternal destruction of the tyrant' (τὸν αἰώνιον τοῦ τυράννου ὄλεθρον). The seventh brother says that because of the tyrant's impiety and wickedness 'justice has laid up for you intense and eternal fire and tortures, and these throughout all time will never let you go' (ταμιεύσεταί σε ἡ δίκη πυκνοτέρῳ καὶ αἰωνίῳ πυρὶ καὶ βασάνοις αἳ εἰς ὅλον τὸν αἰῶνα οὐκ ἀνήσουσίν σε (12:12).

Surely this evidence shows that the destruction language could co-exist alongside the language of eternal torment without limiting the understood duration of God's judgment. The point at issue then is whether Paul means to describe a once-for-all destruction; or an eternally destructive process involving exclusion from God's presence. The traditional interpretation claims the support of the close parallel in 4 *Maccabees* and the congruence with Jesus' teaching just surveyed.

The Apocalypse

Two passages are particularly relevant: Revelation 14:9-12 and 20:9f. These two stand within a whole complex of teaching about judgment within this document, but we cannot consider everything now. I want to make a couple of points in particular.

Revelation knows of no difficulty in the continuing existence of the wicked under the judgment of God (esp. 21:27; 22:14f.); the final triumph of God is not deemed incompatible with a continued

---

[4] = W. Bauer, *A Greek-English Lexicon of the New Testament and other early Christian Literature* (Chicago: University of Chicago Press, 1979), 563.

exclusion and punishment of the godless, on the contrary the final triumph of God's justice is seen in the salvation of the saints and the punishment of the wicked. Revelation calls upon God's people to pray for the execution of his justice now (*e.g.* 6:9f.) and to see in His judgments an occasion for praise and worship (16:4-9; 19:1-5). There is no escaping the fact that Revelation clearly teaches and assumes the continued existence of the wicked in a destructive punishment primarily intended for Satan and his operatives (esp. 14:9-11); permanent exclusion from salvation rest; fire and sulphur, the lake of fire, the second death (19:20; 21:8); eternal torment (20:10ff.).

Conclusion

The purpose of this essay in its original context was to question aspects of some recent approaches to the New Testament teaching about hell, and to provoke further discussion and questions within the context of a friendly open forum. It can hardly be claimed that in its written form it does any more than that. The three basic components of the biblical view of hell are punishment, destruction and exclusion. It is no part of the traditional position to emphasize one of these over the others. Since all these terms are associated in the New Testament with the adjective 'eternal', it is also no part of the traditional position that these horrible judgments of God ever cease. Nevertheless, we should also remember: (1) that God will judge justly and in accordance with deeds and knowledge (leading to a more and less tolerable experience of judgment); and (2) that the eternal fire is designed for the Devil and his angels (God is not a sadist). Human beings experience this judgment by virtue of their association with the Devil as children of wrath and their opposition to Jesus Christ and His gospel emissaries: the fiercest New Testament language is reserved for outspoken and blatant opponents of the gospel and persecutors of Christians.

Section D

CHRISTIAN DOCTRINE

Chapter 11

THE NATURE OF HELL: REFLECTIONS ON THE DEBATE BETWEEN CONDITIONALISM AND THE TRADITIONAL VIEW OF HELL

Tony Gray

Annihilationists have often been representatives of a middle way between universalism and traditionalism. Yet the attempt to 'justify' this on the grounds of a free-will decision runs into the same problems which challenge the traditionalists. However, the texts of Scripture provide imagery which must be faced, and a way out for the traditional case is to look more at the range of imagery used to describe 'personal exclusion' from God.

Introduction

Although recent debate within the evangelical church may have given the impression that conditionalism is a relatively new phenomenon, it has had a role to play in discussions of the nature of hell certainly since the nineteenth century. Edward White, Henry Constable and Emmanuel Petavel-Oliff were notable Victorian conditionalists,[1] and others have argued that the doctrine dates back to the earliest theologians, the church fathers.[2] Yet the recent debate has caused much interest, and has brought to the surface many

---

[1] For an exploration of this material, see G. Rowell, *Hell and the Victorians* (Oxford: Clarendon, 1974).

[2] Most recently, see Ellis in this volume. See also L. Froom, *The Conditionalist Faith of our Fathers,* 2 vols. (Washington: Review & Heal Publishing Association, 1965, 1966), and E. Fudge, *The Fire that Consumes* (Texas: Providential Press, 1982) (revised and compressed edition: Carlisle: Paternoster Press, 1994).

previously hidden assumptions about our understanding of the doctrine of hell.[3]

Conditional immortality is the name given to the doctrine that states that human beings are not inherently immortal, but rather have immortality conferred upon them as part of the experience of salvation. In the debates, immortality is usually taken to mean the inability of the person to perish. Therefore, all the redeemed will be immortal, and life in heaven will be everlasting and consist of a perfect and glorious existence. Those unrepentant will not receive immortality, and hence eventually cease to exist. For this reason conditionalism is linked to the doctrine of hell.

Annihilationism, which is usually associated with conditional immortality states that the wicked will not suffer conscious torment for ever, but that after death and judgment they will be destroyed, ceasing to exist. Annihilationism is thus virtually a corollary of conditional immortality, for if immortality were inherent to human beings, then it follows that annihilation would not be a satisfactory explanation of hell.[4]

The recent evangelical debate was largely stimulated by the tentative endorsement of annihilationism by John Stott,[5] and the much more emphatic case given by John Wenham.[6] Recent support was given to this case by Earl Ellis, and in addition, Clark Pinnock has been a vociferous advocate of conditionalism.[7] Those who have replied from a traditional position include James Packer, Gerald Bray

---

[3]I have explored these issues further in 'Hell: Twentieth Century Attempts to Defend the Doctrine of Hell' (Oxford: D.Phil. Thesis, 1995, unpublished).

[4]Some further clarifications of these definitions can be necessary. See David Powys, who provides a taxonomy of positions in 'The Nineteenth and Twentieth Century Debates About Hell and Universalism', in Nigel M. de S. Cameron (ed.), *Universalism and the Doctrine of Hell* (Carlisle: Paternoster 1992), 93ff. The terms conditional immortality/conditionalism and annihilationism are often used to refer to the same doctrine. The former originates from an argument concerning anthropology, and at times is therefore more helpful in making a distinction between different forms of the doctrine, yet the latter may also utilize this argument. See the observations made by Kendall Harmon, 'The Case Against Conditionalism', in *Universalism and the Doctrine of Hell*, 196-199.

[5]Stott's presentation of the issue came in D. Edwards and J. Stott, *Essentials: A Liberal-Evangelical Dialogue* (London: Hodder & Stoughton, 1988).

[6]J. Wenham, *The Goodness of God* (Leicester: IVP, 1974), and later *The Enigma of Evil* (Guildford: Eagle, 1993).

[7]See Earl Ellis, 'The New Testament Teaching on Hell', in this volume, and for one example of Pinnock's case, see C. Pinnock, 'The Conditional View', in W. Crockett (ed.), *Four Views on Hell* (Grand Rapids: Zondervan, 1992), 135-166.

and Don Carson.[8] Thus the debate has been polarized as an argument between conditionalists and annihilationists on the one hand, and traditionalists on the other.[9] The debate will of course continue, with much important work required on either side. Yet the question remains as to whether it is necessary to be tied to only these two options. The following essay examines issues of justice, immortality and the use of biblical images, all of which cause hesitation about accepting the solutions of conditionalism, and about relying on a traditional doctrine of hell. Is there a third way?

Conditionalism and the Justice of Hell

The impetus for someone reaching a conditionalist position, although always declared as being the testimony of Scripture by evangelicals, can often be discerned to come from elsewhere. Many have often wondered how to reconcile a God of love with the eternal existence of the damned in hell. Just a moment's imagination, and the thought of a close relative or friend suffering eternal conscious pain, will demonstrate the appeal of universalism, or a 'half-way house' such as conditionalism – a traditional hell appears unjust. Rowell notes that in the nineteenth century, conditionalism

> . . . emerged as one of the attempts to find a mediating position between the extremes of universalism and eternal punishment, and, in particular, it was influenced by a revulsion from the cruder forms of missionary theology. Its exponents relied heavily on a learned, though not always discriminating, appeal to Scripture, and were to be found for the most part amongst Congregationalists and Anglican Evangelicals.[10]

Thus the temptation is often to decide for what appears to be a 'softer option', and this has clearly been seen by modern evangelicals. John Stott honestly explains his feelings: 'I find the concept [of eternal conscious torment] intolerable and do not understand how people can live with it without either cauterising their feelings or cracking

---

[8]J. Packer, 'The Problem of Eternal Punishment', *Evangel* 10 (1992), 13-19; G. Bray, 'Hell: Eternal Punishment or Total Annihilation', *Evangel* 10 (1992), 19-24; D. Carson, *How Long O Lord?* (Leicester: IVP, 1991), 101-104, and *The Gagging of God* (Leicester: IVP, 1996), 515-536.
[9]I have supplied a brief survey of the debate in Tony Gray, 'Destroyed Forever: An Examination of the Debates Concerning Annihilation and Conditional Immortality', *Themelios* 21.2, 14-18.
[10]Rowell, *Hell and the Victorians*, 181.

under the strain.'[11] However, he immediately warns that decisions of this nature must not be made on the experience of our emotions, but on what the Bible says concerning the matter. Michael Green is concerned about justice, writing that,

> ... if universalism will not qualify as an authentic Christian option, what about its opposite, the conscious unending torment of all who have never heard the gospel of Jesus Christ? There is no doubt that many earnest Christians hold this view, but all the same I doubt very much if it is a genuinely *Christian* option. What sort of God would he be who could rejoice eternally in heaven with the saved, while downstairs the cries of the lost make an agonising cacophony? Such a God is not the person revealed in Scripture as utterly just and utterly loving.[12]

Stephen Travis decides for conditionalism after a considered evaluation of the issues. Yet even when he takes into consideration arguments that are primarily of a theological nature, they also have a strong emotive force:

> The belief that some, or most, of mankind will suffer in everlasting torment has been felt by many to be both philosophically and theologically intolerable. The seemingly uncreative vindictiveness of eternal punishment . . . might tip the scale in favour of annihilation.[13]

In his large volume on New Testament Theology, the late biblical scholar Donald Guthrie summarized that, 'The doctrine of eternal punishment is not an attractive doctrine and the desire to substitute for it the view that, at the judgment, the souls of the wicked will cease to exist, is understandable.'[14]

This is not to claim that all conditionalists reach such a position due to a hidden emotive force, but only to note the importance of this factor, as most proponents of conditionalism do themselves. John Wenham cautioned theologians to 'beware of the immense natural appeal of any way out that evades the idea of everlasting sin and suffering. The temptation to twist what may be

---

[11]Edwards and Stott, *Essentials*, 314.

[12]M. Green, *Evangelism Through the Local Church* (London: Hodder & Stoughton, 1990), 69 – italics original.

[13]Stephen Travis, *Christian Hope and the Future of Man* (Leicester: IVP, 1980), 124, 135.

[14]Donald Guthrie, *New Testament Theology* (Leicester: IVP, 1981), 892.

quite plain statements of Scripture is intense. It is the ideal situation for unconscious rationalising.'[15]

Defenders of the traditionalist position have also been too swift to accuse conditionalists of being susceptible to this hidden agenda.[16] On the other side of the fence, the universalist Nels Ferré has accused conditionalists of desiring 'to escape the Christian contradiction in eternal hell'.[17] For some, this may be the deciding factor, yet this is not necessarily so for all on the conditionalist side.

If it is not the deciding factor, then the claim which all should applaud is that annihilationism is a doctrine reached because of the weight of Scripture. For many of those evangelicals proposing this doctrine, it is not a case of a premeditated exegetical mistake, forcing the texts to fit a predetermined scheme. Rather, it springs primarily from the conviction that Scripture teaches annihilation. Stott writes that, 'as a committed Evangelical, my question must be – and is – not what does my heart tell me, but what does God's word say?'[18] Ellis, in his essay in this volume, makes a similar claim:

> More important . . . is the teaching of canonical Scripture which, rightly understood, is for evangelical Protestants the infallible revelation of God from which all Christian doctrine must be vetted. The issue for evangelicals, then, is one of biblical interpretation.[19]

Yet it then seems extremely peculiar that Ellis begins his defense of conditionalism with a survey of patristic theology, and how perhaps some of the church fathers embraced a conditionalist position. Underlying this approach is an important discussion concerning immortality, which shall be examined subsequently.

As has been demonstrated, the belief that conditionalism is a more convincing and just description of hell than traditionalism is held by many. Theologians have been attacked on this matter for using an idea because it seems more reasonable and just, rather than being more scriptural. However, there does appear to be a problem

---

[15]Wenham, *The Goodness Of God*, 38.

[16]See D. Pawson, 'God of Love, God of Justice', *Alpha* (New Malden: Elm House Publications), February 1993, 33, and Packer, 'The Problem of Eternal Punishment', 17: 'Its advocates appear to back into it in horrified recoil from the thought of billions in endless distress, rather than move into it because the obvious meaning of Scripture beckons them'; Bray accuses annihilationists of having shifted their focus from divine justice to human suffering – see Bray, 'Hell: Eternal Punishment or Total Annihilation', 24.

[17]Nels F. S. Ferre, *The Christian Understanding of God*, 243.

[18]Edwards and Stott, *Essentials*, 315.

[19]P. 207

with the justice argument. To cut short the duration of hell does not necessarily provide an adequate statement of the doctrine of hell. Even if that doctrine is something less than traditionally conceived, can such a hell be justified?

The problem is that such an approach to hell does not deal with the *justification* for hell. In terms borrowed from a discussion by Jonathan Kvanvig, although conditionalism alters the nature of hell from eternal conscious punishment to annihilation, the *justification* given for the doctrine of hell usually remains that hell is inflicted as part of God's just retribution. For the fact that the nature of hell has changed, that is, hell is no longer eternal conscious punishment but rather annihilation, does not deal with common objections to hell which have come from universalists and others.[20] These are that an eternity of punishment (whether conscious or not) is not deserved by a finitude of sin. Kvanvig believes that if annihilation occurs, the moral objection against the doctrine of hell still remains. 'Nothing is to be gained in responding to a penal theory by substituting metaphysical capital punishment for metaphysical life imprisonment.'[21]

For those committed to an understanding of hell which sees it in terms of divine retribution, annihilation may initially appear to be a better option. Yet this may be due to the fact that 'nothingness' provides a contrast with images of fire and brimstone, rather than dealing with the specific moral objections themselves. Given the strong view of divine conservation which Kvanvig holds, he also believes that with conditional immortality God is failing to 'immortalize' some persons. There is no distinction between annihilation by commission, and annihilation by omission.

It is clear that some people tackle both the nature of hell (thus making it finite leading to annihilation), and also the justification for hell (thus defending hell using human free-will rather than divine retribution). Pinnock is one such theologian who defends hell by altering several of its more traditional premises. However, those who wish to retain some notion of retribution need to be clear that annihilation does not solve this dilemma. An eternity of nothingness or an eternity of conscious pain is still an eternal punishment for,

---

[20]Hans Küng makes a clear presentation of the objections in *Eternal Life?* (New York: Doubleday & Co., 1984), 136-137; a statement of the universalist attack on a retributive hell is given by John Hick in *Death and Eternal Life* (London: MacMillan, 2nd edn. 1985), 200-201; Jean Delumeau charts the historical critique in *Sin and Fear: The Emergence of a Western Guilt Culture*, trans. Eric Nicholson (New York: St. Martin's Press, 1983), 375.

[21]Jonathan Kvanvig, *The Problem of Hell* (Oxford: Oxford University Press, 1993), 68.

apparently, a finite amount of sin. Whilst there may be arguments used to justify such a retribution, these cannot be side-stepped by appealing to annihilation. For the annihilationist to respond that an eternity of nothingness is not a punishment, because there is no-one in existence to experience such a punishment, is to ignore the *effects* of that action.[22]

Conditionalism and Immortality

Conditionalists make certain claims about the history of Christian theology which demand investigation. Primarily, the claim is made that an over-riding Platonic agenda caused the early church to accept the traditional and prevailing view of hell as a place of eternal conscious torment. Ellis' initial work makes it clear that the historical development of the doctrine is important, and, had an over-riding Platonic theory not been present, then the immortalist assumptions would not have led Christian theology to assume that hell was eternal conscious punishment. Ellis is primarily a conditionalist, rather than an annihilationist, for this argument concerning anthropology and church history is important to him. Before assessing whether this historical argument has value in itself, it will first be helpful to make a brief evaluation of some of his claims.

One of the key elements of Ellis' discussion of Augustine is the charge that his theology is all too influenced by Platonic thought. Whilst we may wish to question what is meant by such an all-embracing term, it would be unfair to charge Augustine with Platonism, if at the same time it is not recognized that both Justin and Irenaeus (discussed by Ellis) could also be guilty of particular influences. That is, they share a stoical view of the soul, an entity which is corruptible and hence not immortal, as the Platonists would argue. Whether this belief is therefore more biblical than the Platonic understanding is open to question. In addition to this inequality in assessment, it may be unwise to push the issue of immortality too far, for the concern of Augustine was with the reuniting of the soul with the resurrection body. The soul *and* the body were important, not merely an immortal soul, and hence there was a theological reason for his concern with immortality. A third point of concern is that whilst we may believe that Augustine was influenced by Platonic

---

[22]One common method to deal with this difficulty argues that those in hell continue to sin. Traditionalists employ this (for example, Carson, *The Gagging of God*, 533), as do people with more developed views of hell, such as C. S. Lewis in *The Great Divorce* (London: Geoffrey Bles, 1946).

immortalist thinking, to argue that Augustine bases his initial assumptions for theology on this, rather than on Scripture, may be pushing the point. Augustine was a theologian of the text, even though, as with all theology, he was subject to other influences.[23]

To illustrate the issue of history further, we examine Ellis' use of other patristic theologians. He quotes Ignatius as writing 'if [God] were to imitate us according to how we act, we would no longer exist'. However, this line of argument does not necessitate the belief in conditional immortality as Ellis understands it. Rather, its implication is that if God were to act as human beings act, we would be destroyed. The point being that God does not judge as humans would.

In the case of Justin, he seems to be making a judgment concerning the nature of the soul. The language of destruction is certainly used, but does this imply a conditionalist understanding? To write, 'Whatever things are or ever shall be, besides God, these things have a perishable nature . . . For this reason souls both are punished and die', Justin compares the soul to the corruptible. That is, souls are more like the body than they are like God – it is corruptible, only God himself is eternal. This need not necessitate Justin holding a conditionalist position.

To claim a conditionalist position from the Irenaeus material is also doubtful. Rather, Irenaeus is considering the condition bestowed upon Adam and the consequences of the fall. The church father is not entering a discussion concerning the outcome at the eschaton, but rather considering the elements of Adam's judgment.

Thus, whilst making careful judgments about the way in which we learn from tradition, it is important that we are clear about historical positions, and about the many different contributing factors that cause a doctrine to develop in a certain direction. Conditionalism does not present itself as a new view, but as a position which has been marginalized due to non-Christian influences.

Having said all this, it may appear that in the end the argument from conditional immortality may be a red herring. For, if Scripture teaches eternal punishment in the form of conscious torment', then other considerations such as immortality are irrelevant.[24] Although many evangelicals who are conditionalists do not

---

[23] At the end of his section on the fathers, Ellis makes a similar comment about Arnobius and Athanasius: 'Both . . . build their arguments more on philosophical than on biblical foundations.'

[24] E. Fudge, a convinced annihilationist/conditionalist, comes to this very conclusion: 'In *either* case – among mortalists or immortality – there is no reason why anthropology should govern eschatology. The true Christian position about

wish to use this as *the* governing principle for all their other arguments, it still has enormous power in their articulations. It may be true that Greek philosophy regarding the immortality of the soul *has* influenced the church's traditional interpretation of the texts, and so then there is a strong case for going against 2,000 years of teaching. Travis writes:

> . . . the claim of the conditionalist is that the 'traditional orthodoxy' of eternal torment arose in the early church precisely because biblical teaching was (illegitimately) interpreted in the light of Platonic philosophy, which involved belief in the immortality of the soul and everlasting punishment.[25]

Nevertheless, a person may acknowledge the Platonic influence on Christian theology at this point (if that is a correct analysis, and it is unclear whether Ellis has demonstrated this), yet fail to be a conditionalist because of his interpretation of Scripture. When analysing the New Testament material, Ellis writes:

> . . . this reading of the New Testament, with glasses ground in Athens, results in a reconceptualization and redefinition of all the New Testament terms and concepts used for the punishment of the unrighteous. It thereby excludes *a priori* the meaning (in an active sense) of extinction of being, that is annihilation, or (in a passive sense) of cessation of being.

Yet the question remains, once we have acknowledged that the spectacles may be there, what, at the end of the day, do the texts say?[26]

The issue of conditional immortality is important regarding our understanding of church history,[27] yet in the final analysis it can prove to be unhelpful. Ellis himself acknowledges this by turning to the issue of biblical interpretation.

---

final punishment must finally stand on a thorough exegesis of the Word of God', Fudge, *The Fire that Consumes*, 196-199.

[25]Travis, *Christian Hope and the Future of Man*, 135.

[26]I am not here supposing that we can approach the text without considering these hermeneutical questions. Powys ('The Nineteenth and Twentieth Century Debates about Hell and Universalism', 135) argues that clear answers will be achieved only when all presup-positions are cleared away, and the text is allowed to speak for itself. However, the possibility of such a task is in principle questionable.

[27]Carson, *The Gagging of God*, 534-535, passes too briefly over the importance of these arguments, both in their historical importance and as to whether Scripture actually does teach immortality.

Conditionalism and Biblical Images for Hell

Some conditionalists accuse traditionalists of interpreting texts too literally. It is possible that Ellis falls prey to this criticism himself. The argument concerning fire is a good case, illustrating the difficulties of interpretation. Ellis writes that 'the purpose and effect of fire is either to purge and refine or, in this context, to destroy utterly although for man pain may accompany the disintegration.' Is there not here the danger of using the image of fire in an overly literal way? To be sure we see fire both destroy material and inflict pain in our own experience. Yet what demands that we take the image literally in either direction – why must we decide that it destroys, rather than inflicts pain?

Carson is helpful in illustrating the fact that some attempts to understand the biblical images of fire lead us to ask strange questions. That is, 'the argument of Stott and others is that the natural inference from the language of fire is that it totally consumes what it burns, that the natural inference from the worms (probably maggots) is that total corruption accompanies their work until there is nothing left to be destroyed.'[28] He proceeds to point out that if we ask such questions, should we then ask what keeps the worms alive once they have eaten all the people, if they are said not to die? 'The question is ugly and silly, precisely because it is demanding a concrete and this-worldly answer to the use of language describing the realities of punishment in a future world still largely inconceivable.'[29] Such literal interpretation can be a double-edged sword.

Surveys of the literature involved in the conditionalist/traditionalist debate highlight how important the interpretation of these images can be. For example, is the worm real? Is it personal, does the devouring exist for ever, what weight does this text give to either the traditionalist or conditionalist side? Yet the question of biblical images forces us to ask the question as to whether we must decide for either conditionalism *or* a traditional understanding of hell? C. S. Lewis has pointed out how Scripture presents us with at least three images for the after-life of unbelievers.[30] Exclusion (Jesus' declaration that those who do not believe will be separated and ordered to depart from him), destruction (as the conditionalists advocate), and punishment (the traditional position). With three apocalyptic images, should we even be attempting to harmonize such a picture, or rather should our hermeneutic approach point to a

---

[28]*Ibid.*, 524.
[29]*Ibid.*, 524-525.
[30]C. S. Lewis, *The Problem of Pain* (Glasgow: Fount, 1940/1977), 99.

different path? Kendall Harmon explores this third way in terms of 'personal exclusion'.[31] Whilst admitting that conditionalism appears to be making a systematic scheme which is not warranted by the biblical witness, he argues strongly:

> A fully biblical theology of hell must do justice to all three images for hell. . . and here is where the traditional view may be faulted, because it focuses too much on punishment and leaves little room for the other two pictures. At this point the conditionalists' critique of traditionalism should be heard when they insist that some New Testament texts do not speak of eternal torment but instead use different language.[32]

Rather, Harmon argues that personal exclusion reminds us that hell is being cut off from the Son of God, hell is God's judgment in that He gives sinners completely over to themselves, and that those in hell are 'not known' by God.

> The crucial point is that the different images each refer to a single reality and that combining different images is not like putting together the pieces of a jigsaw puzzle, but rather like letting the sunlight reflect through a diamond and seeing each ray's colours as pointing towards a single eschatological truth.[33]

Conclusion

Conditionalism cannot avoid the cries of injustice that face a traditional doctrine of hell unless it is prepared to develop a justification for hell in another direction. The argument from immortality, whilst important historically, must be secondary to the interpretation of Scripture. Yet this interpretation itself is often in danger of being too literal, and of ignoring the breadth of the biblical witness. To draw the debate in terms of either conditionalism *or* traditionalism excludes the possibility that there is a third option – the possibility that within Scripture there is a distinction drawn between the clear and the unclear. Images of hell appear to be extremely lucid, yet what they point to is that which is under discussion. Perhaps it is this which could be more fruitfully explored.

---

[31]Harmon, 'The Case Against Conditionalism', 213-224. This whole section is worth consulting for exploring the possibility of a third way within this debate.
[32]*Ibid.*, 216.
[33]*Ibid.*, 224, n. 70.

Chapter 12

THIRTY YEARS OF HOPE: A GENERATION OF WRITING ON ESCHATOLOGY

Stephen Williams

This essay charts some tendencies in eschatological thought since Moltmann's Theology of Hope. *The account is thematic, rather than chronological. Moltmann's work initiated or contributed to fresh thinking about (a) the centrality, (b) the content, (c) the point and (d) the method of Christian eschatology. Correspondingly, the essay describes selected developments in these four areas. It is mostly confined to selected work in academic theology. In order to offer a fair exposition, the author does not, in this essay, enter into critical engagement with the figures and trends discussed.*

Introduction

'At no point is contemporary theology more lacking in candour than in its pronouncements about the "last things".' So writes Charley Hardwick in his recent and acclaimed *Events of Grace.*[1] He echoes a sentiment expressed just over thirty years ago by Schubert Ogden, who offered two reasons for the incredibility of standard treatments of eschatology. Firstly, eschatological statements have no sound basis in human experience or knowledge. Secondly, the mythological elements they contain lack clear conceptual meaning. Ogden wrote just before the boom in theological concern with eschatology. Thirty years of hope have clearly not impressed Charley Hardwick. Without assenting to or dissenting from these judgments, two general observations are in order.

---

[1] C. Hardwick, *Events of Grace: Naturalism, Existentialism and Theology* (Cambridge: Cambridge University Press, 1996), 267f.

First, there seems to be less theological interest in eschatology around – at least in those academic circles that Ogden and Hardwick have in mind – than there was thirty years ago. Dermot Lane, in one of the most recent full-scale treatments of eschatology, says that 'it must be stated – and this is one of the theses of the book – that eschatology is the missing link in much contemporary theology'.[2] Thirty years ago, Moltmann and Pannenberg bore much of the responsibility for generating renewed interest in eschatology, though the interest was certainly around prior to and apart from their contribution. Possibly the publication of the last volume in Moltmann's dogmatics, which is on eschatology, and the translation of the third and final volume of Pannenberg's systematics, which also deals with eschatology, will do the trick again.[3] It remains to be seen.

Secondly, Maureen Junker-Kenny makes effective use of recent German studies of the transformation which western societies are undergoing in the process of modernization. She highlights two characteristics relevant for the theme of hope, namely (a) people's orientation today towards the present instead of the future and (b) the loss of a common vision. 'The second feature', she notes, 'can also take the shape of an explicit farewell to utopian thinking.'[4] Doubtless one could quibble a bit on both counts, asking whether, in fact, a high proportion of people have ever been future rather than present-oriented in a way that is changing now, and to what extent vision has been profoundly common in the past. But she raised important questions. Moving on from the proposition that 'it was easy to identify with the great political ideas of liberty and justice as long as one's personal hopes and the hopes of humanity were still identical', she averred that 'these two levels do not coincide any more. A new ecological analysis of worldwide justice would call for self-denial. It would have to be a utopia of pure duty – for which it is hard to find enthusiastic supporters. The utopias of promise have come to an end' (p. 31f.). This impels her to ask whether hope is an enduring element of human nature or an historical legacy emanating, in the West, from Judaeo-Christianity. At any rate, it is important to restate the Christian hope in a changed context.

---

[2] Dermot Lane, *Keeping Hope Alive: Stirrings in Christian Theology* (Dublin: Gill & Macmillan, 1996), 5
[3] J. Moltmann, *The Coming of God: Christian Eschatology* (London: SCM, 1996). Stanley Grenz has anticipated the translation of Pannenberg's work in *Reason for Hope: the Systematic Theology of Wolfhart Pannenberg* (New York/London: Oxford University Press, 1990).
[4] M. Junker-Kenny (ed.), *Christian Resources of Hope* (Blackrock: Columba, 1995).

With this in mind, we shall survey some developments in theological eschatology in the thirty year period from 1967 to 1997. 1967 was the publication date of the English translation of Moltmann's *Theology of Hope*, but there is more to the choice of this date than Anglophone provincialism. Even as it is, we shall but skim the surface of a selection of works. A starting point in 1964, the original date of publication of *Theology of Hope*, would let in Harvey Cox's *The Secular City*, the fifth edition of Hendrikus Berkhof's *Christ, the Meaning of History*, probably Oscar Cullmann's *Salvation in History* (though I am generally avoiding reference to biblical studies), Vatican II's *Gaudium et Spes*, not to mention the early work of Pannenberg and Rahner. But books translated after 1967, including work by Gollwitzer, Gogarten and Van Ruler are also ignored in what follows. Indeed, the limits are inevitably severe; I am not, for example, glancing at the discussions of eschatology that have featured in the evangelical and other systematic theologies that have flooded the market over these last three decades, nor am I touching on the themes of so-called 'individual eschatology' – life after death, the intermediate state, *etc.*

The title of this essay, and the preliminary remarks on its scope, involve running together two words: 'hope' and 'eschatology'. But is talk of hope necessarily eschatological talk? One characteristic of the discussions of hope and of eschatology is the attempt to relate the mundane language of hope to the language of specifically eschatological hope, so that, even if not all hope is directed to the eschaton, it is stimulated by eschatological hope. One can also ask: is eschatology strictly about hope? For, we could speak of realized eschatology. The answer to this question is something on which Moltmann and most others in our generation have wanted to be clear; eschatology is indeed about the future, and hence its content is the potential or actual object of hope. Moltmann himself looms quite large in the following discussion. In his Ingersoll Lecture of 1984, Pannenberg commented that the eschatological boom of the last two decades 'emerged mainly from the impact of Jurgen Moltmann's *Theology of Hope'.*[5] That sounds familiar enough, but that it should come from Pannenberg effectively banishes any reservation about giving Moltmann pride of place here.

In this volume, Moltmann attempted four things. Firstly, he affirmed the centrality of eschatology – 'Christianity is eschatology'. Secondly, he affirmed its point; it is to stimulate this-worldly action.

---

[5]'Constructive and Critical Functions of Christian Eschatology', *Harvard Theological Review* 77.2 (1984), 119

Thirdly, he affirmed its general content; it embodies promises for this world. Fourthly, he adumbrated its method; it is an exposition of christology, specifically the dialectic of cross and resurrection. We structure the survey that follows by taking these themes in turn.[6]

The Centrality of Eschatology

Formally, the affirmation that Christianity is eschatology did not constitute a complete novelty, although Moltmann gave it a different material content than did Barth, when Barth, in his commentary on Romans said that 'if Christianity be not altogether thoroughgoing eschatology, there remains in it no relationship whatever with Christ'.[7] Moltmann's claim was echoed by Metz, with whom Moltmann has long been associated. 'The orientation of the modern era to the future, and the understanding of the world as history, which results from this orientation, is based upon the biblical belief in the promises of God. The biblical faith demands that theology be eschatological.'[8] If Christianity is eschatological, so, naturally, is theology and in 1970 Herzog edited a whole collection entitled *The Future as Hope: Theology as Eschatology*.[9]

However they have changed, modified or supplemented their scheme over the years, the eschatological orientation of theology and general conviction of eschatological centrality has been main-tained in the work of both Moltmann and Pannenberg. An eschat-ological approach to theology has been influential in diverse quarters. So we find Thomas Finger, in the first volume of his *Christian Theology: an Eschatological Perspective*, appealing first and foremost to *Theology of Hope* and explicitly endorsing Moltmann's claim that 'Christianity is eschatology'.[10] In a different tradition again, Peter Jensen, Principal of Moore College in Sydney, published lectures in 1991 under the title *At the Heart of the Universe*.[11] Jensen did not speak of Moltmann's influence, but rather unexpectedly began his general exposition of Christian doctrine with eschatology. According to Jensen: 'The advantage of this procedure is that it captures the biblical sense of

---

[6]For a different kind of survey covering a slightly longer period of time, see Klaas Runia, 'Eschatology in the second half of the twentieth century', in *Calvin Theological Journal* 32.1 (1997), 105-135.

[7]Karl Barth, *The Epistle to the Romans* (Oxford: Oxford University Press, 1968), 134.

[8]*Theology of the World* (London: Burns & Oates, 1969), 87.

[9](New York: Herder & Herder, 1970).

[10](Scottdale, Pa.: Herald, 1985), 101ff.

[11]These were published in the United Kingdom in 1994 (Leicester: IVP).

purpose in God and the corresponding dynamic of history.' But the concluding reason he gave in defending this procedure was that 'it makes it more likely that ethical and existential considerations will emerge from the treatment of doctrine rather than philosophical ones' (p. 11). That leads us on to the second characteristic of Moltmann's approach; the point of eschatology.

The Point of Eschatology

Inasmuch as theologians have emphasized the eschatological dimension of Christian faith these last thirty years or so, it has often been with a view to showing how it makes an impact on our world, specifically by stimulating, generating or steering social action and responsibility over its widest range. As Nicholas Lash put it, eschatology is a stimulant and not a narcotic.[12] He is parrying the Marxist attack on religion as an opiate and, of course, the challenge and critique of Marxism often formed the context for at least the earlier reflections on eschatology in our period.

Such was the perceived point of eschatology in the decade and more following Moltmann's *Theology of Hope*, that Ratzinger, in his 1977 publication on *Eschatology: Death and Eternal Life*, sounded a stern warning.[13] He noted that it was possible in his day to write theological eschatology in dialogue with the theology of futurity, the theology of hope and theology of liberation. No doubt, said Ratzinger, the relation of the future to the present and the question of the praxis of hope, are parts of eschatology. But he did not intend to 'surrender to the transformation of perspectives implied in the reduction of eschatology to these things.'[14] Eschatology must continue – and major on – its reflections on death, hell, the intermediate state and immortality. Ratzinger's worry was that eschatological belief was being hijacked in a political cause. But:

> The Kingdom of God, not being itself a political concept, cannot serve as a political criterion by which to construct in a direct fashion a programme of political action and to criticize the political efforts of

---

[12]N. Lash, *A Matter of Hope: A Theologian's Reflections on the thought of Karl Marx* (London: Darton, Longman & Todd, 1981), 161.

[13]J. Ratzinger, *Eschatology: Death and Eternal Life* (Washington DC: Catholic University of America, 1988).

[14]*Ibid.*, 4.

248

THE READER MUST UNDERSTAND

other people. The realisation of God's Kingdom is not itself a political process.[15]

We may insert two observations here. First, Ratzinger's reasoning is not stringent. From, 'the Kingdom of God is not a political concept' it may well follow that 'it cannot serve as a political criterion by which to construct in a direct fashion a programme of political action . . .', if we emphasize *'direct'*. But one could maintain that the kingdom is a political concept and criterion without claiming that the realization of that kingdom is a political *process*. That is, the putatively political nature of the kingdom and of criteria do not dictate a judgment on how it will be realized.

Secondly, one wishes that Ratzinger had documented his claim specifically. The kingdom of God has long been a (probably the) central eschatological concept in the work of Pannenberg and certainly in some of the material published in *Ethics* he deduces conclusions about European union from his beliefs about the eschatological unity of humankind.[16] But it is not clear that the kingdom was precisely functioning as a political concept when Pannenberg did so. And in his important essay – admittedly after the German, but prior to the English version of Ratzinger's book – Pannenberg warned against indentifying 'a certain line of political action unequivocally as [even] approximating the Kingdom of God'.[17]

As for Moltmann, even when he came to his detailed exposition of 'Historical Eschatology' under the rubric of 'The Kingdom of God' in *The Coming of God,* he still did not view it as 'the integral hope of Christians'; what constitutes that is the new creation of all things.[18] Whether it was Gustafson, writing on theology and ethics, or liberation theologians, chiding European theologians of hope, the accusation was made against Moltmann that insufficiently detailed moral or political deductions were drawn from his eschatological premises and promises.[19] As for Metz, Schillebeeckx could take for granted, in this early period, that he was refusing to derive from the gospel (including its eschatological) message any 'direct programme of social and political action'.[20] If Ratzinger principally had liberation theologians in mind, there would have been a

---

[15]*Ibid.,* 58.
[16](Philadelphia: Westminster, 1981), chap. 7.
[17]See the Ingersoll Lecture: 'Constructive and Critical Functions', 125.
[18]Moltmann, *The Coming of God,* 132.
[19]See below on liberation theology. For Gustafson, see *Theology and Ethics* (Oxford: Blackwell, 1981), 53-58.
[20]See Schillebeeckx, *God the Future of Man* (London: Sheed & Ward, 1969), 157.

need to show that political conclusions were being significantly derived from eschatology, specifically kingdom eschatology.

I am not saying that Ratzinger was altogether wrong, just that examples were needed and that work was needed to show that he was right. However, it has been widely held in general, from within a whole variety of conceptual schemes in the last thirty years, that a cardinal point of eschatology is the generation of this-worldly activity. But this, of course, was a principle apparently or frequently parasitic on a particular construction of the content of eschatology, to which we now move.

The Content of Eschatology

The this-worldly point of eschatology derives from its this-worldly content, and with the phrase 'this-worldly' we are into real thickets of semantic ambiguity. The problems here that have arisen over the last thirty years have done so quite generally on two scores. One is the question of whether religious language in general and eschatological language in particular are being used literally, symbolically, in some combination or in some other way. The other is whether 'this-worldly hope' refers to an ultimately eschatological state, the ultimate quasi-territorial fulfilment of hope, or to proximate hope, or to both; and, if the latter, how does or should one distinguish the usages in the literature? Further, if we are referring to ultimate hope, does it refer to a continuity between what presently is and what ultimately will be or is it compatible with a strong assertion of discontinuity (while maintaining corporeality) on a literalistic analysis? I mention this last point in our context of starting with Moltmann's concerns, because Delwin Brown, for example, in *To Set at Liberty*, quite rightly pressed the question of the meaning of 'this world' in Moltmann's theology, averring that its radical discontinuity made talk of the future of *this* world validly talk of this world only in 'a very odd sense, if at all'.[21]

Now it may be judged that either by the time Brown wrote or with *The Coming of God*, Moltmann was able to rebut the charge, but there is undoubtedly a lack of appropriate conceptual analysis in the theological eschatologies of the last thirty years. The concept of 'possibility' illustrates this. 'Hope', said Kierkegaard, 'is passion for the possible'. 'The possible' here appears terminologically to stand in contrast to 'the promised' to which specifically Christian hope, in its primary theological sense, is correlated. But it is not as simple as that.

---

[21]Delwin Brown, *To Set at Liberty: Christian Faith and Freedom* (Maryknoll: Orbis, 1981), 116.

As Ricoeur noted, in his discussion of hope, 'possibility' is contrasted to 'necessity' here.[22] It is also semantically possible to make 'possibility' the opposite of 'impossibility' or the opposite of 'certainty'. Add the option of a technical Blochian use of the word 'possibility' and, whether one is thinking in English or in German, there is plenty of potential for confusion.

Why are the concepts surrounding hope, the concept of hope itself and of this-worldly hope, given far less analysis than they need? There are two reasons, I think.[23] First, there is a fear of dualism, a separation of hopes which, by stating the distinction, will subordinate worldly concerns to avowedly ultimate ones. This has been a standard fear in the last thirty years of hope. It is reflected, for example, in the work of Dermot Lane at the end of our thirty year period. He quotes Gerald O'Hanlon: '. . . Our primary hope is directed towards God . . . this will be realized definitively in heaven; . . . in a secondary sense we may hope for this-worldly anticipations of this primary hope.'[24] Lane's response would be unaffected if we were to substitute 'consummation in a new heaven and new earth' for 'heaven'. Lane said: 'To talk about primary and secondary hope runs the risk of playing down the seriousness of hope for this life.'[25] His following comments reveal the conceptual confusion involved here. What he terms 'hope for this life' may not be realized and is not, on a theological account, the object of promise. The 'hope of heaven' is a different matter, being, on a traditional theological account, a matter of certainty. The perfectly legitimate concern – that the non-proximate object of Christian hope does not rob present life and its hopes of their importance – is ill-served by blurring this distinction of hopes, however firmly we relate them. But, in Lane's analysis, there is a hint of another factor that may be responsible for the blurring of the distinction, one that also comes to light with my reference to a 'traditional account'. That is the epistemic status of things ultimately hoped for.

---

[22]Paul Ricoeur, 'Freedom in the Light of Hope', in *Essays on Hermeneutics* (Evanston: Northwestern University Press, 1974), 407ff.

[23]A third point would be unduly provocative. Those who work mainly within the analytic tradition of philosophical theology will note that these debates often have their provenance in theological circles little affected by that tradition and will conclude that this accounts for the general lack of stricter conceptual analysis. If this point is justified, it neither amounts to an endorsement of that tradition *tout court* or suggests that only within it can an appropriate rigorous analysis occur.

[24]Lane, *Keeping Hope Alive*, 123.

[25]*Ibid.*, 128.

Second, in speaking the language of promise and certainty, one is sounding as though no epistemological questions arise in contemporary theology in relation to the knowledge of God. But, of course, they do, and questions about the grounds for hope enter into theological attempts to relate and distinguish different kinds of hope. However, much of the time they do not *systematically* enter into those attempts. Consequently, the distinction between what we may be assured will ultimately come about and what we desire will proximately come about, frequently lapses or leads a fuzzy existence. The kinds of epistemological considerations involved are indicated in Nicholas Lash's work, to which we have referred, *A Matter of Hope*.

Lash takes on Karl Popper, who attacked historicism on the grounds that 'by substituting certainty for hope, it denies man's moral responsibility for the construction of his future'.[26] Lash responds that hope can be certain, but we need to explore different modes of certainty. 'In so far as hope is to be considered as a mode of knowledge of "the meaning of history", it is hermeneutic, interpretative knowledge, and not "explanation".'[27] Later, Lash speaks of 'the knowledge to which Christian faith lays claim (which forms the substance of hope). . .'[28] But Lash also contrasts hope with assertion,[29] and says that 'hope may, indeed, be questionable, but, if it is to remain hope, it can only take the form of a question. For the Christian, that question is cast as request: "Thy Kingdom come."'[30] It is characteristic of hope never to relinquish the 'interrogative mood'.

All this risks distortion by abstraction, and it would be unfair to remark here on the coherence of Lash's exposition. I cite it as illustrative of epistemological awareness, an awareness present in Lash more than most over these last years. As for the broad content of eschatological hope, we can pick up three areas for discussion.

The Nature of This-worldliness

I have referred to and simply bracketed the question of literal and symbolic language. But talk of ultimate this-worldly hope *prima facie* involves belief in a continuity between the present and the new earth, a literal continuity which yet allows for radical transformation and symbolic representation. This whole question has been taken up with

---

[26]Lash, *A Matter of Hope*, 68.
[27]*Ibid.*, 69.
[28]*Ibid.*, 150.
[29]*Ibid.*, 261.
[30]*Ibid.*, 270.

some verve in conservative evangelical discussion. In 1982, leading participants in the Lausanne movement debated the relation of evangelism to social action. The report highlighted one area of disagreement and that pertained to eschatology. Amidst general agreement on eschatological questions, there was disagreement on whether or not the new earth would be markedly continuous with this one, or whether the annihilation of this earth is in prospect. Continuity allegedly furnished an incentive for action; the works of our hands will endure, albeit in a transformed mode.[31]

The discussion, however, is not limited to conservative evangelical circles. Moltmann, working with different methodological presuppositions, touched on it in *God in Creation* as well as in *The Coming of God*.[32] For, after all, we are dealing with a question with historical anchorage in differences between the Lutheran and the Reformed communions in the seventeenth century. Reformed theologians over the last thirty years have sustained an interest in these questions. The Dutch Calvinist tradition, in particular, has made a very prominent contribution in this area. None is more important than that of Hendrikus Berkhof. We have excluded discussion of *Christ, the Meaning of History*, whose editions were produced prior to 1967. *Well-Founded Hope*, which escaped the ban by being published in 1969, contained some notable material, but is too scanty on the present topic to help us out.[33] But in *The Christian Faith*, translated in 1979, Berkhof, modifying a rather stronger continuist line in *Christ, the Meaning of History* wrote as follows: 'We can say that our culture provides the scaffolding for the coming structure, a scaffolding that will later be torn down again. It is also possible, however, to view our culture as providing the building materials for a coming kingdom.' He settled finally for 'the fact that all of cultural development will prove to be meaningful in the light of eternity. But that is the limit of what can be said about it.'[34]

---

[31]*Grand Rapids Report, Evangelism and Social Responsibility: an Evangelical Commitment* (Exeter: Paternoster, 1982), 40-42.
[32]*God in Creation* (London: SCM, 1985), 90-93; *The Coming of God*, 267ff.
[33]H. Berkhof, *Well-Founded Hope* (Richmond: John Knox, 1969).
[34]Berkhof, *The Christian Faith: an introduction to the study of the faith* (Grand Rapids: Eerdmans, 1979), 539. I correct an account in my 'Evangelicals and Eschatology: a contentious case', in A. N. S. Lane (ed.), *Interpreting the Bible: historical and theological studies in honour of David Wright* (Leicester: IVP, 1997), 291-308, where I say that Berkhof tacitly qualifies the position that he took in *Christ, the Meaning of History* (306); as a matter of fact, the qualification, if not loud, is certainly explicit (518).

The All-embracing Nature of Hope

Interestingly, an example of the second area to which I refer also contains a strong assertion of continuity. There has been interest in the all-embracing nature of this worldly hope, extending its scope to the cosmos, and going beyond hope for history to a hope for nature, matching socio-political concerns generated by hope for history with ecological concerns, generated by hope for nature.[35] The specific link with the continuity question is forged by Peter Phan in an article recently published in the *Irish Theological Quarterly*, 'Eschatology and Ecology; the Environment in the End-Time.'[36]

Phan argued that, while attention has been given to the eschatological destiny of the non-human cosmos, the 'biblical *metaphor*' of 'a new heaven and new earth' has been picked up,

> but the precise nature of the new cosmos and its relationship to the present earth are left rather vague. Indeed, it may be asked why, morally speaking, efforts, sometimes extraordinary, should be undertaken to save the environment, if in the end it will disappear, or to use a biblical metaphor, will be reduced to ashes in a universal conflagration.

Accordingly, Phan, taking up that strand in the tradition which emphasizes the intrinsic, not just the instrumental, value of the cosmos, argues for its final transformation and for its 'material and spatial' nature.

Not only our work, especially our work of love, will remain, but also 'all creation', hence material beings included, is set to be freed from bondage to decay; it will not be destroyed nor will it disappear. 'All creation' certainly comprises more than humans; minerals, plants, animals, mountains and rivers, the heavenly bodies, the sun, the moon and the stars, from the microcosm to the macrocosm, are included in this process of liberation. In terms of St Francis' 'Canticle of the Sun', should we not think that in this 'new heavens and a new earth' there will be the same brother sun, the same sister moon, the same water and the same air? And will there not be the birds and fishes that Poverello preached to, the bees the Saint fed with the finest sugar, the wolf he tamed, and the worms upon which he poured out the tenderest love, all of them freed from decay and sharing in eternal beatitude?

---

[35]Francis Bridger offered an evangelical contribution here in 'Ecology and Eschatology: a neglected dimension', *TynBull* 41.2 (1990), 290-301, but it was very general.
[36]62.1 (1996).

Human achievement will also endure. Why should the architecture of Taj Mahal or Saint Peter's Basilica, the music of Beethoven and Mozart, the tragedies of Sophocles and Shakespeare, the sculptures of Michelangelo and Rodin, the philosophies of Confucius and Plato, and the scientific discoveries of Galileo and Einstein, just to cite a few things at random, not perdure for ever?[37]

Phan's work illustrates, then, the fusion between concern for continuity and the concern re the implications of eschatological belief for the environment.

The God of Hope

A shift towards a cosmocentric eschatology is naturally, though not necessarily, associated with a revisionary doctrine of God. In a work like Ruether's *Gaia and God: An Ecofeminist Theology of Earth Healing*, anything like a traditional eschatology has effectively disappeared, but she was explicit on the restructuring of theology many years before that.[38] Whether or not it is particularly connected with cosmocentrism, the content of this-worldly hope in the last thirty years is frequently linked with some revisionary notions of deity.

Moltmann, in *Theology of Hope*, picked up Bloch's phrase about God as one with 'future as his essence', although I think that the significance for *Theology of Hope* emerges more in an essay in *The Experiment Hope* which introduces *Theology*, than in the volume itself.[39] Be that as it may, the trinitarian conceptuality adumbrated by Moltmann in *The Crucified God* and in later work formed the doctrine of God in a different way, making it a dynamic trinitarianism amounting to a dynamic panentheism. In the era of *Theology of Hope*, there was a clear interest abroad in the connection between a doctrine of God and the future. Harvey Cox, struggling to come to terms with the death of God, announced in his own *Secular City*, admitted that 'if theology can leave behind the God who "is" and begin its work with the God who "will be". . .' he could get interested in God again: 'An exciting new epoch in theology could begin.'[40] Metz, in his chapter on 'An Eschatological View of the Church and the World', in *Theology of the World*, expressed his preference for translating Exodus 3:14 as 'I will be who I will be.' On this supposition, 'God revealed Himself to Moses more as a power of the future than as being dwelling beyond

---

[37]Phan, 'Eschatology', 13.
[38]See her *Sexism and God-Talk* (London: SCM, 1983).
[39]See *The Experiment Hope* (London: SCM, 1975) ch. 4.
[40]H. Cox, *On Not Leaving it to the Snake* (London: SCM, 1968), 11.

all history and experience. God is not "above us" but "before us". His transcendence reveals itself as our "absolute future".'[41] History, in the Son, is 'the actual destiny of the unchanging God'.[42]

The excitement of discovery here is captured all the more effectively for its eager, yet not over-dramatic or uncritical, statement in Schillebeeckx' work, *God – the Future of Man*. Schillebeeckx, pushing 'Gaudium et Spes', agreed that

> the eschatological expectation is not a brake on this building up of a
> human world, but rather the fulfilment of it by adding new motives;
> it is a more intensive stimulus towards the building up of the world
> and this promotion of all nations because the *eschaton* stimulates us
> to bring about a better earthly future.[43]

He found himself simultaneously moved, as he sought to understand and communicate God in the era of His death, to speak of God as 'our future', the 'wholly New', not 'wholly Other', 'the One who is to come'. Nevertheless, this adds a dimension to God, as it were, rather than providing a wholesale revision; Schillebeeckx was reluctant to let go of the divine presence, so we must think of God as 'our future' without 'overlooking the fact that, according to the Bible, the foundation of the eschatological expectation is the certainty in faith of communion with God here and now'. For 'the foundation of *hope* is *faith* in Yahweh who reveals himself as the living God of the community'. Schillebeeckx held that the neglect of this biblical foundation is an unmistakable drawback in some of the recent 'theologies of hope' and further that 'this neglect fosters an unjustified identification of the promotion of the well-being of all people with the coming of the Kingdom of God.'[44]

Here, too, we must include the massive contribution of Karl Rahner who refused to detach God as Absolute Future from the future of this world and united immanence and transcendence. In Rahner's theology, God is interpreted eschatologically – He is first God of the future rather than present, the 'power of the future', His being intrinsically related to history, His being and actualized sovereignty (that is, His kingdom) one. As Spirit is transcendent in His immanence, so, for us: 'The immanent consummation of a history worked out in freedom by a being endorsed with spiritual faculties is

[41]Metz, *Theology of the World*, 88.
[42]*Ibid.*, 22.
[43]Schillebeeckx, *God – the Future of Man*, 144.
[44]*Ibid.*, 188f.

its transcendent consummation because the immanence is its transcendence.'[45]

Finally, we mention another massive contribution, that of Wolfhart Pannenberg. There are features similar to what we find in Rahner. The end witnesses not only the revelation, but the coming into fulness of God's being; God's future kingdom and future of the world are God's future. At the same time there is, I think, more ambiguity here. The brief communication published as an appendage to Tim Bradshaw's study of *Trinity and Ontology* indicates as succinctly as can be the ambition to maintain the futurity of God's being, not just revelation, but the conceptual formulation of the doctrine seems to me quite unclear.[46] At the same time, a leading conservative and quite sympathetic commentator from the North American continent, Stanley Grenz, finds even panentheism – still more pantheism – 'somewhat wide of the mark' in characterizing this position.

> For Pannenberg . . . God's self-realisation in the world is the revelation in the historical process of the eternal self-realisation present in the innertrinitarian life . . . In his understanding the world process does not so much contribute to the reality of God as it reveals what is always present, albeit in a hidden manner, in God's eternity. For Pannenberg, then, God is affected by the world process but not in the sense that this process adds to the divine reality. Rather, the effect of the process lies in the demonstration of the relationship of God over creation, without which God would not be God and cannot be 'all in all'.[47]

Clearly, we should ideally need to probe this further by investigating the semantics of 'lordship' and the relationship between time and eternity which has always had a prominent place in Pannenberg's thinking. Instead, we take up the reference to 'process', which moves us to a final word on the immediate discussion before we take up the fourth and final point in the wider discussion. Pannenberg has been a natural conversation partner for process thinkers. But a rather distinctive perspective emerges in at least some process thinkers in relation to this-worldly hope. Without regarding all

---

[45]See Peter Phan, *Eternity in Time: a Study of Karl Rahner's Eschatology* (Selinsgrove: Susquehanna University Press, 1988), 195.
[46]Tim Bradshaw, *Trinity and Ontology: a comparative study of the theologies of Karl Barth and Wolfhart Pannenberg* (Edinburgh: Rutherford House, 1988), 402.
[47]See Grenz, *Reason for Hope*, 211.

process thought as undifferentiatedly one, let us turn to John Cobb's *Process Theology as Political Theology*.[48]

Spurred on by theology of hope, political theology and liberation theology, Cobb, in 1982, announced his aim of becoming 'a political theologian in the tradition of process theology'.[49] He took up Sölle's phrase 'the indivisible salvation of the whole world' as a guide to the direction political theology should take. For all his support and admiration for political theologians, Cobb, in his very irenic work, warned that 'the conceptual formulations by the three German political theologians [Sölle, Metz and Moltmann] are so vague [on the idea of God] that the consequences could be dangerous for the future of Christian faith in God.' In the case of these three, 'it is hard to determine how seriously we may expect or hope for the promised world. Yet the meaning of hope for us depends on whether it is a real possibility'. Cobb is clear that we cannot confidently anti-cipate the consummation of the historical process. 'Indeed, history is *really* open.' 'We stand, therefore, before a radically open future with no assurance that our efforts for justice will succeed or even that human history will long continue.' We could well destroy ourselves, so Christian hope 'cannot assure us of the meaningfulness of our actions by pointing towards a future kingdom of God on the planet.' With Whitehead; our resurrection is not on this planet. It is in God.[50]

Two things must be said about this. First, it is clear that we need to go into process thought – more precisely Whitehead's thought – to grasp the full meaning of the claim that our resurrection is in God. Secondly, the commitment to a this-worldly hope is admittedly tenuous here. We certainly need an eschatological basis for socio-political and ecological engagement (Cobb pushed for the inclusion of an ecological dimension in political theology), but the eschatological basis is not a dogmatic assertion of divine this-worldly promises. The eschatological basis is God: 'For Whitehead also the eschaton is virtually identified with God.'[51] I think that in terms of our *earth*, the this-worldly/other-worldly option is nugatory; we should have to say that God, a this-worldly entity in His consequent nature, is our hope. We have plenty of incentive for this-worldly commitment; things *may* get better, and that is worth working for.

Now I think that the desire of some process theologians – Brown, Ogden and Cobb – to strengthen liberation, as well as polit-

---

[48]J. Cobb, *Process Theology as Political Theology* (Manchester: Manchester University Press, 1982).
[49]*Ibid.*, xi.
[50]*Ibid.*, 71-81.
[51]*Ibid.*, 78.

ical, theology by giving it a sounder metaphysical basis, indicates an interesting convergence of concerns between process and liberation theologians to which we shall shortly advert. Mention of liberation theology conducts us to our final section, on the question of method.

Eschatology and Method

Moltmann's method of deducing eschatological statements can no doubt be variously described, but the christological dialectic of cross and resurrection undoubtedly featured prominently in the early work. Debate over method in relation to eschatology has encompassed many things. Thus perhaps Karl Rahner's best known contribution to eschatology is his discussion of the hermeneutics of eschatological statements, with its anthropological focus and christological control, rejecting any attempt to make eschatological statements descriptions of the future underived theologically from anthropology and christology.[52] Moltmann took a different route: eschatology and christology are correlated by thinking out of the promise, as it were, not by rooting eschatology in a doctrine of the human person, whose fulfilment is attained eschatologically. Pannenberg discovered sharply contrasting approaches here, with promise and anthropology as rivals, but he thought they could be synthesized.[53]

Rubem Alves, the Protestant liberation theologian, was quite sharply critical of Moltmann in *A Theology of Human Hope*,[54] which appeared not long after *Theology of Hope*. From the outset, we note how differently Alves set about things, beginning with commitment to humanization, elaborating a political humanism and trying to bring the language of promise into this messianic humanism. Hope, the language of political humanism, is from the beginning hope for the qualitatively new and better in history.[55] So how does Moltmann fare?[56] For political humanism 'the transcendent in man is thus deeply rooted in his present . . .'; 'for Moltmann there is no transcendent in the present'. For political humanism 'the powerful present . . . projects itself in the direction of a hopeful future'; for Moltmann it is the transcendent promise that opens up man's future – the present in

---

[52]Phan, and see Rahner, *Theological Investigations* IV (London: Darton, Longman & Todd, 1974), chap. 13.
[53]'Constructive and Critical Functions', 121.
[54]R. A. Alves, *A Theology of Human Hope* (Washington, DC: Corpus Books, 1969).
[55]*Ibid.*, 25.
[56]Although Alves also discusses Metz, we restrict ourselves to mention of Moltmann here, as Bonino, whom we discuss below, treats of Moltmann.

itself is closed and contains only the possibility of death. For political humanism: 'Man . . . creates the future, which is never determined . . . Moltmann, however, sees the future as already determined.'[57]

When Gutierrez, not long afterwards, came to examine Moltmann, in his classic *A Theology of Liberation*, he overtly supported Alves against Moltmann, but the criticism is far more muted.[58] Gutierrez emphasized single world history, a history of salvation. And the category of Promise is apt: 'The Promise orients all history towards the future . . . Human history is in truth nothing but the slow, uncertain, and surprising fulfilment of the Promise.'[59] Gutierrez cited Moltmann in support here and averred that 'the Bible presents eschatology as the driving force of salvific history radically oriented towards the future. Eschatology is thus not just one more element of Christianity, but the very key to the Christian faith.'[60] This is not explicitly directed against Alves; a kind of middle ground between Moltmann and Alves is potentially in the claim: 'The liberating action of Christ – made man in this history. . . – is at the heart of the historical current of humanity; the struggle for a just society is in its own right very much part of salvation history'.[61] Theology, as a critical reflection on the praxis of liberating struggle, begins with the validity of hopeful human agency. The eschatological kingdom, present in history, transcends limited historical realizations, but historical realizations belong to it, as does human agency, though it is God who ultimately fulfils the transcendent promise.

Much needed to be analysed and clarified here, comprehensively taking in the theme of salvation and liberation.[62] But, to return to Moltmann, the problem, as far as Gutierrez was concerned, was not that he got the wrong end of the stick (Alves' criticism) but that he was one-sided. Moltmann 'has difficulty finding a vocabulary both sufficiently rooted in man's concrete historical experience, in his present of oppression and exploitation, and yet abounding in potentialities . . .'[63] However, it was Bonino's *Doing Theology in a Revolutionary Situation*, published in 1975, that finally provoked a

---

[57]*Ibid.*, 67f.
[58]G. Gutierrez, *A Theology of Liberation* (Maryknoll: Orbis, 1973), 217.
[59]*Ibid.*, 160.
[60]*Ibid.*, 162.
[61]*Ibid.*, 168.
[62]See the specific study by Leonardo and Clodovis Boff, *Salvation and Liberation* (Maryknoll: Orbis, 1984). I do not regard liberation theology as a single entity. See J. L. Segundo, *Two Theologies of Liberation* in A. T. Hennelly (ed.), *Liberation Theology: a documentary history* (Maryknoll: Orbis, 1980).
[63]Gutierrez, *Theology of Liberation*, 217.

response from Moltmann.[64] Bonino's eschatology does not appear to differ substantially from Gutierrez' in terms of material content. So we can concentrate on his criticism of Moltmann, which was that he failed to relate his eschatological theology to the concrete situation. 'If theology means to take history seriously, it must incorporate . . . a coherent and all-embracing method of sociopolitical analysis. Moltmann does not seem conscious of this need.' He fails to give concrete content to identification with the oppressed. He, with most European theologians, is content to state the critical function of theology 'independent of a structural analysis of reality'. We need more than a new idealism of Christian theology and 'a clear and coherent recognition of historical, analytical and ideological mediation'.[65]

Moltmann's response was instructive.[66] Inasmuch as he engaged in methodological issues, he focused on the use by liberation theologians of European Marxism and of other European thinkers. They stand accused of failing to be authentically Latin American. The hermeneutical question of an engaged reading of texts, clear in Bonino and vital for method, is not touched on, yet it, along with the principle of socio-analysis in theology, was crucial for Bonino's over-all argument. What Moltmann does say is that Bonino and his comrades have failed to show how it does not all come out in the wash in exactly the same way, when it comes to the practical content of theology. For, he averred, scrutiny of the liberation theologians' position reveals that they speak of fragments and anticipations in history, of the kingdom, and not the identification of the historically particular with the eschatologically fulfilled. That is his own position exactly!

His response raises the importance of method. If Moltmann is right, and if, starting from promise, you get where liberation theologians get starting from elsewhere (or elsewhere plus promise) and with different methodological principles, what is the existential importance of methodologically proper procedure here? If the *point* of eschatology is not principally to inform, but is practical, and methodological differences do not generate practical differences, how important is the strife over method?[67] Will not human hope, not just action, phenomenologically shape up in much the same way, whether history is 'broken open' by, for example, incarnation or eschaton? Or

[64]*Revolutionary Theology Comes of Age* (London: SPCK, 1975).
[65]*Ibid.*, 147-149.
[66]'An Open Letter to Jose Miguez Bonino', in Hennelly (ed.), *Liberation Theology.*
[67]This has interesting ramifications for Moltmann's various treatments of Barth and Bonhoeffer, from whose conceptual schemes he differs somewhat.

are the differences involved really important, registering not here but at another point in theology and practice?

It remains to remark, as promised, on a similarity between process and liberation theologies in this connection. In 1988, Bonino published his essay on 'Love and Social Transformation in Liberation Theology'.[68] Consistent with *Doing Theology in a Revolutionary Situation*, he documented the commitment for change as a work of love. The difference between Latin American and European theology may be quite narrow, but it exists. 'In one case the primary reality is the present awareness of God's love that opens the eyes of hope; in the other, it is the proclamation of the final victory that awakens the commitment to love.'[69] Process theology and liberation theology both emphasize divine love and corresponding human love as motivation for action. European theologies frequently seem to require that the motivation be placed in the framework of eschatological hope for the future of this world, and gain strength therefrom.

We are within sight of wide pastures here, and we must stop at the sight. For we should soon stumble upon such things as the dialogue between Moltmann and Brunner which Douglas Schuurman set up.[70] In his *Faith, Hope and Love*, Brunner declared his conviction that love needs no stimulus other than itself.[71] His work is too early in our century for consideration, but reflection on Schuurman's discussion and on at least some writings in liberation theology provokes the question of whether an emphasis on love in liberation tends first to the demotion, then the marginalization, then the irrelevance of eschatology, for social and political purposes. Indeed, in some modern theology that highlights liberating praxis, it seems to be theologically dispensable.

With these thoughts suspended over us, we are conducted to a concluding reference to feminist theology. In 1975, Letty Russell wrote that 'God's promise leads us to a confidence that the future is open, but not to an exact knowledge of how liberation will be accomplished or what it will look like.'[72] She wrote in consistent,

---

[68]In F. Burnham *et al.*, *Love: the Foundation of Hope: the Theology of Jürgen Moltmann and Elizabeth Moltmann-Wendel* (SanFrancisco: Harper & Row, 1988).

[69]*Ibid.*, 72.

[70]D. Schuurman, *Creation, Eschaton and Ethics: the ethical significance of the Creation-Eschaton relation in the thought of Emil Brunner and Jürgen Moltmann* (New York: Lang, 1991).

[71]E. Brunner, *Faith, Hope and Love* (London: Lutterworth, 1957), 57 and see *Eternal Hope* (London: Lutterworth, 1954), 85: 'Whoever lives in the power of love asks no question about meaning because he possesses truth and puts it into effect.'

[72]L. Russell in T. McFadden (ed.), *Liberation, Revolution and Faith: Theological Perspectives* (New York: Seabury, 1975), 94.

though not identical, vein in an essay on 'Authority and Hope in Feminist Theology', published in 1988.[73]

But Ruether, to whom Russell refers in this latter essay, struck a different note. In *Sexism and God-Talk*, this is the problem with historical eschatology. Either (1) 'the end point occurs outside of history altogether and so fails to provide a point of reference for historical hopes' or (2) 'the final era of salvation is identified with a particular social revolution. The revolution thereby becomes absolutised'.[74] The moral of this is that we should avoid flight into an unrealized future and concentrate on getting relations just and right on the basis of nature. 'This concept of social change as conversion to the centre, conversion to the earth and to each other, rather than flight into an unrealized future, is a model of change more in keeping with the realities of temporal existence.'[75]

The whole nature of hope-talk changes with God-talk in this enterprise. It takes on different dimensions.[76] Should we connect this with the shift from future to present orientation alluded to earlier? I do not know; the question is somewhat flat-footed. Certainly, however, the story of thirty years of hope can and should be told in tandem with ruminations on justice and on freedom. Gispert-Sauch is surely not untypical, in an account of 'Asian Theology', in stating that any eschatology must be justice eschatology.[77] Alfred Hennelly subtitles his book on *Liberation Theologies* 'The Global Pursuit of Justice'.[78] As we face the new millennium, there is no doubt that the quest of justice and freedom will go on. The question is whether eschatology will still be part of the universal theological endeavour.[79]

---

[73]In Burnham, *Love*, 79.

[74]See Ruether, *Sexism*, 253.

[75]*Ibid.*, 255.

[76]See J. M. Soskice in T. Elwes (ed.), *Women's Voices: Essays in Contemporary Feminist Theology* (London: Marshall Pickering, 1992), 25, where she remarks that she agrees with Ricoeur about religion and hope.

[77]In D. Ford (ed.), *The Modern Theologians* (Oxford: Blackwell, 1997), 472f.

[78]A. T. Hennelly, *Liberation Theologies: The Global Pursuit of Justice* (Mystic, Connecticut: XXIII Publications, 1995).

[79]I have sought to offer critical discussion on some of these topics elsewhere, but I have limited myself here to a descriptive account. Arguably, those who have oriented Christian eschatology to social action, have given hostages to fortune; action can too easily dispense with an eschatological basis. Note that Moltmann, in his most recent work, avoids that pitfall.

Chapter 13

MUST CHRISTIAN ESCHATOLOGY BE MILLENARIAN? A RESPONSE TO JÜRGEN MOLTMANN[1]

Richard Bauckham

In his recent book The Coming of God, *Jürgen Moltmann offers an innovative reading of the history of Christian millenarianism and suggests that Christian eschatology must be millenarian eschatology. While appreciating Moltmann's theological concerns, this essay argues that they are sufficiently met by the hope of the new creation and do not necessarily require a millennial kingdom prior to the new creation.*

Introduction

According to Jürgen Moltmann, 'Christian eschatology – eschatology, that is, which is messianic, healing and saving – is millenarian eschatology' (CoG 202).[2] This claim concludes Moltmann's discussion of millenarianism in the most recent volume of his dogmatics, *The*

---

[1]The Tyndale Christian Doctrine Lecture for 1997.
[2]I use the following abbreviations for Moltmann's works in English translation, along with page numbers:

CoG =*The Coming of God: Christian Eschatology* (tr. M. Kohl; London: SCM Press, 1996).
HTG =*History and the Triune God: Contributions to Trinitarian Theology* (tr. J. Bowden; London: SCM Press, 1991).
TH =*Theology of Hope: On the Ground and the Implications of a Christian Eschatology* (tr. J. W. Leitch; London: SCM Press, 1967).
TKG =*The Trinity and the Kingdom of God: The Doctrine of God* (tr. M. Kohl; London: SCM Press, 1981).
WJC =*The Way of Jesus Christ: Christology in Messianic Dimensions* (tr. M. Kohl; London: SCM Press, 1990).

Coming of God: Christian Eschatology.[3] The book is a very significant one. It is a mature and full-scale treatment of eschatology by the theologian who, beginning with his first major work *Theology of Hope* (1965), has done more than any other contemporary theologian to restore the dimension of eschatological hope to Christian theology. The subject of *Theology of Hope* was not so much eschatology itself as the eschatological orientation of all theology. In his many subsequent works, Moltmann's theology, while developing in many other ways, has maintained this essential eschatological orientation of all theology towards the eschatological kingdom of God and the new creation of all things. Of course, in developing a theology which has always as a matter of principle an eschatological direction, Moltmann has necessarily written about the content of the eschatological hope, treating various aspects of it in most of his major works. But only with this latest book has he given a comprehensive treatment of the content of the Christian eschatological hope. As well as being one of the most significant of his own works, *The Coming of God* is surely also the most important book on eschatology by a systematic theologian to be published for a long time.

In this essay I intend to focus on Moltmann's extensive discussion of millenarianism, which is notable for the seriousness (rare in a contemporary theologian) with which he treats the Christian millenarian tradition, for his use of millenarianism as a key category for interpreting Christian and western history, and for his advocacy of millenarian hope as an essential part of Christian eschatology. I shall end this lecture by dissenting from his claim that truly Christian eschatology must be millenarian, but I have learned a great deal from interacting with this aspect of Moltmann's work. In contrast to the now somewhat sterile exegetical debate to which most modern discussions of the millennium have been confined, Moltmann brings the millennium fully into the sphere of properly theological concerns and assessment. (In this essay I shall ignore the exegetical issues, even though Moltmann touches on some of them, not because I think them unimportant, but in order to limit my subject and in order to complement the more usual manner in which our subject is discussed.)

---

[3]London: SCM Press, 1996; translated by Margaret Kohl from *Das Kommen Gottes: Christliche Eschatologie* (Gütersloh: Chr. Kaiser, 1995).

A Millenarian Reading of History

It will be helpful to begin with Moltmann's interpretation of millenarianism in Christian and western history. Crucial to his argument – and a relatively novel contribution to the subject – is the distinction he makes and the relationship he envisages between two kinds of millenarianism which he calls 'eschatological millenarianism' (*eschatologische Chiliasmus: e.g.* CoG 146, 192, 193) and 'historical millenarianism' (*historische Chiliasmus: e.g.* CoG 146, 192, 193) or (sometimes) 'presentative millenarianism' (*präsentische Millenarismus: e.g.* CoG 148, 154; *cf.* WJC 32). Eschatological millenarianism is what in the Christian tradition has usually been called millenarianism (or millennialism or chiliasm), that is, the expectation of the universal kingdom of Christ and the saints on earth in the final future of this world, as a kind of this-worldly, historical transition to the new creation at the end of history. This eschatological millenarianism flourished in the patristic period down to the fourth century, but then, especially under the influence of Augustine, largely disappeared until the late middle-ages in the west, when it re-emerged especially in the form of the Joachimist tradition and then in various forms in the Reformation period and especially in post-Reformation Protestantism. Two essential characteristics of it are that it envisages the future reign of Christ as an alternative to the present, a time of fulfilment and unambiguous triumph of all that is good, by contrast with the sufferings and evils of the present, and also that it connects this future reign of Christ within history closely with the end of history and the new creation of all things (CoG 146).

Those who interpret the thousand years of Revelation 20 not as a period in the future, but as a period of history in which the present belongs, have usually been called amillenarians (or amillennialists), that is, those who do not believe in a millennium. Augustine, for example, following the Donatist theologian Tyconius, influentially took the millennium of Revelation 20 to be the age of the church, inaugurated by the resurrection of Christ and continuing until the reign of Antichrist at the very end of history. Such a view can be called amillenarian if the millennium is defined as necessarily a period in the future. Moltmann, however, prefers to call this kind of view 'historical' or 'presentative millenarianism', in order to draw attention to the fact that it conceives the present as the earthly reign of Christ and the saints and as the last age of history. In other words, it is a kind of realized millenarianism,[4] which finds the fulfilment of

---

[4]This idea of realized millenarianism is already adumbrated in HTG 108-109; WJC 25-26, 31-32.

the millennial hope already in the past and the present. The definition can be extended a little to views which do not refer specifically to the thousand years of Revelation 20, but express a triumphalist sense of the goal of history already being realized in the present. Moltmann's point is that such views do not rule out a future millennium merely on exegetical grounds, but because their understanding of the fulfilment of Christ's kingdom on earth already in the present is incompatible with the hope for a qualitatively better future within history. Futurist millenarianism, by insisting that the reign of Christ and the saints is still to come in the future, threatens historical millenarianism's idealization of the present, and this is why it has so often been condemned: 'The condemnations of eschatological millenarianism always have their basis in a historical millenarianism' (CoG 193). Moltmann finds in Christian history, therefore, an oppositional relationship between eschatological and historical millenarianism. Hope for a future millennium, as an alternative to the present, provides the eschatological proviso that qualifies the present as not yet the rule of the saints and the last age of history, whereas the triumphalist claim to the universal rule of the saints with Christ already in the present must outlaw eschatological millenarianism.

Of this realized millenarianism Moltmann says: 'It is not the disappointment that was for two thousand years Christianity's chief problem; it was the fulfilment' (CoG 148). The extent of the problem becomes clear as he discusses three forms of historical millenarianism: political, ecclesiastical and epochal.

First, political millenarianism began when Constantine and his successors adopted Christianity as the political religion of the empire, and Eusebius of Caesarea and others portrayed the Christian empire as the universal kingdom of Christ on earth. Moltmann finds this political millenarianism continued in the east in Byzantinism and Tsarism, and in the medieval west in the Holy Roman Empire, with its mission to subjugate the nations to Christian rule (CoG, 160-167). Among modern examples he pays most attention to America's self-image as the redeemer nation with a God-given universal mission.

Second, the church in the medieval west and the Roman Catholic church down to modern times, with its papal centralism and hierarchical structure, epitomize ecclesiastical millenarianism. In this development the church,

> ceases to see itself as the struggling, resisting and suffering church; it is now the church victorious and dominant. It no longer participates in the struggle and sufferings of Christ, but already judges and

reigns with him in his kingdom. The hierarchical concept of the church is a millenarian concept of the church (CoG,179).

The hierarchical church's claim to rule and judge the nations reveals, says Moltmann, 'a triumphalist, illusory and presumptuous ecclesiology' (CoG 184) which can be understood only as realized millenarianism. So, by contrast with the general view that the millenarianism of the early church petered out around the fifth century, partly in consequence of Augustine's exegesis, Moltmann holds that millenarianism did not die out, but was taken over by the realized millenarianism of empire and church:

> it was transformed into a political and ecclesiastical self-confidence and sense of mission. Once the Christian imperium and the Christian empires themselves become millenarian, they can obviously no longer tolerate any futurist millenarianism; they are bound to see this as profoundly calling in question their own existence, and put an extinguisher on such hope as heretical (CoG 181).

Third, epochal millenarianism is Moltmann's term for the secularized millenarian dream of the modern world which stems from the Enlightenment (CoG 134-135, 184-192). He makes the important, though not novel claim, that the Enlightenment's teleological concept of history is a humanistic transformation of the Christian millenarian tradition. Only the latter provided the idea of a goal of history which will be attained within history. In its sense of the modern world as the last age of history, a qualitatively new period in which progress toward the ultimate goal of history is already under way, the Enlightenment's and the modern west's self-understanding is a form of historical or presentative millenarianism. Its millenarian dream has three elements: imperialism (universal rule over the rest of the peoples of the world, first political, now economic), scientific and technological subjugation of nature, and the project to make human beings the sole subject of history (CoG 185-186, 190). Like the historical millenarianism of the triumphalist church and the Christian empires, the modern ideology of progress is a presumptuous illusion, subject to the disappointments of history. But it is worse than illusory: it justifies violent domination in the realization of universal rule, and leads to the catastrophes – nuclear, ecological and economic – which threaten the modern world.

While historical millenarianism is an ideology used to legitimate power, eschatological millenarianism is a form of resistance to the powers of this world: 'a necessary picture of hope in resistance, in suffering, and in the exiles of this world'(CoG 192). Typically, as in the early church, it is the theology of martyrs (CoG 139, 152-153, 194-195). However, Moltmann acknowledges that it can also be a form of spiritual escapism, as in modern American dispensationalism (CoG 153, 159):

> If the call is no longer to resistance against the powers and their idols, but if instead escapades into religious dream worlds are offered in the face of a world destined for downfall . . . the meaning of the millenarian hope is turned upside down (CoG 153).

Some Critical Comments

Moltmann's millenarian reading of history seems to me broadly convincing and genuinely illuminating. The following critical comments imply merely that at some points it requires refinement or elaboration:

First, Moltmann's argument that the decline of futurist millenarianism in the early church and the suspicion with which it has often subsequently been viewed were solely due to the historical millenarianism of church and empire is one-sided. The pre-Constantinian church was by no means unanimously millenarian,[5] those who did not hold millenarian views in this period certainly did not hold a triumphalist view of church or empire. The popular view that the martyrs ascend at death to be with Christ in His heavenly kingdom may have seemed incompatible with the expectation of an earthly kingdom and may have led to a non-millenarian reading of Revelation 20 already in the pre-Constantinian period, anticipating Augustine's exegesis of the reign of the martyrs as their present rule in heaven (*De Civ. Dei* 20.9).[6] Those who explicitly rejected millenarianism in the pre-Constantinian period (notably Gaius of Rome, Origen and Dionysius of Alexandria),[7] found the millenarian expectation of an earthly paradise too crassly physical and earthly to be appropriate as a Christian hope. The influence of Platonism must be detected here, especially in Origen. This objection to millenarianism

---

[5] See the table in C. E. Hill, *Regnum Caelorum: Patterns of Future Hope in Early Christianity* (Oxford: Clarendon Press, 1992), 194-195.
[6] This is argued by Hill, *Regnum Caelorum*.
[7] Hill, *Regnum Caelorum*, 119-120, 127-132, 141-143; B. E. Daley, *The Hope of the Early Church* (Cambridge: Cambridge University Press, 1991), 49, 60-61.

as materialistic, taken up also by Augustine (*De Civ. Dei* 20.7),[8] continues through to the Reformers and the Protestant confessions (CoG 155), such that (as Moltmann recognizes: CoG 157) futurist millenarianism could only gain respectability in the Protestant traditions in the seventeenth century by carefully characterizing the blessings of the millennium as spiritual rather than worldly. (In this respect it followed the lead of the Joachimist tradition.)

Moltmann maintains that in the post-Constantinian period, 'presentative millenarianism' outlawed futurist millenarianism, and in consequence 'all that was left . . . was hope for souls in the heaven of a world beyond this one' (CoG 147; *cf.* 182). This latter characterization of medieval eschatology is not strictly accurate, since the expectation of bodily resurrection was always firmly maintained, but it is true that the eschatological expectation was dominantly other-worldly and 'spiritual'. What Moltmann misses is that this spiritualizing tendency in the Christian eschatological tradition derives primarily from the strong Platonic influence in the tradition and was itself a reason for the rejection of millenarianism. In other words, in highlighting the historical relationship between 'presentative millenarianism' and futurist millenarianism Moltmann has focused on only one side of the picture, the other side of which is the relationship between futurist millenarianism and the understanding of final destiny or new creation.

Second, Moltmann's critique of historical millenarianism is more thorough and convincing than his account of eschatological millenarianism. We need more examples of the latter to show that in the medieval and modern periods it has functioned as a theology of resistance and suffering. Since non-millenarian eschatological hope has also functioned in this way (*e.g.* for the Protestant martyrs of the Reformation period), the question needs to be probed whether eschatological millenarianism is inherently better suited to function in this way than non-millenarian eschatology is. And since Moltmann recognizes that eschatological millenarianism can function both authentically as a form of resistance and inauthentically as a form of escapism, the roots of these alternative functions need investigation.

Third, Moltmann fails to distinguish between the two types of futurist millenarianism: premillenarianism and postmillenarianism (or premillennialism and postmillennialism). He does use the term 'postmillenarianism', but not in its well-established sense. He uses it

---

[8]Augustine here says that futurist millenarianism 'would be in some degree tolerable' if the rewards it promised the saints in the millennium were spiritual (he himself had held this kind of millenarianism in his youth); the kind of millenarianism he condemns unreservedly is materialistic.

rather in the same sense as 'presentative' or 'historical millenarianism' (CoG 147, 153, 194), apparently treating all futurist millenarianism as premillenarianism. This is not just terminologically
confusing; it also deprives him of a distinction between two kinds of
futurist millenarianism which is essential to an accurate reading of
the Christian millenarian tradition and its relationship to the secular
eschatologies of the modern period.

As Moltmann correctly states, premillenarianism is the
expectation of a millennium to follow the parousia of Christ, while
postmillenarianism is belief in a millennium prior to the parousia
(CoG 147). He also correctly notes that the distinction is very
important (CoG 148, 153). What he fails to notice is that, as normally
used, the term 'postmillenarianism' refers to expectation of a millennium in the *future* before the parousia. Thus, for the most part, the
Joachimist tradition was (in this sense) postmillenarian, as were
Johann Heinrich Alsted, Campegius Vitringa and Johann Albrecht
Bengel, whom Moltmann correctly sees as important figures in the
development of seventeenth- and eighteenth-century Protestant
millenarianism, but misleadingly classifies as premillenarians (CoG
157). He does not notice that, whereas in seventeenth-century Protestantism premillenarianism was more popular than postmillenarianism, in the eighteenth century postmillenarianism became increasingly dominant. It is this Protestant *postmillenarianism* which lies in the
background to the American political messianism which Moltmann
describes and assesses at length (CoG 168-178) and to the secularized
millenarianism of the nineteenth-century idea of progress.[9]

Premillenarianism tends to envisage the arrival of the
millennium as an event for which believers can only hope and pray,
since the visible coming of Christ is to be a sheerly supernatural
event of powerful divine intervention, rupturing the historical process and bringing about a radically novel state of affairs through cataclysmic transformation of the world. Postmillenarianism, on the other
hand, expects the millennium to come about through the activity of
the Holy Spirit prospering the preaching of the Gospel and other
kinds of human activity in history. Postmillenarianism is therefore
more open both to the role of human activity in bringing about the
millennial kingdom and to envisaging the arrival of the millennium
as a gradual historical process, taking place through natural causes
rather than through supernatural intervention. Premillenarians may
believe the parousia to be imminent, but postmillenarians may well

---

[9]*Cf.* R. Bauckham, 'Chiliasmus IV: Reformation und Neuzeit', *Theologische
Realenzyklopädie*, Vol. 7 (Berlin: de Gruyter, 1981), 737-745.

think the millennium to be already dawning in the movements of the Spirit in which they themselves have an active part to play. In this sense only does real post-millenarianism come close to what Moltmann calls 'presentative millenarianism', but nevertheless the two forms of thought are distinct. Though postmillenarians have often thought the process which will bring in the millennium to be already underway, they have rarely, if ever, thought of it as already present.

It will readily be seen that postmillenarianism comes much closer than premillenarianism to the secular millenarianisms of the Enlightenment and the modern period. Whereas premillenarianism enjoyed a major revival in the early nineteenth century as a reaction against the French Revolution and the anti-Christian aspects of Enlightenment ideology, religious forms of postmillenarianism, especially in nineteenth-century America, increasingly approximated to their secular equivalents. The role of affliction and apostasy in the path towards the millennium, which had had a significant place in the older postmillenarianism, was now played down in favour of a simple and steady process of improvement, and the role of human activity in achieving the millennium was played up. In this way nineteenth-century postmillenarianism merged into liberal theology's faith in human progress.

My contention, then, is that Moltmann's millenarian reading of western history would be considerably improved were he to recognize futurist postmillenarianism as a significant category.

Must Christian Eschatology be Millenarian?

As we noted at the outset, Moltmann's claim is that 'Christian eschatology – eschatology, that is, which is messianic, healing and saving – is millenarian eschatology' (CoG 202).[10] Whereas the attempts at premature realization of the millennium within history which he calls 'historical millenarianism' have been disastrous, eschatological millenarianism 'is a necessary picture of hope in resistance, in sufferings, and in the exiles of this world' (CoG 192). We must now consider the theological reasons which lead Moltmann to think the hope of a millennial reign of Christ on earth necessary for Christian eschatology, and ask whether these reasons are entirely conclusive ones.

The fundamental question we shall have to ask is whether the idea of the millennium fulfils a theological need which Moltmann's understanding of the new creation of all things cannot

---

[10]Cf. already HTG 96, 109: 'no eschatology without chiliasm'.

fulfil. It is important to recall that, from *Theology of Hope* onwards, Moltmann has insisted that Christian hope is not for another world, but for the eschatological transformation of this world (*e.g.* TH 21: Christian hope 'sees in the resurrection of Christ not the eternity of heaven, but the future of the very earth on which his cross stands'). The 'integrative eschatology' of *The Coming of God* – which is a principle that the new creation is the eschatological destiny of all things, material and spiritual, human and non-human – surely makes this even more clear and emphatic. It seems too odd that Moltmann can say that when the churches excluded the hope of a future millennium 'all that was left to them was hope for souls in the heaven of a world beyond this one' (CoG 147). Why should the exclusion of hope for a future millennium not leave us with hope for the new creation as Moltmann envisages it – not a purely spiritual other world, but precisely this world renewed and transfigured in all its material as well as spiritual reality?[11] In most of Moltmann's earlier theology, the millennium goes unmentioned,[12] but the eschatological motivation and direction of Christian praxis in the present appears to be supplied by the hope of the eschatological new creation of all things. It seems that Moltmann now thinks the millennium alone, as a this-worldly future prior to the new creation, can supply such motivation and direction: 'Without millenarian hope, the Christian ethic of resistance and consistent discipleship lose their most powerful motivation' (CoG 201). The question we must ask is: what theological function does the millennium fulfil which the new creation cannot?

Moltmann does not systematically set out his reasons for thinking a future millennium theologically necessary, but it is

---

[11]Moltmann's 1982 article, 'Christian Hope – Messianic or Transcendent? A Theological Conversation with Joachim of Fiore and Thomas Aquinas' (HTG 91-109), seems to be important for the development of his thought here. He sees Joachim's eschatology (immanent, messianic and millenarian) and Thomas's eschatology (transcendent and heavenly) as two complementary sides of the Christian hope. His engagement in the controversy between Joachim and Thomas seems to have made him see the eschaton itself, the new creation, in a more transcendent way, focused on the beatific vision rather than the earthly kingdom of God, so that the need for an earthly fulfilment of history has to be met by millenarianism. My question would be: why must these two sides of the Christian hope be kept apart, the millennium being the focus of one of them, the new creation the focus of the other? Does not Moltmann's concept of the new creation, as the eschatological future of *this world* in the immediate presence of God, in fact combine the messianic and the transcendent, the earthly kingdom and the beatific vision?
[12]For references to the millennium before CoG, see TKG 235, n. 44 (first published in 1980) and HTG 96, 108-109 (first published in 1982).

possible to glean a series of such reasons from his discussion. I shall explain and discuss three of them.

First, from Moltmann's millenarian reading of history it is clear that a major function of futurist millenarianism is to supply the eschatological proviso which qualifies all forms of church, state and civilization in the present as at best provisional and penultimate. In particular, this relates to the issue of rule. By maintaining the hope of the universal earthly rule of Christ and His saints as a future, eschatological prospect, millenarian hope qualifies the present as the time in which Christ and His saints do not yet rule on earth. Thus the claims of Christian empires and states to embody Christ's rule, with the implications of absolutism, domination and aspirations to universal dominance which such claims entail, are exposed as presumptuous by the millenarian hope. The claim of a centralized, hierarchical church to embody Christ's earthly rule, with the authoritarian, theocratic and triumphalist implications of this, is exposed as presumptuous by the millenarian hope:

> Before the millennium there is no rule of the saints. Only in the millennium will the martyrs rule with Christ and judge the nations. Before the millennium, the church is the brotherly and sisterly, charismatic, non-violent fellowship of those who wait for the coming of the Lord and in the power of the Spirit, who is the giver of life, enter into Christ's struggle and bear their cross in his discipleship (CoG 184).

Finally, the modern secular millenarian project of domination – the west's domination of the rest of the world and its subjugation of nature – is exposed by the millenarian hope as a kind of eschatological hubris, an attempt to achieve eschatological salvation by the seizure of power. In all three cases the premature usurpation of millennial rule is deadly and destructive. The millenarian ideology serves to justify domination and violence. The claims to universal rule have to be enforced, and the need to maintain the illusion of a golden age achieved requires the suppression of dissent and the silencing and forgetting of the victims of power.

While realized millenarianism allies or assimilates the church to the systems of power and violence that perpetuate the dominance of the powerful, futurist millenarianism offers an alternative to the present which enables Christian resistance to the powers of this world.We might say that realized millenarianism is the expression of a theology of glory, while futurist millenarianism is the eschatological corollary of a theology of the cross (*cf.* CoG 194-195).

This argument seems to me of considerable value, but I would make two comments on it.

(a) The issue of when Christ's earthly rule with his saints occurs – now or in the future millennium – needs supplementing with a discussion of the nature of that rule. Otherwise Moltmann's argument is in danger of suggesting that while it is premature for Christians to attempt to exercise absolutist and violent domination over the world now, they will exercise such domination in the coming millennium. This is a significant issue because some millenarian groups – or their leaders – clearly entertain dangerous aspirations to power, dreaming of ruling in place of the powers that currently rule, and can, with a kind of eschatological impatience, end up trying to put these aspirations into immediate effect. The Anabaptist kingdom of Münster in the sixteenth century is the textbook illustration, to which we may now add the Japanese cult of Aum Shinrikyo, which in 1995 came close to succeeding in killing thousands of people in a kind of trial-run for Armageddon.[13]

(b) I am not convinced that the function of providing an alternative to the present which enables resistance and supplies the eschatological proviso can only be fulfilled by the hope of a millennium, and not by the hope of the new creation, if the latter is envisaged as the eschatological future of this world. After all, according to Revelation, it is not only in the millennium that the saints rule (20:4) but also in the New Jerusalem (22:5). Moltmann argues that the realized millenarianism of the post-Constantinian church resulted in the reduction of eschatology to a purely spiritual, other-worldly hope (CoG 182). But the remedy which Moltmann's own eschatology has always offered for a purely spiritual, other-worldly hope is not to retain such a hope as final destiny, while adding a this-worldly millennium as the penultimate expectation. The remedy is to understand the new creation itself as the destiny of the whole of this present creation, taken into God's immediate presence and transfigured with His glory. Once the new creation is understood in this way, it is not clear why a millennium is necessary.

Second, according to Moltmann, only the millennium supplies a 'goal of history' (CoG 133-134, 137, 193, 197). He does not think of this goal in the sense of a completion of the historical project of the dominant, a prolongation of the present, as the secular millenarianisms that stemmed from the Enlightenment did. Rather, it is the goal for those who participate in Christ's struggle against the powers,

---

[13]See the account in D. Thompson, *The End of Time: Faith and Fear in the Shadow of the Millennium* (London: Random House, 1997), chap. 11.

especially the martyrs (CoG 194), for whom the millennium represents the hope of participating in His resurrection (CoG 195). It is also the goal for Israel, for whom the millennium represents resurrection and redemption, the fulfilment of the messianic promises (CoG 182, 197-198). It is the goal of the moral struggle for justice, freedom and love: at least, Moltmann quotes a passage of Barth, evidently with approval, to this effect. For history to have a goal, Moltmann appears to argue, it must have a goal within history. The eschaton itself is not the goal, but the end of history.[14] The millennium consummates history; the eschaton ends history. The millennium is future history; the new creation is the future of history (CoG 197). But why must history have a goal within history? Why should it not have its goal in the new creation? I can think of two possible reasons.

(a) Since the new creation ends history, it cannot also be its goal. (This, I think, is what Moltmann means in CoG 197.) But this is surely a confusion. The new creation ends the temporal process of history, but it does not end the content of history, that is, all that has existed and happened within the temporal process. In Moltmann's view, all that has lived and happened in history is gathered up into the new creation, redeemed and transfigured. Why should this not be seen as the goal of history?

(b) The new creation is not the goal of history in that human action in history neither achieves or produces it. But nor is the millennium, in Moltmann's understanding, the goal of history in this sense. It is the *God-given* consummation of history. I do not see why the new creation cannot be seen as the goal of history in this sense.

I suspect that at this point it is the development of the secular millenarianisms of the modern period that has influenced Moltmann's thought. (Barth's reference to Kant in the passage Moltmann quotes in CoG 193 may suggest this; *cf.* 188-189). For such secular millenarianisms, the goal of history has, of course, to be within history. It is the immanent *telos* to which human history itself leads, as human action progresses in that direction. For such secular thought, there is in any case no new creation beyond history. But for Christian eschatology which does envisage such a new creation, I do not see why history should not have its goal beyond itself, in God's fulfilment and transfiguration of history in eternity.

Third, a different way in which Moltmann represents the theological necessity of the millennium is to see it as transitional. It 'mediates between world history here, and the end of the world and

---

[14]This distinction is probably influenced by Walter Benjamin, as quoted in WJC 303: 'the kingdom of God is not the *telos* of the historical dynamic; it cannot be made the goal. For historically it is not a goal; it is the end.'

the new world there' (CoG 201). It is 'the eschatological mediation between history and eternity' (CoG 156). This gives it a coherent place in the more general picture Moltmann paints in this book of an eschatological *process* which began with the resurrection of Jesus and will end in the new creation.[15] But that is not enough to demonstrate the necessity of this particular transitional phase. Moltmann claims that if 'we leave out this transition [the millennium], as the non-millenarian eschatologies do, then world history will end – according to modern fantasy – with an abrupt Big Bang', to which he attaches the terms 'Hiroshima images' and 'catastrophe' (CoG 201-202). But (a) God's act of new creation does not destroy; it is not catastrophic; it redeems and renews and transfigures. It ends history – the temporal process; but it does not end the world. (b) Even if Moltmann's millennium is rather more like the new creation than the world at present is, the new creation must still represent a radical transformation. In principle there cannot be a kind of smooth evolution from this world to the new creation. Even the world history that reached its goal in Moltmann's millennium would end with 'an abrupt Big Bang', if that were the appropriate way to conceptualize the end.

In conclusion, it seems to me for the most part, the functions of the millennium in Moltmann's eschatology could be understood as relating to a particular *aspect* of the Christian eschatological hope, but not necessarily an aspect which has to be understood as an interim period in the eschatological process. Moltmann quotes Paul Althaus who said that millenarians rightly stress the 'this-worldly character of the Christian hope', and Walter Kreck who observed that millenarianism 'wards off a docetism in eschatology which abandons the earth' (CoG 193). These, according to Moltmann, 'are not genuine acknowledgements of millenarian eschatology; they are actually a dismissal of it in various polite forms' (CoG 193). But it seems to me they are near the mark. What the millenarian hope does is to focus on the eschatological hope in its more immanent and this-worldly aspect, as the fulfilment of human and historical goals and as the ideal form of the life we live on this earth in this age. This focus is the appropriate one to provide motivation and direction for some aspects of Christian life now, both positively as goal and negatively as eschatological proviso. Other aspects of the eschatological hope, such

---

[15]Moltmann's idea of transitional stages in the eschatological process probably owes something to Joachim of Fiore's three overlapping *status* of world history: see HTG 96 for a formulation of the stages of transition as Moltmann understands them, influenced by Joachim. In TKG, on the other hand, he appropriated Joachim's trinitarian scheme of three *status*, but differed from Joachim in refusing to see them as three *successive* stages (TKG 209).

as the beatific vision and the glorification of all creation in the immediate presence of God, are by comparison more transcendent and in a sense other-worldly. In the millenarian tradition these two sides of the Christian hope have been assigned respectively to the millennium and the eternal state. In the non-millenarian Christian tradition, as Moltmann complains, the more immanent and this-worldly side has been neglected, while in the secular millenarianisms of the modern age, the more transcendent and other-worldly side has been left aside completely.

Christian eschatology needs both sides of its traditional hope, and it needs the millenarian tradition to remind it of the immanent and this-worldly side. But it does not seem to me necessary to follow the millenarian tradition in its temporal distinction between the new creation in eternity and a this-worldly kingdom of Christ which precedes it. If the new creation is understood as God's new creation precisely of this world and this reality, as it is a merit of Moltmann's theology to insist, then it is an eschatological conception in which the this-worldly and the other-worldly are not incompatible, but are the two aspects of the one eschatological reality. Since most eschatological thought is a necessarily imaginative picturing of the un-imaginable, we may have to use alternative images to represent different aspects of the eschatological hope, but we can understand these images as different angles on the one eschatological reality. Irenaeus's earthly paradise, Augustine's heavenly city, Dante's beatific vision, the restored Israel of the dispensationalists, even the classless society of Karl Marx and the ecological reconciliation of the Greens – all these and many more are complementary angles on the eschatological reality, each relating in a different way to the Christian imperative of living hopefully now.

Chapter 14

SCIENCE, WISDOM, ESCHATOLOGY AND THE COSMIC CHRIST

Ernest C. Lucas

Following a brief survey of passages in the wisdom literature which deal with eschatological issues, some modern scientific eschatologies are outlined. Parallels are noted between the approaches to eschatology found in the wisdom literature and among modern physicists. Suggestions are made as to how, in our post-modern context, Christian apologists might respond to the growing interest in scientific eschatologies. It provides an opportunity to enter into a dialogue in which Christians have something positive to say, drawing on the resources provided by the reasoned consideration of eschatology in the wisdom literature and by 'wisdom christology' in the New Testament.

Introduction

F. Tipler, Professor of Mathematical Physics at Tulane University, opens his recent book, *The Physics of Immortality*, as follows:[1]

> This book is a description of the Omega Point Theory, which is a testable physical theory for an omnipresent, omniscient, omnipotent God who will one day in the far future resurrect every single one of us to live forever in an abode which is in all essentials the Judeo-Christian Heaven. Every single term in the theory – for example, 'omnipresent', 'omniscient', 'omnipotent', 'resurrection (spiritual) body', Heaven – will be introduced as pure physics concepts. In this book I shall make no appeal, anywhere, to revelation. I shall appeal instead to the solid results

---

[1] F. J. Tipler, *The Physics of Immortality* (London: Macmillan, 1995), 1.

of modern physical science; the only appeal will be to the reader's reason. I shall describe the physical mechanism of the universal resurrection. I shall show exactly how physics will permit the resurrection to eternal life of everyone who has lived, is living, and will live. I shall show exactly why this power to resurrect which modern physics allows will actually exist in the far future, and why it will in fact be used. If any reader has lost a loved one, or is afraid of death, modern physics says: 'Be comforted, you and they shall live again.'

This is a striking illustration of a recent phenomenon; the interest that scientists are taking in the subject of eschatology. Of course, for a long time they have been interested in the beginning of things – the origin of the universe, the origin of the solar system, the origin of life. What has prompted the recent interest in the end of things, in eschatology? As I have thought about this I have been struck by some parallels between the development of an interest in eschatology among scientists and among the sages or wisdom teachers of ancient Israel.

Wisdom and Eschatology

There is a significant parallel between the activity and interests of the ancient sages and those of the modern scientists. L. Perdue says:

> The sages searched for patterns and consistencies in reality. They sought to discover regularity in the variety of natural and social phenomena and to establish their relationships. Even unrelated phenomena were studied to find correlations that would point to the order and interconnectedness of the world.[2]

This is just what modern scientists are doing too. How did the sages set about their search? To quote Perdue again:

> Normally eschewing prophetic charisma and priestly theophanies, traditional sages believed true wisdom originated with God and was transmitted to them through their powers of observation, reason, and reflection.[3]

---

[2]L. G. Perdue, 'Cosmology and the Social Order in the Wisdom Tradition', in J. G. Gammie and L. G. Perdue, *The Sage in Israel and the Ancient Near East* (Winona Lake: Eisenbrauns, 1990), 461.
[3]*Ibid.*, 460.

Modern scientists, too, rely on observation, reason and reflection. Given these parallels, it would be interesting, and possibly of value to Christian apologetics, to see if there are any discernible parallels between the interest shown in eschatology by the ancient sages and modern scientists. We commence by surveying the role that eschatology plays in Old Testament wisdom books and the Apocrypha.

Proverbs
The great majority of Old Testament scholars would agree with D. Kidner that 'Life after death lies beyond the horizon of Proverbs'.[4] However, there are some places where an eschatological understanding of a proverb has been suggested.

Proverbs 11:7   בְּמוֹת אָדָם רָשָׁע תֹּאבַד תִּקְוָה וְתוֹחֶלֶת אוֹנִים אָבָדָה
There are several uncertainties here. Some think that the first half-line is metrically too long and drop either אָדָם, 'man' (which does not change the sense) or רָשָׁע, 'wicked' (which universalizes the meaning). The more relevant problem for us comes in the second half-line. The meaning of אוֹנִים is disputed. Possibilities suggested are: strength, deceitfulness, wickedness, wealth.[5] Reider[6] suggested emending the word to אֱמוּנִים 'faithful ones' and also taking אָבָדָה as meaning 'last, endure', on the basis of an Arabic root. The proverb would then read: 'When a wicked man dies, his hope perishes, but the expectation of the faithful is everlasting.'[7] This implies belief in some kind of existence beyond death to which the faithful can look forward. However, this suggestion, combining as it does an emendation that assumes a scribal error that has no textual support and a meaning for the root אבד which is unparalleled in biblical Hebrew, is unconvincing. Some scholars follow the LXX (τῶν ἀσεβῶν) and emend אוֹנִים to אֱוִילִים ('fools') to give a synonymous parallelism: 'and the expectation of fools perishes'. One could still read into this an eschatological meaning. The wicked have no hope beyond death, but, by implication, there is something for the righteous to hope for. In the context of Proverbs, however, what this 'better hope' is would seem to be indicated by 10:7, that is, the leaving behind of a blessed memory and a good name. Those who want to avoid emendation have tended to favour the meaning 'riches/wealth' for אוֹנִים, for example the REB translation: 'When someone wicked dies, all his hopes

---

[4] D. Kidner, *Proverbs* (London: Tyndale Press, 1964), 56.
[5] Possible roots are אָוֶן (iniquity, misfortune), אוֹן (strength, wealth), אֲנָה (distress).
[6] J. Reider, 'Etymological Studies in Biblical Hebrew', *VT* 2 (1952), 113-130.
[7] *Ibid.*, 124.

perish, and any expectation of affluence ends.' This is a statement about expectations of wealth, that the wicked are often not allowed to achieve their aim of amassing a fortune (*cf.* Pr. 10:3b and 28b).

Proverbs 12:28 בְּאֹרַח־צְדָקָה חַיִּים וְדֶרֶךְ נְתִיבָה אַל־מָוֶת
There is no dispute about the meaning of the first half-line: 'In the way of righteousness there is life.' M. Dahood has argued that the second half-line should be read as: וּדְרוֹךְ נְתִיבָה אַל מָוֶת 'and the treading of her (*i.e.* righteousness') path is immortality'.[8] He justifies the acceptance here of the very unusual use of the negative particle אַל to negate a noun rather than a verb (resulting in the sense 'not-death') by appeal to 2 Samuel 1:21 (אַל טַל וְאַל מָטָר). However, here it is reasonable to supply an implied verb (יְהִי) between the particle and the noun. His suggested Ugaritic parallels do not carry conviction because they involve the negative adverb בל rather than אל.

Modern English versions offer us three different ways of dealing with this difficult half-line. The NRSV revocalizes the initial word in much the same way as Dahood does, and supplies a verb: 'In the path of righteousness there is life, in walking its path there is no death.' This could be taken to hint at life beyond death, but it seems more likely that it is a stark formulation of the 'two ways' imagery that is used in the wisdom literature (*e.g.* Pr. 2:20-22), having the same meaning as the life/death contrast in Deuteronomy 30:15ff. As Kidner puts it, in the Old Testament 'death is a whole realm in conflict with life, rather than a single and merely physical event'.[9]

The REB revocalizes the negative particle as the preposition אֶל and supplies a verb: 'The way of righteousness leads to life, but there is a well-worn path to death.' The GNB follows the LXX: 'Righteousness is the road to life; wickedness is the road to death.' This assumes that נְתִיבָה is a scribal error, though, among scholars who accept the need to emend it, there is little agreement as to what the original Hebrew word was that might have been corrupted to give the MT. In both of these translations we seem to have expressions of the 'two ways' image.

Proverbs 14:32: בְּרָעָתוֹ יִדָּחֶה רָשָׁע וְחֹסֶה בְמוֹתוֹ צַדִּיק
The first half-line is clear: 'The wicked is overthrown by his evil-doing.' In the MT the second half-line reads, 'but the righteous seeks

---

[8]M. J. Dahood, 'Immortality in Proverbs 12:28', *Biblica* 41 (1960), 176-181.
[9]Kidner, *Proverbs*, 55.

refuge in his death'. This could be taken as indicating a hope of life beyond death for the righteous. Bertram suggested that 'his death' here refers back to the death of the wicked, so that the proverb is asserting that the righteous is protected from the disaster that overthrows the wicked, 'but the righteous finds safety in his (the wicked man's) death'.[10] However, this requires חֹסֶה to mean 'finds safety' instead of 'seeks safety', which is what it means elsewhere. Most scholars follow the LXX, with some support from the Syriac versions, and read 'but the righteous seeks refuge in his integrity'. This means emending במותו to בְּתֻמּוֹ, assuming an accidental transposition of consonants. It produces an apt antithesis.

Proverbs 15:24 אֹרַח חַיִּים לְמַעְלָה לְמַשְׂכִּיל לְמַעַן סוּר מִשְּׁאוֹל מָטָּה
'For the wise the path of life leads upward, in order to avoid Sheol below' (NRSV). This is certainly open to an eschatological reading, not so much because of the use of 'Sheol', which can be just a graphic synonym for 'death', but because of the up/down contrast. That contrast is not present in the LXX version of this verse: 'The thoughts of an intelligent man are ways of life, so that avoiding Hades he may be saved.' This has led to the suggestion[11] that this contrast was added when the proverb was interpreted in terms of later belief in life after death with rewards and punishments. However, taken as it stands in the MT, the verse can be seen as doing no more than expressing graphically the 'two ways' contrast, with the use of 'Sheol' (to which the dead 'go down') prompting the metaphorical use of the up/down imagery.

The sages who compiled and preserved the material in the book of Proverbs seem to have had no interest in eschatological issues, such as life beyond death. They were concerned with 'wisdom' as 'the ability to cope with life', here and now.[12]

Ecclesiastes

Unlike these sages Qoheleth is preoccupied with an eschatological issue – death. He is a great observer of things. The phrases 'I saw' and 'I have seen' recur time and again in his writing. A good deal of what he sees he does not like, hence the pessimism of the book. As M. Eaton says:

---

[10]G. Bertram, 'Die religiöse Umdeutung altorientalischer Lebensweisheit in der griechischen Übersetzung des AT', *ZAW* 54 (1936), 153-167.
[11]W. McKane, *Proverbs* (London: SCM, 1970), 479, quoting Barucq.
[12]R. N. Whybray, *Proverbs* (London: Marshall Pickering, 1994), 4.

It is necessary . . . to accept the pessimistic strand within the book.
For if critical orthodoxy has effectively deleted orthodox elements
within Ecclesiastes, traditional orthodoxy has at times just as
effectively ignored, played down or allegorized its pessimism.[13]

Qoheleth's pessimism arises from at least two different
observations. One is that there is injustice and oppression which goes
unpunished in this life (4:1-3; 7:15; 8:9-11, 14), and Qoheleth has no
hope of retribution and rewards after death (9:1-3a). The second
observation is that, if death is the effective end, it renders meaning-
less much of this life's achievements – wisdom (2:12-17), hard work
(2:18-23), even piety (9:1b-3a). So, life, considered as a self-contained
whole 'under the sun', is rendered 'futile, utterly futile' (1:2) by the
fact of death.

There are a couple of places where some commentators see a
hint of belief in life after death. One is 12:7 with its reference to the
'breath/spirit' (רוּחַ) returning to God at death: '. . . the dust returns to
the earth as it was, and the breath returns to God who gave it'
(NRSV). However, it is very likely that this verse is one of a number of
places where Qoheleth draws on Genesis,[14] especially in chapters 1–
3. In this case the allusion is to Genesis 2:7 and its account of Adam's
creation: '. . . then the Lord God formed man from the dust of the
ground, and breathed into his nostrils the breath of life; and man
became a living being' (NRSV). If so, the most likely meaning is that
death is seen as a form of dissolution which is a reversal of creation,
with no implication of a continuing, disembodied existence. The
second key-verse is 3:21. The LXX, Vulgate, Peshitta and Targum, and
most modern commentators take it as a question in indirect speech:
'Who knows . . . whether. . .?' Eaton argues that it should be taken as
a simple direct question: 'Who knows the spirit of man which goes
upward and the spirit of the beast which goes down to the earth?'[15]
His reasons for this are: (1) if it were a question in indirect speech,
one would expect the inter- rogative particle to come earlier in the
sentence and be prefixed to רוּחַ, as in the question in 2:19. There
seems to be no other example in the Hebrew Bible where the
interrogative is found so late in a sentence; (2) it is more natural to
see the construction here as the common one of the participle with
the article, because the interrogative particle is normally prefixed to

---

[13]M. A. Eaton, *Ecclesiastes* (Leicester: IVP, 1983), 44.
[14]C. C. Forman, 'Koheleth's use of Genesis', *JSS* 5 (1960), 256-263.
[15]Eaton, *Ecclesiastes*, 88f.

an indicative form of the verb; (3) this reading removes what would otherwise be a contradiction with 12:7.

These are weighty points, but they are not unanswerable. Although the interrogative particle is normally pre-fixed to the first word in a sentence or clause, as BDB comments, 'Occasionally, one or more words precede הֲ (in the same clause) for special emphasis'. In this verse the emphasis is on the going up/going down contrast, and if the particle is not to be prefixed to רֹּוחַ it has to come after the construct chain which begins with רֹוחַ, hence its lateness in the clause.

The interrogative particle is used, on rare occasions, with other than indicative forms of the verb, for example, with infinitives absolute in Job 40:2 and Jeremiah 7:9. In Ecclesiastes 3:21 the MT pointing is inconsistent with the prefix being the interrogative rather than the article, since, as Robert Gordis points out, 'the evidence is clear that before Aleph and Yod, there was a tendency to vocalize the inter-rogative *He* with full vowels and dageš'.[16]

If taken as an indirect question, there is no necessary contradiction between this verse, which uses up/down imagery to indicate different destinies for the life-force in humans and animals when they die, and 12:7, which states that the components that make up the human person return to their original sources at death.

In the context of 3:16-22 it does seem more natural to take the clause as an indirect question. If it is taken as Eaton suggests, the thought of the passage gets rather convoluted. Eaton himself has to argue for a far from obvious reading of verse 18.

In any case, even if Eaton's reading is accepted, it is not clear that the difference in the fate of the human and animal life-forces need imply belief in an existence beyond death for humans. Once again Genesis 2 seems to be in the background, where the animals are said to have been made simply 'out of the ground'. The point at stake in the question may then be whether the difference in constitution of humans and animals, as recorded in the creation story of Genesis 2, means that there is any real difference in the nature of humans and animals as they live out their lives 'under the sun'. The implication is that there is no discernible difference.

So, what we find in Qoheleth is that his lack of belief in life beyond death makes life lived according to the patterns he sees in life 'under the sun' seem futile.

---

[16]R. Gordis, *Koheleth: the Man and His World* (New York: Schocken, 1968), 238. He gives as examples: הָאָרַךְ (Gn. 19:9); הַיִּיטַב (Lv. 10:19); הָאִישׁ (Nu. 16:22).

Job

The dialogues in the book of Job are, from one point of view, a clash
of perceived patterns in life. Eliphaz insists that the received wisdom
of the sages is that it is the wicked who suffer (15:17ff.). In this he is
supported by Bildad (18:5ff.) and Zophar (20:4ff.). Job will have none
of this. His observation of life is that all too often the wicked do
prosper, in all kinds of ways (21:7ff.). Added to this, of course, is his
own experience of undeserved suffering. This does not fit the pattern
of how he expects God to behave and so in the depths of his despair
he accuses God of injustice (9:21-24). But his despair also drives him
to consider the possibility of eschatological vindication. The two
passages in which he does this are both the centre of considerable
debate, for different reasons.

Job 14:13-17

> Oh that you would hide me in Sheol,
> that you would conceal me until your wrath is past,
> hat you would appoint me a set time, and remember me!
> If mortals die, will they live again?
> All the days of my service I would wait
> until my release should come.
> You would call, and I would answer you;
> You would long for the work of your hands.
> For then you would not number my steps,
> you would not keep watch over my sin:
> my transgression would be sealed up in a bag,
> and you would cover over my iniquity (NRSV).

It is clear that in chapter 14 the idea of personal resurrection from the
dead is considered. But is it considered and rejected, or considered
and embraced as a true hope? The majority of recent commentators
take the view that the question, 'If mortals die, will they live again?'
(14:14a) is a rhetorical one which expects the answer 'No!' in the light
of verse 12 ('so mortals lie down and do not rise again') and verses 18
and 19 ('. . . so you destroy the hope of mortals'). F. Andersen argues
against this on the grounds that it is imposing western logic on the
book.[17] He regards verses 13-17 as the expression of the author's real
convictions, which are flanked by contrasting opinions which he
rejects. I do not find this convincing. Moreover, verse 13 begins with
מִי יִתֵּן which, as N. Habel points out, 'is a recurring formula in Job

---

[17]F. I. Andersen, *Job* (Leicester: IVP, 1976), 169f.

which marks momentous flights of hope'.[18] So, I think that verses 13-17 express the only hope that Job can see as an answer to his dilemma – the hope of vindication following personal resurrection from the dead. At this point, however, he cannot grasp this hope securely.

Job 19:23-27

This is a much debated *crux interpretum*, full of textual, lexical and exegetical problems which cannot be discussed here. All I can do is state my conclusions, which are as follows. Verses 23-24, with the three-fold repetition of מִי יִתֵּן ('O that . . .'), express Job's strong desire that a permanent record be made of his case: 'O that my words were written down! that they were inscribed in a book! O that with an iron pen and with lead they were engraved on a rock forever!' (NRSV). The reason for this is given in verse 25ff. The emphatic opening, אֲנִי יָדַעְתִּי ('I myself know'), is used elsewhere by Job in quasi-legal contexts to express certainty (*e.g.* 9:2, 28; 13:18). Job is certain that there exists a vindicator[19] who will establish his innocence after his death. It is difficult to be sure whether verses 26 and 27, with their three-fold reference to 'seeing' God, continue this expression of certainty or are a return to an expression of hope. With some hesitation, I take this as an expression of the conviction that, in some way (which is not clear because of the textual problems), Job expects to be aware of his vindication when it comes.

In any case, the relevant thing for us is the fact that there is recognition in the book of Job of the idea of eschatological vindication as a possible way of making sense of the suffering and injustice that occur in this life and meet no remedy before death – even if Job himself does not embrace it.

The Wisdom of Jesus Ben Sirach

Ben Sirach holds to the principle of strict retribution as firmly as did Job's friends (16:11b-14). He also held the belief that there is no meaningful existence beyond death, only the shadowy existence of Sheol (17:27, 28; 30:17; 41:4). Yet he, unlike Job's friends, recognizes that the wicked do sometimes seem to escape retribution. His answer to the dilemma this poses is to argue that it is premature to cast judgment on someone's life and on God's dealings with them until 'the day of death'. On that day God will deal with them according to their deeds (11:20-28; *cf.* 1:13; 3:26; 9:11). This is eschatological

---

[18]N. C. Habel, *The Book of Job* (London: SCM, 1985), 303.
[19]There are various views as to who this is: God, a celestial being, Job's own word of witness personified (*cf.* 16:18, 19).

judgment of a kind – it is concentrated in a person's last moments of life.

The Wisdom of Solomon
Unlike his predecessors in the Hebrew wisdom tradition, this author clearly does believe in a meaningful after-life, with rewards and punishments. In 2:1–3:19 he depicts the wicked, who do not believe that life has any meaning beyond the pleasure one can get out of it or that there is any existence beyond death, ridiculing the righteous. In 2:16-20 they seem to be making fun of the very idea expressed by Ben Sirach of judgment at the moment of death. However, the author says that they are wrong, because there is life after death, with rewards for the righteous and punishment for the wicked.

Wisdom and the Cosmic Christ

It is widely held in New Testament studies that ideas about wisdom played a part in the development of christological understanding in the New Testament period. J. Dunn says:

> It is clear therefore that the *tradition of (pre-existent) Wisdom has been influential at many points in NT christology*. In some of the earlier (i.e. Pauline) passages it may be no more than that *language* or *exegesis* has been prompted by specific language or some particular exegesis used in the Wisdom tradition. But in other cases there can be little doubt that the *role* of Wisdom is being attributed to Christ.[20]

In particular he points to John 1:1-18, 1 Corinthians 8:5-6, Colossians 1:15-17 and Hebrews 1:1-3a as places where a cosmic significance is attributed to Christ by means of a wisdom christology.

The development which lies behind this can be sketched here only briefly. Although in the book of Proverbs wisdom is often no more than a prudential ethical concept, in 8:22-31 wisdom is personified and related to God's creative activity. There is much debate about two key words in this passage,[21] but what is clear is that wisdom existed before the creation of the world, and was with God when it was created. This may be understood in the light of Proverbs 3:19: 'The Lord by wisdom founded the earth;by understanding he

---

[20]J. D. G. Dunn, *Christology in the Making* (London: SCM, 1980), 167.
[21]Verse 22 קָנָה acquired/possessed/created/gave birth to, and verse 30 אָמוֹן master worker/confidant/young child.

established the heavens' (NRSV). Here, however, wisdom is not personified, but is an attribute of God. Job 28:23-28 also speaks of wisdom being used by God in the creation of the world. Ben Sirach speaks of wisdom being with God before all other things were created (1:1-4) and as pervading all creation (24:3-7), but he identifies her with the Torah. In the Wisdom of Solomon the figure of wisdom appears to be hypostatized. She is 'a breath of the power of God, a pure emanation of the glory of the Almighty' (7:25a) and is 'the fashioner of all things' (7:22) who 'pervades and penetrates all things' (7:24b). It is in this book that the 'word' and 'wisdom' of God are brought together in relation to God's acts of creation. The author prays to God as the one: '. . . who has made all things by your word, and in your wisdom fashioned man to have sovereignty over all your creation' (9:1b, 2, REB). In the writings of Philo of Alexandria, of course, ideas about God's word(λόγος) and wisdom(σοφία), and their relationship, are developed further.

So, we can see how a wisdom christology provides a basis for attributing cosmic significance to Christ, but the emphasis is on creation, with no explicit reference to eschatology. We will have to pick this up later.

Science and Eschatology

There are two types of 'secular' end-of-the world scenarios, which I call the 'apocalyptic' and the 'cosmological'. The apocalyptic ones include such things as: a nuclear holocaust (thankfully seemingly much less likely now than a decade ago); the outcome of the environmental stress we are putting on our planet (global warming, ozone depletion); a strike by a comet or asteroid. These are contingent events that might or might not happen, and are to some extent under human control. The cosmological ones are those that are the inevitable outcome of the working of the laws of nature, as far as we understand them. What are they?

To begin with, we have to make a distinction between end-of-the-world and end-of-the-universe scenarios. Thanks to our knowledge of high energy particle physics and the availability of computer simulations, astrophysicists now have a good idea of how stars evolve.[22] Our Sun is a typical fairly low-mass star. It is expected to have a life-time of about 10,000 million years, and is about half-way through its life. In about 4,000 millions years from now it will go

---

[22]P. Davies, *The Last Three Minutes* (London: Phoenix, 1995), 37-48, gives a simple account of this.

through what is call a 'red giant phase', when, as it approaches the
end of its life, it will swell up to about 500 times its present size
before collapsing in on itself to form what is called a 'white dwarf'
star. In the red giant phase it will engulf the Earth, which will be
burnt to a cinder. So, life on Earth must eventually come to an end.

Should human life survive the incineration of the Earth,
presumably by colonizing other planets around other stars, it still
faces eventual demise in one of a number of end-of-the-universe
scenarios. We live in an expanding universe. The great star systems,
the galaxies, are receding from one another. This is happening in a
way that strongly suggests that the universe as we know it began
with a 'Big Bang' some 10,000 million years ago, and there are other
evidence which support this idea. But what of the future?[23] The
answer to that depends on how much mass there is in the universe. If
it is above a certain limit, the attractive force of gravity pulling the
galaxies together will result in the rate of expansion slowing to a halt,
and then the universe will collapse in on itself and end in a big, hot
'crunch'. If the amount of mass is below a certain limit, the universe
will go on expanding for ever because the gravitational attraction will
not be enough to slow it to a halt. But this does not mean that the
universe will go on being inhabitable for ever. The *Second Law of
Thermodynamics* tells us that heat flows irreversibly from hotter
bodies to colder ones, and as it does this there is a loss of what we
can call 'useful energy' – energy that can be used to do work, like just
staying alive. This cannot go on for ever. Eventually there will be no
more 'useful energy' left in the universe and it will have reached the
stage that is called the 'heat death' of the universe. It will all end
with a gradually dwindling whimper. Whether it ends with a crunch
or a whimper, life in our universe is doomed to extinction.

It was in 1856 that the German physicist H. von Helmholtz
pre-dicted the heat death of the universe on the basis of the *Second
Law of Thermodynamics*. For the next 120 years or so the great majority
of scientists took no more interest in eschatology than did the ancient
sages who compiled the book of Proverbs. They were probably too
interested in discerning new patterns in the physical world and
'coping with life' in general.

During the last twenty years or so there has been a growing
interest among scientists in the eschatological implications of modern
cosmology. Why this should have happened I am not certain. I think
that one factor is that in the same period we have seen increasing
recognition of what is called 'the anthropic principle'. This is the fact

[23]*Ibid.*, 67ff.

that we live in a universe that seems spectacularly fine-tuned for life, to quote John Leslie.[24] What is more, there is some evidence that this is a fine tuning, not for just any kind of life, but for carbon-based life in particular. This, perhaps, has provoked the question, 'What is the point of it all?' At the same time, cosmology has advanced on the basis of both firmer observational and theoretical ground, and the cosmological, eschatological scenarios have come into sharper focus. So, there has been a clash of patterns, as in the book of Job – though different patterns are involved. One seems to point to the existence of human life as the reason for the existence of the universe. The other says that life will inevitably be snuffed out as the universe ends with a bang or a whimper. So, how have scientists reacted?

Some, like Qoheleth, find the dilemma beyond resolution, and conclude that everything is pointless, futile. The leading astrophysicist, S. Weinberg, put it this way in 1977:

> It is hard to realize that all this [the Earth] is just a tiny part of an overwhelmingly hostile universe. It is even harder to realize that this present universe has evolved from an unspeakably unfamiliar early condition, and faces a future extinction of endless cold or intolerable heat. The more the universe seems comprehensible, the more it seems pointless.

> But if there is no solace in the fruits of our research, there is at least some consolation in the research itself. Men and women are not content to comfort themselves with tales of gods and giants, or to confine their thoughts to the daily affairs of life; they also build telescopes and satellites and accelerators, and sit at their desks for endless hours working out the meaning of the data they gather. The effort to understand the universe is one of the few things that lifts human life a little above the level of farce, and gives it some of the grace of tragedy.[25]

Interestingly, there is also a parallel here to Ecclesiastes 9:10 with its advice to go on working hard and make the best of life even though it all seems futile. Writing in 1993, Weinberg endorsed his earlier sentiments and added:

> Unlike science, religious experience can suggest a meaning for our lives, a part for us to play in the cosmic drama of sin and redemption, and it holds out to us a promise of continuation after

---

[24]J. Leslie, *Universes* (London & New York: Routledge, 1989), 2.
[25]S. Weinberg, *The First Three Minutes* (London: André Deutsch, 1977), 154f.

death. For just these reasons, the lessons of religious experience seem to me indelibly marked with the stamp of wishful thinking.[26]

He goes on to say that for him it is a point of honour not to give in to the temptation of wishful thinking and accept the consolation the religion offers in the face of our own death and the deaths of those we love.

During the last decade P. Davies has been one of the most prolific writers on the implications of physics and cosmology for religious belief. In one of his early books[27] he expressed the opinion that 'science offers a surer path to God than religion' and that 'science has actually advanced to the point where what were formerly religious questions can be seriously tackled'. Formerly a Professor of Mathematical Physics he now holds a specially created Chair of Natural Philosophy at the University of Adelaide. He was awarded the Templeton Prize for Progress in Religion in 1995. He is so impressed by the way the universe is 'fine-tuned for life' that he believes that there is a cosmic mind behind it and that this mind has a purpose for it. He says:

> The laws which enable the universe to come into being spontaneously seem themselves to be the product of exceedingly ingenious design. If physics is the product of design, the universe must have a purpose, and the evidence of modern physics suggests strongly to me that the purpose includes us.[28]

However, Davies does not believe in a God who is personal, nor does he believe in personal immortality. His eschatological outlook is a kind of cosmic version of that held by Ben Sirach. He argues that if the universe has a purpose, it must have an end, which will come when that purpose has been achieved. So he says:

> If there is a purpose to the universe, and it achieves that purpose, then the universe must end, for its continued existence would be gratuitous and pointless. Conversely, if the universe endures for ever, it is hard to imagine that there is any ultimate purpose to the universe at all. So cosmic death may be the price that has to be paid for cosmic success. Perhaps the most we can hope for is that

---

[26]S. Weinberg, *Dreams of a Final Theory* (London: Vintage, 1993), 204.
[27]P. Davies, *God and the New Physics* (Harmondsworth: Penguin, 1986), ix.
[28]P. Davies, *Superforce* (London: Unwin, 1989), 243.

the purpose of the universe becomes known to our descendants before the end of the last three minutes.[29]

F. Tipler, author of the quotation with which we began, describes himself as an atheist, in the sense of not being a theist.[30] He has, however, put forward a theory which, he claims, shows that according to the known laws of physics personal resurrection is possible. Indeed, he goes further and claims that if his theory is correct, it is inevitable. We do not have time to examine his arguments, especially as they are sometimes quite technical, even abstruse. It must be said that the few physicists who have commented on them think that they depend on assumptions, some say 'speculations', which in turn rest on the use of very particular physical models which may turn out to be totally unrealistic.[31] A wider criticism of his argument is that his definitions of 'life' and of 'immortality' are unsatisfactory. He sees the essence of life to be information processing, and defines life as 'information preserved by natural selection'.[32] He admits that, on this definition, automobiles and various other machines, particularly computers, are 'alive'. His eschatological scenario is that our descendants, perhaps 'successors' would be a better word, will be highly complex information processors which will be able to survive in the dying moments of the 'big crunch' with which the universe will end. In fact, by then there will be a single such entity, the *Omega Point* (term borrowed from Teilhard De Chardin). He/she/it will be able to make use of the vast amount of energy released as the universe approaches the 'big crunch' to produce exact simulations (what he calls 'emulations') of all the people that have existed during the history of the universe. In his view emulations are identical with the original which they emulate, and so he can say that everyone will be resurrected in a virtual reality. But in what sense can they be said to be immortal, since he does not deny that the universe will end? Here he makes a distinction between atomic clock time, by which we measure the history of the universe, and subjective time, a person's experience of time. Subjective time, he says, has to do with our processing of information. The Omega Point will be able to process an infinite amount of information and so, from the subjective point of view, will be immortal, and so keep the emulations in existence for ever.

---

[29]Davies, *The Last Three Minutes*, 155.
[30]Tipler, *Physics*, 305.
[31]See, for example, Weinberg, *Dreams*, 125f.
[32]Tipler, *Physics*, 125.

The interesting thing is that Tipler presents this scenario as a direct response to Weinberg's nihilism. He seems to accept that people need the sense of purpose and the consolation which religion has provided, and for many still does provide. Like the authors of Job and The Wisdom of Solomon he has concluded that life beyond death is an important element in this. His aim is to show that: 'Science can now offer precisely the consolations in facing death that religion once offered.'[33] You can decide for yourself how far he has succeeded.

Conclusions

At this point it is relevant to say something about science and postmodernism, because of their implication for Christian apologetics. In his survey of postmodernism H. Bertens makes an important observation. He says:

> ... the idea that the current crisis in representation has revealed to us that knowledge is impossible must be regarded with the strongest suspicion, even though theoretically it makes perfect sense.[34]

The reason he says this is that the idea itself,

> . . . reflects a narrow point of view, primarily that of the humanities. One can agree that morally, and therefore also politically . . . we lack grounded representations. However, unconditionally to extend non-representation to the cognitive sphere is an imperious manoeuver that may seek to serve the purpose of reasserting the power of the humanities over the sciences in an age in which the former have been relegated to the far background, but that convinces none of those it should convince. This is one of the paradoxes at the heart of postmodernity . . . one does not want to refute the proposition that knowledge is bound up with the knower, is therefore historically and culturally determined . . . and yet we seem to know things. There is one cognitive style, one set of procedural principles that holds the promise of leading us to unconditional knowledge. It is impossible to establish beyond theoretical doubt why these principles work but they would certainly seem to do so: it takes more than the poststructuralist turn to shake the

---

[33]*Ibid.*, 339.
[34]H. Bertens, *The Idea of the Postmodern: A History* (London: Routledge, 1995), 241.

scientific community's belief that we indeed know about, say, the speed of light or the second law of thermodynamics, and for good reasons.[35]

Many in the humanities seem to think that T. Kuhn's book *The Structure of Scientific Revolutions*[36] settled the issue, showing that scientific knowledge is thoroughly historically and culturally determined. However, some historians of science dispute the reading of the history of science on which his thesis is based.[37] His position has also met criticism from some philosophers of science.[38] Philosophically minded practitioners of science do not find it convincing either.[39] They argue that changes in scientific paradigms can be justified rationally, and that paradigms are cumulative, each absorbing and improving upon the one it replaces. In this way, it can be claimed, scientific knowledge becomes increasingly trans-historical and trans-cultural.[40] Its representation of physical reality, while always partial and provisional, becomes increasingly well-founded.

Although there is a good deal of disenchantment with science and technology today, because of the problems they have produced along with the benefits, when it comes to cognitive knowledge most of the population still seem to accept that scientific knowledge is well-founded. Lyotard may define the postmodern as 'incredulity towards metanarratives'.[41] However, the popularity of the books by P. Davies and S. Hawking, which provide a metanarrative from cosmology, and of Richard Dawkins and Stephen Jay Gould, which provide a metanarrative from evolutionary biology, suggests that many people are turning to science for a credible metanarrative. Christian apologists should take this seriously, which is why they should be aware of, and take seriously, the recent interest of scientists in eschatology.

So, what can we conclude from this survey of the writings of sages and scientists? From the sages we learn that eschatology has an

---

[35]*Ibid.*, 240.

[36]T. Kuhn, *The Structure of Scientific Revolutions* (Chicago: University of Chicago Press, 1962, 2nd edn. 1970).

[37]O. Gingerich, *The Eye of Heaven* (New York: American Institute of Physics, 1993), 193-204.

[38]See, for example, W. H. Newton-Smith, *The Rationality of Science* (London: Routledge, 1990).

[39]J. Polkinghorne, *Rochester Roundabout: The Story of High Energy Physics* (New York: Freeman, 1989); Weinberg, *Dreams*, 132-151.

[40]Bertens, *Idea*, 240f., agrees with this claim.

[41]J.-F. Lyotard, *The Postmodern Condition* (Minneapolis: University of Minnesota Press, 1984), xxiv.

important place in a theistic world-view. It can be ignored, as in
Proverbs, while getting on with the pragmatic business of everyday
life. However, when the patterns of life are subjected to the honest
scrutiny of a Qoheleth, or we face the existential questions raised by
experiences of injustice or suffering, even if not as extreme as that of
Job, eschatology becomes a live issue if we are to make any kind of
sense of life. Ben Sirach and the author of The Wisdom of Solomon
show us different options explored by the sages who stood in the
Hebrew wisdom tradition.

The views of the scientists we have considered show that for
a non-theist humanist, eschatology is also important. For some, the
lack of it nullifies the apparent sense suggested by the existence of
patterns in the (physical) universe. For others, the existence of those
patterns provides the basis for asking eschatological questions with
the hope of finding some answers.

This modern interest in eschatology presents Christians with
both an opportunity and a challenge. It provides an opportunity to
enter into a dialogue in which we have something to say. Moreover,
we have something to say not just because Christian eschatology
rests on 'revealed truth', but because in the Hebrew tradition of
which we are joint-heirs there is a reasoned consideration of the need
for it.

The challenge is to ensure that what we have to say is
presented in a way which engages with the current debate. Of course
we have things to say that are not new. Tipler recognizes that the
issue of the historicity of the bodily resurrection of Jesus is a key one,
but says he is not convinced by the Gospel records of it. Here we
need to continue to argue our case as persuasively as possible. But
we must also take seriously the new dimension which modern
science opens up – the ultimate fate of the cosmos and what this says
about the place it has in the purposes of God. The New Testament
writers are aware of this issue, but do no more than allude to it.[42] To
date Christian eschatology has been largely human-centred and
individ-ualistic. We need to follow the example of the ancient sages
and be prepared to grapple with the new issues which challenge our
generation as a result of what modern science says about the pattern
of the cosmos.

For example, how is the 'new heaven and the new earth' of
Revelation 21:1 to be related to our present cosmos? A starting clue
may be found in the recognition that a 'wisdom christology' has a
significant place in the New Testament. As we have seen, there is

---

[42]For example, Rom. 8:18-25; Col. 1:15-20; Rev. 21:1, 2.

nothing explicitly eschatological in this form of christology. However, it inevitably brings together the themes of creation and salvation by attributing a role in creation to the one who is Saviour. It is significant that the wisdom christology of Hebrews 1:1-3a leads into a statement about the Son's soteriological work in verse 3b. The same thing occurs in Colossians 1, where verses 15-17 are the prelude to verses 18-20. Here verse 20 gives cosmic significance to Christ's atoning work, and this can be read in an eschatological light. That it is right to do this seems to be indicated by Ephesians 1:8b-10, where we are told that it is God's 'plan for the fullness of time, to gather up all things in him [Christ], things in heaven and things on earth'. How are we to think of this in terms of the fate of the cosmos as a whole? There are two lines of thought we might pursue. Since Christ is both Saviour and agent in creation, we might consider our being a 'new creation in Christ' (2 Cor. 5:17) as a pattern (or model) for how we can think of the whole cosmos being transformed. This re-creation is not a matter of destruction and replacement, but of continuity and transformation. Of course, the other line of thought to pursue is the evidence provided by the resurrection body of Jesus. Here again continuity and transformation are evident. In the light of this, perhaps we should think in the terms suggested by J. Polkinghorne, one of the very few Christians to have entered into this debate with the scientists, that the new cosmic creation is a creation *ex vetere* rather than another act of creation *ex nihilo*.[43] But to explore what that might mean would require another essay!

---

[43]J. Polkinghorne, *Science and Christian Belief* (London: SPCK, 1994), 167.

Section E

PRACTICAL THEOLOGY

Chapter 15

MISSIONS AND ESCHATOLOGY

Howard Peskett

This essay traces the link between the modern missionary movement and con-
temporaneous end-time expectation. 'Optimistic' post-millennialism gave way to pre-
millennial urgency in preaching, with its Watchword of 'the evangelization of the world
in this generation'. This in turn was replaced by both a social gospel and a more
introverted piety. Today's challenge is to find ways to reach the suffering world with the
message of hope.

Introduction

From 1971 to 1991 my wife and I served in Singapore with a missionary organization called the OMF. It was formerly called the China
Inland Mission, and was founded by Hudson Taylor in 1865, and was
the forerunner of a number of similarly called faith missions. During
most of our time in the mission, numbers were about 1,200; they have
now dropped to about 1,000. In the past twenty-five years there has
been a significant demographic shift in the mission: few serve for a
lifetime; twelve years is about the average; and there has been a
definite tilt towards North America, which is now the largest bloc in
what used to be a predominantly British mission; in addition to this,
there are a large number of Asian members in the mission.

Asia is the largest continent in the world, with the largest
population, the largest number of non-Christians, and the largest
number of adherents of ancient non-Christian religions, amongst
whom evangelism and church-planting has been most difficult. It is
hard to travel on a train through scores of villages in North India, or
to travel all day by bus through the Zhuang mountains in south east

Guangxi, to contemplate the fact that in these places there are hundreds and thousands, millions of people who have not heard of Jesus Christ, and not to ask yourself the question, 'What is the destiny of all these people? What is the significance of all their devotion to their age-old, traditional religions?'

Eschatology used to deal with the four topics: death, judgment, heaven/hell and the last things. The purpose of this essay is to indicate what missionaries and missiologists think about these things, and to what extent the overhang from these four immense and awesome topics affects their work. Missionaries are affected, like everyone else, by today's information overload; there is so much information around, it gets harder all the time to dwell in that which one knows, to feel it in one's bones, to allow the knowledge one acquires to become embedded in experience and expressed in personal transformation.

From time to time I am asked to give a biblical overview of missions, of the story of the church. In this sort of situation I begin with Genesis 12 and end with Revelation 7. I talk about God's choice of Abraham (following the catastrophic rebellion and judgment in the time of Noah), His promise to Abraham of a seed, a land and a blessing, and that in his seed, or through his seed, all the nations of the world will be blessed. Then I talk of how these promises repeatedly were jeopardized and renewed, how these promises peaked and climaxed in our Lord, the suffering Servant, the seed, the land and the blessing; of how God has called out a people for Himself, and how I am animated by this vision of an innumerable crowd in heaven, from every tribe, nation, people and tongue, worshipping around the throne. I talk of the church, spread out through all time and space, 'terrible as an army with banners'. I talk of how Matthew 7:13f. [1] seems to me to be amongst the hardest of all New Testament texts. I suppose I am likely to mention somewhere the verse Habakkuk 2:14.[2] I express the hope that there will be around the throne a crowd that you could no more number than you could number the dust of the earth, the sand on the seashore or the stars in the sky.

The majority of the world's missionaries today are Americans, and the majority of these are premillennial in their theology; a large number are dispensationalists; and there are further

---

[1] 'Enter through the narrow gate; for the gate is wide and the road is easy that leads to destruction, and there are many who take it. For the gate is narrow and the road is hard that leads to life, and there are few who find it.'

[2] 'The earth will be filled with the knowledge of the glory of the LORD, as the waters cover the sea.'

sub-divisions. It is hard to continue in evangelism and church plant-ing, day after day, year after year, especially in communities of inexplicable hardness, without some sort of hope burning inside you. Sometimes when one gets bogged down in the intricacies of alternat-ive eschatologies, and the bitterness of the mutual denunciations they have spawned, one is tempted to flee out of the fire-zone altogether! But I have not found that this has been a big issue inside my mission, or between the missions I have been acquainted with.[3] It is actually the common hope which has united us; it is this which enables us to work on faithfully, without presumption and without despair, those two forms of hopelessness which threaten us from opposite sides.

I will discuss three topics in this essay: the ambiguous legacy of Jonathan Edwards; premillennial pessimism and the rise of fundamentalism; and recent changes of thought in this topic area.

The Ambiguous Legacy of Jonathan Edwards

Jonathan Edwards himself

Jonathan Edwards was a giant.[4] A recent article in the Scottish Journal of Theology[5] compared him to a great mirror in which all sorts of people could see their own faces; although Thuesen did not agree that all readings of Edwards therefore held equal status.

In 1747, in Boston, Jonathan Edwards edited and published a series of sermons which he had preached to his Northampton congregation; the book was entitled (in the generous proportions of the age) *An Humble Attempt to Promote Explicit Agreement And Visible Union Among God's People, In Extraordinary Prayer For The Revival of Religion, And The Advancement of Christ's Kingdom On Earth, Pursuant*

---

[3]It was a pleasure to read a recent eirenical conversation between progressive dispensationalists and three respondents (Craig A. Blaising and Darrell L. Bock, [eds.], *Dispensationalism, Israel and the church: the search for definition* [Grand Rapids, Zondervan, 1992]). In his conclusion (386ff.) Blaising notes the following shared commitments: salvation by grace; the importance of the church in God's plan; the union of redemption and of the people of God; a hope that is both heavenly and earthly; and the hope of eternity with God in a new heaven and a new earth.

[4]Although he was not without precursors, as John F. Wilson insists in Nathan O. Hatch and Harry S. Stout (eds.), *Jonathan Edwards and the American experience* (Oxford: Oxford University Press, 1988), 131-141.

[5]Peter J. Thuesen, 'Jonathan Edwards as great mirror', in *SJT* 50.1 (1997), 39-60.

years previously, in 1739, Edwards had preached a series of sermons (later published) under the title *A history of the work of redemption;* which he had followed up in his *Thoughts on the Revival of Religion in New England* the next year. The innovation which Edwards proposed in these works is that the worst sufferings of the church are past, and a golden age for the church in the world is imminent. There will be a mass conversion of the Jews, a vast dispelling of heathen darkness throughout the world, the most barbarous nations shall become as bright and polite as England, and learning, holiness, peace, love, prosperity and rejoicing shall spread everywhere.[7] Moreover, Edwards believed that,

> This new world is probably now discovered, that the new and most glorious state of God's church on earth might commence there; that God might in it begin a new world in a spiritual respect, when he creates a new heaven and new earth.[8]

Edwards saw a sort of symmetry in the workings of divine providence; he thought that what God began in Asia and Europe, He would conclude in America; he fancifully suggested that the Sun of righteousness would arise in the west, in contrast with the natural sun; and he was even more specific:

> . . . if we may suppose that this glorious work of God shall begin in any part of America, I think, if we consider the circumstances of the settlement of New England, it must needs appear the most likely, of all American colonies, to be the place whence this work (of latter-day glory) shall principally take its rise.[9]

In our library at Trinity College, Bristol, we have a copy of Edwards' *An account of the life of the late Rev. Mr. David Brainerd,* published in 1749. This story, republished scores of times, has had an incalculable effect on missionary motivation in the last 250 years.[10]

Advancement of Christ's Kingdom On earth (1747), in Edward Hickman (ed.), *The works of Jonathan Edwards,* Vol. 2 (London: Banner of Truth Trust, 1974), chap. VII.
[7]C. C. Goen, 'Jonathan Edwards: a new departure in eschatology', in *Church History* 28 (1959), 25-40.
[8]J. Edwards, *Thoughts on the Revival of Religion in New England* (1740), in Hickman, *The Works of Jonathan Edwards,* Vol. 1, chap. X, 382.
[9]*Ibid.,* 383.
[10]E. A. Payne calls it '. . . one of the most influential missionary books of all time', in G. F. Nuttall, *Philip Doddridge 1702-1751: His contribution to English religion* (London: Independent Press, 1951), 98. See also Joseph Conforti, 'Jonathan Edwards's most popular work, "The life of David Brainerd", and nineteenth-century evangelical culture', in *Church History* 54.2 (1985), 188-201.

One particular characteristic of Brainerd which Edwards noted was his 'excitement to earnest prayers and endeavours for the advancement and enlargement of Christ's kingdom in this world'. Edwards candidly admits,

> This is one thing, among others, which gives me great Hope, that God has a Design of accomplishing something very glorious for the Interest of his Church before long. . . . As Mr. Brainerd's Desires and Prayers for the coming of Christ's Kingdom were very special and extraordinary; so, I think, we may reasonably hope, that the God, who excited those Desires and Prayers, will answer them with something special and extraordinary.[11]

With these hopes and aspirations in mind it is not surprising that Edwards was enthusiastic about the Scottish ministers' prayer proposals which had stimulated his Humble Attempt. They had originally asked for two years of prayer; Edwards now proposes that they continue for seven. 'It is evident from the Scripture,' he says, 'that there is yet remaining a great advancement of the interest of religion and the kingdom of Christ in this world, by an abundant outpouring of the Spirit of God, far greater and more extensive than ever yet has been.'[12] He looks forward to the time when '. . . undoubtedly by far the greatest number of them that ever receive the benefits of Christ's redemption, from the beginning of the world to the end of it, will receive it . . .' and he computes in a footnote that there will be one hundred thousand times more believers in that time of prosperity than in the whole of preceding history.[13] How

---

(London: Independent Press, 1951), 98. See also Joseph Conforti, 'Jonathan Edwards's most popular work, "The life of David Brainerd", and nineteenth-century evangelical culture', in *Church History* 54.2 (1985), 188-201.

[11]J. Edwards, *An account of the life of the late Rev. Mr. David Brainerd* (Boston, NE, 1749), 307. At the ordination of Brainerd on 12 June 1744, the preacher, Rev. Ebenezer Pemberton of New York Presbyterian Church, had offered him these words of encouragement: 'When I consider the many prophecies, in sacred Scripture, of the triumphant progress of the gospel in the last ages of the world, I cannot but lift up my head with joy, in an humble expectation, that the day draws near, yea, is even at hand, when the promises made to the Son of God shall be more illustriously fulfilled – when he shall have the heathen for his inheritance, and the utmost parts of the earth for his possession; when his name shall be great among the Gentiles, and be honoured and adored from the rising of the sun to the going down of the same' (Edwards, *A sermon preached in Newark at the Ordination of Mr. David Brainerd* [1744], in Hickman, *The Works of Jonathan Edwards*, Vol. 2, 442ff., 446).

[12]Edwards, *An Humble Attempt* (1747), 284f.

[13]*Ibid.*, 289.

condecent, pious and profitable for Christians to join together[14] to
pray for such an eventuality![15]

Jonathan Edwards believed that the millennium was
approaching: the Reformation represented the fifth vial of Revelation,
and the world was then in the period of the penultimate sixth vial. In
1740 he wrote enthusiastically: 'The New Jerusalem . . . has begun to
come down from heaven, and perhaps never were more of the pre-
libations of heaven's glory given upon earth.'[16] He wrote in 1742 that
the revival '. . . appeared to be the dawning, or at least a prelude, of
that glorious work of God, so often foretold in Scripture, which in the
progress and issue of it, shall renew the world of mankind.'[17]
Edwards,

> . . . asserted that the terrible time of the Church's trials and suffering
> was not still to come, but had already passed . . . Thus Edwards
> brought the Church, in popular expectation, to the dawn of the
> millennium, and made it possible for that millennial expectation to
> become a motive for mission at the end of that century.[18]

---

[14]R. P. Beaver, 'The concert for prayer for missions: an early venture in
ecumenical action', in *The Ecumenical Review* (July 1958), X, 4.
[15]It is sad to report the tensions between David Brainerd and Moravian missionaries, and their disagreements about policy in reaching and serving the Indians.
Zinzendorf considered Brainerd a colonizer. See K.-W. Westmeier, 'Zinzendorf at
Esopus: the apocalyptical missiology of Count Nicolaus Ludwig von Zinzendorf
– a debt to America', *Missiology* 22 (1994), 428. In some ways, Zinzendorf
foreshadowed J. N. Darby in his views on the doom of European Christianity;
this is a topic not touched on by Timothy G. Grass, *The church's ruin and
restoration: the development of ecclesiology in the Plymouth Brethren and the Catholic
Apostolic Church* (Unpublished Ph.D. Dissertation, King's College, London, 1997),
and deserves further research.
[16]Edwards, *Thoughts on the Revival* (1740), 380.
[17]*Ibid.*
[18]Beaver, 'The concert for prayer', 423f. In 1959 Beaver wrote: 'It was in the
middle of the eighteenth century that, on the one hand, there was laid the chief
theological groundwork for later missionary zeal, and, on the other, that missions
became wedded to eschatology for the next century and a half. These developments were both basically due to the writings of Jonathan Edwards . . .' (R. P.
Beaver, 'Eschatology in American Missions', in Jan Hermelink and Hans J.
Margull [eds.], *Basileia: Walter Freytag zum 60 Geburtstag* [Stuttgart: Evangelischer
Missionsverlag, 1959], 60-75, 65). In a yet later article ('Missionary motivation
through three centuries', in Jerald C. Brauer [ed.], *Reinterpretation in American
Church History* [Chicago: University of Chicago Press, 1968]), Beaver says:
'Edwards' *Humble Attempt* stimulated tremendously the eschatological
motivation which had become powerful before the end of the seventeenth
century. The continuing roles of eschatology and apocalyptic expectation require

Northampton and British Missionary Efforts

On 23 April 1784 John Ryland, a young pastor in Northampton, received a parcel of books from Dr John Erskine of Edinburgh. Among them was Edwards' *Humble Attempt* which had a profound effect on Ryland and his friends John Sutcliff of Olney and Andrew Fuller of Kettering. At their Northamptonshire Association meeting in June, Sutcliff proposed a monthly prayer-meeting along Edwards' lines. The idea caught hold, spread quite widely, and by 1789 Sutcliff decided to issue an English edition of Edwards' *Humble Attempt*.[19] The Hickman edition of Edwards' works prints Sutcliff's 1789 Preface;[20] in it he explained that his purpose was to spread the vision for prayer more widely. He did not necessarily agree with every interpretation of Edwards! But he enthusiastically calls: 'Oh for thousands upon thousands, divided into small bands . . . all met at the same time, and in pursuit of one end . . . Grace, great grace be with all them that love the Lord Jesus Christ in sincerity!'

William Carey was one of these young pastors, working in the villages around Northampton: Hackleton, Piddington, Roade, Quinton, Earls Barton, Moulton. He had attended a prayer meeting at Hackleton; travelled to hear Robert Hall preach at Arnesby; he was baptized in Northampton; worked as a shoe-repairer, pastor and teacher in Moulton; and later took a pastorate at Leicester. In the late 1780s he (and his friends) had begun to take leave of the ultra-high Calvinism of the Particular Baptists, and Carey had begun writing a pamphlet about doing something for the heathen. Carey had read Edwards' *Life of David Brainerd*, and he also followed Edwards in believing from his reading in Zechariah that '. . . there shall be an universal conjunction in fervent prayer, and all shall esteem Zion's welfare as their own, (and) then copious influences of the Spirit shall be shed upon the churches . . .' and he believed that he could see already some 'tokens for good'.[21]

---

special attention', which he then proceeds to give them. *Cf.* J. I. Packer, 'Jonathan Edwards and the theology of revival', in *Increasing in the knowledge of God, Report of the Puritan and Reformed Studies Conference*, 1961, 25: 'Edwards . . . looked forward to the conversion of the world; and he confidently predicted that this would be the direct consequence of a mighty revival throughout the whole church, leading to an unprecedented missionary offensive to every quarter of the globe.'

[19]B. Stanley, *The History of the Baptist Missionary Society 1792-1992* (Edinburgh: T. & T. Clark, 1992), 4f.

[20]Edwards, *An Humble Attempt* (1747), 278f.

[21]W. Carey, *An enquiry into the obligations of Christians to use means for the conversion of the heathens* (1792), reprinted with an introduction by E. A. Payne (London: Carey Kingsgate Press, 1961), 78f.

At the Easter 1791 pastors' meeting Carey proposed the formation of a missionary society,[22] which caused considerable discussion; nothing was decided there and then. Carey received encouragement from Samuel Pearce, a Birmingham pastor, fresh from the Bristol Academy, who had himself been inspired by Thomas Coke, Wesley's mission-minded associate. In May, at his ordination into the Leicester church, Carey read to his friends the revised manuscript of his *Enquiry*,[23] and this was later published at 1s.6d. in May 1792. Later that month he preached his famous sermon at Nottingham, and finally in October the Particular Baptist Society for propagating the Gospel among the heathen was formed in Kettering with the princely sum of £13.2s.6d. Carey's name is not on the list of foundation subscribers, Stanley speculates because the half guinea subscription was beyond his limited means.[24]

It is commonplace to begin the story of the modern, western, Protestant missionary era with Carey and the Baptist Missionary Society. The kindling elements of this fire included the Great Awakening, Edwards' writings on revival and on David Brainerd, the prayer-meetings Edwards inspired and encouraged, his hopes for a yet greater outpouring of the Spirit in the end-times, and the feeling that something ought to be *done* for the heathen.

---

[22]In 1742 the well-known, forty-year-old Independent minister, Philip Dod-dridge, had printed some missionary proposals for his Northampton church, asking the question, 'Whether something might not be done, in most of our congregations, towards assisting in the propagation of Christianity abroad, and spreading it in some of the darker parts of our own land?' His proposals came to nothing: his contacts with the Methodists and Moravians, including Zinzendorf, did not fulfil their early promise; and his enthusiasm for Edwards, Brainerd and 'The Society for the Propagation of Christian Knowledge in the Highlands of Scotland, and in popish and infidel Parts of the World' came to nothing because of his early death in 1751. It is tantalizing to have no evidence of the direct influence of Doddridge's thinking on William Carey, although, as S. P. Carey says, 'Doddridge was a household name in his county' (S. P. Carey, *William Carey* [London: Hodder & Stoughton, 1924], 10). See E. A. Payne, 'Doddridge and the missionary enterprise', in Nuttall (ed.), *Philip Doddridge*, 79ff.

[23]Carey, *An enquiry* (1792). Carey refers specifically to 'Edwards on Prayer' as favouring his own personal views about doing something for the conversion of the heathen (12). A close reading of Carey's text shows that Payne misinterprets this passage in his introduction (xii), thinking that it expresses Carey's *doubts* about Edwards' interpretation of prophecy.

[24]Stanley, *Baptist Missionary Society*, 15. Carey's origins were the humblest; a church secretary's minutes in his first charge at Moulton reads: 'Whe met in peas and parted in younity [sic.]' (S. P. Carey, *William Carey*, 47).

Postmillennial Optimism and its Decline

The other side of Edwards' legacy was a patriotic optimism that led to the development of the unstable amalgam called civil millenarianism in America. During America's struggle for independence patriotism and prophecy combined to produce a characteristic brew of interpretations: Lord Bute (from a Scottish island) was the beast from the sea; the Stamp Act was the mark of the beast; King George was the Antichrist; the words 'Royal Supremacy in Great Britain' totalled 666 in Greek and Hebrew.[25] Gradually prophecy speculation was hijacked by patriotic political interests and became secularized. Under the impact of the revolution and its ideas, Edwards' grandson, Timothy Dwight, became an ardent advocate of 'civil millennialism'. 'Arise, shine, for thy light is come,' he exhorted his newly emerging nation enthusiastically, when he was still only twenty-four.

In 1849 an influential American theological periodical asserted that postmillennialism was the 'commonly received doctrine' among American Protestants.[26] In 1854 a Tennessee Methodist minister, Samuel Davies Baldwin, could prove in a 480-page book that the Bible's prophetic references to Israel really meant the United States, and that the timetable of Daniel, correctly interpreted, referred to the interval between the cessation of sacrifices in the temple in AD 68 and 4 July 1776![27] J. P. Philpott in 1864 proved the 'America is Israel' thesis by pointing out that Joseph's son Manasseh had thirteen children, including five girls – which obviously indicated the thirteen colonies, five with female names![28]

Why did this postmillennial consensus break up so quickly? Moorhead suggests that it was 'inherently unstable',[29] combining (early on) a strong sense of natural continuity with a traditional sense of supernatural intervention. However, biblical criticism, distaste and contempt for the genre of apocalyptic and a Ritschlian theology of the kingdom (as a present, ethical reality growing steadily without intrusions) led quite quickly to the view that the New Testament

---

[25]Paul Boyer, *When time shall be no more: prophecy belief in modern American culture,* (Boston: Harvard University Press, 1992), 72.

[26]James H. Moorhead, 'The erosion of postmillennialism in American religious thought, 1865-1925', in *Church History* 53.1 (1984), 61-77, 67. For Britain, David Bebbington (*Evangelicalism in Modern Britain: a history from the 1730s to the 1980s* [London: Unwin Hyman, 1989], 62) says, 'The particular version of (millennial) belief held in the Enlightenment era was uniformly postmillennial.'

[27]Boyer, *When time shall be no more,* 83f.

[28]*Ibid.,* 86. Alexis de Tocqueville observed in the 1830s that American religious and political values were so intertwined as to be inseparable (227).

[29]Moorhead, 'The erosion of postmillennialism', 62.

belief in Jesus' second coming was a mistake, that millennialism was adolescent, and a 'thaumaturgical advent' was not to be expected.

In more personal terms, process was preferred to crisis, conversion was de-emphasized and nurture was emphasized. Death was beatified, and even after death there would be no sudden changes. Thus the evangelical consensus broke up theologically. Meanwhile, society also was changing drastically: there was a proliferation of voluntary organizations, disagreements over slavery, revival(ism) and doctrine, and large-scale secularization. The increasing complexity of urban life and a world war, the rise of social organization on a large scale, the cult of efficiency and the fiasco of the Inter Church Movement after the First World War led to the waning of any sort of supernaturalism or expectation of the miraculous. While evangelicalism was culturally dominant, postmillennialism triumphed; when evangelical influence waned, 'it became the relic of a lost world'.[30]

In the next section I will backtrack and review this process with particular reference to one man.

Premillennial Pessimism and the Rise of Fundamentalism

Arthur Tappan Pierson (1837–1911)

A. T. Pierson was from a New School Presbyterian background. He was licensed to preach (at Binghampton) in April 1860 and married in July of that year. In December that year South Carolina seceded from the Union and on 12 April 1861 the Civil War began. Pierson hoped this would bring about a more Christian America. Before the war, southern Presbyterians tended to be postmillennial in their eschatology; after the war they tended towards a more negative, pessimistic amillennialism or premillennialism[31]. In the north, abolitionism was a decisive prelude to the social gospel.

---

[30]*Ibid.*, 77.

[31]The switch to premillennialism had begun much earlier in Britain; Edward Irving began to stress it in 1827; the repeal of the Test and Corporation Acts in 1828 extended civil rights to non-conformists in 1828; George IV reluctantly signed the Emancipation Act, emancipating Roman Catholics in 1829. The Great Reform bill of 1832 was followed by a cholera outbreak. Soon English Christians were upset by the prospect of the education of Irish children on a non-Protestant basis. How deeply pessimism and social disengagement were related is revealed in a quotation from B. W. Newton: '(Factory children) must suffer and die. The foundations of everything are out of course and no man can rectify them. But we wait for God's Son from heaven.' Quoted in Ian S. Rennie, 'Aspects of Christian

From 1869 to 1883 Pierson was a minister in the mid-West, first in Detroit and then briefly in Indianapolis. His first missions speech (in 1871) showed an emphasis on 'disinterested benevolence', a legacy from Samuel Hopkins. In this period enlightened conservatives were at the forefront of social causes,[32] and it was the urban poor of Detroit who brought Pierson to his first spiritual crisis in 1875. In the following year he met George Müller of Bristol, who later (in about 1878) convinced him to change from a postmillennial eschatology to a premillennial one.[33] According to Dana Robert, Pierson was a first-generation premillennialist 'whose outlook bridged party lines, whose evangelical theology could still be combined with social progressivism'.[34]

In the decade of the 1880s Pierson's involvement in an extraordinarily diverse range of activities in a large, socially engaged, institutional church (Bethany, Philadelphia) *and* in foreign missions increased substantially. Pierson's first commitment was to the Presbyterian Church of the United States (from which he was ousted in 1896 at the age of fifty-nine, after thirty-six years of ministry, following his baptism by James Spurgeon). His friendship with D. L. Moody led to participation in Moody's Northfield Conferences, which were immensely strategic in the development of the student missionary movement. In 1886 he wrote *The crisis of missions* and in 1887 he became the editor of *Missionary Review of the World*, a post which he held until his death in 1911. He held together in his person and ministry on the one hand urban ministry, a stress on Christian unity, denominational loyalty, social action and confident enthusiasm with, on the other hand, a concern for evangelism, prayer, the centrality of the Bible, friendship with interdenominational organizations and a sense of eschatological urgency.

Brethren spirituality', in J. I. Packer and Loren Wilkinson (eds.), *Alive to God: Studies in spirituality, presented to James Houston* (Downers Grove: InterVarsity Press, 1992), 201. See also Grass, *The church's ruin and restoration*, 15ff.

[32]Dana L. Robert, *Arthur Tappan Pierson and forward movements of the late 19th century* (Unpublished Ph.D. dissertation, Yale University, 1984), 85.

[33]Müller became a close friend, and the two prayed for each other daily until Müller died in 1898. Pierson's own words about his change of view were as follows: 'Mr Müller listened patiently to my objections and then said, with his celestial smile: "The only thing I can say is that none of your arguments are founded on *Scripture*. It makes no difference what we think but what does God's Word say?" For ten days he came to my study every day and opened up the truth to me. Ever since that time I have been looking for the Lord's personal return and it has been the inspiration of my life.' Quoted in Delavan L. Pierson, *Arthur T. Pierson: A biography* (London: James Nisbet, 1912), 143.

[34]Robert, *Arthur Tappan Pierson*, 130.

In the 1890s this coalition of causes began to splinter. As the end of the century approached, there were more strident calls for the completion of 'The evangelisation of the world in this generation' (the Watchword, about which I say a bit more below); Pierson played down his premillennial mission theory and painted rosy and action-packed pictures of the church's success in mission. But 'he privately believed that efforts to convert the world were doomed to failure'.[35] Theological toleration became harder, especially after the Centenary Conference of the Protestant Missions of the World in London in 1888, and more so after the World Parliament of Religions in Chicago in 1893, at which Pierson gave a strong, premillennial speech to a pluralistic audience.[36] Pierson's international and interdenominational work brought tensions with the Presbyterian Church of the USA.

Pierson attended the 'Make Jesus King' conference in Liverpool in 1896 and gave an address on the Watchword.[37] Troubles followed his baptism in February 1896. Beginning in 1897 he visited Keswick every year, and his interests shifted towards Keswick spirituality and Bible exposition and writing about the Bible. He was associated with nine Bible schools, mostly premillennial. He was a premillennial dispensationalist, probably (like his friend, A. J. Gordon) of a post-tribulational kind. The split between pre- and post-tribulationism destroyed the Niagara Bible Conferences; the last one was held in 1900. He was one of the seven original consulting editors of the Schofield Reference Bible, published in 1909. But his talks about the End were poetic rather than precise, and he was not a consistent believer in the ruin of the church.

Dana Robert suggests that the mixture of biblical literalism, holiness theology, cultural obscurantism, political conservatism and premillennial pessimism were the constituents of what was later called fundamentalism; some of Pierson's articles were printed in *The*

---

[35]*Ibid.*, 232.

[36]*Ibid.*, 302. See also *Missionary Review of the World* (November 1893), 802.

[37]The title of the conference might lead one to presume that there would be an overheated atmosphere of 'Evangelize to a finish to bring back the King.' But this is not so. In 1889, 500 Japanese students gathered at a conference had sent a telegram to the Northfield Students' Conference in North America, with the words 'Make Jesus King.' A whole series of conferences followed with this as their theme. Pierson gave four talks at the conference, one on 'The plan of God in the ages'; one on prayer; one on the Holy Spirit; and one on the Watchword. His addresses are marked, even at the age of fifty-eight, by a certain wistfulness that he was not himself a missionary. See *Report of the international students' missionary conference, Liverpool, January 1-5, 1896* (London, Student Volunteer Missionary Union, 1896), 19-26 and 178-183.

Fundamentals.[38] But Pierson did not live long enough to become a *bona fide* fundamentalist. *The Missionary Review of the World* had a wide scope and was ecumenically oriented. It was anti-racist, but pro-Zionist, and showed a concern for American Indians. It was socially progressive, not blindly conservative. Pierson mirrored in his own life and history the break-up of the earlier postmillennial consensus, a breakup mirrored also in the differing interpretations of the Watchword.

The Watchword: Evangelization of the World in this Generation
Clifton Phillips remarks, somewhat acerbically,

> The much-flaunted watchword, no matter how variously interpreted, served to epitomize the optimistic self-confidence of a rapidly expanding Anglo-Saxon empire which was bringing both the virtues and the vices of Western civilization to bear on 'backward races' and non-Christian societies all over the face of the earth.[39]

As I have reviewed again the story of how this watchword took hold of a whole generation of students, I have been impressed by the lives of many whom it touched. Robert Wilder, who was finally persuaded to tell the story, and his part in it, in 1936,[40] was a quiet man, who experienced repeated bouts of ill-health. He was convinced that the simultaneous stirring in five countries, which gave rise to the student missionary movement, was a work of God. As the story unfolds, it is very clear that the whole movement developed in an atmosphere of revival, prayer, intense Bible study, much information and openness to the Holy Spirit.

The actual origin of the Watchword itself is slightly complicated. At the famous Mount Hermon Conference in July 1886, A. T. Pierson had given a talk entitled 'All should go and go to all', and his name has been specially linked to the Watchword.[41] But already Royal Wilder, Robert's father, had written in *The Missionary Review* of 1878, 'The life-time of one generation is all the time available for

[38](Chicago, 1910-1915).
[39]T. Christensen and W. R. Hutchinson, *Missionary Ideologies in the Imperialist Era: 1880-1920* (Aarhus: Aros, 1982), 135.
[40]Robert Wilder, *The great commission: the missionary response of the student volunteer movements in North America and Europe: some personal reminiscences* (London: Oliphant, 1936).
[41]He was the leading proponent of the idea (of the Watchword) and the author of a pivotal article in *Missionary Review of the World*, 1881, entitled 'Can the world be evangelized in twenty years?' (Justin Long, Global Evangelization Movement email letter, 14 February 1997).

evangelizing that generation.'[42] In the year previous to this, at the
Shanghai conference of Protestant missionaries in China, the report of
the committee on appeal to the churches had finished off with the
stirring words, 'We want China emancipated from the thraldom of
sin in this generation.'[43] Later, in his defence of the Watchword at the
ecumenical missionary conference in New York in 1900 John R. Mott
extended the pedigree of the Watchword back even further.[44]

Wilder's conviction and commitment were contagious.[45] But
when one reads the reports of the various conferences on both sides
of the Atlantic, there is not a lot of end-times rhetoric. The motives
that are mentioned again and again are the Lord's command, human
need,[46] the reflex effect of missions on the home church; and then
some such words as those of the dying Simeon Calhoun, 'It is my
deep conviction, and I say it again and again, that if the Church of

---

[42]Wilder, *The great commission*, 84.

[43]*Records of the general conference of the Protestant missionaries of China, Shanghai*
(Presbyterian Mission Press, 1878) 478.

[44]'. . . was it not Gordon Hall and Samuel Newell, who in 1818 issued an appeal
to Christians to evangelize the world within a generation? Did not the
missionaries of the Sandwich islands, in 1836, unite in a most impressive appeal
to the Church to preach the gospel to every creature within their generation? Did
not the Shanghai Missionary Conference of 1877 express its desire to have China
emancipated from the thraldom of sin in this generation, and its belief that it
might be done?' (*Report of the Ecumenical Conference on Foreign Missions, New York,
1900* [London: Religious Tract Society, 1900], I, 102). Dana Robert draws attention
to the fact that Pierson himself in an 1891 article refers to something written by
Joseph Angus in 1871. Probably this was a sermon before the Baptist Missionary
Society, delivered on 26 April 1871, in which Angus said, 'The Christians of each
age are to give the Gospel to the people of that age. Every Christian is to tell the
good news to everyone he can reach; and Christians collectively are to tell it, if
they can, to all the world' (D. Robert, 'The origin of the Student Volunteer
Watchword "The evangelization of the world in this generation"', in *International
Bulletin for Missionary Research* 10.4 [1986], 146-149, 14).

[45]Wilder reports: 'Samuel M. Zwemer, the well-known missionary to Moslems,
who volunteered during the year (1886) says that he received the missionary
contagion when sleeping one night in the same bed with me' (Wilder, *The great
commission*, 24).

[46]Wilder refers to a Frederick Curtis, who signed the pledge in 1844, and later
worked for forty years in Japan: 'John Forman said, "I know what ails Curtis; he
sleeps under a chart containing 856 black squares representing 856,000,000
heathen and 170 green squares representing 170,000,000 Mohammedans. Anyone
sleeping under a chart like that must decide to be a missionary or have a
nightmare every night of the week"' (*ibid.*, 16). I have a black and white copy of
an enlarged chart with 1434 squares, in the book *Prophetic studies of the international prophetic conference, Chicago, November 1886* (Chicago: Fleming H. Revell,
1886), 203.

Christ were what she ought to be, twenty years would not pass away
till the story of the Cross would be uttered in the ears of every living
man.'[47] Wilder politely notes that English students were more
conservative than American students, that they thought Americans
were 'below par' and that 'subterranean' methods were needed to get
the same message across in Britain. Nevertheless, the 1896 SVMU
Conference adopted the Watchword.

Wilder notes that there was considerable criticism of the
Watchword by 1912; and that by 1921 it was 'dead, though a certain
sentiment clung to it'.[48] Nevertheless, John R. Mott continued to
defend the Watchword right into the 1930s. He campaigned under
the Watchword umbrella for international and ecumenical unity;
Robert Speer used the Watchword mainly in challenging people to
greater individual dedication; Sherwood Eddy, the least remembered
of these three, became known as another 'world-wandering social
gospel evangelist to students'.[49] The old combination of evangelistic
proclamation and social engagement was breaking up, and variant
eschatological views were a significant demolition instrument: the
more optimistic, idealistic and socially engaged people were tending
towards liberal theology and the 'social gospel'; the more pessimistic,
conservative and introverted were caught up with defending the
truth, living lives of holiness and preaching the gospel. In the
Liverpool meetings of 1912 William Temple argued '. . . that England
and Europe, which were half-Christian, half-pagan, would have the
power to convert the rest of the world only in so far as they
themselves were to become truly Christian'.[50]

---

[47]Wilder, *The great commission*, 40.

[48]*Ibid.*, 88. See Clifton Phillips' contribution in Christensen and Hutchinson,
Missionary Ideologies, 131ff. Sherwood Eddy repudiated the slogan in the SVM
Conference in Detroit at Christmas 1928 and substituted 'world christianization'
which meant, according to one observer, 'a comprehensive gospel in all the
social, economic and political implications that the most advanced prophets have
been preaching since the days of Rauschenbusch'. Quoted in Joel A. Carpenter
and Wilbert R. Shenk, *Earthen vessels: American Evangelicals and Foreign Missions
1880-1980* (Grand Rapids: Eerdmans, 1990), 95.

[49]Denton Lotz, '"The evangelisation of the world in this generation": the re-
surgence of a missionary idea among the conservative evangelicals',
(Unpublished Ph.D. Dissertation, Hamburg University, 1970), 30.

[50]Clifton Phillips in Christensen and Hutchinson, *Missionary Ideologies,* 139.

Recent Shifts in Thinking Regarding Missions and Eschatology

The Great Reversal
David Bebbington asserts:

> The hundred years or so before the First World War . . . deserve to
> be called the Evangelical century. In that period the activism of the
> movement enabled it to permeate British society. Righteousness, as
> Evangelicals might have put it, abounded in the land. Major inroads
> were made on the existing mass of religious indifference.[51]

But towards the end of this period the combination of evangelistic and social energy was already breaking up, as we have seen
in the life and engagements of A. T. Pierson, for a variety of reasons.
Premillennial pessimism and separatism had significantly affected
sections of the church, from the time of E. Irving and J. N. Darby.[52]
Bebbington notes that 'the denominations most affected by Fundamentalism were those most touched by adventism'.[53] He also notes
that futurists, in contrast to historicists, were less concerned with
historical details, and more concerned with the intricacies of
Scripture, and thus removed from commitment to mission. *The
Fundamentals* were published between 1910 and 1915, although the
controversy as such came to a climax after the First World War.[54]
Although this was less virulent in the UK than in the USA, it would
be a mistake to say that the UK was unaffected. Examples of
representative conflicts would be the controversy over the Wesleyan
lecturer at Didsbury, George Jackson, in 1913; the Bible Churchmen's
Missionary Society split from the Church Missionary Society in 1922;
and the ousting of J. Stuart Holden as Keswick chairman in 1928. The
Civil War in the USA had led to serious polarization among
evangelicals; the First World War and the Russian Revolution had
radically deepened arguments about socialism; and Keswick holiness

---

[51]Bebbington, *Evangelicalism*, 149.
[52]See Roy F. Coad, *Prophetic developments with particular reference to the early
Brethren movement* (Christian Brethren Research Fellowship, 1966), and Grass,
The church's ruin and restoration.
[53]Bebbington, *Evangelicalism*, 190.
[54]Sandeen distinguishes the fundamentalist *movement* and the fundamentalist
controversy (E. R. Sandeen, *The roots of fundamentalism: British and American
millenarianism 1800-1930* [Chicago, 1970], 160). His opinion is that the 1919
World's Conference on Christian Fundamentals was the turning point, where
millenarians became fundamentalists.

teaching and its corollaries had produced a lot of aristocratic intro-
version, although there was still a significant emphasis on mission as
well through the convention.[55] Other factors include changing views
of churchmanship and tradition; fast and furious debates on the
relationship between science and religion; and controversy over
ecumenical engagement.

The Reversal Reversed

At about the same time, fifty years ago, as the Tyndale Fellowship for
Biblical Research was getting under way,[56] and a year before the
World Council of Churches was founded in Amsterdam, a young
American professor wrote a slight volume which has turned out to be
pivotal. The title was revealing: *The uneasy conscience of
fundamentalism.*[57] Henry was an example of a new sort of evangelical
emerging in America. His language sounds today somewhat quaint
and archaic, but his tributary of concerns has become today's mainstream. He indicted fundamentalism as 'the modern priest and
Levite, bypassing suffering humanity'.[58] He noted that there was a
growing awareness in fundamentalist circles that 'evangelical Christianity has become increasingly inarticulate about the social reference
of the gospel'.[59] He was particularly eloquent about the embarrassing
divorce between evangelical Christianity and great social reform
movements; he criticized fundamentalism for its loss of a Catholic
Calvinist vision for the whole of life; and he was particularly succinct
in his summary of fundamentalist preoccupation with the intricacies
of the kingdom *then* which had led to the neglect of commitment to,
and mission for the kingdom *now*. He called for a new programme:
an all-inclusive, redemptive context for evangelicals' assault on the
world's ills; total opposition to moral evils, social and personal; and
the offer of a higher ethical standard with Christ providing the
needed energy for these transformations.[60]

---

[55]For example, W. H. T. Gairdner and J. H. Oldham heard R. E. Speer speak at
Keswick in 1894. Gairdner wrote, 'Speer simply God-inspired. . . never heard
anything like it. Joe Oldham and I walk up the road and give ourselves to God.'
Quoted in Timothy Yates, *Christian mission in the twentieth century* (Cambridge:
Cambridge University Press, 1996), 23.
[56]See F. F. Bruce, 'The Tyndale Fellowship for Biblical Research', *Evangelical
Quarterly*, 19 (1947), 52-61.
[57]Carl F. Henry, *The uneasy conscience of fundamentalism* (Grand Rapids:
Eerdmans, 1947).
[58]*Ibid.*, 17.
[59]*Ibid.*, 26.
[60]*Ibid.*, 76. Richard Lovelace was later (in 1979) to publish a much more detailed
review of the important factors leading to a dynamic, engaged orthodoxy:

More Recent Changes

It is hard to believe that it is already fifty years since Henry's little book was published. With hindsight one can see that it presaged a huge shift in evangelical thinking. Most decisive was a shift to this-worldly concerns. We can see this shift taking place in ecumenical thinking in the events leading up to the merger of the International Missionary Council with the WCC at New Delhi in 1961; and the renaming of the *International Review of Missions* as the *International Review of Mission*. In evangelical circles we can see this shift happening through the conferences of the 1960's, of which those at Wheaton, Illinois and Berlin were most influential. We can see shadows of these shifts taking place in the Roman Catholic church through the documents emerging from Vatican II. Perhaps the most striking symbol of this shift of thinking has been the enormous growth of TEAR Fund, which was founded in 1968 and now has a budget of about £20 million per annum. The rising prominence of theologians from the two-thirds world, and their impatience with the dichotomistic thinking of western evangelicals, has been a major factor in this shift, which we can trace most clearly in the Lausanne and inter-Lausanne conferences, and in Lausanne publications, with their demands for, and struggles about integral evangelism or holistic evangelism.[61]

When I was a student in the early 60s I became the missionary secretary of a famous Christian Union with a long history of missionary commitment. There was a special section of the Christian Union with a pledge that 'It is my purpose, if God permits, to serve him in the foreign field.' But the ability and the inclination to make such pledges was ebbing away at the time. It is interesting to look back and peruse a book on missions that was highly influential

---

'Authentic spiritual renewal leads to social and cultural transformation; there is no deep and lasting social change without spiritual awakening; and evangelicals must stress more than church growth and evangelism if they are to duplicate the social triumphs of earlier periods' (*Dynamics of spiritual life: an evangelical theology of renewal* [Downers Grove: InterVarsity Press, 1979]).

[61]Here is a representative voice from the two-thirds world: '. . . I submit that the ultimate test of any theological discourse is not erudite precision but transformative power. It is a question of whether or not theology can articulate the faith in a way that is not only intellectually sound but spiritually energizing and therefore capable of leading the people of God to be transformed in their way of life and to commit themselves to God's mission in the world. As the apostle Paul reminded the Corinthian church many years ago, "The kingdom of God is not talk but power"' (Orlando Costas in Carpenter and Shenk, *Earthen Vessels*, 250).

among students at that time,[62] and to see what the dominant themes of this book were: they were revolution, nationalism, communism, ecumenical Christianity, racism, non-professional (later called bi-vocational) service, cities, students and communications. There was no theological reflection in this book at all. Discussion of eschatological themes was completely absent.

This trend has continued. Interest has shifted away from prophetic issues almost entirely; it is impossible to imagine that a 'prophetic conference' like those held a hundred years ago would draw thousands of participants. There is one exception to this general trend and this is the so-called 'AD 2000 Movement'. This movement consciously harks back to the calls at the end of the last century for the evangelization of the world.[63] Tremendous efforts are being made by all sorts of organizations with all sorts of plans, and with the expenditure of millions of dollars, to reach the unreached before the end of the century.[64] The proliferation of these plans, with their very narrow focus has aroused the criticism of some two-thirds world theologians, who have found this movement insufficiently attentive to larger issues of church and society.[65]

Debates about whether the Lord will return imminently or suddenly or after a specific series of events do not arouse the same degree of interest as before.[66] A. B. Simpson taught that we could

[62]Eric S. Fife and Arthur F. Glasser, *Missions in Crisis* (Downers Grove: InterVarsity Press, 1962).

[63]See Todd Johnson, 1988. The most recent book I have seen in this general area is Jim Montgomery, *Then the end will come: great news about the great commission* (Pasadena: William Carey Library, 1997). The title, of course, is a direct allusion to Matthew 24:14. The book is a headlong rush through a cataract of evangelistic and church-planting projects around the world. The last chapter is entitled 'Then the end will come . . .' and in it Montgomery refers back to a friend mentioned in the first chapter who couldn't find any date in his Bible beyond the date AD 2009.

[64]See David Barrett and James W. Reapsome, *Seven hundred plans to evangelize the world: the rise of a global evangelization movement* (Birmingham, Alabama: New Hope Press, 1988). Weekly and even daily reports can be found at numerous internet sites. By 2 July 1997, 16,790 people had visited the website <http://www.ad2000.org>.

[65]See the discussion prompted by Samuel Escobar's article 'A movement divided: three approaches to world evangelization stand in tension with one another', in *Transformation*, 8.4 (1991).

[66]This is probably not correct for North America. Hal Lindsey's book *Late great planet earth*, published in 1970, had 9 million copies in print by 1978 and 28 million by 1990. Armageddon has been a growth industry. Newsweek talked about the Doom Boom in 1977. Rocket scientists and statisticians do still produce 'proofs' that the world is going to end in 1988 or 1989 or . . . But still my impression is that insistence on particular eschatological views as a precondition

speed up Christ's return by world evangelization, and one of the slogans of C. T. Studd, the founder of WEC International was 'To evangelize the world and have Christ back.'[67] The urgency which the imminence of Christ's return lent to the task of evangelization has ebbed considerably in the last fifty years.[68]

Religious pluralism has made Christians far less certain than they were that the unevangelized will fall straight into hell when they die. In 1894 Hudson Taylor addressed the SVM conference in Detroit memorably with the words, 'There is a great Niagara of souls passing into the dark in China . . . Every day, every week, every month they are passing away! A million a month in China are dying without God.'[69] I have discovered among contemporary students that they are not likely to feel this as a missionary imperative; they are more likely to consider it a problem for theodicy.[70]

Hunter has documented the shift in thinking about hell as well. The affirmation of old orthodoxies and certainties is less certain and definitely less detailed. Jonathan Edwards' famous sermon, *Sinners in the hands of an angry God*, is incomprehensible to many. Statements like 'The hottest parts of hell are reserved for those who have had an opportunity to hear about the Saviour but have not heeded him. There is less severe punishment for the ones in China and elsewhere who have never had a chance to hear about Jesus'[71] would cause embarrassment. Long muted defences of annihilation or conditional immortality have come to the fore, despite assertions that

---

of fellowship is decreasing. Interest in what Hans Schwarz called 'travelogue eschatologies' has declined – see Gabriel Fackre, *The Christian story: a narrative interpretation of basic Christian doctrine* (Grand Rapids: Eerdmans, 1984), 223.

[67]Quoted in K. Fiedler, *The story of faith missions: from Hudson Taylor to present day Africa* (Oxford: Regnum Books, 1994), 277.

[68]Charles van Engen notes that the 1966 Wheaton Declaration cites the eschatological theme, 'but no longer with the frantic eschatological instrumentality of a bygone era' (Carpenter and Shenk, *Earthen vessels*, 214).

[69]Quoted in *ibid.*, 285.

[70]Peter Cotterell confronts this issue in *Mission and meaninglessness: the good news in a world of suffering and disorder* (London: SPCK, 1990), chap. 6. Hunter noticed the shift of thinking among evangelical seminarians; some appeared to hold '. . . that some form of alternative arrangement is provided for those not exposed to the truths of Christianity. God's dealings with the unevangelized are somehow different from his dealings with those who have heard' (James D. Hunter, *Evangelicalism: the coming generation* [Chicago: University of Chicago Press, 1987], 35).

[71]J. K. Moreland, *Millways of Kent* (Chapel Hill, University of North Carolina Press, 1958), quoted in Hunter, *Evangelicalism*, 35.

to minimize the terrors of hell would diminish the sense of responsibility and urgency in evangelization.[72]

Amidst all these debates, with the energy they consume and produce, sensitive Christians are conscious they live in a disordered world of great polarities.[73] The disorders may be hard-to-understand personal tragedies or genocidal conflicts, aided and abetted by the great powers, on a mind-numbing scale. Because of the media and the internet, even without travelling anywhere we have more details about these events more promptly than ever before.

Missionaries, with the Christians they seek to serve, or with those whom they are trying to win, often (not always) live in the border-zone of the conflict between 'the kingdoms of our LORD and of his Christ' and 'the kingdoms of this world'. Often, too, they are conscious of the groaning of the whole creation, for there is a wide correlation between the least-evangelized parts of the world and the areas of greatest poverty. Images spring to mind – of the killing fields of Cambodia; of bodies in their hundreds clogging the rivers of Rwanda; of refugee tents and desperate people clinging to barren, volcanic rock; of a line of Zambian women hoeing soil in a cloud of dust, hoping for rain which never comes.

In reaction to these scenes some hopelessly, hand-wringingly withdraw; others with anger and tears attempt to put a finger in the dyke of suffering. Others, more fortunate and at a greater distance, come up with ideas and schemes that have something genuinely beautiful, something Christ-like about them: a millennial jubilee scheme for the remission of the worst debts of the poorest countries; a 900th anniversary walk through countries devastated by the first Crusade, to confess sorrow and to confess Christ.

---

[72]This is a topic which can only be approached with what Packer calls traumatic awe and passionate sadness; or as John Stott indicates, with great reluctance, a heavy heart and with tears. For the details, see John Wenham, *The goodness of God* (London, Inter-Varsity Press, 1974), chap. 2; J. R. W. Stott in David L. Edwards with John Stott, *Essentials: a liberal-evangelical dialogue* (London: Hodder & Stoughton, 1988), 312ff.; J. I. Packer, 'The problem of eternal punishment', *Crux* 26 (1990), 18-25; and N. M. de S. Cameron, *Universalism and the doctrine of hell* (Carlisle: Paternoster Press, 1992). Philip Hughes, in *True image: the origin and destiny of man in Christ* (Grand Rapids: Eerdmans, 1989), 407, insists that: 'Though held by many, it is a hollow contention that if the death sentence pronounced at the final judgement against the unregenerate meant their annihilation the wicked would be getting off lightly and would be encouraged to regard the consequences of their sin without fear.'

[73]See Peter Cotterell, *Disaster and disorder: the human predicament* (C. R. Batten lecture, 1989, to the London Baptist Preachers' Association).

Walter Brueggemann concludes his book *The prophetic imagination* with a chapter on the practice of ministry. He speaks of the two-fold intention of the Moses movement: to dismantle the oppressive empire of Pharaoh and to form a new community focused on God's freedom, justice and compassion. 'The dismantling begins in the groans and laments of his people; the energising begins in the doxologies of the new community.'[74] It was Jesus our Lord who announced that in Himself, in His life and words and works, the kingdom had arrived; He also taught us to pray 'Your kingdom come.' He is the focal point of all mission and all eschatology.[75]

'Christ Jesus is our hope' (1 Tim. 1:1). All of those who know something of what Dante called 'the thirst, which is instilled into us at our creation, and which never leaves us, for the kingdom whose maker is God'[76] are inspired and energized to love and serve this Lord by the conviction that the hopes of which we already have some foretastes of fulfilment, will one day be fulfilled beyond our wildest dreams.

---

[74]W. Brueggemann, *The prophetic imagination* (Philadelphia: Fortress Press, 1978). N. T. Wright also uses this powerful image of exile as a basic motif in his book, *Jesus and the victory of God* (London: SPCK, 1996).

[75]'. . . the heart of eschatology is not when or what but who, not a schedule or a plan but a person. The gospels move us to contemplate the future not by giving us a blueprint but by relating all to Jesus, Messiah and Son of man.' So, D. C. Allison Jr., in Joel B. Green, Scott McKnight and I. H. Marshall (eds.), *Dictionary of Jesus and the gospels* (Leicester: Inter-Varsity Press, 1992), 209.

[76]Dante, *Paradiso*, II, 19f.

Chapter 16

'THE SEASONS' OF THIS LIFE AND ESCHATOLOGY IN 1 CORINTHIANS 7:29-31

Bruce W. Winter

Attitudes towards what the writer of the book of Ecclesiastes called 'the seasons' of life are profoundly influenced by the perceptions of the nature of the world in which we live. This was no less true in Paul's day where the predominant view of the eternity of the present world and the immortality of the soul provided the framework in which life's important issues were resolved. In 1 Corinthians 7:29-31 Paul provides an eschatological framework for judging matters relating to marriage, sorrow, joy, careers and a correct attitude to the present world. In doing this he connects eschatology with aspects of the seasons of life and provides an enduring framework for Christians who face the same temptation to respond to the seasons of life with other world-views.

Introduction

The nexus between eschatology and ethics provides a key in helping Christians to come to terms with some of the complex issues of their present existence. This final chapter explores a largely neglected aspect of how Paul used eschatology as a pastoral framework for ·handling the immediate and long-term perplexing dilemmas facing Christians in Corinth, and examines briefly its importance for our own situations.

Paul's discussion of the implications of eschatology for the Corinthian Christians (1 Cor. 7:29-31) occurs in the context of a request for a ruling by young men and women who were betrothed. Their dilemma was whether to marry or remain as they were because of the problems created by what Paul describes as 'the present difficulties' in Corinth (1 Cor. 7:26). Up to this point in 1 Corinthians 7 he has provided an important context for the discussion of a number of issues, namely, God's individual gift of singleness or marriedness and His wider callings for individual Christians (7:7, 17-24).[1] He now adds a further perspective from which this problem must be considered.

In foreshadowing the criteria by which those involved will have to make up their own minds (7:27-28a; *cf.* 7:36-37), Paul inserts this new perspective for Christian decision-making early on in his discussion. It is one which radically transforms the perceptions of issues well beyond the one under immediate discussion. In 7:30-31 Paul refers to some of the matters which the ancient preacher in the book of Ecclesiastes called 'the seasons' of life (3:1ff.).

It is proposed to examine, first, the predominant ideological or philosophical view of the nature of the world and destiny of humankind, in the light of which such decisions would have been made in pre-Christian days. We will then consider the contrasting eschatological framework in which Christians were now encouraged to think, followed by the implications for this new world-view on matters relating to marriage, the sorrows and joys of life, and the making of money, all of which were to be determined by a correct 'use' of the present world whose form was 'passing away'. In the concluding section, the implications of eschatology for some of 'the seasons' of life will be discussed over against some popular contemporary Christian thinking which appears to have more in common with the spirit of our age than with the biblical perspective.

The Eternity of the World

While studies in social sciences, and anthropology in particular, attribute to 'culture' different attitudes towards the world in which we live, underlying them are belief systems which go to the heart of perceptions upon which the important decisions of life are made. In the city of Corinth, two systems competed for the minds of the nascent Christian community. One was so ingrained in the thinking of those who were brought up in this highly sophisticated Roman colony, which was the centre of 'Romanitas' in the province of Achaea, that it was regarded as *ipso facto* true. How it worked itself out in 'the way things were done' was not always consciously linked by the Corinthians with that belief system, although a clear nexus can

---

[1]See my '1 Corinthians 7:6-7 – A Caveat and a Framework for "the Sayings" in 7:8-24', *TynB* 48.1 (May, 1997), 57-65.

be established. Another world-view had more recently been embraced by Christians. Its implications for the 'big' issues of life were not clear. The fact that the Corinthians wrote to Paul for rulings on certain pressing matters indicates that, as in the case of young men and women (7:25ff.), they wished to understand what they should do on the basis of their new view of the reality of the world.

The Philosophical Discussion

In the first century, sophisticated arguments surrounded the issue of the eternity of the world, and nowhere is this more so than in Philo's *De Aeternitate mundi*.[2] He himself makes it clear that three traditional views had been entertained in philosophical discussion.

> Some assert that the world is eternal, uncreated and imperishable. Some on the contrary say that it is created and destructible. Others draw from both these. For the latter they take the idea of the created, from the former that of the indestructible and so have laid down a composite doctrine to the effect that the world is created and indestructible (*Aet.* 7).

According to Philo the first perception was that of Aristotle (384-322 BC) (*Aet.* 10), while the second view was supported by Democritus (b. *c.* 460 BC), Epicurus (341-270 BC) and the majority of the Stoic philosophers (*Aet.* 8–9). Plato had argued that the world was 'created and indestructible' (*Aet.* 13). Philo personally believed that 'the cosmos has been created and should in theory come to an end, but is preserved from destruction by the will and providence of the creator'.[3] In the alternative range of possibilities discussed by the ancient philosophers, Philo's view has more in common with Plato's. Given the nature of the discussion in Philo's important philosophical

---

[2]Some of the misreading of this text has arisen from a failure to take cognizance of the fact that Philo structured his discussion along the lines of what was technically called a 'thesis' which fully examined the arguments for and against an idea. D. T. Runia, in an incisive essay, 'Philo's *De Aeternitate mundi*: The Problem of its Interpretation', *Vig.C.* 35 (1981), 105-151, laid to rest the view that Philo contradicted himself within this particular philosophical treatise compared with his view consistently expressed elsewhere in his corpus. For a summary of the discussion, see D. T. Runia, *Philo of Alexandria and the Timaeus of Plato* (Leiden: E. J. Brill, 1986), 394-396.

[3]Philo's *De Aeternitate mundi*, 132.

work, it emerges that a predominant view of his own day filtered down into what A. Dihle had designated the *Vulgärethik*.[4]

After the collapse of the Roman Republic, the philosophical concept of a lasting world was re-enforced by the political propaganda indicating that the commencement of the Empire was, in effect, the beginning of a lasting *Reich*. The actual birthday of its first Principate, Augustus, was declared to be 'the equivalent to the beginning of all things'.[5] He had given it permanence as well as the *Pax Romana*, and this could only re-enforce the concept of the continuity of the 'ordered world' (κόσμος).

The Architectural Replication

Recent studies in 'social' architecture have drawn attention to the fact that town planning and the buildings that comprise a city reflect historical and philosophical values, as well as the ongoing human propensity to impose a sense of order on life which reflects value systems. This is most clearly demonstrated in the effect of postmodernism upon buildings, but is no less true, although perhaps not quite as obvious, in the history of architecture. This is certainly the case for the Roman Empire.[6] They ardently believed in an ordered world, a *kosmos* (κόσμος), and the systematic planning of their cities and design of their buildings reflected their ideological view of the nature of things.

For example, in town planning, the Romans adopted the orderly grid system in laying out their cities. The very city to which Paul wrote 1 Corinthians is a good example of the replication of the orderliness of the natural world in the plan for this new colony, surveyed and laid out in 44 BC.[7] The concept was borrowed from the

---

[4]For an appreciation of Dihle's vast work in this field, see E. A. Judge, '"Antike und Christentum" – Some Recent Research from Cologne', *Prudentia* V.1 (1973), 1-113.

[5]Cited in S. R. F. Price, *Rituals and Power* (Cambridge: Cambridge University Press, 1984), 54-56.

[6]For a general discussion, see J. Metzler, M. Millett, N. Roymans and J. Slofstra (eds.), *Integration in the Early Roman West: The Role of Culture and Ideology* (Luxembourg: Musée National d'Histoire et d'Art, 1995).

[7]For a discussion of the recent recovery of the layout of Corinth based on the traditional grid system, see D. G. Romano, 'Post-146 BC Land Use in Corinth and Planning of the Roman Colony', in T. E. Gregory (ed.), *The Corinthia in the Roman Period*, Journal of Roman Archaelogy Supp. Series 8 (1993), 9-30.

Greeks, who likewise were committed to both the eternity and orderliness of the *kosmos*.[8]

Roman architecture also signalled the same ideological commitment to the symmetry of buildings as well as the layout of city streets. The towering 'tree-like' columns and the ceilings of major buildings, reproducing the natural world in stone, re-enforced an ideological statement about the nature of this world.

The Roman writer, Vitruvius, who produced his work *De architectura* at the end of the Republic, recognised that this subject matter touched not only buildings, but also everything that related to the physical and intellectual life of humankind and its surroundings. It was for this reason that he begins his work with a discussion of first importance, namely, 'The training of architects' (I.1) and includes in the curriculum the study of philosophy. He does this not only because it makes an architect 'high-minded' and not money-minded, but also makes him focus on 'the nature of things' (I.7).[9]

The Personal Continuity

There was also an *a priori* assumption that eternity also rested in the human person with the ancient doctrine of the immortality of the soul. While the first century did not follow Plato's doctrine that the body was the prison-house of the soul, continuity after death was firmly established as part of the folk religion. The important question was, 'What difference did the doctrine of the immortality of the soul make to the way one perceived the present activities of life?' A verbatim presentation of the implications of the immortality of the soul for the present contrasts this disparagingly with another view, namely, a Jewish one. Philo repeats the view of his opponents, the sophists, in his discussion, 'The Worse overcomes the Better' (32-34).

The passage begins with a series of questions, the first one of which had modified Plato's view: 'Is not the body the soul's house?' (not a 'prison-house'). It is followed by another: 'Why, then, should we not take care of a house, that it may not fall into ruins?' The argument then changes from the analogy of 'house' to 'bodyguards and friends': 'Are not the eyes and ears and the band of the other senses bodyguards and friends, as it were, of the soul?' 'Therefore

---

[8]J. B. Ward-Perkins, 'Hippodamos and the Classical Greek City', *Cities of Ancient Greece and Italy: Planning in Classical Antiquity* (London: Sidgwick and Jackson, 1974), chap. 3.

[9]Bk. 9, *Preface* 17-18. He refers elsewhere to Lucretius, *The Nature of Things*, as he acknowledges (9.17). For a wide-ranging discussion, see J. C. Anderson Jr., *Roman Architecture and Society* (Baltimore and London: Johns Hopkins University, 1997), esp. chap. 1, 'The Roman Architects'.

must we not value our allies and friends equally with ourselves?' he says, pushing the argument further. The next statement moves away from Plato to philosophical hedonism. 'Did nature create pleasures and enjoyments and the delights that meet us all the way through life, for the dead, or for those who have never come into existence, and not for the living?' 'And', the series of questions concludes, 'what is to induce us to forgo the acquisition of wealth and fame and honours and public office and everything of that sort of thing which secure for us a life not merely of safety but happiness?'

The questions thus conclude that the lifestyle of this view, and that which they oppose, provide conclusive proof of the validity of what has just been stated. 'The lifestyle is the witness of these things.' Those who were philosophically committed to a first-century brand of platonism outlined above argued that the truth of what they believed was verified from their success. For they were

> men of mark and wealth, holding leading positions, praised on all hands, recipients of honours, portly, healthy and robust, revelling in luxurious and riotous living, knowing nothing of labour, conversant with pleasures which carry the sweets of life to the all-welcoming soul by every channel of sense (34b).

With a series of antonyms they said their opponents were

> almost without exception obscure people, looked down upon, of mean estate, destitute of the necessities of life, not enjoying the privileges of subject peoples or even of slaves, filthy, sallow, reduced to skeletons, with a hungry look from want of food, the prey of disease, in training for dying (34a).[10]

The sophists were referring either to the Alexandrian Jews or possibly the *Therapeutai* community.[11] If the former, then the 'almost without exception' acknowledges only a few notables, and may refer to Philo's family who enjoyed wealth and influence in Alexandria.[12]

---

[10]This last reference to 'training for dying' has been seen as an equivalent statement for ἐπιτηδεύει ἀποθνῄσκειν used of the philosopher in Plato, *Phaedo*. 64a. See *Philo*, LCL, II, 493-494, and Simmias' response that 'this is exactly what my unphilosophical countrymen would say of the philosophers'.
[11]*Contempl.* 14-17, where the *Therapeutai* gave away their possessions.
[12]On the wealth and status of his wider family see J. Schwartz, 'Note sur la famille de Philon d'Alexandrie', *Annuaire de l'Institut de Philologie et d'Histoire Orientales et Slaves, Université Libre de Bruxelles*, 13 (1953), 591-602, and the reservations of S. Foster, 'A Note on the "Note" of J. Schwartz', *SP* 4 (1976-77), 25-32.

If, alternatively, these words refer to the *Therapeutai*, then the transfer of property to their children upon joining that community and the general renunciation of material possessions could explain the language. Philo does speak of 'their longing for the deathless and blessed life' (*Contempl.* 13). Certainly, when taken as a whole, the derogatory comments describe a group without status. The implications are clear. Those who held a view of humankind contrary to the sophists lived radically different lives, and the lifestyles clearly distinguished the philosophical commitment – the despised were Jews. Those who presented the alternative views clearly articulated them on the basis of a particular philosophical basis, 'The lifestyle is the witness of these things' (μάρτυς δὲ ὁ βίος τούτων).[13]

The Duration and Form of this World

We have noted that, in the Graeco-Roman world, a prevailing philosophical world-view profoundly affected the perception of the physical world, and with it a specific anthropology which answered questions concerning the immortality of the soul. Deductions that might legitimately be made from that ideological stance have also been seen to have had far-reaching implications for the conduct of life. Paul refers to an alternative view to the permanence of the world and comments on its relevance in helping to determine an immediate concern, as well as its significance for other important aspects of life (1 Cor. 7:29-31). There was 'the time to embrace and a time to refrain from embracing' (καιρὸς τοῦ περιλαβεῖν καὶ καιρὸς τοῦ μακρυνθῆναι ἀπὸ περιλήμψεως) (Ec. 3:5b LXX). How could they know what 'season' (χρόνος) or what 'time' (καιρός) it was, given that for everything in life there was a season and a time (Ec. 3:1)?

'The Time' (1 Cor. 7:29)
A number of important features need to be noted about Paul's statement that 'the time has been shortened'. First, Paul uses a grammatical construction in this opening section to alert his readers to the importance of what he is about to say. When the neuter demonstrative pronoun 'this' (τοῦτο) is used with verbs of saying, it draws attention to what is being said. In addition, Paul gives very

---

[13]'The mode of life of these two classes is a witness [to the truth of what I say]', II. 225. The Loeb translators of the text are expansive in the rendering of this sentence although the translation captures the import of the argument that has preceded it, and the evidence which follows, to substantiate the nexus between ideology and ethics.

special emphasis when he places the neuter demonstrative pronoun at the very beginning of the sentence in 7:29a:[14] 'And *this* I mean, brethren, (τοῦτο δέ φημι, ἀδελφοί) [that] henceforth the time has been shortened so that . . . (ὁ καιρὸς συνεσταλμένος ἐστιν τὸ λοιπόν ἵνα κτλ). Verbs of saying are followed by 'that' (ὅτι), or, where it is omitted, are understood, so that the first clause is epexegetical.[15] Paul is, therefore, underscoring to the Corinthians the great significance of eschatology for the matter under discussion.

Concerning the matter of 'the time', Witherington notes that συνεσταλμένος ἐστίν has to be translated as 'short' or 'shortened'.[16] The use of this perfect passive periphrastic fills the role of the perfect tense and means that the reference is to the eschatological era *per se*, and not to a short time now before the end of all things.[17] It is not 'short', but 'has been shortened'.

Also, the phrase 'henceforth' (τὸ λοιπόν 7:29) should not be linked with the ἵνα clause and rendered 'that henceforth those who have wives . . .' No texts support the translation of the term within the parameters of the subsequent ἵνα clause concerning 'those who have wives', as is done by translators and exegetes alike.[18] While there are textual variants concerning the actual place of 'henceforth', all locate it within the main sentence, either after[19] or before the verb (συνεσταλμένος ἐστίν).[20] There are interesting examples of the use of 'henceforth' (τὸ λοιπόν) in relation to 'time' (χρόνος). Aeschylus provides two apposite ones. An oath is sworn 'henceforth to the fullness of all time' (τὸ λοιπόν εἰς ἅπαντα πλειστήρη χρόνον), and as a result of an oracle 'Corinth henceforth (τὸ λοιπόν) was to me unknown'.[21] In this verse Paul is drawing attention to Christian eschatology which he sees creates the overarching theological frame-

---

[14]See a detailed discussion of this point in my '1 Corinthian 7:6-7 – A Caveat and a Framework for "the Sayings" in 7:8-24', 59-60.

[15]Manuscripts D E F G include 'that', while the majority do not. G. D. Fee, *The First Epistle to the Corinthians* (Grand Rapids: Eerdmans, 1987), 334, n. 1, suggests that it could be either epexegetical or causal. On the epexegetical use with the neuter demonstrative and verbs of saying, see my '1 Corinthians 7:6-7 – A Caveat and a Framework for "the Sayings" in 7:8-24', 59.

[16]See pp. 173-174.

[17]*BDF*, 352.

[18]A. Robertson and A. Plummer, *1 Corinthians* (Edinburgh: T. & T. Clark, 2nd edn. 1914), 155, do this, and wish to argue that Paul places words before the ἵνα construction for emphasis. The RV and NIV render it 'that from now on'.

[19]*E.g.* P[46], ℵABD*

[20]*E.g.* D.

[21]Aeschylus, *Eumenides*, 763; *cf.* 1031, and Sophocles, *Oedepus Tyrannus*, 795.

work in which this and allied matters are to be judged by the Christian young people who have raised the issue.

'The Form' of this World (1 Cor. 7:31)

What Paul is saying in verse 29 is further illuminated by verse 31 and helps to confirm our understanding of his eschatological comments. He explains the reason for his instructions in verses 29b-31a: 'For the form of this world is passing away' (παράγει γὰρ τὸ σχῆμα τοῦ κόσμου τούτου). Witherington has rightly noted that 'he [Paul] is referring to a process already set in motion, not one about to begin or on the near horizon'.[22]

Verse 26 should also influence our reading of verse 29. In the case of the former verse, I have argued elsewhere that the *Sitz im Leben* that gave rise to the question was the 'present dislocation' in the city itself (7:25-26) – the term 'dislocation' is linguistically used to describe social unrest connected with grain shortages. We have firm evidence for it in Corinth on three occasions during this period.[23] The 'present' difficulties in the former verse should not be taken to mean 'impending' as some have unsuccessfully sought to argue.[24] Rather, what was happening in Corinth at that time was related to anxiety and the accepted social dislocation, along with threats of rioting that accompanied grain shortages.[25]

There are good grounds for suggesting that Paul in 7:29-30 provides a contrasting view to that of the eternity of the world and the soul. Furthermore, he was asserting that young Christians must now look from a new vantage point, *i.e.* Christian eschatology, at the immediate issue to hand and at other matters which could so readily consume them, as they did their contemporaries.

---

[22]See B. Witherington III, 'Transcending Imminence: The Gordian Knot of Pauline Eschatology', p. 173.

[23]For a discussion of the importance of some ten extant inscriptions to Tiberius Claudius Dinnipus erected by the Tribes of Corinth as well as 'the Council and the People', see my 'Secular and Christian Responses to Corinthian Famines', *TynB* 40.1 (May, 1989) 86–106. He was in charge of the famine grain relief on three occasions during this period and this is identified with the present difficulty in 1 Cor. 7:26.

[24]H. Conzelmann, *First Corinthians* (Philadelphia: Fortress, 1975), 132, *contra* Fee, *Corinthians,* 329, arguing on Pauline usage of the term.

[25]As P. Garnsey observes, 'the fear of famine rather than famine itself was enough to send people on the rampage, as in 57 BC or AD 51', *Famine and Food Supply in the Graeco–Roman World: Reponses to Risk and Crisis* (Cambridge: Cambridge University Press, 1988), 31.

The Christian's 'Seasons' in this World

Before discussing the issues that Paul deals with in 7:29b-31a, it is
important to comment on the nature of the group who raised the
question in verse 25. While some have wished to argue that it is the
father or fathers of the betrothed girl, Paul's comments – especially in
7:28 'if you marry', and in 7:36-37 'if need requires he [any man] must
do as he wills', 'having no necessity, but has power as touching his
own will' – would rule that out. Also, the translation of the term
ὑπέρακμος as 'past child-bearing age' in 7:36 has no foundation. It
refers rather to the growing sense of physical closeness and
expectation of sexual intimacy naturally felt as the actual marriage
grew closer.[26] Given the early age at which marriage was contracted
in the first-century Graeco-Roman world,[27] the question has been
raised by young men whether they should marry now.

Who raised the question has an important bearing on the
discussion, because young people were driven by the value systems
and expectations of their secular society. Marriage was everything,
for it secured the much-prized domestic happiness. Sorrow was a
catastrophe for those who pursued joy. The accumulation of money
in order to acquire more possessions was the assured way to 'secure
for us a life not merely of safety but happiness' (Philo *Det.* 32).

Paul deals with four issues and, as Doughty notes in his helpful treatment of this passage, 'the eschatological language functions
to raise up a particular understanding of Christian existence'.[28]
Paul's primary concern here is not to deny the reality or the importance of marriage, sorrow, joy or resources, but to indicate that they
now assume a *relative* importance. They are not everything, for
eschatology puts them in perspective. This contrasts with the
argument of those who hold to the eternity of the world and the soul
and the importance of the pursuit of pleasure now, on the grounds
that these things are inaccessible to the unborn and the dead.[29]

---

[26]For a detailed discussion of these issues, including the meaning of the term
ὑπέρακμος, see my 'The Present Crisis and Consummation of the Marriage, 1
Corinthians 7:25-38', in *After Paul left Corinth: The Impact of Secular Ethics and
Social Change* (Grand Rapids: Eerdmans, forthcoming 1998), chap. 8.
[27]S. Treggiari, *Roman Marriage: Iusti coniuges from the Time of Cicero to the Time of
Ulpian* (Oxford: Clarendon Press, 1991), 153–155.
[28]D. J. Doughty, 'The Presence and Future of Salvation in Corinth', *ZNW* 66
(1975), 69.
[29]'Did nature create pleasures and enjoyments and the delights that meet us all
the way through life, for the dead, or for those who have never come into
existence, and not for the living?' (Philo, *Det.* 33).

What Paul is saying about marriage in 7:29b is perhaps best assessed in the light of his treatment of the remaining issues in 7:30. Considering them first is a legitimate interpretative approach because he uses the same construction in 7:30 as he did in 7:29b for all four issues – 'as if' (ὡς μή). He is not saying that sorrow is nothing and therefore Christians should not weep (*cf.* 1 Thes. 4:13). Those who weep are to recognise that the perspective of the eschatological hope means that their sense of loss is somewhat ameliorated.[30] What has happened is not the end of everything. The same is true of 'joy', which is an aspect of life but again is not everything.[31] Because people's lives do not consist in the abundance of things they possess, securing them cannot be the goal of life. They give no lasting security, and therefore the Christian must take a very different attitude toward them because of the eschatological perspective. There is a proper 'use' of this world, but it is not to be 'abused', *i.e.* exploited, as if this were the only sphere of existence for the Christian (7:31a).

Given that Paul is not rejecting *per se* life's seasons in 7:30-31a, what, then, is to be made of the first issue he dealt with? He states as a consequence of 7:29a 'that *even* those who have wives may be as those who have none' (ἵνα καὶ οἱ ἔχοντες γυναῖκας ὡς μὴ ἔχοντες ὦσιν). The reference here cannot be to a celibate marriage, for however one reconstructs the background of the earlier passage in 7:2-5, what the text says is inescapable – 'the husband must render to his wife her conjugal rights', and the same applies to the wife with respect to her husband (7:3). Sexual abstinence is seen as defrauding the relationship and is therefore permitted for only one reason, and that temporarily. It must be followed by the resumption of sexual relationships (7:5). Paul is certainly not suggesting that marriage is nothing, in contrast to the young people who in secular society regarded it as 'everything' because it gave important signals concerning social class.[32] In the discussion of the meaning of 7:29b, full weight should also to be given to the critical word 'even' (καί). What Paul is saying is that even one of the most important creation ordinances, and, in many ways, a major relationship of life (Gn. 2:20-25), cannot be judged to be everything in the light of the eschatological factor.

---

[30]*Cf.* 2 Cor. 1:3ff. where God is said to be the God of all comfort, and Paul therefore comforts others with the same comfort he receives from God.
[31]The pursuit of 'happiness' (ἡδονή) which is condemned in the New Testament (Lk. 8:14; Tit. 3:3; Jas. 4:1, 3; 2 Pet. 2:13) was a preoccupation of pagan life.
[32]On the importance of rank and wealth, see Treggiari, *Roman Marriage*, 90-100.

Contemporary Importance

If the preacher in Ecclesiastes sets the discussion of the seasons of life within the framework that there is a God-appointed time for everything, and that God has made everything beautiful in its time so that nothing can be added to it and nothing taken away from it (Ec. 3:11, 14), Paul sets his 'seasons' in an eschatological setting.[33]

Much of contemporary Western Christian piety has 'a future hope collapsed into the present' with a demand for fulfilment *now*, emphasising 'the feel-good factor'. Alongside this there has grown a view of great deprivation, tragedy or spiritual disillusionment when the goals of success and happiness are not secured by Christians.

The God-given seasons of life have been replaced for all practical purposes by a view of the eternity of this world and a return to aspects of pagan hedonism. On this view, the amount of enjoyment is proportionate to one's success and 'the lifestyle is the witness' (Philo, *Det.* 34). An expectation has been created that Christians will be 'conversant with pleasures (ἡδονή) which carry the sweets of life to the all-welcoming soul by every channel of sense' (Philo, *Det.* 34). All too often, such teaching is garbed in Christian terminology of a prosperity based on a full exploitation of the opportunities and resources that this world provides, and among its more high profile exponents it has assumed 'gospel' proportions.[34]

If, in the short period before the next millennium, preachers only return to the subject of eschatology in order to refute alarmist teaching about the second coming, especially that linking it to 'the time', there will continue to be a deficiency in the way Christians approach the seasons of life. If, on the other hand, Paul's teaching of the Christian perspective on life in the light of the eschatological hope is addressed seriously, it will provide a crucial paradigm for life's goals and expectations and an awareness of a proper use of the present world. Lifestyle will indeed be the witness of our theological framework, and any framework that excludes the eschatological hope will gravely distort a Christian's perception of the seasons of life.[35]

---

[33]For a critique of aspects of W. Deming's important work, 'Stoic and Cynic Elements in 1 Corinthians 7', in *Paul and Marriage and Celibacy: The Hellenistic Background of 1 Corinthians 7*, SNTS Monograph Series 83 (Cambridge: Cambridge University Press, 1995), chap. 3, see my 'The Present Crisis and Consummation of the Marriage, 1 Corinthians 7:25-38' (forthcoming).

[34]For twentieth-century hedonism's effect on Christianity, see my *Pilgrim's Progress and Contemporary Evangelical Piety*, St. Antholin's 1997 Annual Lecture (London: Barnard & Westwood, 1997), 6ff.

[35]I am grateful to Kent Brower and Tom Coleman for kindly reading this chapter and making helpful suggestions.

Index of Authors

INDEX OF AUTHORS